THE WONDER AND SUPERNATURAL PLAYS OF LADY GREGORY, BEING THE THIRD VOLUME OF THE COLLECTED PLAYS

edited and with a foreword by
Ann Saddlemyer

COLIN SMYTHE
GERRARDS CROSS
1979

Copyright © 1971 The Lady Gregory Estate
Foreword Copyright © 1971 Colin Smythe Ltd.

First published in one volume on 1 March 1971
by Colin Smythe Ltd, Gerrards Cross, Buckinghamshire
as the seventh volume of the Coole Edition
ISBN 0–900675–31–4

First published in paperback format in 1979

British Library Cataloguing in Publication Data

Gregory, Isabella Augusta, *Lady*
    The collected plays
    3: The wonder and supernatural plays of
    Lady Gregory – Coole ed.
    I. Title   II. Saddlemyer, Ann
    822′.9′12   PR4728.G5A19

ISBN 0–86140–018–6

Printed in Great Britain

FOREWORD

"Ah, miracles is gone out of the world this long time with education, unless that they might happen in your own inside."
                                                              (*The Full Moon*)

Lady Gregory's first play was based on the folk legend of St. Colman and King Guaire of Gort, as she heard it from neighbours at Coole; she wrote it, not for "a stage production," but because "a little play in rhyme might perhaps be learned and acted by Kiltartan school-children." Later that same year, in November 1902, she and Yeats were corresponding over a "little Christ play" which, although they first contemplated it together, was tossed from one to the other. Yeats's pagan variant, *The Black Horse*, provided the Rider's song, but Lady Gregory, objecting to her colleague's psychological interpretation of the Garden of Paradise, took the idea back once more and finally, seven years later, reasserted the Christian aspiration in *The Travelling Man*. Again the play is rooted in reality, for despite her insistence on the soul's dissatisfaction with this world once it has been granted a vision of "the Divine Essence," the Stranger follows a familiar path down the long bog road from Slieve Echtge to the rising of the river at Ballylee in Coole demesne. It is not surprising, therefore, when she came to write her most important miracle play, that she should tell the story of Christ's passion in the words of the west of Ireland, as "it might have been told by Brigit, 'the Mary of the Gael', our great Saint, had she been present." In *The Story Brought By Brigit* folk history once more provides a secure base for the inevitable unfolding of the tragic dream, and the cry of Joel the boy from the mountains echoes the pain of all those who see the truth and are helpless: "We wanted him, and we got him, and what we did with him was to kill him. And that is the way it will be ever and always, so long as leaves grow upon the trees!"

The Story Brought By Brigit had been in her mind since the early years of playwriting, but was not finally completed until near the end of her career. It is fitting, therefore, that *Dave* (her last play apart from adaptations), should also carry the dual theme of the dreamer's Garden of Paradise and the "clouds of trouble" that

v

threaten the fellowship of this world. Significantly, Lady Gregory first conceived this morality in a dream. She confided to her diary in 1925: "Another good night, awakening sometimes but happily and without pain. And suddenly I seemed to get the play *Dave* clearly, a ragged woman coming into the house through a storm, faints, believes when revived that she is in heaven and brings the others something to the mind of 'dwellers in that high country'. It seemed to flatten as I wrote it down this morning, yet I think it is the framework I want."[1] The figure of a messenger from another world can be traced throughout her work, from the "tattered, moon-mad beggar" of the early versions of *Kincora* and the patriotic ballad-singer of *The Rising of the Moon*, through Lady Dereen of *The White Cockade* and the chattering Song-maker of *Dervorgilla*, to the ragged mountainy Malachi Naughton with his heart-secret in *The Image* and the kingly Beggar of *The Travelling Man*; but *Dave*'s ghostly Servant of Poverty did not outlast the criticisms of Yeats and Lennox Robinson. And so Lady Gregory's final message to her audience comes more fittingly from the slightly pettish, humanly weary figure of Kate, linking the benediction of "those high countries" with the timeless follies of the world of Cloon: "May friends and angels be around him and steer him to a good harbour in the Paradise of the King!" And Dave himself once more echoes the author's favourite hero, the image-maker: "I will never be content or satisfied till I will come again to that dream."

Only once did she try her hand at a ghost play proper, and although *Shanwalla* is set in the familiar vicinity of Cloon, she had great difficulty with "the shadow that wanders for a while until it has the debts paid it had to pay." Again her fellow directors came to her aid, and a long letter from Yeats after the first production complains of the "muzziness" of Act III: "I confess to an uneasy feeling that your two young women are too expensive a means of alibi, that we get the alibi at the price of that gradual opening. I have had from the very beginning the feeling that the play ought to rise on the fact made apparent from the first sentence, that your hero has been arrested for the crime, and that we want nothing in the first five minutes except the rubbing in of the fact."[2] Reproduced for the first time in this volume is the stronger and clearer third act she later re-worked in her own copy of the play.

Lennox Robinson once described Lady Gregory's children's plays as "laid half-way between Clare-Galway and Fairyland." Certainly the play which first opens the door to that world of wonder lets in at the same time the shimmering elusive clarity of the full

THE COLLECTED PLAYS
III
WONDER AND THE SUPERNATURAL

The Coole Edition
General Editors:
T. R. Henn, C.B.E., Litt.D.
Colin Smythe, M.A.

moon as it touches the little community of Cloon. Through the good offices of yet one more "cracked beggar," Mary, and her brother, the "innocent" Davideen, Hyacinth Halvey is released from the image of his own making and encouraged to heed the call of those "who do not give in to our limitations, are not 'bound by reason to the wheel'," the fools in this world. To witness the miracle of transformation, Lady Gregory calls into *The Full Moon* those wayward characters of the earlier comedies: Shawn Early and the happy melancholic Bartley Fallon from *Spreading the News*, daft Mrs. Broderick from *The Jackdaw*, the bustling "fortied girl" Miss Joyce and the laconic Peter Tannian and his dog from *Hyacinth Halvey*. "Run out now, run," urges Cracked Mary to Hyacinth, "where you have the bare ridge of the world before you, and no one to take orders from but yourself, maybe, and God." Even the earthbound folk around him are touched by the lunar forces of the imagination before Hyacinth escapes into the world of mythology with his two scarecrow dancing guardians from the world of faery. But although Cracked Mary and Davideen sing the sweet song of "The Heather Broom," the citizens of Cloon are left behind with clogged sight and the bewildering cares of "roast and boiled and all the comforts of the day." Indeed Cracked Mary herself is as familiar with the insanity of the asylum as the upside-down moonlit world of her "golden God." The moon's spell is not for all.

There is a wider gateway still into the world of wonder, however, and in her later fairy plays for children Lady Gregory substitutes the magical devices of the enchanter for the awesome "stranger" with his impossible message to this world. Again she dug deep into the folk poetry and tradition of her own people to discover "the wonder tales told in the childhood of the world", as she described her discoveries in *The Kiltartan Wonder Book*. The result of her explorations and newly-found freedom was a new style born of wonder itself, three plays of transformation and spectacle, *The Golden Apple*, *The Dragon*, and *The Jester*, and finally the most complete metamorphosis of all, where even her own favourite heart-secrets are turned upside down, the ballad-play *Aristotle's Bellows*. In these four wonder plays, as in *Damer's Gold*, all is "as simple as a folk-tale, where the innocent of the world confound the wisdom of the wise": the Giant, like the reformed Dragon, has a weak stomach that cannot bear the thought of blood; the Witch, harried by a selfish nagging daughter, faithfully carries out her trade according to the diabolical code of witchery, and the Executioner belongs to a Trade Union; the governess-turned Queen sends runners throughout the wide world advertising the position of cook, but does not neglect to put up tablets in the local Post Office; the hungry King cannot find a quiet corner in his own castle for a comfortable post-prandial nap; the blind Wise Man is only half blind and Fintan the astrologer's prophecy only partially accurate; the young Prince is protected from chills by his Guardian Aunts, for "Kings and princes are getting scarce. They are the most class is wearing away"; and in the Ogre's country matches "won't be invented for the next seven hundred years."

The time is far out of mind, but the setting and language of these plays are as familiar as Kiltartan. The message, too, twinkle though it does through nonsense rhymes and improbable coincidences, is still Gregorian in tone. *The Dragon* is subtitled "A Change of Heart" and was first called "The Awakening of a Soul"; a complete scenario among her papers emphasizes the Queen's interference "for your own good." The mad Jester of Hy-Brasil claims, "I never could know the meaning of that word 'impossible' "; as Manannan, Son of the Sea, whose powers are twice those of the fantastic Ogre's, he is linked in his desire for order and comic technique with yet another myth-maker, the author's close friend Bernard Shaw:

> And when I see a plan make
> The Birds that watch us frown,
> I come and toss the pancake
> And turn it upside down!
>
> In this I follow after
> Lycurgus who was wise;
> To the little god of laughter
> I make my sacrifice!

Finally, in spite of his cranky exterior, there is fault-finding Conan who, when he is given Aristotle's ancient secret of the magic bellows, is as helpless as all mortals who would impose peace and order from without on a disorderly world. "People were harmless long ago and why wouldn't they be made harmless again?" In the creation of Conan, graduate of Trinity College and frustrated miracle-worker, perhaps we see the wry "Grimace called Laughter" directed at the author herself.

The wonder plays came easily to Lady Gregory, partly because her mind "went miching" and "broke through the English hedges into the unbounded wonder-world"; partly also because of their link with her translations of Molière on the one hand and with the ballad structures of her early comedies on the other. For here her knowledge of structure is strong enough to allow dramatic licence in staging and costuming: a well-head and weakly little tree are enough for the Garden at the World's End; a few waving boughs and a cloud of smoke create the fearsome Wood of Wonders; the "Hag of Slaughter" and princes and wren-boys require only paper masks to effect their transformation; *The Dragon* needed simply the theatre's stock costumes, an india-rubber ball, a cocoa-nut and stage carpenter Seaghan Barlow's magnificent mechanical dragon; and the same workshop produced Aristotle's cats out of two old felt hats.

In her use of music and song we can see clearly how close her world of fantasy is to that of musical comedy. In over half her plays song is an integral part of the plot; *Aristotle's Bellows* might well be a ballad opera, while another late play, *On the Racecourse*, uses song to reflect the inner conflict and feelings of the characters. Frequently characters burst into song simply to mark a shift in emphasis or to break the tension; *The Gaol Gate* and *The Story Brought by Brigit* include the keen, with detailed instructions as to its singing. And although she introduces the dance only once, in *The Full Moon*, Lady Gregory early learned the effectiveness of the tableau. But perhaps the greatest similarity of all occurs in the character groupings of the folk-fantasies: the rhyming Guardians of *The Jester* are close cousins to Gilbert and Sullivan, while the two sardonic fiddle-playing cats of *Aristotle's Bellows* belong to the Christmas pantomime. And the final test must also be with that same audience; in her diary for 11 February 1920 the demanding author notes with satisfaction:

"Such a splendid matinée yesterday of *Golden Apple*; crowds of children; I was afraid they would find the play too long, but they didn't seem to, and laughed and applauded."

ANN SADDLEMYER

¹ *Lady Gregory's Journals,* ed. Lennox Robinson (London: Putnam, 1946), p. 323.
² Letter dated 27 April 1915, in the possession of Major Richard Gregory and quoted here by permission of Senator Michael Yeats.

THE PLAYS OF LADY GREGORY
HISTORY OF FIRST PRODUCTIONS BY THE ABBEY
THEATRE COMPANY AND PUBLICATION DATES

Colman and Guaire [1901]. Not produced. Published under title *My First Play* (London: Elkin Mathews and Marrot, 1930).

A Losing Game. Not produced. Published only in *The Gael* (New York), December 1902.

Twenty-Five [*A Losing Game* revised]. Produced 14 March 1903. Never published.

The Poorhouse (with Douglas Hyde). Produced 3 April 1907. Published in *Samhain*, September 1903; with *Spreading the News* and *The Rising of the Moon* as Vol. IX of Abbey Theatre Series (First Series) (Dublin: Maunsel, 1906).

The Rising of the Moon. Produced 9 March 1907. Published in *Samhain*, December 1904; with *Spreading the News* and *The Poorhouse* as Vol. IX of Abbey Theatre Series (First Series) (Dublin: Maunsel, 1906); and included in *Seven Short Plays* (Dublin: Maunsel, 1909).

Spreading the News. Produced 27 December 1904. Published in *Samhain*, November 1905; with *The Rising of the Moon* and *The Poorhouse* as Vol. IX of Abbey Theatre Series (First Series) (Dublin: Maunsel, 1906); and included in *Seven Short Plays* (Dublin: Maunsel, 1909).

Kincora. First version produced 25 March 1905; revised version 11 February 1909. Published as Vol. II of Abbey Theatre Series (First Series) (Dublin: The Abbey Theatre, 1905); revised form in *Irish Folk-History Plays First Series* (New York and London: Putnam, 1912).

The White Cockade. Produced 9 December 1905. Published as Vol. VIII of Abbey Theatre Series (First Series) (Dublin:

Maunsel, 1906); included in *Irish Folk-History Plays Second Series* (New York and London: Putnam, 1912).

Hyacinth Halvey. Produced 19 February 1906. Published in *Samhain*, December 1906; and included in *Seven Short Plays* (Dublin: Maunsel, 1909).

The Doctor in Spite of Himself (from Molière). Produced 16 April 1906. Published in *The Kiltartan Molière* (Dublin: Maunsel, 1910).

The Gaol Gate. Produced 20 October 1906. Published in *Seven Short Plays* (Dublin: Maunsel, 1909).

The Canavans. Produced 8 December 1906; revised version produced 31 October 1907. Published in *Irish Folk-History Plays Second Series* (New York and London: Putnam, 1912).

The Jackdaw. Produced 23 February 1907. Published in *Seven Short Plays* (Dublin: Maunsel, 1909).

Dervorgilla. Produced 31 October 1907. Published in *Samhain*, November 1908; included in *Irish Folk-History Plays First Series* (New York and London: Putnam, 1912).

The Unicorn from the Stars (with W. B. Yeats [a re-working of *Where There is Nothing* written by Yeats in 1912 with the help of Lady Gregory and Douglas Hyde]. Produced 21 November 1907. Published in *The Unicorn from the Stars and Other Plays* (New York: Macmillan, 1908) and included in the Third Volume of *The Collected Works of William Butler Yeats* (Stratford-on-Avon: Shakespeare Head Press, 1908).

Teja (from Sudermann). Produced 19 March 1908. Never published.

The Rogueries of Scapin (from Molière). Produced 4 April 1908. Published in *The Kiltartan Molière* (Dublin: Maunsel, 1910).

The Workhouse Ward [*The Poorhouse* revised]. Produced 20 April 1908. Published in *Seven Short Plays* (Dublin: Maunsel, 1909).

The Travelling Man. Produced 2 March 1910. Published in *Seven Short Plays* (Dublin: Maunsel, 1909).

The Miser (from Molière). Produced 21 January 1909. Published in *The Kiltartan Molière* (Dublin: Maunsel, 1910).

The Image. Produced 11 November 1909. Published as Vol. I of Abbey Theatre Series (Second Series) Dublin: Maunsel, 1910).

Mirandolina (from Goldoni). Produced 24 February 1910. Published separately (London and New York: Putnam, 1924).

The Full Moon. Produced 10 November 1910. Published by the Author at the Abbey Theatre, 1911; included in *New Comedies* (New York and London: Putnam, 1913).

Coats. Produced 1 December 1910. Published in *New Comedies* (New York and London: Putnam, 1913).

The Deliverer. Produced 12 January 1911. Published in *Irish Folk-History Plays Second Series* (New York and London: Putnam, 1912).

Grania. Not produced. Published in *Irish Folk-History Plays First Series* (New York and London: Putnam, 1912).

McDonough's Wife. Produced 11 January 1912. Published in *New Comedies* (New York and London: Putnam, 1913).

The Bogie Men. Produced 4 July 1912 at the Court Theatre, London. Published in *New Comedies* (New York and London: Putnam, 1913). Later revised.

Damer's Gold. Produced 21 November 1912. Published in *New Comedies* (New York and London: Putnam, 1913).

The Wrens. Produced 1 June 1914 at the Court Theatre, London. Published in *The Image and Other Plays* (London: Putnam, 1922).

Shanwalla. Produced 8 April 1915. Published in *The Image and Other Plays* (London: Putnam, 1922). Later revised.

The Golden Apple. Produced 6 January 1920. Published separately (London: John Murray, 1916).

The Dragon. Produced 21 April 1919. Published separately (Dublin: Talbot Press, 1920); included in *Three Wonder Plays* (London: Putnam: 1923).

Hanrahan's Oath. Produced 29 January 1918. Published in *The Image and Other Plays* (London: Putnam, 1922).

The Jester. Not produced professionally. Published in *Three Wonder Plays* (London: Putnam, 1923).

Aristotle's Bellows. Produced 17 March 1921. Published in *Three Wonder Plays* (London: Putnam, 1923).

The Old Woman Remembers. Produced 31 December 1923. Published in *The Irish Statesman*, 22 March 1924; included in *A Little Anthology of Modern Irish Verse*, selected by Lennox Robinson (Dublin: Cuala Press, 1928).

The Story Brought By Brigit. Produced 15 April 1924. Published separately (London and New York: Putnam, 1924).

On the Racecourse [a re-writing of *Twenty-Five*]. Not produced. Published separately (London and New York: Putnam, 1926).

The Would-Be Gentleman (from Molière). Produced 4 January 1926. Published in *Three Last Plays* (London and New York: Putnam, 1928).

Sancho's Master. Produced 14 March 1927. Published in *Three Last Plays* (London and New York: Putnam, 1928).

Dave. Produced 9 May 1927. Published in *Three Last Plays* (London and New York: Putnam, 1928).

PLAYS UNPUBLISHED AND UNPRODUCED

Michelin
The Meadow Gate
The Dispensary
The Shoelace
The Lighted Window
Heads or Harps (with W. B. Yeats)

CONTENTS

Foreword by Ann Saddlemyer   v

History of the first productions and
    publication dates   ix

Colman & Guaire   I

The Travelling Man   19

The Full Moon   29

Shanwalla   53

The Golden Apple   99

The Jester   171

The Dragon   209

Aristotle's Bellows   261

The Story Brought by Brigit   301

Dave   347

Notes and Music   369

First performances at the Abbey Theatre
    and the Casts   403

Appendices
I   Letter from W. B. Yeats   411

II The first version of the third act of Shanwalla   417

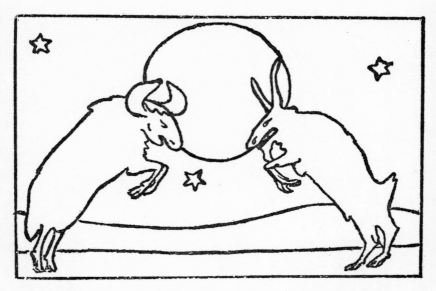

The device by Robert Gregory which first appeared on the cover of Lady
Gregory's *The Full Moon*, which was "published by the author at the Abbey
Theatre Dublin 1911 and sold for sixpence". It was subsequently used by
G. P. Putnam's Sons on all editions of Lady Gregory's plays.

COLMAN AND GUAIRE

COLMAN AND GUAIRE

SCENE: *A hall in the King's house.*

EOGHAN

The King should now be riding through the heather,
  He went out hunting at the break of day,
And if he finds good sport and pleasant weather
  He said that he would stop the night away.

FERGUS

I did not know him gone. I have been dwelling
  Over in Inchy these five days in all,
Watching the woodmen at their task of felling
  Oaks for the beams of the new banquet hall.

And ash and birch logs for the cold nights burning
  And boughs for shelter from the noonday sun.
I will stop here and wait the King's returning
  And give account of all the work that's done.

I wish him luck wherever he is riding
  And a good share of boar and wolf and deer;
His hand is always ready at dividing,
  When he hunts well the poor will have good cheer.

EOGHAN

His tables are still spread with food; he bade me
  Welcome all strangers coming to his court.
His name goes far beyond the bounds of Aidne,
  Guaire, whose bounty gilds the name of Gort.

3

FERGUS

But tell me, Eoghan, for you know I love him
    No less than you, as if he were my own,
What is this cloud that seems to hang above him,
    And makes him often sit in gloom, alone?

You, ever with his father coming, going,
    The man he trusted most of all his men,
Must surely know what troubles him, and knowing,
    Will tell it to me, not to tell again.

EOGHAN

No, Fergus, you lose time in asking, guessing,
    I would not tell it if I knew this thing;
Of this be sure, there never came a blessing
    On one who told the secrets of a King.

FERGUS

I do not ask from any curious humour,
    But there has been much idle talk of late,
And through the country there has gone a rumour
    That Guaire knows of Rhinagh's unknown fate.

They say a bard, lately before him singing
    Said but her name, and had his song cut short—

EOGHAN

Rhinagh! What tale about her are you bringing
    And what is said of her outside the Court?

FERGUS

They tell that Rhinagh, when her lord died fighting,
    And she, a widowed bride, was left to mourn,
Came to her kinsman at his own inviting,
    The old king, Colman, till her child was born.

But he from some wise woman had a warning
    That her son over his should take the sway;
All that is sure is, she went out one morning,
    And never came again up to this day.

4

Some say, her wits gone, she through Burren roaming,
    Losing her way, by hungry wolves was found;
Some say the river, flooded then and foaming
    Swept her to its dark places underground.

Some thought, but feared to say, that Colman's power
    Had, for his son's sake, sent her to her death.
But no one knows for certain to this hour—

EOGHAN

Hush! Walls have ears—or speak with lower breath.

A BOY (*at the Door*)

The King is coming! Haste, make all things ready—
    To bring you warning I ran on before.

EOGHAN

That is the boy went with the hunt—what said he?

FERGUS

No time for talk—the King is at the door!

(*Enter the* KING.)

FERGUS

My lord the King, I humbly bend and greet you;
    Tell me I pray, what drives you back so soon?
For I was told that I would hardly meet you
    Before the coming of to-morrow's noon.

GUAIRE

    While stars still trembled in the sky,
    Before the wood-dove was awake,
    We were abroad, my men and I,
    We passed along by Cutra lake.
    Good luck was with us, two fat deer
    Were brought down by the dogs, and one
    I killed myself with this short spear,
    Just at the rising of the sun.

    In the red bogs our steps ere noon
    Put snipe to sudden, sidelong flight,
    And woodcocks, called there by the moon
    Went back to seek the wood's dim light.

Derreen behind us, and before
The golden mountain, Slieve-nan-or.
We stopped at last to quench our thirst
Beside a stream, when a great deer
Sudden from out the heather burst
And up the thorny bank leaped clear.—
The hounds were after him, and we
Followed, but in the soft bog ground
Our horses struggled, and when free,
He was away, and but the sound
Of the hounds baying led us on
To Dairecaol, where by the lake
We found them baffled, he was gone;
They plunged among the reeds to slake
Their panting sides, and I drew rein,
Angered our chase was all in vain.

Then a mist rose upon the lake
Like white wings hidden in dim rain
And birdlike voices seemed to break
Out into words, "Return again!"
I was afraid then but the boy
That stood beside me, laughed for joy.
Then the mist changed to sudden light
And from its heart there seemed to fly
Great flocks of birds in circling flight
That made a bow across the sky;
Some red like berries on the ash
Some blue like pools the spring rain fills,
Some yellow like the furze that flash
Out into flame along the hills.
Some changed to purple, some to green
And purple mixed into the blue,
And in the glowing arch were seen
Gold wings and silver shining through.
It flashed across from east to west—
I know not what such sign may be,
But, travelling home, we saw it rest
Far off on Burren, by the sea.

For as it faded overhead
We slowly turned and rode away—
Here, bring me wine and meat and bread
For I have fasted all the day.

(*A tray of food is brought in and put before him.*)

FERGUS

This sign may surely have some hidden meaning,
Had we some seer to tell it, old and wise,
Who, grains from the great fields of knowledge gleaning,
Has learned to see with more than earthly eyes.

To-day, as I walked through the Inchy rushes
In the clear sky above I noticed plain
A rainbow swiftly pass like that which flushes
The sky with sudden colour after rain.

You did well to return; a day's sport broken,
A hunt that failed, is a small thing to weigh
Against the chance that you were sent a token
To call you back before the close of day.

(*Enter a* RAGGED MESSENGER.)

EOGHAN

Who is this fellow, all in rags and tatters—
Here, fellow, say, what message do you bring?

MESSENGER

A message for the King on God's high matters.

EOGHAN

Well speak it out then, speak. This is the King.

MESSENGER

God's servant, Colman, over there in Burren
Lies weak with fasting on his limestone bed.
The grain is gone, the beasts are struck with murrain;
He prays you send him and the people bread.

7

There where no tree grows, where no bees are humming
  He looks to heaven from his bed of rocks;
The sea birds scream to tell the storm is coming,
  The badger is his comrade, and the fox.

When daylight touches Burren with pale fingers
  He lies there on his cold, rock-pillowed bed;
But heaven's light on his rough sackcloth lingers,
  The light of stars is shining round his head.

He has been kneeling at the gate of glory
  Praying God's patience for the sins of earth;
Aran and Burren, Aidne and Dunguaire,
  Kiltartan, Coole, Corker that saw his birth.

Earth's food has failed him; he is faint and lonely,
  But if his leanness lets the soul slip through,
True loss not his, King Guaire, but yours only,
  God will have found him other work to do.

GUAIRE

Enough, I do not need so much beseeching,
All men in want are welcome in my sight;
But tell me what his race, that I outreaching
My hand to him, may honour him aright.

MESSENGER

I claim him high enough to claim you brother—
  From Conall, Cormac, Dathi's blood he springs;
The great Fiacra race gave him his mother,
  Rhinagh, the daughter of a hundred kings.

GUAIRE

Beggar! you lie! Begone in shame!
This lying word has you undone—
Here! Call the dogs! Wretch, she you name
In dying left no child, no son.

Would that she had! for he had been
As close in friendship as in blood,
No wanderer, nor poor nor mean,
But sharing half my state and good.

8

Would that she had! I would be free
From the dark deed that shades my life—
Not mine, but done for love of me
Because of foretold jealous strife.

Where are the dogs? Fool, why stand there,
You are not worthy of my sword
Or I had laid your marrow bare
While yet you spoke that lying word.

No man shall dare, no man has dared,
To speak that name before my face—
My father's fame might well be spared
The wakening of his great disgrace!

Here, drag him out and let him whine
His poor false story as he runs—
The son of Rhinagh! Dathi's line!
No begging saints are Dathi's sons!

MESSENGER

That is my message, do your will upon me,
   More than God's will I know you cannot do.
Let your dogs tear me, set your men upon me—
   Death will not make the word I speak less true.

If as your words tell, some old sin or sorrow
   Makes the past weigh so heavy on your head
Will it be lightened when you know to-morrow
   Your kinsman, through your great unkindness, dead?

GUAIRE

No man has ever passed my gate
Or asked help at my open door
But he has had it, early, late,
Friend he, or foe, or rich or poor.
Yes, if the food was at its last,
In time of storm or siege or war
The King himself would sooner fast
Than let a dog go famine sore.

Never till now has it been said
That Guaire has a narrow heart—
That of his meat and of his bread
He would not share one smallest part—
But now through Aidne bards will sing
That Guaire's arm has grown short—
That he is but a niggard King
Unfit to hold a kingly court.

Know, it was not a grudging mind
A closed-up hand that brought this shame,
But wrath that made me passion-blind
At the bare sound of Rhinagh's name.

Speak, Eoghan, speak, and tell the tale
That one dark day I overheard,
That left me grief-struck, horror-pale.
Tell it, spare not one bitter word.
Tell, if at last it must be done,
The father's crime—to shield his son.

EOGHAN

Guaire, to your command I bow,
You give me bitter words to say,
But you well know that then, as now,
What my King bids, I must obey.

It happened many years ago
Some Witch's word made Colman wild,
With threats that Rhinagh's unborn son
Would wrest the kingdom from his child.

I do not know how Rhinagh heard
Some hint of ill, some whispered word,
That made her leave the Court and flee
To seek escape towards the sea.

Far beyond Lydican she passed
But we came up with her at last,
Just where we saw the salt sea tide,
Burren sharp ridged against the grey,
Dunguaire in its lonely pride,
The shadow hills beyond the bay.

My grief! I was bid take her rein
And lead her back towards Gort again,
To where outside the tangled wood
Of Raheen, a great elm tree stood.

I brought her to the tree, and there
Two dark-browed, sullen men we found,
With strange-cut clothes and matted hair.
They pulled her roughly to the ground,
And bid her walk and follow fast;
And stumbling over root and stone,
As through the tangled wood we passed,
I followed, heart sick and alone.

We had come far. The evening's cold,
The pale and clouded silver sky,
The bare blotched rocks, the kine-trod mould,
The withered grass, the moorhen's cry—

All seemed my flesh, my heart to chill.
I wished the dark deed overpast.
When, crossing a long, low-ridged hill
We saw Coole river close at last.

The stone-slabbed bridge not built by men
Over the hidden current set
We crossed, she shrank a little then,
But her rough guards went farther yet;
By the bare twisted thorns of May,
The birch's sudden, ghost-like flash,
To where a heap of grey stones lay,
Grasped in the bare roots of an ash.

And with a rope they made one fast,
And muttering that the day was late,
Over her head the rough loop passed
That made her neck bend with its weight.

She said no word. A sound of strife
To that last hour she would not bring,
Or else too proud to beg for life
Of any lesser than the King.

11

They pointed to the river head,
And there she led the way alone
Fearless and still, with slow grave tread,
Her white hands holding up the stone,
To where the water rises bright,
Dimpling and dancing round and round
As glad to greet again the light
After its dark path underground.

A tall red sallow, where we came
Gilds the dark mud from whence it springs;
She murmured "That is sure a flame
To bear my spirit on its wings".
And where the river's ripples cease
And in its deeper stillness lie
The far-off shadowed, long-branched trees
And deeper yet the far grey sky,
She, stooping low her fair bent head
Searched the strange depth with wondering eyes;
Then, looking still, she softly said,
"Beyond the shadows Heaven lies! "

I would not look—I could not save—
With tear-blind eyes I turned and fled—
I heard the breaking of a wave—
A cry—I slipped and fell as dead.

I know not how that long night passed,
Or many nights. I sought the men
When I awoke to thought at last,
But they were gone, nor came again.
    (*He turns away, putting his hand over his eyes.*)

GUAIRE

Now all is told. That is the hidden story
    That, idly listening, once I overheard.
Since then, no dream of love or fame or glory
    Has brought forgetfulness of one least word.

Men think my pleasure all in feasts and fighting,
    In hunts and jests my harvesting of joy;
They do not guess how dark the hidden writing
    That brought life-anguish to a thoughtless boy.

My father struck through love and fear and sorrow;
   Love of his son, his birthright and his line;
Made his day dark to win me a bright morrow;
   The grief, the load, the penance must be mine.

One night I stood where herons stand and shiver
   Where the cave bats flap dimly overhead,
Where the dark otter swims the moonlit river—
   That winter night when walk the restless dead.

She never came. I thought her soul might hover
   Where by my father's will she felt death's pain.
I thought to ask his son's forgiveness of her,
   But night and my cold watch went by in vain.

MESSENGER

King, you have sure done well in not concealing
   The story of this crime that spoiled your ease.
Now I have leave to give you words of healing
   That, heard aright, will bring you back to peace.

When Rhinagh had been left in that dark hour
   To find within the river-bed a grave,
Then unseen hands came to her and had power
   Even through the stone that weighed her down, to save.

Safe by the shelter of a bush they set her,
   In a green field of Corcar, and ere morn
There, finding strength, since God did not forget her
   The child whose birth the King had feared was born.

And when she woke from the long night of dangers
   And dawning light fell on her infant's head,
She saw two Travelling Men stand by her, strangers,
   One with dim eyes and one with halting tread.

And food and help and comforting they brought her
   One plucked a rush, and in the bush's shade
Rose for the child's baptism a well of water
   And on his face the holy sign they made.

And with the sign, clear sight to her was given,
    She saw no longer old men, blind and lame,
But shining, radiant with the light of heaven,
    The Messengers God sendeth as a flame.

And then, the vengeance of the King still fearing,
    For the first time and last her child she kissed,
And laid him in their hands for his uprearing
    Before they vanished in the morning mist.

She, tired of Courts, took poverty upon her
    And lived a nun, God's handmaid, meek and pure.
But sure in heaven's sight she had high honour
    The servant of the servants of the poor.

I cannot tell where Colman got his learning
    Or where they took him from his place of birth;
It often seems as if his soul was burning
    To its true home beyond the bounds of earth.

FERGUS

I think I saw him once; I stopped in going
    From Duras to Kinvara by the beach
To watch the men from Aran slowly rowing,
    Striving with sailless boats the shore to reach.

And on the sharp-edged rocks I saw one kneeling
    His hands stretched out towards the gates of peace
That show among the sunset clouds, appealing
    To Him who rules the wideness of the seas

I thought at first that it was but a vision,
    But when I saw his pure, uplifted face
I knew him for a Saint on his high mission
    And that I stood beside a holy place.

MESSENGER

That is his life. In prayer and fasting living
    He stays in desert places night and day;
What food I bring, to famished people giving,
    His flesh, his strength, have wasted all away.

I thought this morn that he would see no morrow,
   And, going out, wild herbs and fruits to seek,
I sought his leave some better food to borrow
   From Guaire's bounty, but I might not speak.

"God is my help", he said, "I need no other,
   And life and death in His hands, not mine.
If He would have me seek the King, my brother,
   He will bestow on me some certain sign."

And coming back, for food I had sought vainly
   I saw him from far off lie as one dead;
But running on, where I could see more plainly,
   He was asleep, a rainbow round his head.

The colours faded out at his awaking,
   And as he moved, some far off music ceased;
But the light on his face was like the breaking
   Of morning through the pale clouds of the east.

He said "I thought my earthly life was over,
   That death had come on me in that long sleep,
I felt my spirit leave the flesh and hover
   Outside the body that it still must keep.

"But now I know my work is but beginning
   I know I must not yet lay down the sword
That unseen hands gave to my hand for winning
   A mighty unseen kingdom for our Lord.

"For I am bidden live my life for others,
   And lose no moment for the time is short.
And though all men, God's children, are my brothers,
   Guaire, my kinsman, calls my heart to Gort."

King, I have come. There is his message spoken,
   And if you look upon my words as good,
Send earthly bread, and it will be a token
   You will receive from him the Heavenly food.

GUAIRE

The tale is strange. I would I could believe it.
It has my heart with hope and longing stirred.
Glad would my life be if I could receive it,
But it rests only on a stranger's word.

Sure God would never deal such unjust measure,
Give me a Kingdom, leave him poor and lone;
Heap in my hands such store of earthly treasure,
To his true servant give for bread a stone.

If he my kinsman be and famine-wasted,
I would that God, whose hand my table fills
Would take from me this food that lies untasted,
And set it before Colman in the hills!

(*Two child angels appears and carry away the tray. The
stage grows dark. A vision appears. The Saint seen
kneeling. The child Angels have brought him the
tray.*) *All kneel.*

MESSENGER

The prayer is answered and with no delaying;
The King's food taken, laid there on a stone;
The way to Burren where the Saint is praying
Will as The Way of Angels now be known.

It will be known from this that God is able
To help the fainting, to lift up the poor.
Even in the barren place to set a table
His help, though slow in coming, cometh sure.

For He, whose voice is in the crashing thunder
Whose breath gives lightning and the storm-wind birth,
Works in our sight each year as great a wonder
Calling up harvests from the silent earth.

Happy are we, such miracle discerning,
And happy those, in quiet later days
Who, of the marvels of the old time learning,
Will know that God may work in many ways!

(*Vision fades away.*)

EPILOGUE

This is the tale of Colman and of Guaire,
    Our fathers to their children told it so,
And so from lip to lip the wonder-story
    Came down from fourteen hundred years ago.

Of Guaire's deeds the record is uncertain
    Much good and evil have of him been said
But on the evil let us drop a curtain
    And only say "He gave the poor their bread".

But Colman's work has never yet been barren,
    And here at least his memory never dim.
Churches and wells in Burren and in Aran,
    Kilchriest, Kinvara, take their name from him.

Oughtmana, Kilmacduagh, hold his traces,
    So when you tread the fields his footsteps trod,
Or pass by any of those hallowed places
    For him and all the Saints give thanks to God.

Curtain.

THE TRAVELLING MAN

THE TRAVELLING MAN

A MIRACLE PLAY

PERSONS
   A MOTHER.
   A CHILD.
   A TRAVELLING MAN.

SCENE. *A cottage kitchen. A woman setting out a bowl and jug and board on the table for breadmaking.*

CHILD. What is it you are going to make, mother?

MOTHER. I am going to make a grand cake with white flour. Seeds I will put in it. Maybe I'll make a little cake for yourself too. You can be baking it in the little pot while the big one will be baking in the big pot.

CHILD. It is a pity daddy to be away at the fair on a Samhain night.

MOTHER. I must make my feast all the same, for Samhain night is more to me than to any other one. It was on this night seven years I first came into this house.

CHILD. You will be taking down those plates from the dresser so, those plates with flowers on them, and be putting them on the table.

MOTHER. I will. I will set out the house to-day, and bring down the best delf, and put whatever thing is best on the table, because of the great thing that happened me seven years ago.

CHILD. What great thing was that?

MOTHER. I was after being driven out of the house where I was a serving girl. . . .

CHILD. Where was that house? Tell me about it.

MOTHER (*sitting down and pointing southward*). It is over there I was living, in a farmer's house up on Slieve Echtge, near to Slieve na n-Or, the Golden Mountain.

CHILD. The Golden Mountain! That must be a grand place.

MOTHER. Not very grand indeed, but bare and cold enough at that time of the year. Anyway, I was driven out a Samhain day like this, because of some things that were said against me.

21

CHILD. What did you do then?

MOTHER. What had I to do but to go walking the bare bog road through the rough hills where there was no shelter to find, and the sharp wind going through me, and the red mud heavy on my shoes. I came to Kilbecanty. . . .

CHILD. I know Kilbecanty. That is where the woman in the shop gave me sweets out of a bottle.

MOTHER. So she might now, but that night her door was shut and all the doors were shut; and I saw through the windows the boys and the girls sitting round the hearth and playing their games, and I had no courage to ask for shelter. In dread I was they might think some shameful thing of me, and I going the road alone in the night-time.

CHILD. Did you come here after that?

MOTHER. I went on down the hill in the darkness, and with the dint of my trouble and the length of the road my strength failed me, and I had like to fall. So I did fall at the last, meeting with a heap of broken stones by the roadside.

CHILD. I hurt my knee one time I fell on the stones.

MOTHER. It was then the great thing happened. I saw a stranger coming towards me, a very tall man, the best I ever saw, bright and shining that you could see him through the darkness; and I knew him to be no common man.

CHILD. Who was he?

MOTHER. It is what I thought, that he was the King of the World.

CHILD. Had he a crown like a King?

MOTHER. If he had, it was made of the twigs of a bare black-thorn; but in his hand he had a green branch, that never grew on a tree of this world. He took me by the hand, and he led me over the stepping-stones outside to this door, and he bade me to go in and I would find good shelter. I was kneeling down to thank him, but he raised me up and he said, "I will come to see you some other time. And do not shut up your heart in the things I give you," he said, "but have a welcome before me."

CHILD. Did he go away then?

MOTHER. I saw him no more after that, but I did as he bade me. (*She stands up and goes to the door.*) I came in like this, and your father was sitting there by the hearth, a lonely man that was after losing his wife. He was alone and I was alone, and we married one another; and I never wanted since for shelter or safety. And a good wife I made him, and a good housekeeper.

22

CHILD. Will the King come again to the house?

MOTHER. I have his word for it he will come, but he did not come yet; it is often your father and myself looked out the door of a Samhain night, thinking to see him.

CHILD. I hope he won't come in the night time, and I asleep.

MOTHER. It is of him I do be thinking every year, and I setting out the house, and making a cake for the supper.

CHILD. What will he do when he comes in?

MOTHER. He will sit over there in the chair, and maybe he will taste a bit of the cake. I will call in all the neighbours; I will tell them he is here. They will not be keeping it in their mind against me then that I brought nothing, coming to the house. They will know I am before any of them, the time they know who it is has come to visit me. They will all kneel down and ask for his blessing. But the best blessing will be on the house he came to of himself.

CHILD. And are you going to make the cake now?

MOTHER. I must make it now indeed, or I will be late with it. I am late as it is; I was expecting one of the neighbours to bring me white flour from the town. I'll wait no longer, I'll go borrow it in some place. There will be a wedding in the stonecutter's house Thursday, it's likely there will be flour in the house.

CHILD. Let me go along with you.

MOTHER. It is best for you to stop here. Be a good child now, and don't be meddling with the things on the table. Sit down there by the hearth and break up those little sticks I am after bringing in. Make a little heap of them now before me, and we will make a good fire to bake the cake. See now how many will you break. Don't go out the door while I'm away, I would be in dread of you going near the river and it in flood. Behave yourself well now. Be counting the sticks as you break them.

(She goes out.)

CHILD *(sitting down and breaking sticks across his knee)*. One— and two—O I can break this one into a great many, one, two, three, four.—This one is wet—I don't like a wet one—five, six—that is a great heap.—Let me try that great big one.—That is too hard.— I don't think mother could break that one.—Daddy could break it.

(Half-door is opened and a TRAVELLING MAN *comes in. He wears a ragged white flannel shirt, and mud-stained trousers. He is bareheaded and barefooted, and carries a little branch in his hand.)*

TRAVELLING MAN *(stooping over the child and taking the stick)*. Give it here to me and hold this.

23

(*He puts the branch in the* CHILD'S *hand while he takes the stick and breaks it.*)

CHILD. That is a good branch, apples on it and flowers. The tree at the mill has apples yet, but all the flowers are gone. Where did you get this branch?

TRAVELLING MAN. I got it in a garden a long way off.

CHILD. Where is the garden? Where do you come from?

TRAVELLING MAN (*pointing southward*). I have come from beyond those hills.

CHILD. Is it from the Golden Mountain you are come? From Slieve na n-Or?

TRAVELLING MAN. That is where I come from surely, from the Golden Mountain. I would like to sit down and rest for a while.

CHILD. Sit down here beside me. We must not go near the table or touch anything, or mother will be angry. Mother is going to make a beautiful cake, a cake that willl be fit for a King that might be coming in to our supper.

TRAVELLING MAN. I will sit here with you on the floor.

(*Sits down.*)

CHILD. Tell me now about the Golden Mountain.

TRAVELLING MAN. There is a garden in it, and there is a tree in the garden that has fruit and flowers at the one time.

CHILD. Like this branch?

TRAVELLING MAN. Just like that little branch.

CHILD. What other things are in the garden?

TRAVELLING MAN. There are birds of all colours that sing at every hour, the way the people will come to their prayers. And there is a high wall about the garden.

CHILD. What way can the people get through the wall?

TRAVELLING MAN. There are four gates in the wall: a gate of gold, and a gate of silver, and a gate of crystal, and a gate of white brass.

CHILD (*taking up the sticks*). I will make a garden. I will make a wall with these sticks.

TRAVELLING MAN. This big stick will make the first wall.

(*They build a square wall with sticks.*)

CHILD (*taking up branch*). I will put this in the middle. This is the tree. I will get something to make it stand up. (*Gets up and looks at dresser.*) I can't reach it, get up and give me that shining jug.

(TRAVELLING MAN *gets up and gives him the jug.*)

TRAVELLING MAN. Here it is for you.

CHILD (*puts it within the walls and sets the branch in it*). Tell me something else that is in the garden?

TRAVELLING MAN. There are four wells of water in it, that are as clear as glass.

CHILD. Get me down those cups, those flowery cups, we will put them for wells. (*He hands them down.*) Now I will make the gates, give me those plates for gates, not those ugly ones, those nice one at the top.

(*He takes them down and they put them on the four sides for gates. The* CHILD *gets up and looks at it.*)

TRAVELLING MAN. There now, it is finished.

CHILD. Is it as good as the other garden? How can we go to the Golden Mountain to see the other garden?

TRAVELLING MAN. We can ride to it.

CHILD. But we have no horse.

TRAVELLING MAN. This form will be our horse. (*He draws a form out of the corner, and sits down astride on it, putting the* CHILD *before him.*) Now, off we go! (*Sings, the* CHILD *repeating the refrain*)—

> Come ride and ride to the garden,
> > Come ride and ride with a will:
> For the flower comes with the fruit there
> > Beyond a hill and a hill.

> *Refrain*
> Come ride and ride to the garden,
> > Come ride like the March wind;
> There's barley there, and water there,
> > And stabling to your mind.

TRAVELLING MAN. How did you like that ride, little horseman?

CHILD. Go on again! I want another ride!

TRAVELLING MAN (*sings*)—

> The Archangels stand in a row there
> > And all the garden bless,
> The Archangel Axel, Victor the angel
> > Work at the cider press.

> *Refrain*
> Come ride and ride to the garden, &c.

CHILD. We will soon be at the Golden Mountain now. Ride again. Sing another song.

TRAVELLING MAN (*sings*)—

> O scent of the broken apples!
> O shuffling of holy shoes!
> Beyond a hill and a hill there
> In the land that no one knows.

Refrain

Come ride and ride to the garden, &c.

CHILD. Now another ride.

TRAVELLING MAN. This will be the last. It will be a good ride.
(*The* MOTHER *comes in. She stares for a second, then throws down her basket and snatches up the child.*)

MOTHER. Did ever anyone see the like of that! A common beggar, a travelling man off the roads, to be holding the child! To be leaving his ragged arms about him as if he was of his own sort! Get out of that, whoever you are, and quit this house or I'll call to some that will make you quit it.

CHILD. Do not send him out! He is not a bad man; he is a good man; he was playing horses with me. He has grand songs.

MOTHER. Let him get away out of this now, himself and his share of songs. Look at the way he has your bib destroyed that I was after washing in the morning!

CHILD. He was holding me on the horse. We were riding, I might have fallen. He held me.

MOTHER. I give you my word you are done now with riding horses. Let him go on his road. I have no time to be cleaning the place after the like of him.

CHILD. He is tired. Let him stop here till evening.

TRAVELLING MAN. Let me rest here for a while, I have been travelling a long way.

MOTHER. Where did you come from to-day?

TRAVELLING MAN. I came over Slieve Echtge from Slieve na n-Or. I had no house to stop in. I walked the long bog road, the wind was going through me, there was no shelter to be got, the red mud of the road was heavy on my feet. I got no welcome in the villages, and so I came on to this place, to the rising of the river at Ballylee.

MOTHER. It is best for you to go on to the town. It is not far for you to go. We will maybe have company coming in here.

(*She pours out flour into a bowl and begins mixing.*)

TRAVELLING MAN. Will you give me a bit of that dough to bring with me? I have gone a long time fasting.

MOTHER. It is not often in the year I make bread like this. There are a few cold potatoes on the dresser, are they not good enough for you? There is many a one would be glad to get them.

TRAVELLING MAN. Whatever you will give me, I will take it.

MOTHER (*going to the dresser for the potatoes and looking at the shelves*). What in the earthly world has happened all the delf? Where are the jugs gone and the plates? They were all in it when I went out a while ago.

CHILD (*hanging his head*). We were making a garden with them. We were making that garden there in the corner.

MOTHER. Is that what you were doing after I bidding you to sit still and to keep yourself quiet? It is to tie you in the chair I will another time! My grand jugs! (*She picks them up and wipes them.*) My plates that I bought the first time I ever went marketing into Gort. The best in the shop they were. (*One slips from her hand and breaks.*) Look at that now, look what you are after doing.

(*She gives a slap at the child.*)

TRAVELLING MAN. Do not blame the child. It was I myself took them down from the dresser.

MOTHER (*turning on him*). It was you took them! What business had you doing that? It's the last time a tramp or a tinker or a rogue of the roads will have a chance of laying his hand on anything in this house. It is jailed you should be! What did you want touching the dresser at all? Is it looking you were for what you could bring away?

TRAVELLING MAN (*taking the* CHILD'S *hands*). I would not refuse these hands that were held out for them. If it was for the four winds of the world he had asked, I would have put their bridles into these innocent hands.

MOTHER (*taking up the jug and throwing the branch on the floor*). Get out of this! Get out of this I tell you! There is no shelter here for the like of you! Look at that mud on the floor! You are not fit to come into the house of any decent respectable person!

(*The room begins to darken.*)

TRAVELLING MAN. Indeed, I am more used to the roads than to the shelter of houses. It is often I have spent the night on the bare hills.

27

MOTHER. No wonder in that! (*She begins to sweep floor.*) Go out of this now to whatever company you are best used to, whatever they are. The worst of people it is likely they are, thieves and drunkards and shameless women.

TRAVELLING MAN. Maybe so. Drunkards and thieves and shameless women, stones that have fallen, that are trodden under foot, bodies that are worn with fasting, minds that are broken with much sinning, the poor, the mad, the bad. . . .

MOTHER. Get out with you! Go back to your friends, I say!

TRAVELLING MAN. I will go. I will go back to the high road that is walked by the bare feet of the poor, by the innocent bare feet of children. I will go back to the rocks and the wind, to the cries of the trees in the storm! (*He goes out.*)

CHILD. He has forgotten his branch!

(*Takes it and follows him.*)

MOTHER (*still sweeping*). My good plates from the dresser, and dirty red mud on the floor, and the sticks all scattered in every place. (*Stoops to pick them up.*) Where is the child gone? (*Goes to door.*) I don't see him—he couldn't have gone to the river—it is getting dark—the bank is slippy. Come back! Come back! Where are you? (CHILD *runs in.*)

MOTHER. O where were you? I was in dread it was to the river you were gone, or into the river.

CHILD. I went after him. He is gone over the river.

MOTHER. He couldn't do that. He couldn't go through the flood.

CHILD. He did go over it. He was as if walking on the water. There was a light before his feet.

MOTHER. That could not be so. What put that thought in your mind?

CHILD. I called to him to come back for the branch, and he turned where he was in the river, and he bade me to bring it back, and to show it to yourself.

MOTHER (*taking the branch*). There are fruit and flowers on it. It is a branch that is not of any earthly tree. (*Falls on her knees.*) He is gone, he is gone, and I never knew him! He was that stranger that gave me all! He is the King of the World!

Curtain.

28

THE FULL MOON

TO ALL SANE PEOPLE IN OR OUT OF CLOON WHO KNOW
THEIR NEIGHBOURS TO BE NATURALLY CRACKED OR
SOMEWAY QUEER OR TO HAVE GONE WRONG IN THE
HEAD.

THE FULL MOON

PERSONS

SHAWN EARLY
BARTLEY FALLON
PETER TANNIAN
HYACINTH HALVEY } *All sane.*
MRS. BRODERICK
MISS JOYCE
CRACKED MARY
DAVIDEEN, *Her brother, an innocent.*

SCENE. *A shed close to Cloon Station;* BARTLEY FALLON *is sitting gloomily on a box;* HYACINTH HALVEY *and* SHAWN EARLY *are coming in at door.*

SHAWN EARLY. It is likely the train will not be up to its time, and cattle being on it for the fair. It's best wait in the shed. Is that Bartley Fallon? What way are you, Bartley?

BARTLEY FALLON. Faith, no way at all. On the drag, on the drag; striving to put the bad times over me.

SHAWN EARLY. Is it business with the nine o'clock you have?

BARTLEY FALLON. The wife that is gone visiting to Tubber, and that has the door locked till such time as she will come back on the train. And I thought this shed a place where no bad thing would be apt to happen me, and not to be going through the streets, and the darkness falling.

SHAWN EARLY. It is not long till the full moon will be rising.

BARTLEY FALLON. Everything that is bad, the falling sickness— God save the mark—or the like, should be at its worst at the full moon. I suppose because it is the leader of the stars.

SHAWN EARLY. Ah, what could happen any person in the street of Cloon?

BARTLEY FALLON. There might. Look at Matt Finn, the coffin-maker, put his hand on a cage the circus brought, and the lion took and tore it till they stuck him with a fork you'd rise dung with, and at that he let it drop. And that was a man had never quitted Cloon.

SHAWN EARLY. I thought you might be sending something to the fair.

BARTLEY FALLON. It isn't to the train I would be trusting anything I would have to sell, where it might be thrown off the track. And where would be the use sending the couple of little lambs I have? It is likely there is no one would ask me where I was going. When the weight is not in them, they won't carry the price. Sure, the grass I have is no good, but seven times worse than the road.

SHAWN EARLY. They are saying there'll be good demand at the fair of Carrow to-morrow.

HYACINTH HALVEY. To-morrow the fair day of Carrow? I was not remembering that.

BARTLEY FALLON. Ah, there won't be many in it, I'm thinking. There isn't a hungrier village in Connacht, they were telling me, and it's poor the look of it as well.

HYACINTH HALVEY. To-morrow the fair day. There will be all sorts in the streets to-night.

BARTLEY FALLON. The sort that will be in it will be a bad sort— sievemakers and tramps and neuks.

HYACINTH HALVEY. The tents on the fair green; there will be music in it; there was a fiddler having no legs would set men of threescore years and of fourscore years dancing. I can nearly hear his tune. (*He whistles* "The Heather Broom.")

BARTLEY FALLON. You are apt to be going there on the train, I suppose? It is well to be you, Mr. Halvey, having a good place in the town, and the price of your fare, and maybe six times the price of it, in your pocket.

HYACINTH HALVEY. I didn't think of that. I wonder could I go —for one night only—and see what the lads are doing.

SHAWN EARLY. Are you forgetting, Mr. Halvey, that you are to meet his Reverence on the platform that is coming home from drinking water at the Spa?

HYACINTH HALVEY. So I can meet him, and get in the train after him getting out.

(MRS. BRODERICK *and* PETER TANNIAN *come in.*)

MRS. BRODERICK. Is that Mr. Halvey is in it? I was looking for you at the chapel as I passed, and the Angelus bell after ringing.

HYACINTH HALVEY. Business I have here, ma'am. I was in dread I might not be here before the train.

MRS. BRODERICK. So you might not, indeed. That nine o'clock train you can never trust it to be late.

HYACINTH HALVEY. To meet Father Gregan I am come, and maybe to go on myself.

MRS. BRODERICK. Sure, I knew well you would be in haste to be before Father Gregan, and we knowing what we know.

HYACINTH HALVEY. I have no business only to be showing respect to him.

SHAWN EARLY. His good word he will give to Mr. Halvey at the Board, where it is likely he will be made Clerk of the Union next week.

MRS. BRODERICK. His good word he will give to another thing besides that, I am thinking.

HYACINTH HALVEY. I don't know what you are talking about.

MRS. BRODERICK. Didn't you hear the news, Peter Tannian, that Mr. Halvey is apt to be linked and joined in marriage with Miss Joyce, the priest's housekeeper?

PETER TANNIAN. I to believe all the lies I'd hear, I'd be a racked man by this.

MRS. BRODERICK. What I say now is as true as if you were on the other side of me. I suppose now the priest is come home there'll be no delay getting the license.

HYACINTH HALVEY. It is not so settled as that.

MRS. BRODERICK. Why wouldn't it be settled and it being told at Mrs. Delane's and through the whole world?

PETER TANNIAN. She should be a steady wife for him—a fortied girl.

SHAWN EARLY. A very good fortune in the bank they are saying she has, and she having crossed the ocean twice to America.

BARTLEY FALLON. It's as good for him to have a woman will keep the door open before him and his victuals ready and a quiet tongue in her head. Not like that little Tartar of my own.

MRS. BRODERICK. And an educated woman along with that. A man of his sort, going to be Clerk of the Union and to be taken up with books and papers, it's likely he'd die in a week, he to marry a dunce.

BARTLEY FALLON. So it's likely he would.

MRS. BRODERICK. A little shop they are saying she will take, for to open a flour store, and you to be keeping the accounts, the way you would not spend any waste time.

HYACINTH HALVEY. I have no mind to be settling myself down yet a while. I might maybe take a ramble here or there. There's many of my comrades in the States.

MRS. BRODERICK. To go away from Cloon, is it? And why would

you think to do that, and the whole town the same as a father and mother to you? Sure, the sergeant would live and die with you, and there are no two from this to Galway as great as yourself and the priest. To see you coming up the street, and your Dublin top-coat around you, there are some would give you a salute the same nearly as the Bishop.

PETER TANNIAN. They wouldn't do that maybe and they hearing things as I heard them.

HYACINTH HALVEY. What things?

PETER TANNIAN. There was a herd passing through from Carrow. It is what I heard him saying——

MRS. BRODERICK. You heard nothing of Mr. Halvey, but what is worthy of him. But that's the way always. The most thing a man does, the less he will get for it after.

PETER TANNIAN. A grand place in Carrow I suppose you had?

HYACINTH HALVEY. I had plenty of places. Giving out proclamations—attending waterworks——

MRS. BRODERICK. It is well fitted for any place he is, and all that was written around him and he coming into Cloon.

PETER TANNIAN. Writing is easy.

MRS. BRODERICK. Look at him since he was here, this twelve-month back, that he never went into a dance-house or stood at a cross-road, and never lost a half-an-hour with drink. Made no blunder, made no rumours. Whatever could be said of his worth, it could not be too well said.

HYACINTH HALVEY. Do you think now, ma'am, would it be any harm I to go spend a day or maybe two days out of this—I to go on the train——

MISS JOYCE (*at door, coming in backwards*). Go back now, go back! Don't be following after me in through the door! Is Mr. Halvey there? Don't let her come following me, Mr. Halvey!

HYACINTH HALVEY. Who is it is in it?

(*Sound of discordant singing outside.*)

MISS JOYCE. Cracked Mary it is, that is after coming back this day from the asylum.

HYACINTH HALVEY. I never saw her, I think.

SHAWN EARLY. The creature, she was light this long while and not good in the head, and at the last lunacy came on her and she was tied and bound. Sometimes singing and dancing she does be, and sometimes troublesome.

MISS JOYCE. They had a right to keep her spancelled in the asylum. She would begrudge any respectable person to be walking the street. She'd hoot you, she'd shout you, she'd clap her hands at you. She is a blight in the town.

HYACINTH HALVEY. There is a lad along with her.

SHAWN EARLY. It is Davideen, her brother, that is innocent. He was left rambling from place to place the time she was put within walls.

(CRACKED MARY *and* DAVIDEEN *come in.* MISS JOYCE *clings to* HYACINTH'S *arm.*)

CRACKED MARY. Give me a charity now, the way I'll be keeping a little rag on me and a little shoe to my foot. Give me the price of tobacco and the price of a grain of tea; for tobacco is blessed and tea is good for the head.

SHAWN EARLY. Give out now, Davideen, a verse of "The Heather Broom." That's a splendid tune.

DAVIDEEN (*sings*)

> Oh, don't you remember,
> As it's often I told you,
> As you passed through our kitchen
> That a new broom sweeps clean?
> Come out now and buy one,
> Come out now and try one—

(*His voice cracks, and he breaks off, laughing foolishly.*)

MRS. BRODERICK. He has a sweet note in his voice, but to know or to understand what he is doing, he couldn't do it.

CRACKED MARY. Leave him a while. His song that does be clogged through the daytime, the same as the sight is clogged with myself. It isn't but in the night time I can see anything worth while. Davy is a proper boy, a proper boy; let you leave Davy alone. It was himself came before me ere yesterday in the morning, and I walking out the madhouse door.

SHAWN EARLY. It is often there will fiddlers be waiting to play for them coming out, that are maybe the finest dancers of the day.

CRACKED MARY. Waiting before me he was, and no one to give him knowledge unless it might be the Big Man. I give you my word he near ate the face off me. As glad to see me he was as if I had dropped from heaven. Come hither to me, Davy, and give no heed to them. It is as dull and as lagging as themselves you would be maybe, and the world to be different and the moon to change its courses with the sun.

BARTLEY FALLON. I never would wish to be put within a mad-house before I'd die.

CRACKED MARY. Sorry they were losing me. There was not a better prisoner in it than my own four bones.

BARTLEY FALLON. Squeals you would hear from it, they were telling me, like you'd hear at the ringing of the pigs. Savages with whips beating them the same as hounds. You would not stand and listen to them for a hundred sovereigns. Of all bad things that can come upon a man, it is certain the madness is the last.

MISS JOYCE. It is likely she was well content in it, and the friends she had being of her own class.

CRACKED MARY. What way could you make friends with people would be always talking? Too much of talk and of noise there was in it, cursing, and praying, and tormenting; some dancing, some singing, and one writing a letter to a she devil called Lucifer. I not to close my ears, I would have lost the sound of Davideen's song.

MISS JOYCE. It was good shelter you got in it through the bad weather, and not to be out perishing under cold, the same as the starlings in the snow.

CRACKED MARY. I was my seven months in it, my seven months and a day. My good clothes that went astray on me and my boots. My fine gaudy dress was all moth-eated, that was worked with the wings of birds. To fall into dust and ashes it did, and the wings rose up into the high air.

BARTLEY FALLON. Take care would the madness catch on to ourselves the same as the chin-cough or the pock.

MRS. BRODERICK. Ah, that's not the way it goes travelling from one to another, but some that are naturally cracked and inherit it.

SHAWN EARLY. It is a family failing with her tribe. The most of them get giddy in their latter end.

MISS JOYCE. It might be it was sent as a punishment before birth, for to show the power of God.

PETER TANNIAN. It is tea-drinking does it, and that is the reason it is on the wife it is apt to fall for the most part.

MRS. BRODERICK. Ah, there's some does be thinking their wives isn't right, and there's others think they are too right. There to be any fear of me going astray, I give you my word I'd lose my wits on the moment.

HYACINTH HALVEY. There are some say it is the moon.

SHAWN EARLY. So it is too. The time the moon is going back, the blood that is in a person does be weakening, but when the moon is strong, the blood that moves strong in the same way. And it to be at the full, it drags the wits along with it, the same as it drags the tide.

MRS. BRODERICK. Those that are light show off more and have the talk of twenty the time it is at the full, that is sure enough. And to hold up a silk handkerchief and to look through it, you would see the four quarters of the moon; I was often told that.

MISS JOYCE. It is not you, Mr. Halvey, will give in to an unruly thing like the moon, that is under no authority, and cannot be put back, the same as a fast day that would chance to fall upon a feast.

HYACINTH HALVEY. It is likely it is put in the sky the same as a clock for our use, the way you would pick knowledge of the weather, the time the stars would be wild about it.

MRS. BRODERICK. That is very nice now. The thing you'd know, you'd like to go on, and to hear more or less about it.

MISS JOYCE (*to* H. H.). It is a lantern for your own use it will be to-night, and his Reverence coming home through the street, and yourself coming along with him to the house.

MRS. BRODERICK. That's right, Miss Joyce. Keep a good grip of him. What do you say to him talking a while ago as if his mind was running on some thought to leave Cloon?

MISS JOYCE. What way could he leave it?

HYACINTH HALVEY. No way at all, I'm thinking, unless there would be a miracle worked by the moon.

MRS. BRODERICK. Ah, miracles is gone out of the world this long time, with education, unless that they might happen in your own inside.

MISS JOYCE. I'll go set the table and kindle the fire, and I'll come back to meet the train with you myself.

(*She goes. A noise heard outside.*)

HYACINTH HALVEY. What is that now?

SHAWN EARLY (*at door*). Some noise as of running.

BARTLEY FALLON (*going to door*). It might chance to be some prisoner they would be bringing to the train.

PETER TANNIAN. No, but some lads that are running.

(*They go out.* H. H. *is going too, but* MRS. BRODERICK *goes before him and turns him round in doorway.*)

MRS. BRODERICK. Don't be coming out now in the dust that was formed by the heat is in the breeze. It would be a pity to spoil your Dublin coat, or your shirt that is that white you would nearly take it to be blue.

(*She goes out, pushing him in and shutting door after her.*)

CRACKED MARY. Ha! ha! ha!

37

HYACINTH HALVEY. What is it you are laughing at?

CRACKED MARY. Ha! ha! ha! It is a very laughable thing now, the third most laughable thing I ever met with in my lifetime.

HYACINTH HALVEY. What is that?

CRACKED MARY. A fine young man to be shut up and bound in a narrow little shed, and the full moon rising, and I knowing what I know!

HYACINTH HALVEY. It's little you are likely to know about me.

CRACKED MARY. Tambourines and fiddles and pipes—melodeons and the whistling of drums.

HYACINTH HALVEY. I suppose it is the Carrow fair you are talking about.

CRACKED MARY. Sitting within walls, and a top-coat wrapped around him, and mirth and music and frolic being in the place we know, and some dancing sets on the floor.

HYACINTH HALVEY. I wish I wasn't in this place to-night. I would like well to be going on the train, if it wasn't for the talk the neighbours would be making. I would like well to slip away. It is a long time I am going without any sort of funny comrades.

(*Goes to door. The others enter quickly, pushing him back.*)

BARTLEY FALLON. Nothing at all to see. It would be best for us to have stopped where we were.

MRS. BRODERICK. Running like foals to see it, and nothing to be in it worth while.

HYACINTH HALVEY. What was it was in it?

SHAWN EARLY. Nothing at all but some lads that were running in pursuit of a dog.

BARTLEY FALLON. Near knocked us they did, and they coming round the corner of the wall.

HYACINTH HALVEY. Is it that it was a mad dog?

PETER TANNIAN. Ah, what mad? Mad dogs are done away with now by the head Government and muzzles and the police.

BARTLEY FALLON. They are more watchful over them than they used. But all the same, you to see a strange dog afar off, you would be uneasy, thinking it might be yourself he would be searching out as his prey.

MRS. BRODERICK. Sure, there did a dog go mad through Galway, and the whole town rose against him, and flocked him into a corner, and shot him there. He did no harm after, he being made an end of at the first.

SHAWN EARLY. It might be that dog they were pursuing after was mad, on the head of being under the full moon.

CRACKED MARY (*jumping up excitedly*). That mad dog, he is a Dublin dog; he is between you and Belfast—he is running ahead— you couldn't keep up with him.

HYACINTH HALVEY. There is one, so, mad upon the road.

CRACKED MARY. There is police after him, but they cannot come up with him; he destroyed a splendid sow; nine bonavs they buried or less.

SHAWN EARLY. What place is he gone now?

CRACKED MARY. He made off towards Craughwell, and he bit a fine young man.

BARTLEY FALLON. So he would too. Sure, when a mad dog would be going about, on horseback or wherever you are, you're ruined.

CRACKED MARY. That dog is going on all the time; he wouldn't stop, but go ahead and bring that mouthful with him. He is still on the road; he is keeping the middle of the road; they say he is as big as a calf.

HYACINTH HALVEY. It is the police I have a right to forewarn to go after him.

CRACKED MARY. The motor cars is going to get out to track him, for fear he would destroy the world!

MRS. BRODERICK. That is a very nice thought now, to be sending the motor cars after him to overturn and to crush him the same as an ass-car in their path.

CRACKED MARY. You can't save yourself from a dog; he is after his own equals, dogs. He is doing every harm. They are out night and day.

SHAWN EARLY. Sure, a mad dog would go from this to Kinvara in a half a minute, like the train.

CRACKED MARY. He won't stay in this country down—he goes the straight road—he takes by the wind. He is as big as a yearling calf.

MRS. BRODERICK. I wouldn't ever forgive myself I to see him.

CRACKED MARY. He is not very heavy yet. There is only the relics in him.

HYACINTH HALVEY. They have a right to bring their rifles in their hand.

CRACKED MARY. The police is afraid of their life. They wrote for motor cars to follow him. Sure, he'd destroy the beasts of the field. A milch cow, he to grab at her, she's settled. Terrible wicked he is; he's as big as five dogs, and he does be very strong. I hope in

39

the Lord he'll be caught. It will be a blessing from the Almighty God to kill that dog.

HYACINTH HALVEY. He is surely the one is raging through the street.

PETER TANNIAN. Why wouldn't he be him? Is it likely there would be two of them in it at the one time?

SHAWN EARLY. A queer cut of a dog he was; a lurcher, a bastard hound.

PETER TANNIAN. I would say him to be about the size of the foal of a horse.

MRS. BRODERICK. Didn't he behave well not to do ourselves an injury?

BARTLEY FALLON. It is likely he will do great destruction. I wouldn't say but I felt the weight of him and his two paws around my neck.

HYACINTH HALVEY. I will go out following him.

SHAWN EARLY (*holding him*). Oh, let you not endanger yourself! It is the peelers should go follow him, that are armed with their batons and their guns.

HYACINTH HALVEY. I'll go. He might do some injury going through the town.

MRS. BRODERICK. Ah now, it is not yourself we would let go into danger! It is Peter Tannian should go, if any person should go.

PETER TANNIAN. Is it Hyacinth Halvey you are taking to be so far before myself?

MRS. BRODERICK. Why wouldn't he be before you?

PETER TANNIAN. Ask him what was he in Carrow? Ask was he a sort of a corner-boy, ringing the bell, pumping water, gathering a few coppers in the daytime for to scatter on a game of cards.

HYACINTH HALVEY. Stop your lies and your chat!

MRS. BRODERICK (*to* TANNIAN). You are going light in the head to talk that way.

SHAWN EARLY. He is, and queer in the mind. Take care did he get a bite from the dog, that left some venom working in his blood.

HYACINTH HALVEY. So he might, and he having a sort of a little rent in his sleeve.

PETER TANNIAN. I to have got a bite from the dog, is it? I did not come anear him at all. You to strip me as bare as winter you will not find the track of his teeth. It is Shawn Early was nearer to him than what I was.

SHAWN EARLY. I was not nearer, or as near as what Mrs. Broderick was.

MRS. BRODERICK. I made away when I saw him. My chest is not the better of it yet. Since I left off fretting I got gross. I am that nervous I would run from a blessed sheep, let alone a dog.

SHAWN EARLY. To see any of the signs of madness upon him, it is Mr. Halvey the sergeant would look to for to make his report.

HYACINTH HALVEY. So I would make a report.

PETER TANNIAN. Is it that you lay down you can see signs? Is that the learning they were giving you in Carrow?

MRS. BRODERICK. Don't be speaking with him at all. It is easy know the signs. A person to be laughing and mocking, and that would not have the same habits with yourself, or to have no fear of things you would be in dread of, or to be usingg a different class of food.

PETER TANNIAN. I use no food but clean food.

HYACINTH HALVEY. To be giddy in the head is a sign, and to be talking of things that passed years ago.

PETER TANNIAN. I am talking of nothing but the thing I have a right to talk of.

MRS. BRODERICK. To be nervous and thinking and pausing, and playing with knicknacks.

PETER TANNIAN. It never was my habit to be playing with knicknacks.

BARTLEY FALLON. When the master in the school where I was went queer, he beat me with two clean rods, and wrote my name with my own blood.

MRS. BRODERICK. To take the shoe off their foot, and to hit out right and left with it, bawling their life out, tearing their clothes, scattering and casting them in every part; or to run naked through the town, and all the people after them.

SHAWN EARLY. To be jumping the height of trees they do be, and all the people striving to slacken them.

HYACINTH HALVEY. To steal prayer books and rosaries, and to be saying prayers they never could keep in mind before.

MRS. BRODERICK. Very strong, that they could leap a wall—jumping and pushing and kicking—or to tie people to one another with a rope.

SHAWN EARLY. Any fear of any person here being violent, Mr. Halvey will get him put under restraint.

PETER TANNIAN. Is it myself you are thinking to put under restraint? Would a man would be pushing and kicking and tearing his clothes, be able to do arithmetic on a board? Look now at that. (*Chalks figures on door*). Three and three make six! —and three—

41

MRS. BRODERICK. I'm no hand at figuring, but I can say out a blessed hymn, what any person with the mind gone contrary in them could not do. Hearken now till you'll know is there confusion in my mind. (*Sings*.)

> Mary Broderick is my name;
>> Fiddane was my station;
> Cloon is my dwelling place;
>> And (I hope) heaven is my destination.
> Mary Broderick is my name,
>> Cloon was my——

CRACKED MARY (*with a cackle of delight*). Give heed to them now, Davideen! That's the way the crazed people used to be going on in the place where I was, every one thinking the other to be cracked.

HYACINTH HALVEY (*to* TANNIAN). Look now at your great figuring! Argus with his hundred eyes wouldn't know is that a nought or is it a nine without a tail.

PETER TANNIAN. Leave that blame on a little ridge that is in the nature of the chalk. Look now at Mary Broderick, that it has failed to word out her verse.

MRS. BRODERICK. Ah, what signifies? I'd never get light greatly. It wouldn't be worth while I to go mad.

(BARTLEY FALLON *gives a deep groan*.)

SHAWN EARLY. What is on you, Bartley?

BARTLEY FALLON. I'm in dread it is I myself has got venom into my blood.

HYACINTH HALVEY. What makes you think that?

BARTLEY FALLON. It's a sort of a thing would be apt to happen me, and any malice to fall within the town at all.

MRS. BRODERICK. Give heed to him, Hyacinth Halvey; you are the most man we have to baffle any wrong thing coming in our midst!

HYACINTH HALVEY. Is it that you are feeling any pain as of a wound or a sore?

BARTLEY FALLON. Some sort of a little catch I'm thinking there is in under my knee. I would feel no pain unless I would turn it contrary.

HYACINTH HALVEY. What class of feeling would you say you are feeling?

BARTLEY FALLON. I am feeling as if the five fingers of my hand to be lessening from me, the same as five farthing dips the heat of the sun would be sweating the tallow from.

HYACINTH HALVEY. That is a strange account.

BARTLEY FALLON. And a sort of a megrim in my head, the same as a sheep would get a fit of staggers in a field.

HYACINTH HALVEY. That is what I would look for. Is there some sort of a roaring in your ear?

BARTLEY FALLON. There is, there is, as if I would hear voices would be talking.

HYACINTH HALVEY. Would you feel any wish to go tearing and destroying?

BARTLEY FALLON. I would indeed, and there to be an enemy upon my path. Would you say now, Widow Broderick, am I getting anyway flushy in the face?

MRS. BRODERICK. Don't leave your eye off him for pity's sake. He is reddening as red as a rose.

BARTLEY FALLON. I could as if walk on the wind with lightness. Something that is rising in my veins the same as froth would be rising on a pint.

HYACINTH HALVEY. It is the doctor I'd best call for—and maybe the sergeant and the priest.

BARTLEY FALLON. There are three thoughts going through my mind—to hang myself or to drown myself, or to cut my neck with a reaping-hook.

MRS. BRODERICK. It is the doctor will serve him best, where it is the mad blood that should be bled away. To break up eggs, the white of them, in a tin can, will put new blood in him, and whiskey, and to taste no food through twenty-one days.

BARTLEY FALLON. I'm thinking so long a fast wouldn't serve me. I wouldn't wish the lads will bear my body to the grave, to lay down there was nothing within it but a grasshopper or a wisp of dry grass.

SHAWN EARLY. No, but to cut a piece out of his leg the doctor will, the way the poison will get no leave to work.

PETER TANNIAN. Or to burn it with red-hot irons, the way it will not scatter itself and grow. There does a doctor do that out in foreign.

MRS. BRODERICK. It would be more natural to cut the leg off him in some sort of a Christian way.

SHAWN EARLY. If it was a pig was bit, or a sow or a bonav, it to show the signs, it would be shot, if it was a whole fleet of them was in it.

43

MRS. BRODERICK. I knew of a man that was butler in a big house was bit, and they tied him first and smothered him after, and his master shot the dog. A splendid shot he was; the thing he'd not see he'd hit it the same as the thing he'd see. I heard that from an outside neighbour of my own, a woman that told no lies.

SHAWN EARLY. Sure, they did the same thing to a high-up lady over in England, and she after being bit by her own little spaniel and it having a ring around its neck.

PETER TANNIAN. That is the only best thing to do. Whether the bite is from a dog, or a cat, or whatever it may be, to put the quilt and the blankets on the person and smother him in the bed. To smother them out-and-out you should, before the madness will work.

HYACINTH HALVEY. I'd be loth he to be shot or smothered. I'd sooner to give him a chance in the asylum.

MRS. BRODERICK. To keep him there and to try him through three changes of the moon. It's well for you, Bartley, Mr. Halvey being in charge of you, that is known to be a tender man.

PETER TANNIAN. He to have got a bite and to go biting others, he would put in them the same malice. It is the old people used to tell that down, and they must have had some reason doing that.

SHAWN EARLY. To get a bite of a dog you must chance your life. There is no doubt at all about that. It might work till the time of the new moon or the full moon, and then they must be shot or smothered.

HYACINTH HALVEY. It is a pity there to be no cure found for it in the world.

SHAWN EARLY. There never came out from the Almighty any cure for a mad dog.

(BARTLEY FALLON *has been edging towards door.*)

SHAWN EARLY. Oh! stop him and keep a hold of him, Mr. Halvey!

HYACINTH HALVEY. Stop where you are.

BARTLEY FALLON. Isn't it enough to have madness before me, that you will not let me go fall in my own choice place?

HYACINTH HALVEY. The neighbours would think it bad of me to let a raving man out into their midst.

BARTLEY FALLON. Is it to shoot me you are going?

HYACINTH HALVEY. I will call to the doctor to say is the padded room at the workhouse the most place where you will be safe, till such time as it will be known did the poison wear away.

BARTLEY FALLON. I will not go in it! It is likely I might be

44

forgot in it, or the nurses to be in dread to bring me nourishment, and they to hear me barking within the door. I'm thinking it was allotted by nature I never would die an easy death.

HYACINTH HALVEY. I will keep a watch over you myself.

BARTLEY FALLON. Where's the use of that the time the breath will be gone out of me, and you maybe playing cards on my coffin, and I having nothing around or about me but the shroud, and the habit, and the little board?

HYACINTH HALVEY. Sure, I cannot leave you the way you are.

BARTLEY FALLON. It is what I ever and always heard, a dog to bite you, all you have to do is to take a pinch of its hair and to lay it into the wound.

MRS. BRODERICK. So I heard that myself. A dog to bite any person he is entitled to be plucked of his hair.

HYACINTH HALVEY. I'll go out; I might chance to see him.

MRS. BRODERICK. You will not, without getting advice from the priest that is coming in the train. Let his Reverence come into this place, and say is it Bartley or is it Peter Tannian was done destruction on by the dog.

SHAWN EARLY. There is a surer way than that.

MRS. BRODERICK. What way?

SHAWN EARLY. It takes madness to find out madness. Let you call to the cracked woman that should know.

HYACINTH HALVEY. Come hither, Mary, and tell us is there any one of your own sort in this shed?

MRS. BRODERICK. That is a good thought. It is only themselves that recognise one another.

BARTLEY FALLON. Do not ask her! I will not leave it to her!

MRS. BRODERICK. Sure, she cannot say more than what yourself has said against yourself.

BARTLEY. I'm in dread she might know too much, and be telling out what is within in my mind.

HYACINTH HALVEY. That's foolishness. These are not the ancient times, when Ireland was full of haunted people.

BARTLEY FALLON. Is a man having a wife and three acres of land to be put under the judgement of a witch?

HYACINTH HALVEY. I would not give in to any pagan thing, but to recognise one of her own sort, that is a thing can be understood.

MRS. BRODERICK. So it could be too, the same as witnesses in a court.

BARTLEY FALLON. I will not give in to going to demons or druids or freemasons! Wasn't there enough of misfortune set before my path through every day of my lifetime without it to be linked with me after my death? Is it that you would force me to lose the comforts of heaven and to get the poverty of hell? I tell you I will have no trade with witches! I would sooner go face the featherbeds.

HYACINTH HALVEY. Say out, girl, do you see any craziness here or anything of the sort?

CRACKED MARY. Every day in the year there comes some malice into the world, and where it comes from is no good place.

MRS. BRODERICK. That is it, a venomous dew, as in the year of the famine. There is no astronomer can say it is from the earth or the sky.

HYACINTH HALVEY. It is what we are asking you, did any of that malice get its scope in this place?

CRACKED MARY. That was settled in Mayo two thousand years ago.

MRS. BRODERICK. Ah, there's no head or tail to that one's story. You'd be left at the latter end the same as at the commencement.

HYACINTH HALVEY. That dog you were talking of, that is raging through the district and the town—did it leave any madness after it?

CRACKED MARY. It will go in the wind, there is a certain time for that. It might go off in the wind again. It might go shaping off and do no harm.

BARTLEY FALLON. Where is that dog presently, till some person might go pluck out a few ribs of its hair?

CRACKED MARY. Raging ever and always it is, raging wild. Sure, that is a dog was in it before the foundations of the world.

PETER TANNIAN. Who is it now that venom fell on, whatever beast's jaws may have scattered it?

CRACKED MARY. It is the full moon knows that. The moon to slacken it is safe, there is no harm in it. Almighty God will do that much. He'll slacken it like you'd slacken lime.

SHAWN EARLY. There is reason in what she is saying. Set open the door and let the full moon call its own!

BARTLEY FALLON. Don't let in the rays of it upon us or I'm a gone man. It to shine on them that are going wrong in the head, it would raise a great stir in the mind. Sure, it's in the asylum at that time they do have whips to chastise them. (*Goes to corner.*)

CRACKED MARY. That's it. The moon is terrible. The full moon cracks them out and out, any one that would have any spleen or any relics in them.

46

MRS. BRODERICK. Do not let in the light of it. I would scruple to look at it myself.

CRACKED MARY. Let you throw open the door, Davideen. It is not ourselves are in dread that the white man in the sky will be calling names after us and ridiculing us. Ha! ha! I might be as foolish as yourselves and as fearful, but for the Almighty that left a little cleft in my skull, that would let in His candle through the night time.

HYACINTH HALVEY. Hurry on now, tell us is there any one in this place is wild and astray like yourself.

(*He opens the door. The light falls on him.*)

CRACKED MARY (*putting her hand on him*). There was a great shouting in the big round house, and you coming into it last night.

HYACINTH HALVEY. What are you saying? I never went frolicking in the night time since the day I came into Cloon.

CRACKED MARY. We were talking of it a while ago. I knew you by the smile and by the laugh of you. A queen having a yellow dress, and the hair on her smooth like marble. All the dead of the village were in it, and of the living myself and yourself.

HYACINTH HALVEY. I thought it was of Carrow she was talking; it is of the other world she is raving, and of the shadow-shapes of the forth.

CRACKED MARY. You have the door open—the speckled horses are on the road! —make a leap on the horse as it goes by, the horse that is without a rider. Can't you hear them puffing and roaring? Their breath is like a fog upon the air.

HYACINTH HALVEY. What you hear is but the train puffing afar off.

CRACKED MARY. Make a snap at the bridle as it passes by the bush in the western gap. Run out now, run, where you have the bare ridge of the world before you, and no one to take orders from but yourself, maybe, and God.

HYACINTH HALVEY. Ah, what way can I run to any place!

CRACKED MARY. Stop where you are, so. In my opinion it is little difference the moon can see between the whole of ye. Come on, Davideen, come out now, we have the wideness of the night before us. O golden God! All bad things quieten in the night time, and the ugly thing itself will put on some sort of a decent face! Come out now to the night that will give you the song, and will show myself out as beautiful as Helen of the Greek gods, that hanged herself the day there first came a wrinkle on her face!

DAVIDEEN (*coming close, and taking her hand as he sings*).

> Oh! don't you remember
> What our comrades called to us
> And they footing steps
> At the call of the moon?
> Come out to the rushes,
> Come out to the bushes,
> Where the music is called
> By the lads of Queen Anne!

(*They look beautiful. They dance and sing in perfect time as they go out.*)

PETER TANNIAN (*closing the door, and pointing at* HYACINTH, *who stands gazing after them, and when the door is shut sits thinking deeply*). It is on him her judgment fell, and a clear judgment.

SHAWN EARLY. She gave out that award fair enough.

PETER TANNIAN. Did you take notice, and he coming into the shed, he had like some sort of a little twist in his walk?

MRS. BRODERICK. I would be loth to think there would be any poison lurking in his veins. Where now would it come from, and Cracked Mary's dog being as good as no dog at all?

PETER TANNIAN. It might chance, and he a child in the cradle, to get the bite of a dog. It might be only now, its full time being come, its power would begin to work.

MRS. BRODERICK. So it would too, and he but to see the shadow of the dog bit him in a body glass, or in the waves, and he himself looking over a boat, and as if called to throw himself in the tide. But I would not have thought it of Mr. Halvey. Well, it's as hard to know what might be spreading abroad in any person's mind, as to put the body of a horse out through a cambric needle. (HYACINTH *looks at them.*)

SHAWN EARLY. Be quiet now, he is going to say some word.

HYACINTH HALVEY. There is a thought in my mind. I think it was coming this good while.

SHAWN EARLY. Whisht now and listen.

HYACINTH HALVEY. I made a great mistake coming into this place.

PETER TANNIAN. There was some mistake made anyway.

HYACINTH. It is foolishness kept me in it ever since. It is too big a name was put upon me.

PETER TANNION. It is the power of the moon is forcing the truth out of him.

HYACINTH HALVEY. Every person in the town giving me out for more than I am. I got too much of that in the heel.

SHAWN EARLY. He is talking queer now anyway.

HYACINTH HALVEY. Calling to me every little minute—expecting me to do this thing and that thing—watching me the same as a watchdog, their eyes as if fixed upon my face.

MRS. BRODERICK. To be giving out such strange thoughts, he hasn't much brains left around him.

HYACINTH HALVEY. I looking to be Clerk of the Union, and the place I had giving me enough to do, and too much to do. Tied on this side, tied on that side. I to be bothered with business through the holy livelong day!

PETER TANNIAN. It is good pay he got with it. Eighty pounds a year doesn't come on the wind.

HYACINTH HALVEY. In danger to be linked and wed—I never ambitioned it—with a woman would want me to be earning through every day of the year.

SHAWN EARLY. He is a gone man surely.

HYACINTH HALVEY. The wide ridge of the world before me, and to have no one to look to for orders; that would be better than roast and boiled and all the comforts of the day. I declare to goodness, and I'd nearly take my oath, I'd sooner be among a fleet of tinkers, than attending meetings of the Board!

MRS. BRODERICK. If there are fairies in it, it is in the fairies he is.

PETER TANNIAN. Give me a hold of that chain.

MRS. BRODERICK. What is it you are about to do?

PETER TANNIAN. To bind him to the chair I will before he will burst out wild mad. Come over here, Bartley Fallon, and lend a hand if you can.

(BARTLEY FALLON *appears from corner with a chicken crate over his head.*)

MRS. BRODERICK. O Bartley, that is the strangest lightness ever I saw, to go bind a chicken crate around your skull!

BARTLEY FALLON. Will you tighten the knots I have tied, Peter Tannian! I am in dread they might slacken or fail.

SHAWN EARLY. Was there ever seen before this night such power to be in the moon!

BARTLEY FALLON. It would seem to be putting very wild unruly thoughts a-through me, stirring up whatever spleen or whatever relics was left in me by the nature of the dog.

PETER TANNIAN. It is that you think those rods, spaced wide, as they are, will keep out the moon from entering your brain?

BARTLEY FALLON. There does great strength come at the time the wits would be driven out of a person. I never was handled by a policeman—but once—and never hit a blow on any man. I would not wish to destroy my neighbour or to have his blood on my hands.

SHAWN EARLY. It is best keep out of his reach.

BARTLEY FALLON. The way I have this fixed, there is no person will be the worse for me. I to rush down the street and to meet with my most enemy in some lonesome craggy place, it would fail me, and I thrusting for it to scatter any share of poison in his body or to sink my teeth in his skin. I wouldn't wonder I to have hung for some of you, and that plan not to have come into my head.

(*Whistle of train heard.*)

HYACINTH HALVEY (*getting up*). I have my mind made up, I am going out of this on that train.

PETER TANNIAN. You are not going so easy as what you think.

HYACINTH HALVEY. Let you mind your own business.

PETER TANNIAN. I am well able to mind it.

HYACINTH HALVEY (*throwing off top-coat*). You cannot keep me here.

PETER TANNIAN. Give me a hand with the chain.

(*They throw it round* HYACINTH *and hold him.*)

HYACINTH HALVEY. Is it out of your senses you are gone?

PETER TANNIAN. Not at all, but yourself that is gone raving mad from the fury and the strength of some dog.

MISS JOYCE (*at door*). Are you there, Hyacinth Halvey? The train is in. Come forward now, and give a welcome to his Reverence.

HYACINTH HALVEY. Let me go out of this!

MISS JOYCE. You are near late as it is. The train is about to start.

HYACINTH HALVEY. Let me go, or I'll tear the heart out of ye!

SHAWN FARLEY. Oh, he is stark, staring mad!

HYACINTH HALVEY. Mad, am I? Bit by a dog, am I? You'll see am I mad! I'll show madness to you! Let go your hold or I'll skin you! I'll destroy you! I'll bite you! I'm a red enemy to the whole of you! Leave go your grip! Yes, I'm mad! Bow wow wow, wow wow!

(*They let go and fall back in terror, and he rushes out of the door.*)

MISS JOYCE. What at all has happened? Where is he gone?

SHAWN EARLY. To the train he is gone, and away in it he is gone.

MISS JOYCE. He gave some sort of a bark or a howl.

SHAWN EARLY. He is gone clean mad. Great arguing he had, and leaping and roaring.

BARTLEY FALLON (*taking off crate*). He went very near to tear us all asunder. I declare I amn't worth a match.

MRS. BRODERICK. He made a reel in my head, till I don't know am I right myself.

SHAWN EARLY. Bawling his life out, tearing his clothes, tearing and eating them. Look at his top-coat he left after him.

BARTLEY FALLON. He poured all over with pure white foam.

PETER TANNIAN. There now is an end of your elegant man.

SHAWN EARLY. Bit he was with the mad dog that went tearing, and lads chasing him a while ago.

MISS JOYCE. Sure that was Tannian's own dog, that had a bit of meat snapped from Quirke's ass-car. He is without this door now. (*All look out.*) He has the appearance of having a full meal taken.

BARTLEY FALLON. And they to be saying I went mad. That is the way always, and a thing to be tasked to me that was not in it at all.

MRS. BRODERICK (*laying her hand on* MISS JOYCE'S *shoulder*). Take comfort now; and if it was the moon done all, and has your bachelor swept, let you not begrudge it its full share of praise for the hand it had in banishing a strange bird, might have gone wild and bawling like eleven, and you after being wed with him, and would maybe have put a match to the roof. And hadn't you the luck of the world now, that you did not give notice to the priest!

Curtain.

SHANWALLA

BRIDE. There was a woman from the North used to be telling me that every time you see a tree shaking there is a ghost in it.

CONARY. When one goes that has a weight on the soul that is more than the weight of the body, it cannot get away, but stays wandering till some one has courage to question it.

BRIDE. That is what the woman told me. To have courage to question them you must, or they will have no power for to speak.

CONARY. I knew one Kearney met a woman, a stranger. "Is there anything I can do for you?" says he, for he thought she was some country-woman gone astray. "There is," says she. And she told him of some small debts she had left unknown to her friends, not more than ten shillings in all, and when she died no more had been said about it. So her friends paid these and said masses, and shortly after she appeared to him again. "God bless you now," she said, "for what you did for me, for now I am at peace." But if Kearney did not question her, she would not have power to tell what ailed her. And it is certain that a mother will come back to care the child that is left after her.

BRIDE. I never saw my mother that was taken at the very hour of my birth.

CONARY. It is likely she had a hand in you; for a child that gets help from the other side will grow to be the best in the world.

BRIDE. They must surely be uneasy about those left after them, or why would they quit for one minute only that good place where they are gone.

CONARY. Coming back to give help, that is what they do be doing. Believe me, if it is good to have friends among the living, it is seven times better to have them among the dead.

BRIDE. Whist now! Larry will say no one will be talking of such things unless it might be a woman or a fool!

SCARRY (*coming in*). Is that you Owen Conary keeping the woman of the house in talk?

CONARY (*changing manner*). Myself it is, Lawrence Scarry! Calling to mind I was the grandeurs of this place in the long ago, the time the Darcys' hounds would be putting a fox in trouble! (*Sings.*)

> Hark, hark, the sounds increase
> Each horn sounds a bass
> Away to Chevy Chase
> Poor Reynard is in view;
> All round the sunny lake

Lough Cutra then he takes
But they without mistake
His footsteps did pursue.
'Twas on Ballyturn hill
Poor Reynard made his will . . .

SCARRY. Stop your noise now and get out of sight. I saw the Master coming and he crossing the bridge!

BRIDE. Come with me Owen till I'll lead you to where there is a warm wad of straw in the shed beyond. You can rest yourself there for a while. You might miss your step if I brought you up the ladder into the loft.

(*They go out.*)

SCARRY. That's it, put him out of sight in some place. (*He takes bit and stirrups and rubs them with a chamois leather, humming as if grooming a horse.*)

DARCY (*at door*). Are you there Larry?

SCARRY. I am, sir.

DARCY (*coming in*). What way is the horse today?

SCARRY. Grand, sir. Grand out and out.

DARCY. I'd be here sooner but for having to attend the Bench in Cloon. Magistrates are scarce these times.

SCARRY. There's good daylight yet. You can take a view of him.

DARCY (*going to side and opening door comes back, shutting it*). He doesn't look too bad.

SCARRY. Is that all you have to say? He's altogether a beauty!

DARCY. Oh, Larry, do you think can he win in the race?

SCARRY. He to fail I'll give you leave to do your choice thing on me.

DARCY. There will be good horses against him.

SCARRY There's a good breed in him. Never fear he'll best them.

DARCY. That dealer in Limerick owns a bay mare has a great name.

SCARRY. You may bet your estate on Shanwalla.

DARCY. That mare won all before her at Turloghmore.

SCARRY. Shanwalla that will get the victory over all Ireland.

DARCY. You are likely making too much of him.

SCARRY. There's no one can go stronger than him, and you to be trotting him itself; and as gentle as that you could bridle him with the ashes of a spent thread of silk.

DARCY. It would frighten you to see the leaps they are putting up on the course.

SCARRY. There isn't a leap in any part would baulk *him*.

DARCY. It will be a fierce race, a fierce pace.

SCARRY. I'll pity them that will make their start with Shanwalla! They to try and catch him, he'll take the cracked strain, and away with him.

DARCY. He to win I'll have my pocket well filled. And believe me, you'll be no loser.

SCARRY. It's time indeed you to do some good thing for me, and I wedded and joined with a wife.

DARCY. It wasn't I that bade you take a wife.

SCARRY. It was you put me stopping in this bare barrack of a deserted old kennel, till I near died with the lonesome.

DARCY. Well you have company now, whatever complaints she may put out of her.

SCARRY. The time she was a poor serving girl in your own kitchen she was better treated than to be housed under rafters in a loft.

DARCY. A loft is an airy place.

SCARRY. A loft the crows wouldn't stop in, but to be going in and out of it with the breeze.

DARCY. It to be airy you will not be stopping in it wasting your time of a morning.

SCARRY. It is gone to rack too. It was made since God made the world. It's as old as Adam. There's a great traffic in it of rats, till they have it holed like a sieve.

DARCY. Holes are very handy for you to be looking down into the manger to see is Shanwalla eating his feed.

SCARRY. And no way to go up in it but only a ricketty ladder does be shaking like a bough in a big wind.

DARCY. That is great good. It will keep you sober more than if you gave your oath to the missioners. You would be in dread to go face it and you after taking a drop.

SCARRY. I tell you I wouldn't care if I had to climb a rope to the skies if it wasn't for my woman of a wife.

DARCY. I'm not too well pleased with you, Larry, for bringing in a companion till after the race would be won. Take care would she be chattering about the horse.

SCARRY. You need be in no dread. Wise head and shut mouth. That's the way with her.

DARCY. I wouldn't wish her to be bringing company around the place.

SCARRY. No fear of her coveting to ask any person to come see the poor way she is lodged.

DARCY. That's a good reason to keep you down. I have no mind anyone to come peeping and prying, striving to see him and to give out a report of him.

SCARRY. There is no one will get any sight of him till such time as he will come sparkling on to the course, and he tossing his head, like as if you were pitching buttons.

DARCY. Take care would you let anyone come next or near him.

SCARRY. I know my business better than that.

DARCY. Give no one leave to touch or to handle him. It is a little thing would put a horse astray.

SCARRY. Ah, horses in this country is a hardy class. They wouldn't die through swallowing a buttercup the same as they do out in France.

DARCY. It's impossible to be too careful.

SCARRY. It wasn't myself lamed the chestnut, leaping on to the road, that the sinews spread on him.

DARCY. It's not of making leaps I am afraid. There are other things might lame him such as a thorn in the knee.

SCARRY. He got no thorns under my care.

DARCY. A hayseed in the eye might bring blindness on him.

SCARRY. It might, and my eyes being blind.

DARCY. A prick of a nail.

SCARRY. He's done with shoeing for this time.

DARCY. A pinch of some poison in the drinking water.

SCARRY. Without they'd poison the whole river it would fail them to bring that about.

DARCY. I tell you I'll be easier in my mind when next Friday will be passed.

SCARRY. So you would be too. It's best not praise or dispraise a crop before the June will be out.

DARCY. I am wakeful fearing for him in the night time.

SCARRY. I wonder you wouldn't shift him over to your own yard and you being so uneasy.

DARCY. I wouldn't say but it might be best.

SCARRY. Do it so, and I'll get my sound sleep.

DARCY. He might get cold in the new stable.

SCARRY. Let him wear his blanket.

DARCY. Sure enough, there's no eye like the master's.

SCARRY. I often heard you say that.

DARCY. It's hard trust anyone.

SCARRY. Please yourself.

DARCY. It might not be worth while for the short time till the race.

SCARRY. This is Tuesday. There's three days to it yet.

DARCY. Wait till I'll take another look at him.

SCARRY. Look here now Master Hubert. You'll bring him out of this tonight or I myself will go out of it.

DARCY. What are you talking about?

SCARRY. I will not stop in charge of him, and I not to be trusted.

DARCY. Who said you were not trusted?

SCARRY. You said it now.

DARCY. I did not.

SCARRY. I say that you did.

DARCY. That's a big lie.

SCARRY. Your own is bigger again.

DARCY. That's no way to speak to me.

SCARRY. I'll put up with it no longer.

DARCY. All right so. You can go tomorrow.

SCARRY. I'll go here and now.

DARCY. You cannot till tomorrow. I have no one to care the horse tonight.

SCARRY. Where is the trainer you had engaged?

DARCY. That's nothing to you. You have to keep charge till morning.

SCARRY. Let him earn the big money he is paid.

DARCY. You know well he is gone this fortnight.

SCARRY. Let you send and call him back.

DARCY. He is gone for good and all.

SCARRY. My share of trouble with him! It's little we'll cry after him, myself and Shanwalla.

DARCY. Go your own road tomorrow but you cannot quit my service till then.

SCARRY. If I do stop it is not to oblige you Mr. Darcy, but because I have a great regard for that horse.

DARCY. All right! We'll say good-bye to one another in the morning. I've stood enough of you and of your tongue! (*Goes.*)

SCARRY. Ah, my joy go with you! (*Sings ostentatiously:*)

The lands he did forsake, and swam across the lake
But to his great mistake the hounds kept him in view,
Our County Galway joy
Is Persse of Castleboy . . .

(BROGAN *and* O'MALLEY *come in.*)

O'MALLEY. Fine evening, Lawrence.

SCARRY. Is that you Pat O'Malley? Is it up from Limerick you are after coming, James Brogan?

BROGAN. Going on to the fair of Loughrea I am, where I have business with a dealer from Cappaghtagle.

O'MALLEY. We just called in to see what way yourself and Bride agree together. It is what they were telling me, your life is like marriage bells.

BROGAN. We were waiting beyond behind the little wall of bushes till Darcy would be gone. You might not be well pleased he to have seen us.

SCARRY. Little I'd care he to see you or not to see you!

O'MALLEY. They are saying he gives you no leave so much as to cross the threshold of the door.

BROGAN. There is surely some great treasure in this old kennel of a place that he has no mind to let slip from him. His eyes stuck to the window and his ears to the hinges of the lock.

SCARRY. Whatever he does I had enough of it! I have a mind to break out loose and let the whole world get a view of that great treasure at the fair of Loughrea tomorrow!

BROGAN. Is that the way with you? But you'd be in dread of him to do it.

SCARRY. I'm in no dread of him. It is his most enemy I would make welcome on this night.

O'MALLEY. I thought he had a great smack for you. Ye that were two comrade lads in your young days, as near as the tree to the bark.

SCARRY. He went too far in the way he went on. I have a temper of my own. There's an end of my service in this place.

BROGAN (*sitting down*). I wonder now is the horse as good as what they say?

SCARRY. He's good enough.

BROGAN. Darcy is in dread they were telling me of letting so much as his shadow be seen on the wall in any place there might be humans passing.

O'MALLLEY. A foolish man, a foolish man. It is not putting a wall around the field will stop the cuckoo from quitting it.

(BRIDE *comes in. She has put on the dress she had been working at, and dressed her hair. She is startled when she sees guests.*)

BRIDE. Is that yourself, Pat? I didn't know there was anyone in it.

O'MALLEY. It is so. And here is another kinsman of your own that you didn't see this good while. A great pity it failed him to come to the wedding and the dance.

BROGAN. Will you give me a welcome, Bride?

BRIDE. It is my custom to give a welcome to all that come in at Lawrence Scarry's door.

SCARRY. Well now aren't you very dressed out today more than any other day?

O'MALLLEY. It is the wedding-dress she is wearing sure enough.

BRIDE. I was putting a few wilts in it where it was too wide and I am after fitting it on.

O'MALLEY. Thinking to wear it you are I suppose on the day of the Inchy races.

BRIDE. I am, so long as the weather will be good. I would not wish the rain to interfere with the flowers (*strokes dress*).

BROGAN. Grandeur and finery to be so plentiful with you it is a great wonder you not to have silk shoes on your feet.

SCARRY. So she will have them, and a suit of changing colours, that she will be laughing with the delight of them.

O'MALLEY. I wonder you to go handle that skillet that might spoil the neatness of your gown.

BRIDE. Put it on the fire, you, Lawrence, where you'll be in need of a drop of warm water, for it is time for you give Shanwalla his feed. (Goes.)

BROGAN. Shanwalla! That is a name is well known through the five provinces!

SCARRY. There's little known about him yet.

BROGAN. More than you think.

SCARRY. No one saw him since he came back from the trainer. It is within in the demesne he gets his exercise since then.

BROGAN. If they didn't see him they heard of him.

SCARRY. I gave out nothing or spoke his name at all since the time he was brought back into my charge.

BROGAN. There is maybe one that did speak.

SCARRY. Who was that?

BROGAN. The man that owns him.

SCARRY. You're out. It is he himself forbade me to let one word about him out of my mouth.

O'MALLEY. There are other ways of giving out news besides with the tongue. To be looking down as if there was a secret between yourself and the depths of the earth, and to be whispering with yourself and starting, and to be giving little hints about something you could tell if you had a mind; and to be as if deaf and dumb every time the race is so much as spoken of. That's what makes the lads that meet him full sure he has the winner in his hand. There's not a man within the seven counties but has got wind of him.

BROGAN. Whether or no, it's impossible at this time to get any odds against Shanwalla.

O'MALLEY. Did you put anything on him yourself, Lawrence?

SCARRY. I did not. Where would I meet with anyone to make bets with? I was hoping for good odds.

BROGAN. You're hoping for what you won't get. There is but one way for you to make your profit on the race.

SCARRY. The one way is to back him.

BROGAN. It is not, but to bet against him.

SCARRY. He will surely win.

BROGAN. That was said of many a horse that it failed after to get the goal.

SCARRY. There'll be no failing in him. The jockey is one that will ride him steady and will not let him renege.

O'MALLEY. I knew a man out in Athlone had not so much as a red halfpenny, and it was a horse he backed at Mullingar races, and that had no great name, put a large fortune into his hand.

BROGAN. I remember the race. It was a grey was the favourite, Hill of Allen is the name was on him. There was no other horse fit to come near him.

O'MALLEY. My man that bet against him.

SCARRY. What way did he win so?

BROGAN. He had knowledge of the horse and that he was fidgety at the start—nervous like—till he'd set out. So he made objection to every start that was made, till he had him dancing wild, rearing up to the skies, and flakes flying from his bit. By the time the real start was made, in place of going forward it is a side leap he made, and threw the jockey, and no more about him.

SCARRY. That was a very roguish thing to do.

O'MALLEY. Ah what roguish! If God allotted riches for some

64

people and allotted more to be in poverty, it is best for a man to look out for himself. That man I tell you had debts down on him, and since that time he grew into riches and is his own master.

BROGAN. No one putting orders on him to go there or hither, and no need ever to humble himself to another.

SCARRY. The man that would make me an offer to do a trick of the sort it would be the worst day ever went over him. It's a thing I wouldn't listen to from the Queen under her crown.

BROGAN. Ah, by your own telling, Darcy doesn't give you such good treatment you should be slaving your life out for him the way you do.

SCARRY. Whatever I do for him this is the last night I'll be doing it. The horse will be going to his own stables in Ravahasy tomorrow.

O'MALLEY. Is it that this is the last night you have charge of him?

SCARRY. That's what I said. And I'll take good charge of him. There's no enemy will make any headway putting *him* astray. I'll stop waking with him through the night time.

BROGAN. We'll stop along with you. I have here a pack of cards.

O'MALLEY. There's a drop here in the bottle I have. You won't feel the time passing.

SCARRY. I'll be best stopping alone. The night is not long passing since the days took a stretch.

BROGAN. It's more likely sleep will come upon you than if you would be taking a hand with the cards.

SCARRY. I'll bid Bride to put down black tea for me that will keep me waking. The tea is very lively.

O'MALLEY. That is a poor thing to go drink. It will set the heart uneasy and leaping within you.

SCARRY (*pointing to door*). Well, boys, I'll put you on your road as far as the river, where I'll be getting a pail of pure water in the pool that is below the bridge. The skillet is on the boil that I can take the chill off it. It is time for the horse get his feed.

BROGAN. I'll engage it is good feeding he is getting. What is it you are giving him?

SCARRY. Everything of the best.

O'MALLEY. There's some says new milk to be very serviceable.

SCARRY. Ah, it's not fattening a pig I am. I wouldn't go as far as that. But meal and water and good oats having mixed up with them an odd time a couple of fresh eggs.

O'MALLEY. That's great diet, God bless him!

BROGAN. How often now would you give him that in the day?

SCARRY. Three times, and no muzzle but to let him measure his own belly. It's a poor thing to send a horse out hungry to a race.

O'MALLEY. A naggin' of whiskey is a thing now I saw give great courage at the start.

BROGAN. There was a red mare I used to be with throve on nothing so well as split peas. A great horse—she'd ate you if she had a foal.

SCARRY. The oats we have is as hard as any sort of peas you could meet. It was harvested in the heat of last August two years.

BROGAN. Is that it within in the sack?

SCARRY. It is not, but within in the bin it is.

BROGAN. A lock on it the same as if it was coined gold. I suppose Darcy gives it out himself?

SCARRY. He does not. (*Unlocks it.*)

BROGAN (*looking in*). And the sieve locked up along with it.

SCARRY. That's the master's orders. And Bride that has to scald it every day.

BROGAN (*fingering oats*). It is seemingly middling good.

SCARRY. Ah, what middling? Sure it weighs near fifty pound to the bushel. (*Shakes sieve.*) Do you hear it rattling the same as grains of shot?

BROGAN. Will you be giving it to him now?

SCARRRY. I will not till I'll have the water drawn and give him a drink. I must go get it now.

BROGAN. I'd like well to get one view of him. Open now the door.

SCARRY. I will not do that. He's someway nervous; he to be aware of a stranger late or early it would startle and disturb him.

BROGAN. I am well used to handling horses.

SCARRY. You wouldn't handle this one. You to go in to him offering to give him a feed or a drink, you should keep your seven yards out from him or you'd get his hocks in your face!

O'MALLEY. He must be very violent and hurtful.

SCARRY. It's only with strangers he does be that way. The minute he'll feel them coming he'll show a very roguish eye. But as to myself, he'd give me leave to let off gunpowder in his manger, or to squeal the bagpipes around his stall.

O'MALLEY. It is given in to Brogan that he has a way with him.

SCARRY. The trainer himself would not get leave to comb his mane or his tail. It's the work of the world to get a blacksmith with courage to put a shoe on him. Come on now, it's time for me draw the water.

BROGAN (*sitting down*). I'll follow you. I should take out of my shoe a pebble that preyed on me and I coming the road.

SCARRY (*at door*). Hurry on so. I'm waiting.

O'MALLEY. Is that now the old forge is in the corner of the yard?

SCARRY. It is, and there used to be two smiths working in it every day of the year.

O'MALLEY. The bellows should be broke by this. Or is there a bellows in it at all?

SCARRY. The handle is in it,—wait till I'll show you.

(*They go out,* SCARRY *taking pail.*)

BROGAN (*calling out*). I'll be after ye! (*Gets up, looks out door, takes lid off the saucepan. Takes a couple of small packets wrapped in blue paper from his pocket. Puts one back and shakes contents of other into saucepan.* BRIDE SCARRY *has come to other door, and stands looking at him.*)

BRIDE. What is that you are doing, James Brogan?

BROGAN (*startled*). I am following after Lawrence that went on to the bridge.

BRIDE (*going between him and door*). I saw you putting something into the skillet.

BROGAN. There's some see more than is in it to see. It is your sight that spread on you.

BRIDE. I am surer of my own sight, James Brogan, than I am of your word.

BROGAN. Is it since you joined with the Scarrys you are grown so proud to be running down your own breed?

BRIDE. It is well I know, whatever brought you here, you are at no good trade.

BROGAN. Is it to rob you think me to be come? I see no great sign of riches about the place. It is to a better house than this I would go and I searching out profit for myself. I tell you Bride Scarry for all your pride it is no great match that you made.

BRIDE. I got an honest man, and that is what you never were yourself. For you did not deal right and fair with them that trusted you and employed you.

BROGAN. It is you yourself drove me from honest ways the time you turned your own face against me.

BRIDE. My face was against you from the time I knew your ugly behaviour, an army man—a deserter—I know what it was

67

brought you into Liverpool gaol. I tell you I am well satisfied having my face turned towards a better man.

BROGAN. You could have made a good man of me and a well doing man if you had but taken me in hand. I give you my oath you are the only woman was ever shut up in my heart.

BRIDE. Do you think with this foolish talk to turn me from what I saw? I know well you have the mischief in your mind.

BROGAN. Is it living near Darcy has put these suspicions into you?

BRIDE. It is not, but only what I know about yourself.

BROGAN. What high notions you have learned since you quitted Munster? A great judge you are of good or bad, as if you were the biggest in the world!

BRIDE. It is Lawrence will judge your behaviour. I will tell him what I saw. How do I know was it to do him some injury you put that—whatever it was—into the water.

BROGAN. You'll tell him no such thing.

BRIDE. I will, and let you make out your own case.

BROGAN. Didn't you get very cross and bold! Your voice raised and shrill the same as some fierce woman in a fight!

BRIDE. It is he will take you in hand so soon as he will come back.

BROGAN. Whatever I may want to do, never fear I'll do it in the spite of his teeth!

BRIDE. I will bring all your bad deeds to light!

BROGAN. You are making a great mistake! Give me your promise to be quiet or I'll gag your mouth. I'll master you!

BRIDE. You might not get leave to do that. It is the Almighty is our master in everything.

BROGAN. You need not think to escape me! I'll come down on you! I'll put right fear on you. I'll make you go easy from this out—I'll banish you out of the world.

BRIDE. God will not forgive you those threats.

BROGAN. I'll destroy Lawrence along with you!

BRIDE. Living or dead I'll be against you, and you trying to do injury to my man! (BROGAN *clutches her, she calls out*) Lawrence! Lawrence!

BROGAN. I'll put you under the clay! I'll have the life of you.

BRIDE (*trying to free herself*). It is hard to quench life!

DARCY (*calling from the yard*). Are you calling Lawrence, Mrs. Scarry? He's not here.

BROGAN (*releasing her*). It's Darcy! What way will I get out of this!

BRIDE. You can go out the coach-house door. I'll give you time to escape, and let you never let me see one sight of you again! (BROGAN *goes*.)

(BRIDE *puts lid on kettle, puts it aside*.)

DARCY (*coming in*). Where is Larry?

BRIDE. He'll be here, sir, in a minute.

DARCY. Did he tell you he had a falling out with me this morning?

BRIDE. He did not, sir.

DARCY. He is too short in his temper.

BRIDE. That would be a pity.

DARCY. He is too full of suspicions.

BRIDE. I wouldn't think that.

DARCY. The minute I say a word he thinks I mean more than is in it, and up with him like a bursting bottle, that you daren't go near him or speak reason to him.

BRIDE. Oh you could, sir. He has a great respect for you.

DARCY. So have I a great respect for him. But I am not without a spirit of my own, and some of these days he'll maybe go too far.

BRIDE. He would be sorry to do that.

DARCY. Well now if you wish to help him——

BRIDE. That is my wish indeed, to be a helper to him.

DARCY. I'd be glad you to keep a watch on him, and to quieten him down any time he will be getting these high notions into his head, and make him keep that sharp tongue of his in order.

BRIDE. I will do that, sir. He would be sorry to give you any annoyance. He thinks the world and all of you.

DARCY. And another thing. Any time he might be cross or have a drop taken, or be anyway put out at all, let you keep him out of my way, for I'd be sorry to have words with him again, or any quarrel at all.

SCARRY (*coming in with pail*). Give me here the skillet, Bride.

BRIDE (*taking it and holding it behind her*). I have to heat some more water.

SCARRY. What is in it will do.

BRIDE. It will not. (*She pours it into a pan and puts on shelf.*) It won't take only a minute. There is the big kettle you can pour some in.

SCARRY (*pouring and putting on fire*). Hurry on now. Did you bring the eggs?

69

BRIDE. I have a couple in the loft, I'll go get them.

SCARRY (*sarcastically*). Let you hurry so, till Mr. Darcy will be satisfied we are not neglecting his horse.

DARCY. It's not that brought me. I'll not be stopping.

BRIDE. Do not go sir, till I will come back. I have a thing that must be told out, and that it is right for you to hear.

SCARRY. Go do your business now, and don't mind talking till you'll come back. (*Pushes her out half playfully. Then stoops, takes up paper* BROGAN *had thrown in ashes, takes dip candle out of a tin candlestick, puts paper under to steady it and puts back on mantleshelf.*)

DARCY. You were put out, Larry, a while ago at me saying I was uneasy about the horse.

LARRY. He is your own property.

DARCY. That's not it, but there are things you don't understand.

SCARRY. It's likely enough I have bad understanding.

DARCY. There's a bad class of people going through the world.

SCARRY. I don't need understanding to know that much.

DARCY. Have done with humbugging. I have been given sure information that there will be an attempt made against Shanwalla.

SCARRY. Let them do their best. The ruffians!

DARCY. Do you see now that it is best to bring him over to my own yard? But I depend on you to come along with him. I have no one I could trust him with but yourself.

SCARRY. I'll come so. But why didn't you tell me that in the commencement?

DARCY. You'll come now, tonight?

SCARRY. I cannot until morning, till I'll ready a lodging there beyond for the wife.

DARCY. Come early so, before there will be people moving about. Here is the key of the stable. I have another for my own use. Don't let it out of your own hand!

SCARRY (*putting key on a nail*). I will come at the brink of dawn.

DARCY. There is some noise like a fall.

SCARRY. It is likely the rats. You would swear at some times there to be armies battling in the house.

DARCY. Like a little scream I thought I heard.

SCARRY. You'd hear every class of noise in this place. There's no doubt but rats are a terror. I don't know why is it they are in the world at all.

CONARY (*bursting door open*). Come out here for the love of

God, Lawrence Scarry, and see what has happened your wife!
(SCARRY *rushes out.*)

DARCY (*seizing* CONARY). What is the matter? What has happened? Where is she?

CONARY. Out there abroad on the stones. A fall I heard.
And like a little cry. . . I made my way to it from the shed where
I was . . . and my foot struck against something that was the ladder
that had fallen to the ground.

(*A low cry heard outside.*)

DARCY. My God!

CONARY. I stooped down my hand, and I felt a little head that
I knew to be her head, and I raised it up but it fell back this way
(*makes sign with hand*) on the flags. . . What is this that is wet
on my palm?

DARCY. It is blood.

SCARRY (*coming in with her body in his arms*). Make way for
her! She is gone out of our hand! (*Lays her down.*)

DARCY. My God! That cannot be!

SCARRY (*kneels and lays his head on her breast*). O Bride! My
darling and my first love!

CONARY (*kneeling*).

Brigit, break the battle of death before her!

　　Let the cloak of Mary be under her head!

Come young Michael lead her by the hand

　　To the country of the angels, to the white Court of Christ!

Curtain.

ACT II

SCENE. *Two days later. Same as last, but a settle bed in the
room. There are bottles and pipes lying about, and ends of five
large candles in brass candlesticks.* SCARRY *is sitting by the fire
with head in hands.* O'MALLEY *comes in.*

O'MALLEY. It should ease your mind, Lawrence, the wake to
be over and all to have passed so nice and so comfortable. (*Pauses
but* SCARRY *is silent.*) Ah, no wonder you to be lonesome and lone-

some looking! Very sudden she went indeed; never a word out of her they were telling me, from the time you brought her from where she was lying on the stones and laid her down upon the floor. (*Another pause.*) But there is no one but must say you did your best for her, living or dead, putting a good coffin on her and leaving her down with her own people in the graveyard of Eserkelly. And everyone is talking of the wake—nothing scarce in it but all plentiful. But with all the drink was in it there was no leaping or playing or funning, for there was no one but was sorry for her. Is it a fact now that Darcy himself sent provision from the big house, even to the five white candles that were kindled and burning around her? (SCARRY *nods.*) Well it was a mournful thing to happen, but we cannot have our own way always, and you have a right not to neglect yourself, but to give over fretting, for it's likely you have a long life before you.

SCARRY (*with a bitter laugh*). A long life is it? That is a thing my most enemy would wish to me.

O'MALLEY. Ah, your grief will wear itself out after a while, where it was the will of God.

SCARRY (*with another laugh*). That's the talk of women and of fools! And why would God have any spite against me more than any other one?

O'MALLEY. Well there's no one at all, they do be saying, but is deserving of some punishment from the very minute of his birth.

SCARRY. And is it for the sin of the apple you are drawing down that curse upon me? There is no fair play in that.

O'MALLEY. Sure it is allotted to every Christian to meet with his share of trouble.

SCARRY. It is a bad lot that fell upon myself! It is no way fair trouble to have been settled for me in the clouds of the sky at the time I made my first start in the world.

O'MALLEY. You maybe did some contrary deed yourself, without putting blame upon the skies.

SCARRY. I tell you I made no bad deed to drag me down more than another. I was no robber or treacherous friend! I harmed no person young or old or did this or that! I coveted no gift from the riches of the kings of the earth, or broke the bars of the treasury of heaven!

O'MALLEY. Ah, where's the use of talking?

SCARRY. God to have any grudge against me wouldn't it be enough to let it fall on myself and not to leave it on my companion to pay the penalty? What call had the armies of heaven to bring away the woman had no sharpness in her mouth? It is a great loss to the world that little laugh to be banished out of it!

O'MALLEY. It will not serve you to be roaring and running this way and that way like a mare would be screeching after her foal athrough the rocks.

SCARRY. What way did it fail the harm to fall on the horse was in it and that I took delight in? Hadn't he a name big enough to satisfy the pride and the covetousness of death? Oh, Bride, my heart is linked to you yet, that you could draw me to the ends of the grey world!

O'MALLEY. Lie down now on the bed and take your rest, where you never closed an eye the two nights since she went from you. It is the passion of sleep that has you racked and that is turning you to be mad and wild.

SCARRY (*stumbles over to side of bed, then turns back*). What way would I lie in my warmth, and she being frosty cold in Eserkelly, and a made grave all that is left to her!

O'MALLEY. There is no one but will tell you that you will surely come to her again, on the far side of the world.

SCARRY. There is no world of the living on the far side! That is a deception and a vanity! She to be living she would not leave me my lone, if she had to break through the flags of the floor of heaven! We to die there is nothing left of us but as if a breeze of wind that is passed away, and no more about it.

O'MALLEY. Take but one half hour's sleep I say, and your senses will come back to you and your reason.

SCARRY. I wish to God you could put me in my sleep for seven years or seven quarters of the year itself! That would be very good. Is there drink enough left in the wake-house to bring down sleep and forgetfulness? (*Seizes bottle and pours into a pewter mug, then puts it down again.*) Oh, Bride, what am I saying? What way can I lie down in my sleep when it is far from you will be my waking! There is nothing will befriend me only death—my life to burn out in a minute the same as the tails the children do be kindling in the barley gardens! It will be best let it out from me with some little sharp bit of iron! (*Goes to door.*)

BROGAN (*who has been at door for a moment or two comes in*). Here let you sit down. (*Pushes over mug to him.*) Drink it now. It's little but you'll fall in your standing with the weakness. (*Pushes him into chair.*) Have courage man! You are shaking like the tree of the Crucifixion! (SCARRY *drinks.*)

O'MALLEY. That's right. It will bring the senses back into him.

BROGAN (*sits down and lights pipe*). Tell me now, Pat O'Malley, what way is the world shaping? Have you any new tidings of the big races of Inchy tomorrow?

O'MALLEY. Sure there is no talk of any other thing. There is quality gathered into all the big gentlemen's houses.

BROGAN. Would you say now Shanwalla to be the favourite yet?

O'MALLEY. Why wouldn't he be the favourite? He's a great sort. He is far beyond any one of the blood horses will be in it.

BROGAN. You heard nothing against him I suppose?

O'MALLEY. Sure there is nothing can be brought against him. You know that before.

BROGAN. A touch of the strangles they were telling me he has got. It's a bad thing to get quit of or to cure.

SCARRY. That's a damned lie they told you saying that. He never had any such a thing.

BROGAN. Ah, it's hard to believe all the lies that is in the world. I suppose you didn't see him since he went out of your care?

SCARRY. I did not.

O'MALLEY. I got a sketch of him myself that night, the night of the misfortune that came on this place. It was Darcy himself was leading him away by the river path. It was Lawrence Scarry had more hand in him than any trainer or tribe of trainers. He behaved very mean doing that.

SCARRY. He did not. He behaved fair and square to me.

BROGAN. That's very good. It is the neighbours I heard talking, saying that he someway mistrusted you.

SCARRY. He behaved good and honest. He said to me to move over to his own yard so soon as I would have done . . . this business here. It is there I should be going at this time.

BROGAN. They are saying he tried to bring back the trainer from the Curragh in your place, and that he would give you no more leave to attend the horse.

SCARRY. Little they know, so full as they are of fancies.

BROGAN. Well, I'm only telling you what is said.

SCARRY (*taking key from nail*). Look at that key. Do you know what is it?

BROGAN. What way would I know?

SCARRY. It is the key of Shanwalla's stable beyond. Darcy gave it into my hand, and he gave with it full leave to go in at any minute of the night or day. Was that now mistrusting me?

BROGAN (*touching key*). You are not telling me he did that much?

SCARRY. He knows well the love I have for that horse! I'll like well to see the way he'll put defeat on the whole rout of them!

BROGAN. That's right! Go see the race tomorrow. You'll get some life in you with the shouting of the crowds upon the course.

SCARRY (*drinking again*). Shouting "Shanwalla" they will be! It is I will give out my own shout. I'll lay my bets with the best of them. I'm not put out yet!

BROGAN. That's it! . . . There's no one on the course will make bigger money than what you will, and you to take courage in your hand.

SCARRY. Money? What would I want getting money! I would not stoop my back for it, and it to be shining on the grass!

BROGAN. That now is a solid key. . . . Let me take it in my hand a minute.

SCARRY. I will not do that. (*Puts key in pocket.*)

BROGAN. What way could I harm it?

SCARRY. The man that gave it to me said not to let it out of my own hand. I will hold to that command.

BROGAN (*sneeringly*). You are very faithful to Hubert Darcy.

SCARRY. He trusted me with it and he can trust me.

BROGAN. If he has trust in you, it is you yourself maybe put too much trust in him.

SCARRY. The thing he gave into my care, I will never give it up to any other one. There is no book or no paper will ever have me pictured doing that.

BROGAN. I am saying you maybe think too much of Darcy.

SCARRY. He is my master and my near friend. He will never be hurted or harmed by enemy or illwisher so long as I'll be living in the world.

BROGAN. A pity he not to have been as faithful to yourself.

SCARRY. He to say a sharp word to me, it is short till he would come back to make it up with me in some friendly way.

BROGAN. Indeed he was very often visiting this old kennel.

SCARRY. Evening or morning he was never hardly without taking a course around the place.

BROGAN. If you are a man at all, Lawrence Scarry, you will rise up and draw down a revenge on the man was offering temptation to your wife!

SCARRY. That's a blasted lie!

BROGAN. I say he was offering temptation to Bride Scarry.

SCARRY. It is not to my wife he would speak a word of the kind! I'd have the life of any man thought that.

BROGAN. I am but saying what I know.

SCARRY. She would have turned him out the door if he had but said one word. She would have told myself.

BROGAN. That is the very thing she was about to do. The time you came up from drawing water in the river who did you find before you in this place? Was it Darcy? And he and herself talking together.

SCARRY. What harm if he was in it?

BROGAN. You had but just gone out when he came in—all the same as if he had been watching you. I that was taking a pebble from my shoe made away through the coachhouse door. I came back there again in a short while to know was he gone out. He was there yet.

SCARRY. Why wouldn't he be there?

BROGAN. What he had said to her I don't know, but I heard well what she herself was saying—she had a very clear sweet voice.

SCARRY. She had that.

BROGAN. She was saying at that time: "I have my face turned to a better man." And after she said, "I was certain you had some mischief in your heart"; and after that again, "It is Lawrence will be the judge." He broke out angry then and gave up his whisper and called out, "If you say one word to him it will be the worst word ever you said in your life. I'll put right fear on you, I'll master you!"

SCARRY. Is it Darcy that was my friend said that!

BROGAN. You yourself came in then at the door, and I made away by the bridge over the river.

SCARRY. He said that to her! If you are lying I'll squeeze the breath out of you! (*Seizes him.*)

BROGAN. So help me God I heard the woman that was your wife giving out those words in this place. I'll swear it in any court in Ireland!

SCARRY. Let me out of this! I'll go task him with it! I'll take his life!

BROGAN. You will find it hard to do that, and his people being around him in the big house.

SCARRY. My seven curses on him and on his house and his four-footed beasts and his means and upon his soul! I'll put my heavy vengeance on him! I'll make an attack on him at the racecourse in the sight of all!

BROGAN. You will not. You will draw down on him a surer punishment than that. To put him back, and to lessen his means, and to bring down his pride, till he will quit the country being vexed and ashamed.

SCARRY. What way will I do that?

BROGAN. You have but the least little thing to do. Just to go into the stable beyond on this night, and to put what is in this paper (*takes out packet*) into the horse's flour and water or into his feed of oats the way he will fail in the race. That is the only best thing to do, and you not being too tender with the horse.

SCARRY. Darcy's horse is it! My curse upon him! It's well pleased I'd be seeing him sunk in the river below, or to struggle and smother in a bog!

BROGAN. That's right now.

SCARRY. I'll go do it! I'll drag Darcy down!

O'MALLEY. You cannot go out at this time. It isn't hardly up to ten o'clock. They would see you coming in the yard. There is brightness in the young moon. You must wait till farther out in the night. They will all be in their sound sleep that time. The horse himself will make no outcry, you being no stranger coming to the stall.

SCARRY. It is long to me till I'll set out, till I'll go do my revenge.

BROGAN. We'll stop along with you.

O'MALLEY. We cannot. Here is Owen Conary coming to the door.

BROGAN. Let you get shut of him, Lawrence, throwing yourself on the bed saying you have need of sleep, and that much is no lie! We'll come back here to you, and he to have gone his road. (*They go by left door.*)

CONARY (*groping at door*). Is there anyone within?

SCARRY. Is it in here you are coming, Conary? This is a bad place for one that is questing to fill his bag. It is not a great share of leavings is here after the great throng was in it, and the great feast we had these two nights back!

CONARY. It is not food I am craving, Lawrence Scarry.

SCARRY. Drink it should be so, and tobacco! There's no one comes into this place without coveting to bring something away out of it. There were some had an eye on the horse and another coveted—curse him—a nearer thing and a thing he never could reach to. And as to what you yourself are coveting (*turns up bottles*) it is gone, and no more to be got.

CONARY. That is a sort of welcome should drive me out the door! I'm not one to be bothering or giving trouble! It is now and forever I will turn my back on you!

SCARRY (*seizing and dragging him to hearth*). Stop there now by the fire. (*Pushes him into chair.*) I've no mind to be left my lone to please any man or any two men, and I going to lie down in my sleep . . . (*Sits on bed.*) What sort is the weather without?

CONARY. Fair enough now, but there is a mist coming up from the west.

SCARRY. Dry your feet there from the damp of the road. Waken me after a while, and I to be too long sleeping. I'll be wanting to go out in the darkness, for a night ramble. That's the time all will be quiet and no one to meddle or put you back . . . that's the time for mischief and for the fox to get his prey! (*Lies down.*)

CONARY. It might be best. It's hard lie quiet through the hours of the night, when you are down and a care on top of you. . . . If I didn't know you to be racked and wore out I would put the beggar's curse on you! But God help you! There never was such trouble in anything ever a man put over him! A little saint she was and a loughy woman besides. Surely it was God called her, and His Lady. I could cry down my eyes thinking of her. The priest getting no leave to overtake her and not a good-bye in the world wide. (*Listens.*) That is good! The sleep is the best friend to any troublesome heart. But as to her that is gone, to be a day in her company would lengthen your life. A strange thing she to be holding the cup to me but three days ago; and in what world I wonder is she now? It is quiet and easy she should be at this time as it is well she deserved it. What call would she have to go walking? No children to care or to nourish; no debt that would be a weight on her mind. . . . (*Goes over and listens to* LAWRENCE *then comes back.*) Let him sleep on now while he can do it. God is the best and maybe after a while he'll quieten things all over! (*He nods over fire.* BRIDE *comes in. She stands by* LAWRENCE. *Then stoops a little.*)

BRIDE. Lawrence! Lawrence! Waken! It is I, myself, Bride your wife! (*There is no movement from* LAWRENCE. CONARY *still sits over fire.*)

BRIDE. Conary! (*He does not answer, she comes nearer.*) Conary! It is I myself, Bride Scarry!

CONARY (*uneasily*). Is there anyone anear me?

BRIDE. It is Bride, your friend. Speak to me now, speak to me!

CONARY (*getting up and shrinking*). It is but a voice in my ear. Let me get out of this!

BRIDE. Speak to me; question me! I can do nothing without you question me.

CONARY. I am affrighted, hearing the voice of the dead.

BRIDE. My heart is living, Conary. I have not passed the mering of the world. It is to serve Lawrence I am come and to give him a warning—to save him from bad handling and from harm, to save him from doing a great wrong. Question me, question me!

CONARY. There is something before me—some whiteness, it might be the flame upon the hearth. Lawrence! Waken!

BRIDE. He to waken itself he cannot see me, he cannot hear me. Look now I am here before you. Many a yesterday I took the hunger off you, and now you will not do this little thing for me!

CONARY. What is it? Who is it? Is it that I have my eyesight? Oh, the darkness is come upon me again! Let me go away out of this! (*He shrinks away groping out of door.*)

BRIDE. Is it not a hard case I to be a stranger now, and it is short since I was the woman of the house! (*Goes back to side of bed.*) Lawrence! Lawrence! have you no word at all for me! You would not be in dread of me. Lift up your lips to me that is your wife! ... My grief, he cannot hear me—he cannot feel my hand! Who is there now to help me unless it might be his friends on the other side. (*She stands straight and lifts her hand.*)

> I call now to the family of Heaven
> To put ridges of mercy around him on every side;
> Any bad thing might be coming from the left hand,
> I put the King of the Graces between himself and itself!

> Listen Martin and Patrick that do be praying for us,
> Do not let him be in bad case at the last!
> He is all one with a bird has a trap closing around him.
> Stretch out now and turn him to the lucky road!
> (*Sound of talking at door. She goes to corner.* BROGAN *and* O'MALLEY *come in.*)

BROGAN. Is he in here at all?

O'MALLEY. He is in his sound sleep on the bed.

BROGAN. That is very good. He will be fresh and lively for the work is before him.

O'MALLEY. It was a good thought you had, making up that story about Darcy.

BROGAN. We could not have brought him to our way without that.

O'MALLEY. A foolish man he should be to give credit to it, and he knowing Darcy so well as what he does. But there was confusion in his mind with all the trouble he put over him.

BROGAN. The jealousy to come on a man, it is easy make him believe all.

O'MALLEY. I was in dread we might have to do the job ourselves.

BROGAN. I wouldn't ask to bring him into it if we had power to do it without him.

O'MALLEY. He having the key of the stable there'll be no stay in doing it.

BROGAN. It's easy to get the key. It's likely it's in the pocket where he left it a while ago. (*Takes key from coat hanging by bed.*) It's as good for me to keep it myself. (*Puts it in pocket.*)

O'MALLEY. We can go on without him so.

BROGAN. The horse that would rouse the whole place with kicking and clattering, and he seeing strangers coming anear him. There is no one only Lawrence can handle him, and keep him quiet, he being used to his ways. (*Shakes him.*) Rouse yourself up now, Lawrence Scarry!

SCARRY. What is it?

BROGAN. Let you waken!

O'MALLEY. It is time to stir yourself.

SCARRY. Is the night gone by?

BROGAN. It is not. You have it before you.

SCARRY. I was in deep sleep.

BROGAN. We are come back sooner than we thought. It is dark the night is turned. There is come a clout over the moon.

SCARRY. I was through the world in my sleep.

BROGAN. You are wakened out of it now.

SCARRY. I was as if in some white place. It is likely it was a dream.

O'MALLEY. Let you rise up now.

SCARRY. The sweetest sound of music ever I heard. (*He is sitting on side of bed.*)

O'MALLEY. Put on your coat now and come on along with us.

SCARRY (*puts on coat*). I am going out in the night.

O'MALLEY. Come on so.

SCARRY. It is not with you I am going. I am going my lone.

O'MALLEY. So you can go—over to the big stables.

SCARRY. It is not there I am going.

BROGAN. Where is it so? Is it to lay a complaint against us and a warning?

SCARRY. It is not. But I will not go in your company.

BROGAN. Is it that you are going to renege and you after giving us your word?

O'MALLEY. Is it that you are falling back from drawing down your revenge?

SCARRY. That plan of revenge is as if gone from my mind. I have no desire to hurt or to harm any person at all. (*Gets up.*)

BROGAN. Ah, come along, man, with us and it will come back to you.

SCARRY. It is over to Eserkelly I am going. I have a mind to go look at Brigit's grave.

BROGAN. Making excuses you are. What would bring you there at this hour of the night?

SCARRY. I am uneasy without going there.

BROGAN. Scheming you are. What can you do for her? She is safe enough in the grave.

SCARRY. The world wouldn't put it out of my head that she came anear me in my sleep.

BROGAN. That is but vanity and foolishness. There is no one comes back from the dead.

SCARRY. So nice she looked and so calm and so mournful. I am going to you now, Bride, till I will cry my fill for you! God knows, she to come back I would give her a good welcome, shadow and all as she might be!

O'MALLEY. It is that he is a coward and is afeard to do what he took in hand.

BROGAN. He has us made fools of. He has us robbed.

O'MALLEY. It is easier save yourself from a rogue than from a liary person would not hold to his word.

BROGAN. Is it that you are a traitor or in dread to keep your purpose?

SCARRY (*turning from door*). Is it of the like of ye I would be afeard?

O'MALLEY (*taking his arm*). Come on now, Lawrence.

SCARRY (*shaking him off*). Don't touch my clothes or don't come anear me!

BROGAN. Come on and do what you have to do or you'll repent it.

O'MALLEY. A renegade you are!

SCARRY. Let you quit talking to me before I'll make you!

BROGAN. No wonder he to be so cross and craven! It's likely what I said was no news to him. It's likely he knew well Darcy was after the wife. It's likely he had it planned to let her go with him before he wed with her!

SCARRY. I'll have your life on the head of those words out of your lying mouth! (*Strikes at him*).

BROGAN (*at door*). You may believe me this time! There is short-
ness of life before you. I'll send you to the slaughter. If ever you
leaped high on any horse you'll make a higher leap again with the
hangman! (*Flings him back and goes out banging door.*)

Curtain.

ACT III

SCENE. *A few days later. The office at* DARCY'S. *A desk and one
or two chairs and benches.* 1ST POLICEMAN *looking from window.
Two* GIRLS *come in.*

1ST GIRL. Is this now the Magistrate's Court?

1ST POLICEMAN (*pompous*). It is so. It is here Mr. Darcy will
find proof who is it is guilty of destroying his horse Shanwalla, the
way he would not win the race.

1ST GIRL. It is Lawrence Scarry done it. The World is saying
that.

1ST POLICEMAN. Keep your mouth shut until such time as the
court is sitting.

1ST GIRL. My uncle Pat O'Malley is laying down it will be
proved by sure token.

1ST POLICEMAN. Pat O'Malley! Let him have a care will it be
proved against himself.

1ST GIRL. It will not. Aren't we after coming here purposely to
swear his alibi and that he could not be near the stable at all. We
met Pat O'Malley coming home last Thursday night. (*To* 2ND
GIRL) Isn't that so now?

1ST POLICEMAN. Be silent now. There can be no word spoken
in this place until such time as the Magistrate will be on the Bench.

1ST GIRL. A great wonder it was Mr. Darcy to bring the horse
out to the race and not to leave him in the stable the way he was.

1ST POLICEMAN. They thought there to be nothing on him and
he leaving the yard.

1ST GIRL. Sure you saw the way it was, that he couldn't so much
as raise a gallop, and all the world travelling to Inchy to see him,
and all the bets that were on him gone astray.

1ST POLICEMAN (*excited*). Is it that ye were in it? I got no leave to go myself, but sent patrolling the Loughrea road.

2ND GIRL. A great pity you to have missed it. There was no one but had a bet upon that horse.

1ST POLICEMAN. I wasn't without a bet on him myself.

1ST GIRL. I myself that put a shilling on him. Word I had from a knacky man that got a tip from the stand. I think I never will chance a bet again.

2ND GIRL. I was late myself coming to the entrance gap and everyone pressing through it; and there came a great noise of talking among the crowd that I thought the race to be ended. The throng parted then and the light-weight came passing out, and he wearing Darcy's colours, grey and yellow. Very mournful looking he was, and his eyes going into the ground. Some man that was behind me on the road called out and asked what was the honour of Mr. Darcy doing at the leaps. And the jockey made as if an oath to himself and gave no answer at all.

1ST POLICEMAN. What would he say? It was no wonder the heart to be broke in him.

1ST GIRL. No but wait till I tell you. I that was there at the commencement and that saw the whole thing. I went up on some barrels the time I heard a great cheer for Shanwalla that was coming down the road; prancing up he was and his coat shining. If Darcy had a mind to sell him that time I tell you he'd have his full price got!

1ST POLICEMAN. It would be lucky for Darcy if he did sell him.

1ST GIRL. The weighty part of the crowds came running to see him, such a welter and such a killing you never saw as was in it; climbing and knocking the wall they were, till there was nothing left standing only gaps.

1ST POLICEMAN. So I saw it myself after. That is the way it was.

1ST GIRL. Shouting Shanwalla they were, that was for Galway, and all Munster against him! But all of a sudden it is to go wild like he did, and to stop and rear up, and Lawrence Scarry that was leading him strove to soother him down. But as he came into the field it is to go into a cold sweat he did, and then he went round in a sort of a megrim, the same as a man that would have drink taken.

1ST POLICEMAN. So he had drink taken . . . of *some* sort.

1ST GIRL. And is it true so that it is to poison him they did?

2ND GIRL. If they did itself he is as well nearly as he was before. The farrier from Craughwell that came and attended him. Sure my grandfather was in it that is better again for cures, and he gave me the story down.

1ST POLICEMAN. It is the farrier makes a claim to have brought him round.

2ND GIRL. Shivering he was, and they couldn't keep a drink with him he was that drouthy, and they gave him castor oil, for whatever you put before him, if it was soot and water, he must drink it. But the world wouldn't make him vomit, and it was my grandfather brought him round at the last, giving him a pint of forge water, and whisky and the white of an egg. And everyone that heard it said there was surely poison within him.

(2ND POLICEMAN *comes in*.)

1ST POLICEMAN (*to* GIRLS). Go back there now out of the way. Let ye mind yourselves. If it is as witnesses ye were brought here the less talk ye let out of yourselves the better it will be for the cause of justice. (*To* 2ND POLICEMAN) Did ye find another Magistrate to sit along with Mr. Darcy.

2ND POLICEMAN. Out searching for one we were the whole of the morning and no one to be found, where they were all gone to the meet of the hounds at Rahasane.

1ST POLICEMAN. It wouldn't hardly be according to law Mr. Darcy to judge his own case.

2ND POLICEMAN. Sure he has but to commit whoever is thought to have a hand in it for trial to the Galway assizes. A week is no great hardship in gaol.

1ST POLICEMAN. Did the Head Constable come yet?

2ND POLICEMAN. He did not. He is in pursuit after some trace or track of the guilty person that was put into his hand.

1ST POLICEMAN. We were thinking it might be Brogan or O'Malley.

2ND POLICEMAN (*drawing him aside and putting his mouth close to his ear*). What would you say hearing it to be Lawrence Scarry.

1ST POLICEMAN. Do you tell me so! That's what the little girl was laying down a while ago, but I paid no attention.

2ND POLICEMAN. There isn't hardly a doubt about it.

1ST POLICEMAN. I wouldn't be the one to tell that to Mr. Darcy.

2ND POLICEMAN. Whisht! Here he is coming! (*They stand to attention*.)

DARCY (*coming in*). Is Lawrence Scarry here?

2ND POLICEMAN. I didn't see him, sir.

DARCY. I'll want him to sift out evidence along with the Head Constable that might help us to find out who was it did this thing.

2ND POLICEMAN. I believe the Constable is of opinion he all to has his hand laid upon the rogue.

DARCY. That's right. It is long to me till I'll have him before me. I won't be long sending him to his rightful place, that is gaol.

1ST POLICEMAN. He'll be best there, surely.

DARCY. He must be a terrible ruffian! I never heard of a worse case in my lifetime! To come breaking into my stables and to try and do away with my horse!

2ND POLICEMAN. It was a very ruffianly deed.

DARCY. To go hurt a *man* you would want to put out of the way it would be bad enough. But I think it seventeen times worse to make an attack on an innocent creature that gave no provocation to anyone. You'd have been sorry to see the way he was!

1ST POLICEMAN. I was well pleased to hear he is at this time on the mending hand.

DARCY. That has nothing to do with it! It's no thanks to the villain if he did escape. There was enough of poison left in the pail he drank from to do away with all the horses on the green of Ballinasloe!

2ND POLICEMAN. So the Constable is after telling me.

DARCY. The black-hearted ruffian! It is crooked law that wouldn't mix that same poison into the diet of the man used it on Shanwalla! He'll get hanging, anyway. There's some justice in that.

1ST POLICEMAN. The law is very severe in those cases.

DARCY. It couldn't be too severe! I wouldn't grudge it to my own brother, and I to have one, and he to have done such a deed!

1ST POLICEMAN. Here is the Head Constable coming, and a couple more along with him. They are bringing with them . . .

DARCY. The men they suspect, I suppose. Go tell them to hurry. And try can you find Lawrence Scarry.

1ST POLICEMAN. I'll not have far to go look for him. He is close at hand.

CONSTABLE (*coming in*). I couldn't get here any sooner, sir. I have been searching the whole matter out.

DARCY. That's right. Have you got hold of the man that did it?

CONSTABLE. In my opinion I have.

DARCY. I was in dread you might not be able to put your hand on him.

CONSTABLE. No fear of that. There is one thing sure in this world—when there's a crime there's a criminal.

DARCY. It's not always so easy to find him.

CONSTABLE. In some cases it is not. But it was easy enough this time. I've got him.

DARCY. I thought there were two suspected.

CONSTABLE. O'Malley and Brogan you are thinking of. But they can clear themselves. They have their alibi as good as proved.

DARCY. Who are you going to charge so?

CONSTABLE. It is Lawrence Scarry.

DARCY. Scarry! ... *My* Lawrence Scarry!

CONSTABLE. The same one.

DARCY. Rubbish! You might as well say that I myself did it!

CONSTABLE. The case is strong against him.

DARCY. Some one has made up false witness.

CONSTABLE. There is no need for that. There is proof.

DARCY. There couldn't be proof of what didn't happen. Larry loved that horse!

CONSTABLE. That makes the crime the worse.

DARCY. Where is he? He will be able to disprove it.

CONSTABLE. We have him now at hand. I am after making a search in the room at Cahirbohil where he was housed. I found this piece of blue paper stuck under a candle. It was in a tattered condition and smelling of stale porter. It fits in shape and similitude with the twisted paper we found on the stable floor and that had some remains of the poison in it yet. There are some grains of the same sort here. This is the document proves the case through and through.

DARCY. If I thought it possible—but I don't—that he had gone out of his wits and done such a thing I would sooner withdraw the case than have it proved against him!

CONSTABLE. It would be impossible to do that. I have my report made to the inspector. It will be in the hands of the Crown.

DARCY. I tell you he couldn't have done it! It was in the night time it was done, after ten o'clock, between that and early morning.

CONSTABLE. It was within that time sure enough. You took notice yourself, sir, some of the flour was spilled from the box where it was.

DARCY. If I did I thought it might be a rat or a mouse or a thing of the kind. I knew no one could have come in. I had locked the door myself. I had the key all the time.

CONSTABLE. There was no other one, I suppose, has a key?

DARCY. No one—except Lawrence Scarry.

CONSTABLE. So I was thinking. (*Writes note.*) I wasn't rightly sure till now.

DARCY. It makes no difference. He wasn't near the stable. I was expecting him. He never came till morning. He told me he was tired out after the burying—and low-hearted—no wonder . . . and the day over, he had laid down to sleep on his bed.

CONSTABLE. We'll soon know can he give proof of that. I'm not one to rush at a thing without sure evidence.

DARCY. Why don't you go look for proofs against these other men? Had you no information against them? We might be able to prove it. Bring them in.

CONSTABLE. All I heard was, they had bets put on against your own horse in the race. There was ill-feeling against them among those that lost their money. I was advised to make enquiry about them. I did that. I got no information was enough to charge them on.

DARCY. Bring them here, I might make out something. (*They are brought in.* O'MALLEY *is brought forward.*) Now look here, my man, if you were brought in here, it is that there is something against you. What is it? Do you know anything of what happened my horse? Did you ever see him or handle him? Say yes or no.

O'MALLEY. I will. Previous to the day of the races I never laid an eye on him.

CONSTABLE. He says he can give proof he was not out of his own house that night.

O'MALLEY. So I can, too. There are two little girls of the neighbours can bear testimony to that.

DARCY. Who are they? Will they be honest witnesses?

1ST POLICEMAN. Very decent little girls, sir, and well-spoken. Nieces of Pat O'Malley, I believe they are.

DARCY. What have they to say?

1ST GIRL. It was Thursday night. We met Pat O'Malley coming home, where he had been to the burying at Eserkelly; and he having a pain in the jaw and it going athrough his head.

2ND GIRL. That is so. Cold, I suppose he got.

1ST GIRL. We turned into the house with him, and we sat there for a while.

DARCY. For how long?

1ST GIRL. A middling while, and he telling us newses of the burying.

2ND GIRL. Giving us an account of all the people that were in it.

DARCY. That's enough. All I want to know is what time it was.

2ND GIRL. I couldn't know . . . only the middling right time.

1ST GIRL. It was just on the stroke of ten o'clock we went in——

2ND GIRL. I was forgetting that. Just up to ten o-clock.

1ST GIRL. The wife put a hot plaster to the jaw and he went in to his bed, and we went away then, and the door was closed after us. Closed and locked; and he never left the house till morning.

2ND GIRL. Till it was time to make a start for Inchy races. We were together going the road.

CONSTABLE. You see, sir, it is hardly worth while going on with this case.

DARCY. Go on then with the other, Brogan. Can he prove where he was that night?

CONSTABLE. That is a thing was laid down against James Brogan. He was seen coming out through a gap in the demesne wall at Cahirbohil about twelve o'clock Thursday night.

DARCY. That is better. He is likely the man we want. Have you any witnesses?

BROGAN. You need bring no witness to that. I did come out that side. I thought it no harm where it was a mile of a short-cut. I had gone in to see a friend.

DARCY. At that time of night?

BROGAN. No, but earlier. I went to visit him. I was coming back from the fair of Loughrea. Darkness overtook me on the road; I went to ask a lodging of him.

DARCY. What friend had you inside my demesne?

BROGAN. I should sooner say kinsman by marriage. His wife's mother and my mother were mixed, blood thick, they were, two cousins. Anyone that has learning can read it on the headstone in Eserkelly. He was Lawrence Scarry.

DARCY. What time was that?

BROGAN. The time I went there it was close on ten o'clock. I stopped a good while, maybe two hours.

DARCY. Then Scarry was in his own room where you were with him all that time! I knew he never left it. I knew he was speaking the truth!

BROGAN. I took my rest there for a while. But I did not say I was with him. I won't tell you one word of a lie. There was no one in the place but myself.

DARCY. Where was he then?

BROGAN. The Lord be praised, I do not know, and that I cannot tell.

DARCY. He might have gone to some neighbour's house.

BROGAN. To be sure he might. That's what I was thinking myself. It will be easy for him call that neighbour to witness.

1ST POLICEMAN. Owen Conary, the dark man that goes quest-ing on the roads was talking abroad in the yard. I heard him give out he himself was the latest person was with Lawrence Scarry on that night.

DARCY. Call him in then. He might settle the matter.

CONSTABLE. He will, I'm thinking. One way or another. (CONARY *comes in.*)

DARCY. What time were you with Scarry at Cahirbohil Thurs-day night?

CONSTABLE. If ever you were there at all.

CONARY. Why wouldn't I be there? I was in it surely. The time I went in it was near to ten o'clock.

CONSTABLE. What way do you know that?

CONARY. I know it by the number of steps I made, and I coming the road from Kilchriest.

CONSTABLE. And Scarry was in it?

CONARY. He was to be sure.

DARCY. How long did you stop with him?

CONARY. I don't know was it an hour, half an hour? I couldn't be rightly sure.

CONSTABLE. Try and call up your memory now.

CONARY. I wouldn't be sure. My mind was on other things be-sides time.

DARCY. You maybe stopped with him up to ten o'clock.

CONARY. I did and later, I can be certain of that.

DARCY. This man Brogan says he was there at that time.

CONARY. He did not come in when I was in it. Lawrence Scarry was there in his lone. I talked with him a short while, till being tired and down-hearted he stretched himself in sleep on the bed through the night.

DARCY. That's what he told me. It is certain he slept in his bed last night. This Brogan must be making a mistake or making up a story. He says he came in. You say no at all came in.

CONARY. No one—unless. . . .

CONSTABLE. Unless who? Tell it out.

CONARY. I thought I saw . . .

CONSTABLE. He is getting away from the truth. You know that you cannot see, and you having the eyesight lost, and being as you are stone dark.

CONARY. I never did before in my natural life. But I give you the bail of my mouth I saw that time, or it seemed to me that I saw.

DARCY. Go on. What did you see?

CONARY. I saw Bride Scarry walking.

CONSTABLE. This is superstition and a mockery. We all know her to be dead.

CONARY. I tell you she came in the spirit.

DARCY. I'm afraid his mind is rambling.

CONARY. Why would she not come and the spirit not long gone out of her, where it is known God will blow His breath into those that are dead a hundred or two hundred years?

DARCY. Did you speak to her?

CONARY. I did not; and it is a great pity that it failed me to do it. But it was all strange to me. It is often I coveted to see the flames of the fire on the hearth, and there it was before me, and the walls of the house on every side. And as to her, I saw her as I never saw anyone in this life. But there being no one waking along with me, the fright went into my heart, and it failed me to question her, and I went out the door and made no stop or delay.

CONSTABLE. You are certain it was Bride Scarry? What sort was she?

CONARY. She seemed to me to be coming from the south, and to have on her the lovely appearance of the people of heaven.

DARCY. He is given over to dreams and visions. We are getting nothing from him at all.

CONSTABLE. He was trying to befriend Scarry but there is nothing in what he says that can serve him.

DARCY. Stop a minute. Scarry did not leave the house? He was in bed asleep when you went out?

CONARY. He laid himself on the bed. But he said he would not be long in it. He bade me waken him. He said he would be going out later in the night.

CONSTABLE. So he did go out later, and did the crime. I was full sure of that.

DARCY. It is hard for me to give up trust in him. He to have turned against me, I will never have faith in any other man in the living world.

CONSTABLE. He will give you his own account now of himself.

SCARRY (*coming in between two policemen*). Will you tell me what is going on, Mr. Hubert, or if it is by your orders it is going on? These peelers dragging me here and there! First they would not give me leave to come to you, and now they are shoving me in, the same as a thief on the road! (*To Policeman.*) Leave go your hold!

CONSTABLE. Keep a quiet mouth now and behave yourself!

SCARRY. What call have you to be putting orders on me? It is Mr. Darcy is my master. I take orders from no other one.

CONSTABLE. It is likely you'll give heed to my orders from this out!

SCARRY. Let you keep that thought for robbers and law-breakers! I'm not one of that class! I never gave a summons or got a summons or gave my oath in a court!

CONSTABLE. It is not with a court but with a gaol you will be making acquaintance this night!

SCARRY. Divil a fear of me! Whatever you have against me or make out against me, it is Mr. Darcy is well able to bring a man from the gallows!

DARCY. You need expect no help from me, Scarry, if the grave was there open before you!

SCARRY. What in the world wide! What at all is it you have against me, Mr. Hubert?

DARCY. You will know that at the Assizes when you will be brought before the judge.

SCARRY. Tell me out what it is, and I'll show you I am clear from blame!

DARCY. You'll show me! I would not believe one word coming out of your mouth!

CONSTABLE. There's no use talking. We know what way you passed the night before the race.

SCARRY. Is that it now? Is that what has put you out, sir? You are vexed I did not come to mind the horse. It is very sharp blame you are putting on me for that!

DARCY. You need not try to put a face upon it! You cannot come around me now that I have knowledge of what you are!

SCARRY. I had a right to have come, and you uneasy as you were.

DARCY. That's not it, I tell you!

SCARRY. I told you I thought to come . . . and that I was racked and tormented . . . and maybe I had a drop taken . . . and sleep came upon me.

DARCY. I wish to God you had stopped in your sleep!

SCARRY. I give you my oath, I'll never quit your yard again but to be minding your business night and day.

DARCY. You'll never be helper or head lad again in any stable I may own.

SCARRY. That is hard judgment when all I did was to drowse awhile.

DARCY. It is not your drowsing and sleeping goes against you! It is the deed you went out for after your rising up!

SCARRY. What way did you know I went out?

CONSTABLE. There now, he has allowed it.

SCARRY. I never denied it.

CONSTABLE. What time now did you go out?

SCARRY. It seemed to me like the dead hour of darkness, but it might not be so far out in the night.

CONSTABLE. What brought you out at all?

SCARRY. I was troublesome in the mind.

CONSTABLE. You came then to Mr. Darcy's stables.

SCARRY. No, it was not this side I came. It was to the old church of Eserkelly I went, to the side of Bride my wife's grave.

CONSTABLE. You can maybe bring witness to that?

SCARRY. Who would I bring? There was no one in it, unless God, and the dead underneath.

CONSTABLE. What did you go doing there?

SCARRY. Asking her forgiveness I was if ever I was anyway unkind, and saying prayers for the repose of her soul.

CONSTABLE (*to* DARCY). This seems to be a humbugging story, sir, made up to get at your soft side, the way you will get him off.

O'MALLEY. Ah, what getting off! He said one time he was asleep and he says now he was rambling the fields.

BROGAN. Let him tell that story to the birds of the air, for there is no one on the face of the earth will believe it.

SCARRY (*seeing them for the first time*). Is it you yourself, you red rogue, is at the bottom of this mischief? I should have known that where there was bad work you would be in it, yourself and your comrade schemer! (*To* DARCY.) They are two that would swear away a man's life for a farthing candle! There is no nature in them! They are two would think no more of giving false witness than of giving a blow from a pipe. Tell that story to the birds of the air is it! I will and to the magistrate that is my master!

BROGAN. He gave little belief to all you told him up to this.

SCARRY. I have more to tell and maybe he will believe it!

BROGAN. You have nothing to tell but what will bring your own head into the loop!

SCARRY. Maybe it's your own head it will bring into it!

BROGAN. Do your best so, and see will your lies serve you.

SCARRY. What brought you into the house that night? Why did you waken me? What did you ask of me? Was it to come along with you to Darcy's stable?

BROGAN. Stop your slandering mouth!

DARCY. Maybe there is something in it.

BROGAN. I say this man has made up this false witness and that story because we have knowledge of what would hang him twice over, and we being willing to tell it out!

SCARRY. You have nothing to tell against me, if it is not that for one half hour, God forgive me! I consented to your wicked plan.

BROGAN. What I have to say I would sooner not say, because it concerns her that was near in blood to me, if she was mixed in marriage with yourself.

SCARRY. Keep your tongue off her, you villain! Have some shame in you!

BROGAN (*to* DARCY). Have I leave to speak?

DARCY. Go on.

SCARRY. No! It would not be for honour her name to be spoken out of your false mouth, you that are a disgrace to the world! I know what you have in your wicked mind, and what when I was mad and crazed with trouble you made me give credit to for one minute only! I declare to heaven that if you say it in this place it will be the last lie in your throat!

DARCY (*to* BROGAN). Speak out.

BROGAN. It is loth I am to do that, and I would not, without that I am forced by your honour's commands and this man's treachery. I know and I tell you out, it was he himself that made away with his wife!

SCARRY. My God Almighty! (*Stumbles and holds a chair.*)

BROGAN. Look, sir, at the way she died! Gone in the snap of a finger. Well as she was that you would take a lease of her life, as supple walking as a young girl. What was it happened her? Is it that the ladder was settled in a way it would go from under her, and to slip on a slippy flag, the way she would be quiet and dumb and could not hold to her word and tell out to her master that it was Lawrence Scarry himself had engaged for money to put injury on the thing was in his charge!

SCARRY. Let me out till I'll choke him!

BROGAN. Search your mind, sir, did she say she had something to lay before you! Was it he sent her out of the door? Was it he himself brought her in dead? Put away she was, before she could give out that word.

DARCY (*to* SCARRY). You understand what he is saying. What answer have you?

SCARRY. The twists and tricks of a serpent he has! Didn't I

speak before and what did it serve me. (BRIDE *comes in and stays near door*).

DARCY (*getting up*). The case looks bad and black. It has gone beyond me. (*He looks at Constable's notes; the others whisper together.*)

BRIDE (*coming to* CONARY). Can you hear me what I say, Owen Conary?

CONARY. I do hear you and know your voice, indeed.

2ND POLICEMAN (*touching his shoulder*). No speaking now.

BRIDE. But there is great need for us to talk together. We must have leave to do that. (*Turns and stands a moment near door.*)

A BOY (*coming to the door*). The horses are getting uneasy in the stable. Lawrence Scarry come and quiet them down. (LARRY *starts up, and goes to door.*)

DARCY. No, not you. Never again. (LARRY *leans against wall his arm over his face.* DARCY *and* CONSTABLE *go out.* 2ND POLICEMAN, BROGAN *and* O'MALLEY *follow them.*)

1ST POLICEMAN (*to* SCARRY). Here you can stand outside the door but I'll keep a grip on you. (*They go out. The Girls come towards door.*)

2ND GIRL. We got out of it well. I thought it was for a bit of funning Pat O'Malley put all that in our mouth about him being within his own house. How would I know if he was in it at all?

1ST GIRL. I declare I'd nearly be sorry for poor Larry if it was not for the black deed he has done. (*They go to door, look out and whisper with* 1ST POLICEMAN.)

BRIDE (*coming to* CONARY). Here I am now that you may question me.

CONARY. I will do that, and I give great praise to God that sent you back to me. For I am in no dread of you this time.

BRIDE. You need be in no dread of me, indeed; and it is to save my man I am come, for he is at the rib end of the web, and no woof to be got, and not one to save him without your help and my own.

CONARY. Answer me and tell me now what is to be done for him, and what way can he stand up to the judge, and he it may be going to his hanging tomorrow?

BRIDE. I am come here to stand between himself and his ill-wishers, and the man that put the curse of misfortune upon him.

CONARY. Do that, for he is the worst God ever created, and it is bad is his behaviour and you could not beat upon his cunning. And it is a great wonder the Lord to allow all the villainy is in the world.

And that they may meet with all they deserve at this time, and in the cold hell that is before them.

BRIDE. Let you not call out a judgment against them, but let you leave them to the Almighty; and I myself never will put my curse on them; but that He Himself may change everyone for the best!

CONARY. Stretch out now and give aid to the boy that had the sea of the world's troubles over him, since you yourself went from him to the other side, and that was a boy did not deserve it from God or man.

BRIDE. I will do that. For he was fair and honest until the man that is his red enemy put a net around him with lying words, and he broke away from it after. And he was a kind man to me, for a headstrong man, while I was with him, and I liked him well. Do now my bidding and I will leave you my blessing by day and by night, in the light and in the darkness, for from this out I will be free from the world's trouble and at peace.

CONARY. I will do your bidding, indeed. And it is not lonesome I will be from this out, but I to be going the long road it will be as if I did not belong to the world at all; for it seemed to me the time I looked at you, the heavens to have opened then and there! (*They go up to corner. She is seen to be speaking to him. Presently they both go out.* DARCY, CONSTABLE *and the rest come in.*)

CONSTABLE (*to* SCARRY). Come over here now and hear what Mr. Darcy has to say.

DARCY. After the testimony given about the poison, there is nothing for me to do but to commit you to gaol.

SCARRY. My mind is as if gone blind. I can keep no thought in my head. This is surely the crossest day that ever went over me. I can make no stand against such treachery.

CONARY (*coming forward*). Will I get leave to say one word . . .? A message I am after being given . . .

DARCY. Have you anything new to tell?

CONARY. A message I am after being given for Patrick O'Malley. I am bidden to tell you, Pat O'Malley, to give up now the thing that is in your hand, that is the sign and the token of your treachery, and of the deed you have joined in and that you have done.

O'MALLEY (*taking his hand from his breast where he had thrust it*). There is nothing in it.

CONARY. Let those that have eyesight say if there is! (CONSTABLE *goes over to* O'MALLEY.)

O'MALLEY (*flinging a letter at* BROGAN). It is you betrayed me!

It is you gave it to me! There is no one had knowledge of it only yourself. (CONSTABLE *takes up and gives paper to* DARCY.)

DARCY (*reading*). It is a promise to pay £50 to him so soon as Inchy races will be over, if so be the horse Shanwalla will not have been able to make a start.

O'MALLEY. It was poverty brought me to it, and the children rising around me.

BROGAN. Keep your tongue quiet, you fool!

CONARY. I hear your voice, James Brogan. I am not without a message to yourself.

BROGAN. Some lie you have made up. Who is there in the living world would go send me a message in this place?

CONARY. You will know who sent it, hearing it. It was given to me but now.

BROGAN. There was no one came in or went out. I swear to that.

CONARY. It failed you to see her; but she was here.

BROGAN (*uneasily*). She . . . What are you saying? What are you talking about?

CONARY. She gave me this message: "Were you not a foolish man, James Brogan, to knock the ladder from under me, and I but just after saying to you that it is hard to quench life!"

BROGAN. She did not—she could not——

CONARY. You know well who it was spoke that word. Have a care! She is maybe not far from you.

BROGAN (*falling on his knees and looking towards the door*). I give my faith and my solemn oath, Bride, that the time I got wild and faced you I never thought to leave a hand on you, to kill you, but only to put fear on you, the way you would not tell on me, and but to quiet you for a while!

DARCY. Do you understand what you are saying?

BROGAN. "Living or dead I'll be against you," you said, and I threatening to do injury to your man. Oh, Bride, you were always against me, and you are against me yet, and it is through you I will give myself up to the Judge and will go to my punishment as it is well I have earned it! (*The two policemen stand at each side of him as he stands up, and lead him and* O'MALLEY *to door.*)

CONARY (*to* SCARRY). Surely God has some great hand in you, giving leave to the woman to keep her promise for your help. And didn't she behave well, coming challenging through myself your enemies in the court, the way you got over them all, and you so near your last goal!

SCARRY. Through you is it? Stop your raving. She to have left her standing in Heaven it is not with you she would have come speaking, or with any one at all only myself!

DARCY. It is a good thought he had facing them. But it's no wonder he to be apt at riddles, there is great wit and great wisdom in the blind. And it's little he could have done for you, Larry, but for knowing that I myself was on your side.

CONSTABLE (*to the two* POLICEMEN). I'm full sure the beggar was in league with them and knew their secrets, and turned on them and betrayed them for his own safety, seeing me searching out the matter to the root.

2ND POLICEMAN. I never heard in my time a spirit to give any aid to the law or to the police.

1ST POLICEMAN. There's nothing in the world more ignorant than to give any belief to ghosts. I am walking the world these twenty years, and never met anything worse than myself!

Curtain.

THE GOLDEN APPLE

TO

GEORGE BERNARD SHAW

THE GENTLEST OF MY FRIENDS

THE GOLDEN APPLE

PERSONS
  THE KING OF IRELAND
  SIMON MAOR. *His Steward.*
  HIS DOCTOR.
  THE WITCH.
  PAMPOGUE. *Her Daughter.*
  THE GARDENER.
  FATACH MOR. *The Giant.*
  BRIDGET. *His Wife.*
  MUIREANN. *The King of Spain's Daughter.*
  RURY. *The King of Ireland's Son.*
  THE KING OF SPAIN'S FIVE SONS.
  SERVANTS AND GUARDS.

ACT I

SCENE I. *The Witch's garden. A little tree,* CENTRE, *with leaves and blossom and one golden apple. A well before it.* GARDENER *potting plants. He is singing a little song. He bends over well.*

GARDENER. What way is it with you, my poor little five fishes? Looking up to the sunbeams ye are. Is it that ye remember yet the King's Court in Spain? I am thinking ye have sense and memory like any person walking the earth. Are you saying it is long ye are here in the garden, through seven springs of planting and seven summers of growth? (*Sings another verse.*) Have patience now and the young lady your sister will be coming to visit you and to speak to you unknownst to the Witch. Ah, you draw down under the water hearing that word! Is it that you are saying she done Druid tricks on you, changing your shape and bringing you from your country, and the little Tree of Power along with you? It's a pity now some to have too much talk, and ye that are a king's sons having none at all of it. It is likely enough living down in that well ye will grow blind and deaf in the heel. Five little red-mouthed trouts! That is a bad way for a king's sons to be! —— Mind yourselves now. It's the Witch is after coming from her journey. (*He sings and works.*)

> (WITCH *comes on. She is wearing a cloak of badger skins, and a mask with long teeth and a pair of goat's horns.*)

WITCH. What way is the little tree?

GARDENER. The best. I have it well cared. I am after putting a prop to it. If you would not support the head the neck of it would be staggery.

WITCH. Blossom on it and an apple—the golden apple that will cure any sickness at all or any wound.

GARDENER. Well cared I have it; flowery above and not cranky in the stalk the way some trees do be.

WITCH. I have a mind to shift it and to plant it under my own window pane where I can be looking at it every day.

GARDENER. It's best leave it where it is, and not to be combing or rising the roots.

WITCH. It has too much of shades and of shelters. It was used to the country of the sun.

GARDENER. Wait till the month of March comes at it and you'll see it's a great persecuting it will get, and it not to be minded the way it is.

WITCH (*throwing off her cloak and mask*). Hide that under the branches. It is my daughter is coming—— Come hither to me, Pampogue.

PAMPOGUE. You are come back to the garden?

WITCH. I am always glad to come back within its walls.

PAMPOGUE. Walls! So there are enough of walls around us.

WITCH. It is a good shelter for yourself they are as well as for the little tree.

PAMPOGUE. I would sooner be outside whatever way it is, than to be closed up with no company but green plants.

GARDENER. Sure the seed we sowed will soon be flourishing up. There will be roses and posies and every sort that is pretty blooming out all around.

PAMPOGUE. I am seven times tired with the sight of your roses and posies and of the white sun itself going up and going down.

GARDENER. You will not find the seven days of the week too long, and some king's son to come courting you.

PAMPOGUE. It is near time indeed for some one to bring me out from this.

WITCH. Don't be in so great a hurry, child, to go out into the dangers of the world.

PAMPOGUE. You yourself go out gathering news or making news far and wide. It would be more fitting I to be doing that, and you that are up in age to be sitting spinning at the wheel.

WITCH. No, I will not do that. I to begin to give in to age, it is likely it would run through me too quick.

PAMPOGUE. Bring me out with you so. I would like well to travel among neighbours and to go visiting at country houses by the roadside.

WITCH. Have patience, child, for a while.

PAMPOGUE. To be with myself only I'd think the day as long as a year! Where is the benefit of all the power you own, when you cannot get me settled in a good place? It is time for me to be giving out food to company and keeping the keys of a house.

WITCH. I did not see the husband yet I thought to be worthy of you.

PAMPOGUE. You never gave me a sight of any one at all, only the gardener. All the fair-haired men I hear talk of finding comrades on the round world, and I myself hidden from them among trees!

WITCH. It is foretold to me it is love for some man of the round world will put you under trouble and torment. Wait a while, and when the right stars will be up in the heavens I will find you a lucky match.

PAMPOGUE. You are making excuses with your stars! I to have been seen before this I would have my choice of husbands!

WITCH. You have very proud, hardy talk! Is it Splendour, son of the King of the Greeks, you are looking for, or the King of Prussia's son?

PAMPOGUE. You to have given me royal blood it would be easy for me make a match with a king's son.

WITCH. There is not a woman of my race that had not a king under her feet! But as to yourself, I will give you no leave at all to wed with any man of Adam's race.

PAMPOGUE. I heard it said my father was of that breed.

WITCH. If he was, it is on his account I am at war with the whole tribe of men, striving to draw away their life.

PAMPOGUE. If you pleased yourself, why would not I please myself in a man?

WITCH. Do so, and he will leave your heart to walk barefoot over a hard highroad of flints.

PAMPOGUE. Is it that you are looking for some man in the fairies for me? Or gone out of the body? Or one coming from the country Underwave, having a skin the colour of coal?

WITCH. I have no desire to give you up at all. If I had, as to matches, I was offered one but yesterday.

PAMPOGUE. Who was that?

WITCH. Fatach Mor the Giant——

PAMPOGUE. He has a wife of his own.

WITCH. He is but the matchmaker. It is for a friend he came asking, that is coming to his castle looking for a wife.

PAMPOGUE. Has he a good way of living?

WITCH. He has put a rent upon the whole of Scotland. There are some say he has laid it upon the birds of the air.

PAMPOGUE. Is he a natural man?

WITCH. He is nearer to the class of the giants. He is the Grugach of the Humming.

PAMPOGUE. Is he anyway well looking?

WITCH. Middling only. Wait, and I will find you a better match in a quarter or three-quarters of a year.

PAMPOGUE. I'll take him. To see the daffodils sprouting in this place again it would surely bring me to my death. Gardener!

GARDENER (coming). What is it?

PAMPOGUE. I'm going out of this! I'm going to make a great match! I will never come inside a garden again, but be driving in carriages through crowded streets.

GARDENER. Is that a fact?

PAMPOGUE (to WITCH). You will want to give me some good clothes. Let them be made the same as the King of Spain's daughter had the time you brought her here. A cloak of the colour of the foxglove she had, and roses worked around the hem of her skirt.

GARDENER. So she had. There is nothing left to her now, only her little golden mittens. There was no one but would turn his head to look at her.

PAMPOGUE. There is no one would look at her now. She is nothing at all in her suit of a girl of the ducks and ashes. Get me clothes the same as she had, till I'll show out well.

WITCH (to GARDENER). Go, seek some bundles of silks and satins are inside the door of the house. Bring here the serving girl with you. (GARDENER goes.) You can make your choice of the dearest sort of silk that is pleasing to you.

PAMPOGUE. Let the girl herself sew the dress for me.

WITCH. She will, and you will become it well. Turn up your hair now and make a ball of it. It is true enough you are grown out of being a child.

(MUIREANN *comes, dressed in tattered sacking, with* GAR-
DENER *who carries bundles.*)

PAMPOGUE. Rinse now the dirt from off your hands, the way
they will be fit to handle silk clothes.

MUIREANN (*showing her hands*). They are roughened with the
sods and ashes, but they are clean.

WITCH. Look now at these silks that are the grandest nearly in the
world. You have to shape and to sew a dress for Pampogue such as
they wear at the Court of Spain.

MUIREANN. It is long since I saw a suit of the kind.

WITCH. Put your mind to it now. This dress must be made ready
by evening, by the time of the gathering of the crows.

MUIREANN. I think that is not enough of time.

WITCH. That is sluggishness. If the work is not done by then
your bed will be the iron harrow.

PAMPOGUE. If it fails her to do this, bid her go clean out the
seven cowhouses that never were cleaned for seven years.

MUIREANN. Give me thread and needles.

PAMPOGUE (*to* GARDENER). Give her a few threads from that
pound ball that is tied to the stem of the tree.

WITCH. There are needles. Have a care of them. My father gave
me the full of a ship of them, and I lost none and broke none and
there are but those five left, where they are all worn out sewing
and making and mending my clothes. (*She goes.*)

PAMPOGUE (*watches girl work. Takes up scissors*). What call has
a girl carrying turf and herding geese to have on her such a head
of hair? (*Snips a lock from it.*) There! (*Throws it on grass.*) The
birds will take it to be hemp or oakum and will carry it away, lining
their nests. (*She tries to cut another lock.*)

MUIREANN. Do not touch it! If I am poor in the world to-day, it
was a queen was used to smooth out that hair.

PAMPOGUE. It is much if I leave you your golden mittens.

MUIREANN. It is only my hand they will fit.

PAMPOGUE. Be civil now and mannerly and maybe I will bring
you to attend me and sew my clothes where I am getting a great
match out in Scotland.

MUIREANN. I was brought to this place by the power and the
spells of the witch that is your mother. It is all one to me where I
go, or do not go, as long as I am not free from that power.

PAMPOGUE. You are loth to leave your little brothers maybe in
the well.

105

MUIREANN. There is no one in this place under sorrow but only themselves and myself.

PAMPOGUE. Give me a thread of your threads.

MUIREANN. Here it is, and a needle.

PAMPOGUE. No, it is a pin I am wanting. Here now is one. I will crooken it and put a berry on it and go fishing for pinkeens in the well. There is nothing at all in the fashion, they were telling me, but gloves made of the skin of a fish.

MUIREANN (*jumping up and seizing thread*). You will get no leave to do that! The witch herself will get no leave to do it! Go away out of this!

PAMPOGUE (*spitefully and frightened*). There now, you have the five needles lost! I will go tell of you that through crossness and through spite you cast them down into the well. You will surely be sent cleaning out the seven cowsheds! (*Goes.*)

MUIREANN. My grief and my sorrow!

GARDENER (*coming forward*). That one would spit out poison would wither up the grass!

MUIREANN. Did you hear her tormenting me?

GARDENER. I did. I'd sooner a venomous mist to come and to slaughter the crops. She's as cross as a bag of weasels.

MUIREANN. She threatened to cast down her line and her hook, and I started, and lost the Witch's needles in the well!

GARDENER. That she may be worse this day twelvemonth!

MUIREANN. I cannot get a view of them at all. They are stuck down in the sand and in the stones.

GARDENER. That herself and all belonging to her may wither off the face of the earth!

MUIREANN (*with a shout of joy*). They have brought them back to me! My needles! Every one of the five little fishes put up his head, and he having a needle in his mouth!

GARDENER. Is that a fact?

MUIREANN. Aren't those now the good little brothers? By and by when the work is ended I will play a little tune to you, that we used to hear in our father's house.

GARDENER. It is a hard thing you to be left to the kindness of fishes. It is a king's son in his own shape should be coming to your aid.

MUIREANN (*standing up*). It is near the fall of evening. Look at the flight of the wild ducks across the sky. (*A sound of cawing.*) There now are the crows gathering to the high elms.

GARDENER. Whisht! They travel far. I am listening to their news of the world.

MUIREANN. I am lost now and destroyed. I have made no way at all with the work. The Witch will show no kindness. She will put trouble and hardship on me through the night. But I will not give in to her to shed tears or to give out any cry at all! (GARDENER *laughs*.)

MUIREANN. It is a bad time you chose for laughing!

GARDENER. There is many a one would laugh, having knowledge of the talk of the birds.

MUIREANN. Teach it to me so.

GARDENER. I will do that. I learned it from a blue hawk that was my grandmother.

MUIREANN. A while ago there was no one would laugh, the time I would be under any of the little troubles of a child.

GARDENER. There is news will set a man laughing at any time because he knows it will turn to good.

MUIREANN. Is it news that will help my case?

GARDENER. It is. It is news of a dying king. (*He goes off singing his little song.*)

(MUIREANN *sits down and sews desperately.* GARDENER *comes back dressed as a ragged messenger with broken breeches and tattered shoes, his ears sticking through his cap.*)

GARDENER. I am going a journey.

MUIREANN. Oh, bring me along with you! Bring me away from the Witch's garden!

GARDENER. It would be no use. You cannot stir unknownst to her.

MUIREANN. I would run fast, very fast.

GARDENER. Old as she is, she is as supple-walking in her limbs as a young girl.

MUIREANN. I could hide.

GARDENER. You could not. She is a very fierce woman. There is not a wall in any part would keep you safe from her rage.

MUIREANN. There is no help for me so.

GARDENER. It is time for me get it for you.

MUIREANN. What way can you travel so far?

GARDENER. I didn't live these seven years under a witch without learning some of her trade. There are wild geese on the wing to-night. It is along with them I will go.

MUIREANN. Oh, will you save me out of this!

GARDENER. I promise you that. I give you as bail the four quarters of the heavens and of the sea and of the land against my own body and my soul! (*Goes.*)

(WITCH *and daughter come in.*)

WITCH. Where are the needles I gave you?

MUIREANN. They are here. I am sewing with one. The rest are stuck in my mitten.

WITCH (*to* PAMPOGUE). You deceived me, saying she had lost them, and bringing me here from my rest that I was in need of, where the day was long on me.

PAMPOGUE. She has not the sewing near done. Send her to clean out the seven sheds.

WITCH. Keep quiet. I am tired with your peevishness. I will listen to no more of your talk. Mind yourself, girl! I will let you off punishment to-night, but the rods will be ripe and ready for you to-morrow!

(WITCH *and* DAUGHTER *go.*)

(MUIREANN *takes her little silver pipe, bends over well, and plays "The little old mud cabin by the hill."*)

SCENE II. *A room in the Court of the King of Ireland. The* KING *lying on a bed.* DOCTOR *sitting beside him.* SERVANTS. SIMON MAOR *comes in and looks at him.*

SIMON. Is there life in the King yet?

DOCTOR. There is, but hardly.

SIMON. He shrunk greatly in the days past. He reduced very much in the face.

DOCTOR. No wonder in that, and he lying on the bed through the three quarters of the year. He never made a laugh since he was in it. It is a heavy wound he got.

SIMON. It was bad to him to be beat in the battle. And his seven packs of hounds at the same time to be swept from him and lost.

DOCTOR. It was worse to him, the two eldest sons to be killed in the same fight where he got the wound.

SIMON. The son that is left to him is worth the whole of them.

DOCTOR. He's not much. It's hard lead him. The father himself is more apt to take my counsel and advice. It is long till he will be fitting to be King.

SIMON. It is not long till he will be that. That old remnant in the bed lost a power of money over you, but there isn't left of him now but the same as a shadow in a bottle. Not an ounce of flesh on him, but only skin and bones.

DOCTOR. He would be a great loss to Ireland. I might bring him around yet.

SIMON. It would maybe give him relief to quit the world. To die in your bed is the safest death. It would be nearly a pity he not to go, and all prepared so nice.

(A SERVANT *brings in a sheepskin*.)

DOCTOR. Give that to me. (*He takes skin and begins to wrap it round* KING.)

SIMON. What skin is that?

DOCTOR. The skin of a sheep that is after being killed, fresh and warm. I am about to wrap it about his body. It might put some heat into his blood.

SIMON. Whose orders were those to go killing a sheep?

DOCTOR. My own orders, as the King's doctor.

SIMON. If you are itself, I am the King's steward. I will bear no meddling with my flocks.

DOCTOR. I will meddle and have a right to meddle, where it is for the service of the King.

SIMON. Out of what flock did they go bring it?

DOCTOR. Tush! What way would I know? A sheep is a sheep— a four-footed beast in the field, and mutton when it is served on the table. When it is but the skin I am in need of, it makes no difference what sort they will go kill.

SIMON. It makes a big differ to myself. A doctor that is stuck in the house has no call to interfere with the stock. Let me see now, did you take one of the culled ewes I have ready for October fair, or the wethers I am fattening against Shrove? (*Pulls at sheepskin*.)

DOCTOR. Don't be stirring it now, letting in the draught.

SIMON. I wouldn't begrudge a horny hogget from the mountain; a hardy class that go foraging on furze and heath.

DOCTOR. I tell you I don't care what it is so long as it has warmth within it, and a weighty fleece.

SIMON. A weighty fleece! (*Feels it.*) Have a care is it my Ormond ram!

DOCTOR. I'll tell the King on you, and that you begrudge him his own.

SIMON. I'll tell the King's son you went killing and destroying what will be *his* own! It's likely it will not be *this* King will be reckoning the lambs' tails next Easter!

DOCTOR. He might not be as near it as you think.

SIMON. Signs are he might. It's the world will be changing around you. I tell you a true word, it is not everybody would drink *your* medicines!

DOCTOR. Go on now till he'll hear you! He is wakening.

(KING *feebly stirs.*)

SIMON. There is hot stones on the hearth. Wait till I will put them to his feet. (*He brings stones and puts them at end of bed.*)

KING. Where is Rury, my son ?

DOCTOR. Out hurling, I suppose; or fowling with his horse and his dog.

SIMON. He never was far out in the country since the bad turn came, but around the gardens and the house.

KING. Send out looking for him. He is all the son that I have.

SIMON. And you are all the father he ever had. He dotes down on yourself.

DOCTOR. It is natural a young lad to be sporting and rambling.

SIMON. You know well that through the night time, and the King sleeping, he was sitting by the brink of the bed.

DOCTOR. If the King would charge myself with any message to him, or any commands as to his behaviour, there would no mistake be made.

KING. Is it certain I am going out?

DOCTOR. I am striving to keep the life in you. I have death baulked and baffled up to this. I have kept him back from the pillow, but he is at the foot of the bed.

(*A horn heard.*)

KING. What is that?

SIMON. It is the big horn is at the grand gate. It is long since it was sounded out before.

DOCTOR. It is likely it is some king sending to ask news of your health.

KING. A king is it?

DOCTOR. I would say by the sound it is one of the big men of the world.

KING. Put me sitting up against the pillow.

(DOCTOR *and* SIMON *raise him.*)

DOCTOR. Take care would you let him slip down!

KING. What is this you have put around me?

DOCTOR. The skin of a sheep newly killed.

KING (*with a roar*). Is it that you thought me to be dead that you dared to dress me up as a sheep? Is that the way you have made me a fool of so soon as you thought my senses to be gone?

DOCTOR. It was the skin that brought you around.

SIMON. It was not, but the hot stones.

KING. A sheepskin! Had you no lion from the Eastern World to go skin, or a bull itself would be sending out challenges, tearing up the sod with his horns?

DOCTOR. I thought to be doing what was right.

KING. Let ye put some face upon my bed! Kings do not die like flies in a heap, one the same as another. Every king has a separate death, and should have it! How would you know what time it would be put in a story or a song?

(*They arrange armour and rough skins about his bed.*)

DOCTOR. Here is the big shield, the Wheel of Battle. I will put it beside your hand.

KING. Let in now the king or the king's messenger that is come maybe from Arthur of Britain or from the Crown of France.

(*Door is opened and* GARDENER *appears in his dress as a ragged man.*)

Who is that?

DOCTOR. A ragged green man!

SIMON. Broken breeches on him, and puddle water in his shoes.

DOCTOR. Turn him out!

SIMON. Put him out the door!

KING. Let the crows make their supper of him to-night!

(ALL *push him towards door.* RURY *appears coming in and pushes him back.*)

DOCTOR. Who is stopping him?

SIMON. It is Rury, the King's son.

RURY. He is a messenger. He has the right to give his message.

GARDENER. I have an advice to give.

KING. Is it sent by a comrade king?

GARDENER. It is not.

DOCTOR. Are you doctor to any king?

GARDENER. I am not.

SIMON. Or steward to any king?

GARDENER. I am not.

SIMON. Then you have no word that is worth saying.

RURY. Let him speak.

GARDENER. The birdeens of the air brought word where I was, that the King of Ireland is all but in the grip of death.

DOCTOR. It is no wonder the birds themselves to be crying him.

GARDENER. It is not crying or keening they were, but laughing.

KING. What is he saying?

GARDENER. Laughing to think there is a great king going out, and he not sending some messenger to the lucky apple tree in that place.

RURY. What way would that help him?

GARDENER. The cure of the world is in it. There is a golden apple of that tree would raise a man it had failed all the doctors to rise.

RURY. Is that a true story?

GARDENER. It's as true as I'm telling you. To make a sound man of him it would, and to give him lengthening of life.

KING. It is hard to believe it at all.

DOCTOR. With all the cures I am doing through the years I never heard of it.

SIMON. Who is it owns the apple?

GARDENER. It is owned presently by the Witch that is called in Ireland the Hag of Slaughter, that has it robbed from the Royalty of Spain.

RURY. Is it east or west the garden is?

GARDENER. It is not knowledge of the roads will bring you to that far foreign place that is called Garrdin-dearead-an-domhain, the Garden at the World's End.

(RURY *goes aside, puts on cloak, takes up and tries some weapons.*)

KING. It should be a long way off.

GARDENER. To go for the apple and to get the apple and to bring it to this place would need the length of a year and a day.

SIMON. Will the King last out that long?

DOCTOR. I'll engage to keep him for that time through the power of my physic, that is maybe as good as apples in the heel.

KING. If you do not, I will leave it in my will, every doctor in Ireland to be hanged!

SIMON. And who now will go look for the apple?

GARDENER. It is a man having courage should do that. There is a giant in the way, Fatach Mor. There is danger in passing by his house.

SIMON. I wouldn't think much of giants; I never heard of a giant having stock enough to keep a steward, or a herd itself, employed.

GARDENER. There are the tricks of the Hag of Slaughter.

SIMON. The people do be full of stories of her. But I never could be in dread of a witch.

GARDENER. There is the Wood of Wonders to be passed, that is full of monsters and of shadow-shapes.

SIMON. I never would believe in that sort. I am going about through the dark night every lambing time, and I never met with anything worse than myself.

GARDENER. There is the Hill of Fire to be crossed that sends up a blast of flame; and the Mountain of Spearheads that are sticking up through the ground.

SIMON. It is the one in charge of the King's health should go in search of what will stiffen out his life. We reckon the doctor that much use.

KING. Let him go so without delay.

DOCTOR. It would fail me to do it in the time. I am no good stepper on the road, let alone upon spearheads and fiery flames. I am too far out in years.

SIMON. It is lively it will make you. There is no one rightly young, only those that will travel.

DOCTOR. Send out the captains of the King's army.

KING. They have no drill or preparation to protect them against unnatural things.

SIMON. The Witch to change them into grasshoppers they would be crushed under the weight of their armour—and they to shrink so much in bulk!

DOCTOR. Let you yourself go, where you are making a mock of danger.

SIMON. Is it I myself? What about my hay? My stacks? My haggard? With the milk to be regulated and all the cows that are about to calve!

DOCTOR. You are in dread of the Giant and the Witch.

SIMON. I am not. But I am loth to meddle with apples after what happened in Adam's Paradise. (KING *sinks back*.)

DOCTOR (*to the* SERVANTS). It's as good for you lay out the sheets.

RURY (*coming forward and speaking to* SIMON). Take good care of my white greyhound till I come back. You may put out the horses at grass.

SIMON. Where is it you are going?

RURY. Keep in the red colt through the heat of the day. He goes crazy when the flies come around him.

KING. You are not going away, Rury?

RURY. I will be back in a year and a day.

SIMON. Is it that you are going for the apple?

KING. You cannot go. It is not according to right rule the heir to go, and the King himself not having strength in his hand to notch his name or his command upon a stick.

DOCTOR. It is right he should go. Everything that can be done should be done to save the King's life.

SIMON. Is it that you have it in your mind to make him banish the son?

KING. I crave and command you not to go into those dangers.

RURY. Who would not to hell for a cure if one belonging to him was sick?

SIMON. Hasn't the lad great courage?

KING. I will not let you go! You that have always earned my blessing and that never have earned my curse.

RURY. Keep your heart up and rouse yourself, and you won't feel the year passing. For the latter end of the world to be tomorrow, I would go out in the same way.

KING. Do not let him out the door! He will never bring his life away out of all that!

SIMON. You would as easy put a gad around sand, or keep a hold of a sunbeam in your fist.

KING. His two brothers went out laughing, and it was to meet with their death.

SIMON. And he not knowing so much as where is the garden!

RURY. If it isn't in the east I'll go west, and if it isn't in the west I'll go south, and from that again to the north! I will not eat two meals in the one place or sleep two nights in the one bed till I will bring back the cure for your healing!

SIMON. Take comfort, King. I myself will go with him for to take charge of him on the road.

DOCTOR. That's right. The King will give you the lend of him, Rury, for the length of a year and a day.

SIMON. I will walk every whole step of Ireland, but I'll bring him back safe and sound!

KING. Lift the flagstone from the hearth and give him out the sword was cooled with three drops of lions' blood.

SIMON. Ask him along with that to give you the costs of the road. (KING *points to a purse, and* DOCTOR *gives it to* SIMON.) I leave it on the King this is travelling charges, and should not be put to my account as steward.

RURY. The messenger is gone. We must overtake him, till we learn what way we should make our start for the Garden at the World's End!

SIMON (*to the* GUARD). Let you strike up now, boys, the "Shan van voght"!

(*March played. They go out. The* KING *sinks back weeping.* DOCTOR *stands over him.*)

SCENE III. *The Wood of Wonders. An open space. Evening darkening.* WITCH *and* PAMPOGUE *come in with branches.*

PAMPOGUE. Is this what they call the round world? It is a lonely looking sort of a place.

WITCH. You gave me no rest till I would bring you with me, and now you are not content.

PAMPOGUE. What made you choose this wild spot?

WITCH. It is best for the work I have to do.

PAMPOGUE. You didn't tell me yet what is that work.

WITCH. A thief that is coming the road to bring away the apple from the garden. What I have to do is to put him backward.

PAMPOGUE. What ails you that you cannot rise up in the air like a mist and come down and turn him into a green stone?

WITCH. We have our own way to contend with. There are some things it is hard for me to touch.

PAMPOGUE. They give out you have power over all things.

WITCH. I am under orders like the rest. There is an order that we cannot meddle with the royal blood of Ireland, that is protected since the time of the Danes; unless it will come into our power through fear or through tasting our food.

PAMPOGUE. Is it one of that blood is coming the road?

WITCH. Not at all—not at all—just a thief, a pair of robbers. It will be easy frighten them, putting these branches around them, that they will think themselves to be in a wood. (*She makes branches into bundles.*) To drive the wits from them with fear, that will be best of all. I will raise a sound in the air, they will think it to be a storm of wind.

PAMPOGUE. Give me some branches to be shaking at them. I will flutter up my apron till they will feel a blast.

WITCH. Do not. To hear the sound of wind and not to feel it would put more dread into the heart.

PAMPOGUE. What made you gather that bag of rush cotton?

WITCH. We will make with it the appearance of snow.

PAMPOGUE. What at all are you putting around you? I never saw that ugly dress.

WITCH (*putting on badger skin, cloak, and mask*). That is the way the men of the earth have me pictured. The skin of badgers around me and two goats' horns going out through my head.

PAMPOGUE. I would not like to be looking at you. Keep away from me.

WITCH. That is the story they give out about the Hag of Slaughter. It is for the like of them we that are ever-living must put on the ugly image of age. Let them see me as they have made me out to be.

PAMPOGUE. Whisht! There is some one coming.

WITCH. Come back here out of their sight. (*They take up bushes and branches and stand behind them.*)

(*Enter* RURY *and* SIMON.)

SIMON. I wish we could see some lodging. There is a queer sound from the sky. I heard like a blast of wind that would lay the thistles low.

RURY. It is but a storm is rising.

SIMON. To come a sudden darkening of the light there did.

RURY. It is but a cloud over the moon. You are losing courage to be in dread of that.

SIMON. I did not, but sore in the heart with walking I am. My legs are near worn to the knee. I might as well be a car-wheel on the road.

RURY. If there is a long road behind us it is likely the road before us is longer again.

SIMON. The soles of my boots is near wore out.

RURY. They will have to last a good while yet.

SIMON. They will, where they lasted near thirty years already, for they will be but the soles of my two feet.

(*Branches waved around them.*)

RURY. We would seem to be gone astray in some forest.

SIMON. In some terrible wilderness of a wood.

RURY. Hush! I am thinking it should be the Wood of Wonders. There is some music playing of itself.

(*A wild air is played.*)

SIMON. I would say it to be the sea roaring as if all the people of the world were to be drowned. Believe me, it is best for us turn back.

RURY. You came out boasting you were in dread of nothing.

SIMON. I am not, and the sun to be in the heavens. The day is getting as dark as if all the men in the King's jail were being hanged!

116

RURY. That was a branch fell upon my head.

SIMON. It was no branch fell on myself, but some person hit a stroke on my back.

RURY. There is no person here to do that.

SIMON. There is another—and another!

RURY. Do not give in to fancy. There is no one hitting you at all.

SIMON. It is you yourself is doing it! It is an unkind thing doing that!

RURY. I feel strokes coming on myself. They are given with a whip of thorns.

SIMON. Turn back I tell you, bring your life out of this!

RURY. I will bring it out on the other side. I will not go doubling like a hare.

SIMON. There is a lion of roaring!

RURY. I wish he would come before my sword.

SIMON. There is like the howling of red-haired wolves! There is a shiver of fright going through me! I don't wish to be killed, where I was not brought up to it like kings' sons.

RURY. We cannot lose our life spending it in dread of death.

SIMON. The thirty walls of heaven to be lighting bonfires to be welcoming me, I would sooner go back to my own parish.

RURY. The doctor would make fun of you, seeing you now.

SIMON. That he himself may be put under curses and spells and the unnatural creatures of the air!

RURY. All I would ask is light to recognise them.

SIMON. Natural things to come against me I would not know fear or fright—— Do you hear that now?

RURY. They are but shapes and spirits. They can do us no bodily harm.

SIMON. There is a hand touched me.

RURY. It was of no living person. The feel of it was like the feel of ice.

SIMON. There is like a shivering come upon me—— What is that passed by?

RURY. Three bald clowns having three hounds in their hands, and three reddened spears.

SIMON. Who is there? Keep yourself away from me!

A VOICE. I am a man of the hurlers without heads. Four-and-twenty men of us, and the ball we are playing with is my own head. (*Sound of sticks upon a ball.*)

SIMON. I wouldn't wish to be hunted through Ireland by hard bristly heads without legs!

RURY. What do you want of us?

VOICE. Dig a grave for us! Dig a grave for us! (*They go off.*)

SIMON. There is a foot with a spur on it.

RURY. Take that foot out of my path! (*Strikes at it.*)

ANOTHER VOICE. I tell you, this time yesterday there was no one dared meddle with that foot!

RURY. There are horrible things about us!

MANY VOICES. Go back! Go back! There is no road for you here!

(*WITCH appears.*)

SIMON. Look at her, look! That one would make a hare of you! She is the Hag of Slaughter!

RURY. I will never turn back for any Witch's bidding!

A VOICE. Many a better thief than yourself went the same journey and not a one ever came back!

(*There are shrieks, and snow is thrown about them, then a thick smoke.*)

RURY. It is like the smoke of elder-wood. We will go on.

SIMON. Wait awhile—my heart is panting. I thought the world was going down!

RURY. The smoke is clearing away.

SIMON. Oh! There came a smell from it like as if all the dead people of the world were there!

(*Smoke clears away. WITCH seen sitting by a fire singing a lament. She is not wearing mask and horns, but has a black shawl over her head. Her grey hair is hanging.*)

WITCH. Stop here and eat a bit with me, King of Ireland's son!

SIMON. Do not stop with her. She is no way pleasing to look at, and her hair down to her heels.

RURY. I am hurrying on my journey, I have no time to stop in any place.

WITCH. I to have grandeur about me, and a grand big dinner to give you, you would stop. But because I am poor and miserable and have but a bone to offer you, you will not stop.

RURY. That is not so; it is that I am in haste.

WITCH. The man that will not show respect to those who are low, even if he is high, he will get no respect for himself.

SIMON. Do not stop with her! She will work on us a charm or a spell! (*WITCH goes on keening.*)

RURY (*pushing him off*). It is a habit of my habits never to listen to the call of a lone woman without getting knowledge of her case. What name have you?

WITCH. My name is Sighing and Sorrow, Black Night of Winter, White Night of Snow; Grief, Groaning, Keening, and a Grave!

RURY. What is it ails you?

WITCH. Sit down till I will tell you. Twelve sons I had and they are all after being brought away to their death.

RURY. What way can I help you?

WITCH. Go back, bring the armies of the King of Ireland, till they will go against the armies of the Dogheads that brought them away.

RURY. I cannot do that. I must go on until my business will be done. I will come then and help you.

WITCH. You are deceiving me.

RURY. I never left a lie after me in any place.

WITCH. Take this bone in your hand; put this flesh I offer you in your mouth.

RURY. I will not deny you because you are in trouble and grief.

(RURY *is putting a bit in his mouth when* PAMPOGUE *comes behind him and snatches it from him.*)

PAMPOGUE. Use none of her food or you are a gone man! It is best throw it in the fire. (*She throws it away.*)

WITCH. My seven curses upon you, you have freed him when I all but had him in my hands!

RURY. You are lying to me, and deceiving me! You are no lone woman wanting help.

WITCH. I will get you yet! I will tear the heart out of you! I swear it by the earth that holds the graves of the dead!

RURY. There is no fear on me. I know who you are. You are the Hag of Slaughter.

WITCH. I am that! And I tell you I myself will set the ravens croaking over your grave.

RURY. They will never croak and call out in Connacht that I was brought down by a hag! Have a care now! I am loth to shed the blood of a woman, but it would be right for me to strike at a witch! (*He takes* SIMON *by the shoulder and goes off waving a sword.*)

WITCH (*to* PAMPOGUE). That is what you have done with your meddling and your want of wit.

PAMPOGUE. You lied to me! He is a king's son. I would not give you leave to put poison in his mouth.

WITCH. Fool! You think to manage me and to set yourself over me! It was no poison. It was the food that would put him under my power for ever, and he taking and eating it from my hand.

PAMPOGUE. Get him into your power again and put the seven

spells of love on him. I will have nothing to do with your Giants and Grugachs, it is with that man only I will wed.

WITCH. You are on the path of destruction now. My grief that I let you leave the garden!

PAMPOGUE. Go, get me that king's son!

WITCH. Have you no thought at all for her who cared and reared you, and gave in to everything you would ask?

PAMPOGUE. Get me what I want! You filled me with the things I did not want. It is my own way I will go now!

WITCH. It will be a bad way for you and for yourself. But take your own way. I will get him for you, if striving will do it. I will give him the golden apple. It will buy for you his love. But I thought the man was not born in Ireland that would stand against my spells as he did.

(*The same wild music is heard.*)

SCENE IV. *A room in the* GIANT'S *castle. He and Wife are playing Fox and Goose on a large blackboard with chalk.*

WIFE. This and this blots out that——and one for the good of my make. I rub out your noughts and put in my own crosses.

GIANT (*throwing down his bit of chalk*). I'll play no more Fox and Goose. You had me beat last time. (*He yawns.*)

WIFE. What now would you wish to be doing?

GIANT. Couldn't you draw down a new story or an old story out of the book.

WIFE. The History of the Giants is it? It's a holy terror to be reading them. (*Takes book and sits down.*) Which now will be your choice? There's as many of them as my fingers and toes. This one is the story of Fuath of the Seven Heads and Seven Humps and Seven Necks, that was one of the best giants ever counted in Ireland.

GIANT. I heard that before.

WIFE. You did not, but of the Scotch giant of the Seven Glens and Seven Bens and Seven Bogs.

GIANT. What now did he do?

WIFE (*looking in book*). He used to be dragging six bullocks by their tails at the one time, and to go harrow the ground with the bristled body of two wild boars he would tie to the two strings of his shoe.

GIANT. Am I now as strong as that one?

WIFE. You are to be sure, my dear, you are.

GIANT. Sound me out another.

WIFE. Would you wish Head-without-Body, son of King of the Castles, that came home from his morning ramble driving seven kings in a gad?

GIANT. Could I now do that much?

WIFE. You could, my dear, you could.

GIANT. This is such a backward place I would hardly meet with a king in a twelvemonth, where they are all banished, I suppose, to their own countries. Go on now.

WIFE. There is a very pretty little story of one Dearg Mor. His head and his hands that were after being cut off came playing cards with Finn Mac Cuil on a ship.

GIANT. I wouldn't wish my head and hands to be cut off. It is often I do be thinking since I turned to be a giant I might have followed some better trade.

WIFE. You might have gone as a billeted soldier in the line army, to be a bully in the service of a king.

GIANT. I am thinking it is a middling easy job to be a king.

WIFE. There are giants left as good a name after them, such as Polyphemus that was killed by the great Greek.

GIANT. Kings go from father to son, and one that is slack in his wits might not be found out for a long while. But you have to be a giant of yourself, and to put up your own name.

WIFE. So you do put it up, my dear, so you do.

GIANT. I am thinking there is a reflection on giants, now people are getting to be so cranky and so enlightened. What story now will be written in the book of myself, the great Giant, Fatach Mor?

WIFE (*jumping up*). I myself to write the book, I would say he was a great bother stopping all through the day in the house, and not to go and cut a few heads of cabbage for the dinner.

GIANT. Ah, what dinner? I am not able to lessen on anything worth while this long time. I have the appetite lost.

WIFE. To move about and to stir yourself you should, and to lend a hand turning the hay.

GIANT. I cannot grabble with everything at once. Little you care if I got as thin as a fishing-rod. I, now, suffer more than any common man. There is more room for the pain to work by reason of the height of my body and the length there is in my limbs.

WIFE. Let you send for a doctor so, if you are not satisfied with the attendance I am giving you.

GIANT. A doctor should have more knowledge.

WIFE. Never fear, he'll have knowledge enough to take your money, giving your sickness every name longer than another.

GIANT. It is yourself begrudges them the fee.

WIFE. Fee enough not to cut the head off them. Giving you, maybe, medicines were in bottles on the shelf these sixty years, that you hardly could read the labels on them.

GIANT. There is a physician, they were telling me, at the King of Ireland's Court. The capital doctor of the country he is. He is greatly beloved with the King.

WIFE. He should be free by this, for I heard a good while ago the King was in a dying state under his hand.

GIANT. Can't you give your mind now to send your pigeon messenger to bid him put on his coat of healing and come hither without delay. Give me some sort of a note or a writing for him.

WIFE. Ah! Get out the door, will you, and I'll give you anything you'll ask outside heaven!

GIANT (*at door to left*). It is on you it will fall, any harmless person to get their death seeing me on the road—through terror of my height and of my size.

WIFE. Close the door after you!

GIANT (*putting in his head again*). Don't forget, now, setting out the yard as a giant's yard should be set out, every fork but one having a head on it.

WIFE. Have a care! I am about to throw scalding water out the door! (*She lifts pot from fire.* GIANT *slams door and goes.*) (*Sitting down.*) My joy go with you in a bottle of moss, and if you never come back you'll be no great loss! (*She takes out a little stocking, turns out money into her lap and counts it. There is a knock at door to right.*) Come in!

(RURY *and* SIMON *enter, very travel-stained and tired.*)

RURY. We are travelling a long time. Can you give us food and rest?

WIFE (*jumping up and curtseying low*). My hundred thousand welcomes to you, King's son from Ireland!

RURY. What way do you know me?

WIFE. Why wouldn't I recognise the signs of a king, and I reared in Connacht? You are the highest blood in Ireland, by your father anyway.

RURY. It is a good thing to meet with a welcome.

WIFE. You never were more welcome, and if there were ten of you, you would be welcome! But is it that you came riding spread-legs down a rainbow, or what way at all did you come?

RURY. We travelled a queer long way coming here.

SIMON. We did surely. We have half the world walked.

WIFE. You should have come through great dangers.

SIMON. If we did, we came through them all. That lad, my master, would face anything, dog or Christian, he would meet.

WIFE. I didn't hear a Connacht man's voice the seven years I am a Giant's wife.

SIMON. What giant?

WIFE. This is the house of Fatach Mor.

SIMON (*uneasily*). Is it that there is within that door a full room of skulls?

RURY. Give us something to eat, and we will go on our road.

WIFE (*putting porridge from a saucepan into bowls*). You couldn't eat healthier than the oatmeal. It will give you nice courage for a while. We don't have meat in the house but one day in the week, and that day is yesterday.

SIMON. I suppose the Giant devours his meal abroad, tearing and rending it where it falls. It should be a terrible thing to be wed with a man the like of that.

WIFE. Indeed, I'd sooner be at my own liberty than confined in this place. Whisper—— I am trying to fill a little stocking against the time I'll go back to Connacht.

RURY. Can you give me news of the Garden that is at the World's End?

WIFE. It is I myself can give it.

RURY. I have to get an apple there for my father's healing. Is it far?

WIFE. You never would be able to reach it, and you not getting help on the way.

RURY. You don't know, I suppose, the Witch that owns it, that is said to be the Hag of Slaughter?

WIFE. I myself know her, and it's well I know her, and it's I do know her.

RURY. Is she as bad as what they say?

WIFE. She is, and worse.

SIMON. Sure we got a sketch of her below in the Wood of Wonders; a horned, twisted hag.

WIFE. That's not her. The wasting of time does not touch her. She kept her youth through being thorny-hearted, and taking an odd sleep through seven years.

RURY. What way will we know her?

WIFE. You couldn't know her. When she has a mind she looks

as innocent as a little child would be picking strawberries in the grass. She does be coming here often of late.

SIMON. To this house?

WIFE. The Giant that is turned matchmaker through her means, where his kinsman the Grugach of the Humming is coming looking for a woman of a wife. To put us to the expense of the wedding they will, that will have a year's firing used in a week.

SIMON. Is it with the Witch he will go wed?

WIFE. He will not, but with the daughter. Much good may it do her! And he having but one foot and one eye, and it in the middle of his head.

RURY. It should be hard for him find a wife.

WIFE. Ah, he has the riches. And the girl is no great blood, where her father was but a well-looking Munster man, coaxed the Witch with a sweet note in his voice.

RURY (*putting down bowl and mug*). It is time for us go on towards the Garden.

WIFE. Did you get warning of the dangers of the road?

RURY. We got news of them, the Blazing Mountain and the Hill of Spearheads.

WIFE. Look now what I will do for you, if I put my own neck in the rope. I would like well that you would get the better of the witch-woman and put an end to her matches and her meddling. Do you see what is there hanging on the wall?

RURY. It is a ball of flax.

SIMON. Twisted it is on a crooked holly stick.

WIFE. It is not any size at all to be looking at, but it will give out a thousand miles of thread.

SIMON. Is it that there is enchantment in it?

WIFE. It has that much of a charm it would bring you through all the world. It is the Witch left it there, the way Fatach Mor would be able to go up and down giving her news of the coming of the Grugach, where it is tethered to an apple tree in the Garden. Go throwing it before you, and come up with it as far as it goes.

RURY. It will bring us to that tree?

WIFE. As straight as a bullet. It will be a high bridge over fire, and as to the spearheads, you passing over them they will turn their points straight downwards. What, now, do you say to me?

SIMON. Very good. It is a man without sense would go climbing a fence would be hard, and a fence would be low and easy being beside him.

RURY. I will tell the King, my father, it was you that saved his life.

WIFE. You are welcome, dear, you're welcome. Well, God enable you! And that you may put nettles growing upon the Witch's hearth!   (*Three roars heard.*)

SIMON. What at all is that?

WIFE. It is Himself coming in.

RURY. It is best for us go on. I have no wish to do hurt to your man.

WIFE. You are late. He is at the door.

SIMON. Put us in hiding till he will be gone.

WIFE. Get in here to the chest of bog deal. (SIMON *slips in.*)

RURY. I will stop here behind the dresser. I might make a run past.

WIFE. You cannot, but wait till I will put him asleep. You can make a leap then out the door.

GIANT (*coming in*). I am thinking you gave me a good advice. I am feeling some desire for my meal.

WIFE. That is great. What now will I make ready for you?

GIANT (*throwing down some heads of cabbage*). I took down a few of the heads are on the forks since yesterday. Let you put them in the pot to boil.

> (SIMON *who has lifted an inch of the lid of chest shuts it again, terrified.*)

(*Excited.*) Fru, Fra, Fashog! I smell the smell of a melodious lying Irishman!

WIFE. Oh no, my dear. It is but a breeze passed over a boat sailing from Connemara, and brought a hint of the smoke from the turf.

GIANT. I have no mind friends of your own to be coming to pick knowledge of myself and my ways. That is the way they get to lose their respect for us.

WIFE. Oh no, but more respect for yourself they would get.

GIANT. Give me here the knife. I will be slicing and cutting the heads.   (SIMON *peeps out again, terrified.*)

(*Turning.*) Fru, Fra, Fashog! I smell the smell of the melodious lying——

WIFE. Oh no, my dear. It is but the little root of shamrock I brought in my box, that is blooming out in the green plot abroad in the yard.

GIANT. Those men of Ireland are getting too saucy altogether!

Look now till you'll see the way I'll take a hold of this by the neck and will cleave it with one stroke!

> (*Holds up a cabbage:* SIMON *again tries to peep.*) (*Throwing down cabbage.*) It is lies you are telling me! I am certain I smell the smell!

WIFE (*putting hand on his arm*). Oh, my dear, I was in dread you would be jealous if I told you. It was a little bird from Ireland perched upon my shoulder a while ago, and I out bleaching the tablecloths for the Grugach's wedding feast. Go out now and put a few more heads upon the forks before any person will pass by.

GIANT. I to mind you I would have my feet wore to flitters running here and there.

WIFE. Come over here, my dear, and I will sing you Grania's little sleepy song she used to be crooning over Diarmuid, to soothe him till the dinner would be boiled.

GIANT. I will sit down here on the chest.

WIFE. No, but come here out of the draught of wind is coming in at the door. (*He sits down in easy-chair.*) Here is a pillow for your head. (*She sits on arm of chair and sings*) "Sleep a little, my blessing on you, my lamb from beside the pool; Oh, heart of courage beyond all courage, there is not a woman but envies me to-day."

GIANT (*sitting up proudly*). I to fall asleep, waken me with three blows of a hammer from the Forge of the Four-and-twenty Smiths.

WIFE. I will, my dear, I will. (*Sings*) "Let your sleep be like the sleep in the east, of the great hero was called the Sluggard. A pair of tongs he had upon his back, and a squealing pig between the two hands of the tongs!"

GIANT (*looking up*). If that song puts me to sleep, waken me with letting fall on me a beam from the roof!

WIFE. If that doesn't waken you I'll cut the toe off you—— (*Sings*) "Let your sleep be like the sleep in the west, of Halfman that carried a churchyard on his back!"

GIANT (*looking up*). That is a giant you would call a giant!

WIFE (*speaking rapidly*). The best sleep ever he got was through the rattling of an iron candlestick having three branches, and nine apples weighing nine stone upon every branch! (*She takes poker and tongs and rattles them upon iron pot.*)

> (GIANT *seems to sleep profoundly. During the clamour,* SIMON *scrambles out of chest, and he and* RURY *go to door.* WIFE *puts down fireirons and waves a hand to them.*)

SIMON (*at door*). That was the longest hour that ever was on the hands of the clock!

(GIANT *starts up.* RURY *and* SIMON *rush out of door, locking it after them.*)

GIANT. There is some one gone out the door!

WIFE. You are dreaming, my dear, through your sleep.

GIANT (*at window*). Two of them that are in it!

WIFE. Oh, the villains! Go after them and stop them!

GIANT. They have the door locked!

WIFE. It's easy for you wrench it open.

GIANT. I have no time to put on my battle dress.

WIFE. You could go a short-cut through the window.

GIANT. I wonder at you! You know well to go out of the window I would have to take off my tree-legs—— (*Shows stilts under his clothing.*) The people to see me that way, it is likely they would be saying me not to be a real giant!

Curtain.

ACT II

SCENE I. *The Garden.* WITCH *and* GARDENER. *The* WITCH *is richly dressed.*

WITCH (*looking at apple tree*). The thread is tightening. Some person is coming here having the ball in his hand.

GARDENER. It might be Fatach Mor the Giant. It was to him you gave the use of it.

WITCH. It is not. I know by the feel of the flax it is a man with a heart of courage has a grip of it.

GARDENER. It can be no one but some friend of your own, ma'am, would have the string.

WITCH. It is no friend. I know well who it is. If I refuse him the apple, it is likely he will rob it in spite of me. He has robbed me of more than that, more than that. I will lose her. It fails me the strength to cross her. I must give him to her, I will bid her make ready to meet him. My grief that she ever laid an eye on him! He will vex her heart yet. (*Goes left.*)

GARDENER (*looks after* WITCH *and shakes his head*). You have that slip of a daughter too much petted. A peevish colleen, a peevish colleen! It is often a woman cut a rod would beat herself in the end. (*He goes aside.*)

(RURY *and* SIMON *come on right.*)

RURY. There now at last is the apple!

SIMON. I wonder is it of solid gold.

RURY. It is better than that, having healing in it.

SIMON. That is so. The health is the only riches.

RURY. What is that shining at the foot of the tree?

SIMON. It is but a curl of hair.

RURY. It is shining of itself.

SIMON. Pluck down now the apple and come out of this.

RURY. There must be some great beauty in the garden. I will go seek her.

SIMON. I am in dread of the Hag. Get the apple and come.

RURY. I am certain I will wed with no other one but the woman that owns this curl.

SIMON. Come on now for pity's sake.

RURY. Stop here till I will go look for her among the trees. (*Goes.*)

WITCH (*coming in*). It was not you had a hold of the end of the thread?

SIMON. It was not, your honour my ladyship. It was my master. He is taking a view of the beauties of the garden.

WITCH. What brought him here?

SIMON. For a cure he came. A lovely garden it is—a very grand place. I wonder now where is the witch-woman that owns it?

WITCH. Would you recognise her if you saw her?

SIMON. I would to be sure. Didn't she rise spirits before us in the wood beyond. It isn't easy mistake her. A beautiful lady like yourself, ma'am, would get your death to be looking at her like. A flattened bluish sort of a nose. Hair the same as a horse's tail.

WITCH. Is that the way she is?

SIMON. The ugliest you would see in the world. You wouldn't be the better of it in a year. Nails like the tips of cows' horns. A greenish tusk shaped like a reaping-hook going back to her ear. Six foot of goats' horns going back from her head.

WITCH. That is enough of talk. Tell me this, has your master himself promised to any one?

SIMON. He has not. Sure he is only hardly a boy!

WITCH. Has he any secret love?

SIMON. He wouldn't look at a woman's face, and Helen to be

walking the road from Troy; but at hounds, at the hunting, or horses making their leaps.

WITCH. Go, call him here.

SIMON. Here he is coming. It is himself will tell your honourable ladyship I am telling no lie.

RURY. I am come to ask for that apple.

WITCH. That is a great thing to ask.

RURY. It is for the cure of a wounded king.

WITCH. It is for one like yourself it has been waiting, a man with daring and with good luck.

RURY. I am thankful for that word. I will pluck it and bring it away.

WITCH. Hold your hand. Whoever will get that apple has one promise to give.

RURY. Tell it out to me.

WITCH. He must put himself under bonds to wed with the young girl that is here with it in the garden.

RURY. That is what I would wish, and she being the great beauty I take her to be.

WITCH. She is, and better again.

RURY. Tell me where can I get a sight of her.

WITCH. Go over west to the butt of a yew tree that is shaped like a table. I will bid her bring you meat and wine.

(Goes left, RURY *is going right.)*

GARDENER. Come hither, King's son of Ireland!

RURY. I cannot stop.

GARDENER. Have a care! Have a care!

RURY. I see nothing to be in dread of.

GARDENER. There is a great deal a man should be in dread of and he thinking to take a wife.

RURY. If that is all the danger I will face it.

GARDENER. There are some that might be dressed up with all the colours of the birds, might not be as good as one might be wearing a poor girl's suit.

RURY. It is not dress I would think of, beside beauty and courage and sweet speech.

GARDENER. That is so. To be mannerly and not to have anything to say with any one, but to carry your own character.

RURY. I must go to the butt of the yew tree.

GARDENER. Do not. Stop here behind this cluster of bushes. It's the young lady herself that is coming, you will see her on the minute.

RURY (*going behind bushes*). There are two coming.

(PAMPOGUE *and* MUIREANN *come in.*)

PAMPOGUE. Stop now till I will see my face in the well. (*Looks in.*) Do I look good to-day?

MUIREANN. You can see the shining of your jewels in the water.

PAMPOGUE. Will you come herding geese for me the time I will be wedded with the King of Ireland's son?

MUIREANN. If I go it will be for the reason I stop here, the strength of your mother's power.

PAMPOGUE. You are right to be in dread of her. She that can put upon you the shape of a whale of the ocean, or of a midge of the air.

MUIREANN. That power might not be lasting.

PAMPOGUE. She will have pith and power so long as she owns the Three Rods of Magic and Mastery.

MUIREANN. Some one who is stronger again might bring them away from her.

PAMPOGUE. They are well hidden. You would never make out where they are.

MUIREANN. It is likely she keeps them close at hand.

PAMPOGUE. She does not. She thinks no person knows where they are—but I know.

MUIREANN. How can you know if she did not tell you?

PAMPOGUE. She did not tell me, but I put my eye to the keyhole one night she was talking to the Wizard of the Withered Knee. She gave them to him wrapped in holly bark. I put my ear to the hole.

MUIREANN. That was a wrong thing to do.

PAMPOGUE. If I did not do it I would not have heard what she said. "Go, put them," she said, "in the farthest room of the house of the Sidhe that is in the hill of Knockmaa." I have a mind to go look for them myself, the way I will get the mastery over the King of Ireland's son.

MUIREANN. I will leave down these dishes on the yew tree and go back to my work.

PAMPOGUE. You will not! I would wish you to see the prince who will be my husband, and that you yourself will never get the like of. You can take a view of him, but he will never cast an eye on yourself.

(*A bird sings.*)

MUIREANN. Listen! There is joy in his little sweet song.

PAMPOGUE. Give me that stone.

MUIREANN. What do you want with it?

PAMPOGUE. I want it to fire at that bird. (*Throws stone.*)

MUIREANN. Come on to the yew tree.

PAMPOGUE (*with a scream*). There is a snail! Put your foot on it!

MUIREANN. No, I will put it among the ivy leaves.

PAMPOGUE (*trying to slap her*). I'll call your owner to give you cruelty, where you will not do my commands. Goose girl! Goose girl! (*Goes mocking.*)

(RURY *and* GARDENER *come on.*)

GARDENER. Which now of the two has the seven blessings going along with her?

RURY (*to* MUIREANN). It is you surely are the young queen.

MUIREANN. I am daughter and granddaughter and great-granddaughter of kings.

GARDENER. It was easy for *him* to recognise the stock of kings.

MUIREANN. I am kept here in the garden by the malice and treachery of a witch.

RURY. Will you come to be wife of a king and mother of kings to come?

MUIREANN. What way can I escape from her spells?

RURY. I will bring you away from her power. I will make an end of her.

GARDENER. It is hard treatment she should get. To take a poor child up in her hand and to torment her the way she does.

RURY. O Flower of the raspberry! It is in my heart you are come to harbour. There was never the like of you on the face of the earth! Your shadow only would set all the kings of the world quarrelling.

MUIREANN. It is empty I would be coming to your house. I that was used to golden vessels, I have not now of the goods of the world but my five brothers only, that are turned to fishes in the well.

RURY. I will make a sunny-house for you, thatched with the feathers of the birds! I will put a carpet of silk under your feet.

MUIREANN. That is the way it was with me, and I in the Court of Spain.

RURY. I will give red wine to the horse you will ride; it is on flowers he will set his golden shoe.

MUIREANN. If I knew you to have no wife, I would not wed with any man but yourself.

RURY. There is the love of hundreds in your face and there is the promise of the evening star.

MUIREANN. My face that was sheltered and my hands that were under no weight, only gold rings, are brown with the weather and hard.

RURY. The driven snow on the mountain is nine times blacker than the blackberry beside your whiteness! All the women of the world are rushlights in an iron socket, but you are a candlestick of gold on a queen's table.

MUIREANN. It is long since I heard talk like that.

RURY. Neither star nor sun shows half as much light as your shadow!

MUIREANN. I think your name should be Honeymouth out from Ireland.

RURY. When the men of Ireland see me bringing you back to them, their hearts will be under the sole of your shoe.

MUIREANN. Will you surely bring me there with you?

RURY. I will surely. It is you will make every happy thing happier. All the days of the years to come are waiting for your footstep to tread upon them.

MUIREANN. To have been under unkindness and reproach for so long and to hear you say those words, it is like as if the dead quarter of the year is gone by, and the birthday of the spring at hand.

RURY. You are a little silver birch tree all alone upon a rock, washed in the white rays of the moon.

MUIREANN. I have been alone indeed and as desolate as a bare bush left in a gap.

RURY. There is many a woman would go cranky and bitter under such hardness.

MUIREANN. There is no hardship coming on me now but I would laugh at it, as happy as the rising sun.

GARDENER. Make no delay, King's son. The Witch is coming here. Pluck down the apple and go.

RURY. I will bring this queen-woman with me to my father's house. I must bring her away from danger.

MUIREANN. Oh yes, bring me away! They will never let me come to you again.

GARDENER. She must not quit the garden at this time. There is danger about her on the road. To bring her away you must come again with power that is greater than the power of the Witch.

RURY. If I do not get her I will not leave a head on any one in the place!

GARDENER. Listen to the sound of her stick stirring the dead leaves—— It is like hammering nails in a coffin. It is not swords can go against that one, but to shoot her with a bullet having three times nine curses on it. Go, do your work, and I will find the secret of her magic. I think I have come near it now.

MUIREANN. He is maybe right. He has wisdom and knowledge. But oh, isn't it a great pity!

RURY. I will be back with you as swift as the swallow.

MUIREANN. You will forget me, going away.

RURY. I will never forget you while green grass grows.

MUIREANN. You will maybe turn away from me, seeing I am not so nice looking as what you think.

RURY. That will happen when it is the shadow of the hollow that will fall upon the side of the hill.

GARDENER. Hurry, hurry, it is a long road.

MUIREANN. Take these little cakes, two of them to eat on the road, and one to bring back to Ireland. I have left on them three drops of honey, where I touched them with three fingers of my hand. And take with them my little pipe of music. I will come to you whenever I hear its call.

WITCH'S VOICE. The bride is gone to the butt of the yew tree. Where is the bridegroom, the King's son of Ireland?

(RURY *and* MUIREANN *go out of sight.*)

(*Coming on.*) The bargain is made and the promise given. What are you doing there, Gardener? Where is the King of Ireland's son?

GARDENER (*pointing upwards*). Listen, listen!

WITCH. What would I listen to?

GARDENER. To the talk of the filibines and stairs overhead!

WITCH. They have no news or message for me.

GARDENER. I suppose not, I suppose not. They are but crying that the house of the Sidhe is on fire, that is in the hill of Knockmaa.

WITCH (*with a shriek*). The hidden house at Knockmaa!

GARDENER. The houses of the witches are blazing up, they are crying, and all their furniture and their goods!

WITCH. My Rods of Magic and Mastery that are in it! Ochone, my grief! (*She rushes off.*)

GARDENER. That was a lucky lie. She will go out on the wind to Knockmaa. The bands of death on her, and whatever part of her the crows will not eat, let the dogs of the wilderness devour!

(RURY *and* MUIREANN *come back.*)

RURY (*kissing her*). My hundred loves, my share of the world!

MUIREANN. Oh dear black head!

(RURY *plucks the apple from the tree and goes.*)

SCENE II. *Same room in the Giant's castle.* GIANT *sitting in high easy chair with pillows and medicine bottles. A catapult in his hand.*

WIFE (*bringing in doctor*). Here is the doctor after coming from the King of Ireland's Court.

GIANT. Wait a minute. (*Fires a stone through window.*) I was just taking aim with my catapult at a pet blackbird is perched on the shoulder of an enemy I have out in the far-off Indies. Could the King of Ireland now do that much?

DOCTOR (*pompously*). He being a King has no need doing that sort of thing for himself, where he has his ships and his armies to go torment and put down his enemies.

GIANT (*dropping catapult*). May be so—— It should be a very nice thing to be a King of armies.

DOCTOR. I cannot be losing time stopping here from the side of the King's bed. What is it ails you?

GIANT. Slack enough in the health I am. Some weeks fair enough and some weeks no action—— Has the King now any sickness on him of that sort?

DOCTOR. The King is on the broad of his back, last harvest was a year.

WIFE. Let you put a face on yourself and speak up to the doctor.

GIANT. On and on sickly I am. A day in bed—a day out of bed.

DOCTOR. Do you go walking or leaping or running, for to give exercise to your limbs?

GIANT. I do—some times. Herself that sent me but yesterday gathering kippeens.

WIFE. If I did, you did not bring in enough of them to make a crow's nest.

GIANT. It is the way I spent the time, knotting trees together. It is as good for me bring in the whole forest at the one time.

DOCTOR. Have you the appetite lost?

GIANT. That is the most thing ails me.

DOCTOR (*to* WIFE). You have a right to boil down old hens for him. But maybe hens is nothing to a giant. What now are you used to take at your meal?

GIANT (*taking hold of book*). Oh, I might bring in a wild boar for my dinner and draw it through the ashes and leave nothing of the four quarters of it but the bones. Or to tear a bullock in two halves, and to boil the one half of it and roast the other half, and devour them bit about.

WIFE. Don't be showing off now. Tell out your case fair and plain.

DOCTOR. I would wish to look at your tongue.

GIANT (*standing up*). Bridget, put up here the stepladder for the doctor.

WIFE. That you may be forgiven.

GIANT. Would you put him to the trouble to make a staircase, cutting notches in the backs of my legs?

(DOCTOR *climbs ladder and looks at tongue.*)

DOCTOR (*coming down*). To give up using so much meat you should. It is too much blood it is making. Wait now till I will notch on an elder stick the diet for your days. Not more now than one sucking pig for breakfast; and for dinner, one quarter of beef; and at supper, a sheep boiled in cow's milk. (GIANT *gives a groan.*) Or two sheep—not to be too hard on you in the commencement. I will stop and see you eating this day's meal myself.

GIANT. That would be too troublesome; it would be hardly worth while change my diet between this and the feast I will be giving in a few days for the wedding of the Grugach of the Humming.

WIFE. Ah, give over fooling. What ails you not to speak out the truth to a doctor that should know what you eat as well as if he was inside you.

GIANT. I am not willing.

WIFE. I tell you it doesn't signify giving out your case to a doctor, that is bound under bonds to betray your secret to no other one.

GIANT. One person to know it, and you to know him to know it, is the same as if it was known to all the world.

WIFE. He is ashamed telling you meat does not suit him. His talk of boars and of bullocks are from the stories and vanities of the books. He does not use but a pot of stirabout in the morning and a hen's egg, maybe, for kitchen with his barley bread at night.

GIANT. A goose's egg! A goose's.

DOCTOR. I knew well he was but humbugging and talking foolishly.

WIFE. You need not be making little of him on the head of it. It does not lessen his courage if he uses no meat, he having a weak stomach, since the time he was a child.

DOCTOR. Give me a hold of your pulse. It is much if I do not put you under a curse of blisters for striving to hide from me your case.

WIFE. There is some doctors who can recognise what sickness is on a man by the smoke they see going out of the chimney of his house. I knew of one could tell it by measuring you.

DOCTOR (*sarcastically*). He would! Or by the colour of your hair.

GIANT. It is a hard thing I to use so little, not like some would-be gluttonous, and to have that pain and depression on my chest.

DOCTOR. Does the pain be leaping from side to side?

GIANT. It does.

DOCTOR. There does be no leaping at some times, but quiet?

GIANT. That is so.

DOCTOR. I knew well I would come at it. It is in great danger you are. Did you ever go asleep in a meadow, and your mouth to be open, and you to be stretched alongside a running stream?

GIANT. It is likely I might.

DOCTOR. I was sure of that. It is what I am thinking, you have swallowed a water-worm or an eel.

GIANT. Do you say so?

DOCTOR. That is what is destroying you.

GIANT. So it will be too. It to be growing in bulk within me till it will get to be the size of a sea-serpent, and I myself getting to be as thin as thin!

DOCTOR. When he does be uneasy, the place being strange to him, that is the time you feel the pain.

GIANT. That's it! That it is.

DOCTOR. And the time he does be quiet is the time he does be consuming everything that you will eat.

GIANT. I feel it—I can nearly hear it! It is leaping in me the same as a little bird!

WIFE. What way will you do a cure on him?

DOCTOR. I will lay my mind now to that.   (*A knock at door.*)

GIANT. Who at all is this?

WIFE. I wouldn't wonder it to be the witch.

DOCTOR. Is it the Hag of Slaughter? It is best for me go back out of this.

GIANT. No, but stop there alongside the hearth till she will be gone, and you can work on me my cure. She will not meddle with you at all.

WITCH (*coming in*). Death and destruction on you, Fatach Mor, where you parted with my ball of thread to a thief!

WIFE. There you have your answer. If it was a thief got it, it was a thief took it.

GIANT. What was it he stole?

WITCH. He stole more than riches. There is one thing he stole will fall heavy upon yourself.

GIANT. What now is that?

WITCH. He has taken my daughter's fancy. She would give him her share of the world and herself along with it. He has stolen her love.

WIFE. Why would that fall heavy on Fatach Mor?

WITCH. She has her mind made up not to marry and wed with the Grugach of the Humming, since she threw her eye on one of the world's men.

GIANT. Is it that she will break off the match?

WITCH. That is what I am telling you.

WIFE. There will be no need, so, for us to make ready the supper and the feast. You can put him off on the long finger.

GIANT. Do you want to make an end of me altogether? The Scotch are no way favourable to deal with, and they are apt to be tricky in the finish, not getting their own way.

WIFE. Find him another wife so.

GIANT. That is not so easy as you think. If he is no way handsome himself, he expects the youngest and the grandest in the world.

WITCH. It is well you have earned trouble, and it to fall on you, where you gave a harbour to the King of Ireland's son.

DOCTOR (*coming forward*). Is it that you are acquainted with the King of Ireland's son?

GIANT. To steal my ball of flax he did, and made his escape through that side door.

WITCH. He has stolen another thing. The golden apple from the Tree of Power.

DOCTOR. He has got that?

WITCH. To snap it away he did, and to go.

DOCTOR. He brought away the apple of healing?

WITCH. If he did I will get it back again. It is for that I am come here. This road is partly on his way home. Let you make a trap for him.

GIANT. Myself is it?

WITCH. He will be in need of provision. I have the money in his purse changed into pebbles of flint. It is likely he will turn up to this door.

GIANT. I have no mind to see him at all. Let him go on his way.

WITCH. I thought to get more thankfulness after all I have done for you, promising my own daughter to your kinsman.

GIANT. That promise is broke. He to come here itself it is likely he would refuse me the apple.

WITCH. He will refuse it surely. It is to fight him you must.

GIANT. I have no mind to go join in other people's quarrels.

WITCH. All you want is the courage. You are well able to best him. He is but a lad. No sign of a beard on him unless he would paint himself with blackberry juice.

GIANT. What way can I go killing and fighting, and a live worm being within me, is leaping on every side?

DOCTOR. Are you looking for a certain cure?

GIANT. Why would I send for you if I was not?

DOCTOR. There is but one cure for you to be found. Not having it, you will waste and wither and be that water-worm's prey.

GIANT. Give it to me without delay.

DOCTOR. It is that apple that is after being stole.

GIANT. What use is that, and it not being in my hand?

DOCTOR. You have to fight and put down the man that has it.

GIANT. Wouldn't some other apple do?

DOCTOR. If you set no value on your own life I may as well say good-bye to you.

WITCH. I will go bring the young lad a challenge from you. It is not long till he will blow the horn of battle at the door. (*Goes.*)

GIANT. I will refuse! To force me is no fair play.

DOCTOR (*to* WIFE, *putting on hat*). He will not be long with you. But you will be free from the cost of burying him, for you will find no coffin will fit himself and the water-worm. It is best throw them into the tide. (*Is going.*)

GIANT. Do not go! I'll make an attack on him! I'll put him down, if he is a king's son! I'll devour him first and the apple after!

DOCTOR. No, but to do that would destroy you entirely. The monster is within you would get strength by that, and the lengthening of life. He will live to the womb of judgment! It is to me myself you have to give the apple.

GIANT. And what way will you rid me of him?

DOCTOR. To eat bacon and herrings and every salty thing you should, till there will be a great drought on him, and to lie down on the grass outside, and your mouth to be open, and the apple convenient to it.

GIANT. What will happen me then?

DOCTOR. To go wild mad with the drouth he will; getting the smell of the apple that is full of juice, he will make a leap out of your mouth, and, believe me, he will never enter into it again.

GIANT. That is a great plan now.

WIFE. Can you find no other way to cure him? A great shame and a great pity the lad to have gone through such hardships for the apple, and not to bring it home to his father after all, that is lying at the point of death. There must have been great need on the King when he sent the man is dearest to him in the world into such danger for his sake.

GIANT. That's the way with the wife I have, thinking of every other person's health before my own.

WIFE. Have you no kindness in you at all?

GIANT. It would be an unkind man would not be kind to his own life. (*Horn of battle is heard.*)

DOCTOR. Here is he coming! It is best for me not to be seen. I would not wish to be taking a side.

GIANT. Is it after shoving me into danger that you will not lend me a hand?

DOCTOR. I have here some ointment. I will rub it upon the boards. Let you drive him out this door, and it will be easy knock him. (*Rubs near door, right.*)

WIFE. A black shame on you. That you may die hard and die as you deserve it!

(*Horn heard again.* DOCTOR *hides.* WIFE *opens door, left.* RURY *and* SIMON *come in.*)

GIANT (*standing up*). Did you take notice of those forks outside?

RURY. I did not.

GIANT. Every one of them having a head on it but the one that is waiting for your head.

RURY. Is it my head or your own head that will go on the top of that spike?

GIANT. Give me up the apple you are after stealing, and I will let you go free out of this.

RURY. I will give you nothing at all, only a green sod over your head!

GIANT. Come on till I will put you under my long cold teeth!

RURY. Don't be thinking it's on feather beds I'll put yourself the time I will bring you down!

GIANT. I think you too big for one mouthful and not big enough for two mouthfuls! It is snuff I will make of your bones.

RURY. There are three shares of dread on you and not a share at all upon myself!

GIANT. It is boiled blood I will be drinking with my supper to-night!

SIMON. Go on, Rury, go on! I will come behind and tickle his ankles till he will stoop down to be scratching them!

GIANT. Is it fighting on fiery flagstones you are used to, or sticking red-hot knives into one another's hearts?

RURY. It is with this sword I will fight, that was cooled with three drops of lions' blood!

GIANT. So I have a sword of my own that nothing can stand against! I am after drawing it through the heart of the last man of three hundred!

SIMON. Go on, till we'll see Prince Rury's noble white silken feet go up, and your big ugly feet go down!

RURY. Come on, now!

GIANT. Go, take your stand on that spot beside the door.

RURY. No, but it is yourself I will put out through the door!

SIMON. If it fails you to knock him, try can you stagger him! (*Tries in vain to tickle stilts.*) There is great stand in him.

GIANT. If you are a half of the world, I am three-quarters of the world!

SIMON. Make a ball of him till his toes will be telling mischief and misfortune into the holes of his ears!

GIANT (*with a roar*). Make ready the big pot to boil him in!

(RURY *rushes at him.* GIANT *backs through door, left,* RURY *and* SIMON *rush after him. A heavy fall is heard and roar. They come back dragging* GIANT *by the stilts.*)

RURY. It is much if I give you your choice of two sods of the earth to die on!

SIMON. That's it! Tie him with the five knots!

GIANT. Leave me my life and I will give you my sword that will cut through a black stump of a log!

RURY. I see nothing blacker or uglier than your own head. (*Lifts sword.*)

SIMON. Strike the head off him! Put the cold of the sword to the marrow after that, till it will freeze and be scalded with cold!

WIFE. As you are strong, be merciful!

RURY. Do you give in altogether?

GIANT. I give you the victory and my seven thousand curses!

RURY. Didn't you know I was a Connacht man?

SIMON. It's as good for you to kill him out and out.

WIFE. Do not. There is no great harm in him except for a time he would be showing off. Ask mercy now and promise better behaviour.

GIANT. If I am a third of the world, yourself is the half of the world. Let me off now and I'll give my seven oaths I will never lay a cross finger on you again.

RURY. I am satisfied so. I am in a hurry to go on my way.

(RURY *is going out quickly by right door. He slips and falls with a cry. The apple rolls out.* DOCTOR *steals from corner and seizes it while* WIFE *and* SIMON *stoop to help* RURY.)

SIMON. It is the ankle is twisted on him. Rise up now if you can.

WIFE. Come out here, Doctor, and do your best for him.

DOCTOR. It is best bring him out by the side of the road and put a bed of green rushes under him.

(*He puts apple in his pocket and goes to door, right, as they help* RURY *to rise and go out, left.*)

GIANT (*mournfully*). He brought away the apple in the heel!

DOCTOR. You are not in need of it. I have the worm banished in another way. Believe me, you will not feel it leaping any more. (*Steals out quickly as* RURY *is helped out at other door.*)

SCENE III. *A roadside.* RURY *sitting up, half leaning on the grass.* SIMON *looking at him.*

SIMON. You are not fit to rise up at all, with weakness and want of sleep.

RURY. I have too much time lost. We must go on our journey home to Ireland.

SIMON. I don't know at all what was it knocked you.

RURY. It is the floor was as slippery as the flesh of eels.

SIMON. No wonder you to be left in a weakness, lying by the road out through the clouds of night.

RURY. Were we here all through the night-time?

SIMON. We were, till the night kissed the dawn, and beyond that again. There is red showing now in the evening sky.

RURY. It is far from my darling I will see the dawn of every day!

SIMON. I would wish us to be farther again, and our back to the garden and all that we have gone through.

RURY. I am lonesome after her. I to have seen her once it is a pity I do not see her every minute.

SIMON. It is lonesome enough I am myself. Lonesome after my supper I am.

RURY. Full or fasting we must go on till we bring the cure to my father.

SIMON. I would like well to be in the King's house, but I would not like to be travelling to it. It's there you would not be hungry or dry!

RURY. It is time for us set out.

SIMON. What ails you to be in such a hurry! Is it that the King gave you for a mother the wind of March? I wonder now what are they eating for their meal at this time? Roasted pork with the cracklings, black puddings and rounds of beef!

RURY. Barley bread would be enough to give us strength if we but had it.

SIMON. There is an old story carrying among people, that when a prince went meeting enchantments he would be apt to be given a tablecloth would be covered with every choice food, boiled and ready. Ah, what am I talking about. I'd be in heaven having a sheep's trotter in my hand, and a bit of a sixpenny loaf.

RURY. Why wouldn't you traffic for food in some place and then we will go on.

SIMON. Give me the purse so. If ever I get the chance of food again I will eat my seven enoughs!

RURY. Here it is. (*Gives purse.*)

SIMON (*opening it*). What happened the money! What now is this!

RURY (*looking*). There is nothing but pebbles of flint.

SIMON. As sure as you're living that is an enchantment put upon us by the Witch!

RURY. It is gone, whatever happened.

SIMON. We may as well, so, give in to famine. We'll be that thin by morning they can play cards with our corpses at the wake.

RURY. Give me my little crossbow. It might chance me to make a shot at a wild duck or at a swan.

SIMON. Don't make little of a crane itself, or a marten cat or a coney. I think that I have stood upon the hungry grass. (*Listens, then calls out*) Come back now! I hear the trots of horses! There is a knot of people coming.

(*Voices heard and some well-to-do people come in.* SIMON *has sunk down on the roadside, swaying his body.*)

1ST STRANGER. Is this the path leading to the house of Fatach Mor the Giant?

SIMON. It is—I believe.

1ST STRANGER. Is it far?

SIMON. It is not.

IST STRANGER (*to others*). Come on so, we'll be there as soon as the Grugach of the Humming.

2ND STRANGER. He came sooner than was thought. It is a wedding in a hurry it will be.

IST STRANGER. It may be there will be no wedding at all in it. They were telling me below in the drinking tent, it has failed the Giant to find him a wife.

2ND STRANGER. It is a bad man to anger he should be. It is to cut the head off of the guests he might.

IST STRANGER. No but another was saying the Hag of Slaughter has taken it in hand, and her promise given to find him one that will be to his liking.

2ND STRANGER. So long as the supper is ready and the music, we are all right, bride or no bride. I'll chance it. Come on.

(SIMON *gives a low keen.*)

IST STRANGER. What is on you?

SIMON. Enough of trouble is on me, where the King's son of Ireland is after meeting with his death.

IST STRANGER. Is that so! The King's son dead?

SIMON. In this far foreign place. No one to keen him or to lay him out, because of his own people being far away.

IST STRANGER. We will turn aside and go three steps with the corpse.

SIMON. It is a good way from this, a half a day's journey—in the wide middle of a bog.

IST STRANGER. We cannot go so far. We have to be at the Giant's house by supper-time.

SIMON. What signifies, what signifies? It is not company he will want going home to the Court and Castle of the King. All the strands of Ireland will be fretting after him till they will go down and be lost under the tide. But to leave him the first night with no one to wake him, in the wide middle of a bog!

IST STRANGER. Are there no neighbours to call in?

SIMON. Turf-cutters and chair-makers I could call, and I having food and drink to give them. But I never would be willing to call any one to a hungry wake!

2ND STRANGER. I will give you something for that and welcome. Here is meat and bread.

SIMON. To lay him out I would wish as a King's son—a bag of gold under his head, a bag of silver under his feet.

STRANGERS. Here, take this, and this, and this (*they give him money*) for the King of Ireland's sake. If it was not for dread of the Grugach and the Giant we would travel with you every foot of the way. (*They go.*)

SIMON (*calling after them*). It is not losing money you are, giving it this time! It is well it will be remembered in Ireland. (*Sound of crows cawing as they go away.*) Go on with your cawing, ye thieves of the air! Is it looking for the dead prince ye are? Is it that ye will tell that story out to the world at large?

WITCH (*coming in dressed as a harper*). Who is it you are waiting for, Bird-Alone?

SIMON. My master that is gone fowling. He is not gone far. Why now are you yourself and your harp going away from the great feast, and every other one facing towards it?

WITCH. So I was in it. I will maybe go back after a while.

SIMON. What way is the Giant?

WITCH. Middling only. I heard some talk of a fight he had.

SIMON. Sure it is with my own master he had it. It was my master beat him. It is on the head of an apple the fight was.

WITCH. He is letting on he won the day.

SIMON. What way did he win the day when he did not win the golden apple?

WITCH. Has your master got the apple with him yet?

SIMON. He has, to be sure. Where it was before, within in the pocket of his body-coat.

WITCH. He should be tired with all he went through.

SIMON. He is, and spent. His heart will rise when he has food taken. It is a great pity they left me no wine.

WITCH. You can buy it down below. There is wine and beer selling in a little cabin made of green branches to refresh the people are on their way to the Giant's feast.

SIMON. I wouldn't wonder but they'd want it, the Giant's wife being no great housekeeper.

WITCH. Go on now for it.

SIMON. Here is my master coming. (RURY *comes.*)

RURY. All I got was this cormorant. (*Throws it down.*)

SIMON. That much wouldn't take the hunger off us. See now am I a good forager on the road! See what I got myself, with no weapon at all—only lies. (*Gives him food.*) I will go now get wine that will hearten you.

RURY. Let you hasten so. We have enough of time lost. (SIMON *goes.*)

WITCH. I will rise a tune now for you, King of Ireland's son.

144

RURY (*lying down on the grass and eating*). I never refused music up to this; but let it be a short tune. (WITCH *lays down harp, it begins playing of itself.*)

WITCH (*in a drowsy tone*). Play, little harp of willow wood, that lived sleepy with love of your own likeness and your shadow in the stream—— Play on! Give the Prince rest for a while. Play every one of you, strings (*she waves her hands over* RURY) that were drawn from the beasts rocking in the slumberous sounds of the sea. Play a little song would put him in his sleep through the sawing of timber in a pit, or the screeches from the Island of Cold. (RURY *sleeps profoundly.* WITCH *kneels and searches his clothes. She gets up.*) It is not here! The apple is not here! They are all deceiving me! The Giant is deceiving me; he has maybe got it in his house. I'll tear it from his keeping! I'll master him! (*She rushes off, leaving harp, which goes on playing softly.*)

(MUIREANN *comes in. She has her arms out as if distracted. She is dressed in rich clothes.*)

MUIREANN. Where is he? Where is he? Where is Rury, my darling that is dead?—— Oh! He is there! The crows of the air were telling no lie saying you were dead and gone! (*She keens and makes her lament.*) Oh, Rury! Oh, my first love! My first darling of the men of the world! There is no night in the year I would not burn a penny candle looking at your beauty! It is what I will be bringing with me from this out, the full of my two shoes of sorrow!

The first day of summer will come, the first day of winter will come. Every bird will come back to its own nest, but Rury my darling will not come back to me for ever!

It is a withered world it is! It is not long I will stay living in it. I to be left my alone, the same as the last tree of a wood! Let the two of us be laid in the one grave!

Good-bye to you, my five little fishes. (*She takes fishes which are tied in a bunch hanging by her waist.*) I am thinking you will not live after me. It is near a pity I did not leave you where you were in the well. My grief! If I had but the loan of a little silver lake!

SIMON (*coming back*). The King of Spain's daughter! What in the world wide brought you here, ma'am, and what is it ails you?

MUIREANN. The birds overhead that told me the King's son of Ireland was dead.

SIMON. You grew to be very skilful picking knowledge from the air.

MUIREANN. What are you yourself doing, not to be crying and

keening him? It is a bad friend and a bad servant you are letting him die! You to have had the smallest wound in the world, he would have searched out herbs of healing to put round about you. Why did it fail you to go search the whole face of the world for a cure for the King's son?

SIMON. Is it that you think it is to die he done? He did not, but a fit of slumber that came upon him.

MUIREANN. Why did the birds say it?

SIMON. Chatterers they are, running telling that I said him to be dead. If I did, I was letting on all the time.

MUIREANN. You had no right even for a playgame to say out such a terrible thing!

SIMON. I not to have said it, it is likely it would be true before this. I gave out his death for to keep life in him.

MUIREANN. He will not move. What way can I believe you?

SIMON. He is but getting his quiet and his comfort in a fit of slumber that came on him after eating his meal. There is no harm at all in that. The sleep is the health of all. He to be awake, there is no knowing what battle or fight he might be in!

MUIREANN. It fails me to waken him in any way.

SIMON. I wouldn't wonder if it was the playing of that harp. (*Takes it and covers with a cloak.*) More enchantments! I having a bit of tow in my ear against the toothache it did not take the same effect upon myself.

MUIREANN. Waken, Rury! You will waken when you hear my voice!

SIMON (*shaking him*). Rise up now and see who is before you!

MUIREANN. Listen, listen, I am in great danger. It is the Witch that dragged me as far as this. She bade me put on good clothes—— She said it was to meet you I was coming. And then——

SIMON. What plan had she in her head?

MUIREANN. Rury! Waken! Help me! I heard her telling some person a while ago she was bringing me to be a wife to the Grugach that her own daughter had refused to wed.

SIMON. The curse of the crows on her! Isn't she the black villain!

MUIREANN. She left me under a bush of shelter in the valley beyond; it is there I heard the talk of the birds. She will be coming back. Rise up now out of your sleep!

SIMON. Rise up, indeed. I am in dread the Giant is not asleep.

MUIREANN. Did I give you my love and will you fail me? (*He moves.*) (*A roar is heard.*)

146

SIMON (*looking down the road*). That is the Giant, sure enough. I partly guessed his roar.

MUIREANN. They are coming! Oh, save him if they take me! Cover him over with branches or with grass! Here I will put my golden mitten in your hand, that you will know I was with you——

GIANT (*coming in with* WITCH). Is it this one is to be given to the Grugach?

WITCH. It is. Let him take her or leave her.

GIANT. It is easy matchmaking there will be, and she to be put into my hand.

WITCH. There is the King's son in his sleep on the grass.

GIANT. I have nothing to say to him. I am under bonds not to do him hurt or harm. Let him sleep on through the length of the year.

WITCH. Bring away the girl so.

GIANT. Well now you have spared me a good deal of trouble. She has a lovely face. (*To* MUIREANN) Come on now.

MUIREANN. Do not bring me away! Leave me here! I would sooner go to my death.

GIANT. The guests are come and the tables are spread. There is nothing wanting, only yourself. I will lift you into the air the same as a wisp of straw. (GIANT *and* GIRL *go*.)

MUIREANN (*heard calling*). Rury! Rury! Rury!

RURY (*stirring*). Who is that calling me?

SIMON. The Lord be praised he didn't waken sooner. He'd be made an end of surely, and he to go following after them the way he is.

RURY. There was some one calling me by my name.

SIMON. Ah! It was dreaming you were, or listening to the grass-hoppers in the grass.

RURY. I am certain I heard a call. It was nearly like Muireann's voice.

SIMON. It is close to the fall of night. Come on now on your journey.

RURY. Muireann! How happy I would be if I was going back to her now—to find her by the brink of the well.

SIMON. Is it that you are forgetting the King that is watching the windows till he will see you come?

RURY. You are right. I must go on to him. I will give him the cure. I will set out again the very same day.

SIMON. You might or you might not. Every new meeting is a new bargain. I would be wary of going back again into the Witch's garden, where she might chop a tree against your life. It might be best find some other young beauty on our own side of the world.

RURY. I have but to give him the apple of healing. I can turn my back then, my message being done.

SIMON. Fatach Mor had a great opinion of himself, thinking to take it from you.

RURY. Where is it? I put it in here——

SIMON. It was in no other place. (*They search.*) A sore heart and cold flesh on them! As sure as you are standing there, they have the apple whipped.

RURY. The Witch, or Giant, or whoever took it must have snapped it away as quick as a hawk.

SIMON. As sure as you live it was stole by that little cannat of a doctor. It is going through me that he was near us at that fight.

RURY. It might be so. I thought I saw some unkind face through my faint. But why would he rob it?

SIMON. To bring it home to the King I'll engage, and to let on he to have won it himself. It's best for us hurry on after him by the shortest road, that is here by this path to the west.

RURY. We should overtake him if we travel on through the night.

SIMON. We'll make a start anyway.

RURY. Give me my sword. What is that on it? A little golden mitten——

SIMON. So it is too.

RURY. It was Muireann left it here. She was surely here in this place.

SIMON. It might have come in some other way.

RURY. It was her call I heard! Where is she? You know, and you do not tell me! She was here when I was asleep!

SIMON. Leave choking me! If I did not tell you it was for your good. You are no way fit to go fighting. If you have no wish to be scalded it's best not go stir the pot.

RURY. Where is she? Tell me or I will drive the life out of you!

SIMON. The Giant that brought her away to his castle.

RURY. Why did he do that?

SIMON. It was that Hag of Wickedness put her into his hands.

RURY. What made her do it?

SIMON. She gave her to be bride to the Grugach of the Humming, that her own daughter was after refusing to wed.

RURY. Oh, my first love! I am coming! (*He goes following her.*)

SIMON. I would give the full of Ireland of horned cattle, the lad never to have learned the nature of love!

SCENE IV. *Night. Outside Giant's castle. A lighted window. Guests seen inside and music heard.*

(RURY *and* SIMON *come on.*)

RURY. It is up there she should be at the supper.

SIMON. It would be hard come to her. There is a great troop of men having steel suits on them beside the door.

RURY. I will break my way through them.

SIMON. What way could you do that, and they that close as that they are touching one another?

RURY. If I have to kill them I will do enough of killing! I will make heaps of their feet and of their heads.

SIMON. You would be no better off. You to lay a hand on the young lady it is likely the Hag has put spells on her that she would go from you like a bird into the air.

RURY. If I could but bring her down out of that and steal her away——

SIMON. Here is some person coming out the door; he maybe would give us news of her.

RURY. It is but a cook from the ovens.

SIMON. If he is, he might be no bad friend.

RURY (*to* COOK). What is it that is going on inside?

COOK. It is a great wonder you not to know this is the night of the great wedding. A grand quality dinner that is in it. The freshest of every meat, the oldest of every drink, the food you think of and the food you would not think of. Myself and the rest of the cooks are destroyed making and baking and with the want of sleep.

SIMON. I never saw much in that house. You'd get more plenty of a fast day in the King of Ireland's servants' hall, and you but a party of one.

RURY. Are there many in it?

COOK. There are that. The Grugach out from Scotland and two of his first cousins. Fatach Mor is but a chicken beside them.

SIMON. He has a bad name that Grugach of the Humming.

COOK. He'd be a bad one to cross or go against. But as they are now, himself and the Giant are as great as two pickpockets. Sure it is the Giant has found a wife for him.

RURY. She will not wed with him.

COOK. If she does it will not be of her own fancy. Any lady in Ireland that would rear a son to that one would be sorry.

RURY. Does she seem to be fretting?

COOK. She looks as if she would sooner to go drown herself than to be joined to the like of him. She was crying a while ago, but they have her sorrow hid with the dint of the music they have raised.

SIMON. The Grugach now, is he striving to come around her and to comfort her?

COOK. He is not. He is picking the bones of a deer. He'll have time enough to tame her. Himself and his men will bring her away to-morrow in their fleet of ships to Lochlann, or some place in the North.

RURY. Will you carry a message to her?

COOK. I cannot do that. I have to go trying the ovens. There is not a tint of bread left in the place. That I may be forgiven for the lies I told! It is the hungriest feast ever I saw.

RURY. I have here three cakes of bread. Will you bring them in and give them to the young queen?

COOK. I will not. It is a kish full of them I would want to satisfy those.

RURY. I would give you a good reward.

COOK. What use would it be to me, and I after being made an end of maybe by the Giant or the Hag of Slaughter, where they would think me to be making a mockery of them.

RURY. Give me your clothes and I will bring them up myself.

COOK. Give me the reward and I will.

RURY. Give him out money from your purse.

SIMON. Is it to hide yourself under a cook's suit you think to do?

RURY. That is the way I will go unknownst through the door.

COOK. It is short till they will make an end of you and they to recognise you. A great troop of the Grugach's people there are; Fawgauns and Blue Men.

SIMON. I'm in dread that by the walk of you they will know you to be one used to giving orders.

COOK. Let the clothes be put on yourself, so, that is more of my own shape and build.

SIMON. I don't care. I'll engage no one will lay down that I am not a cook. I'll go in, sooner than send my master to his death.

COOK. Here now. I'll rub a grain of flour on your face.

(SIMON *puts on smock and cap.*)

RURY. Give her the cakes into her hand—whisper in her ear to come down as if to take the air. I will bring her away in a crack.

COOK (*to* RURY). Go back now, let no person see you watching here.

RURY (*going off*). She will know the three honey-drops on the cakes.

SIMON. Is it to knock at the door or to blow the horn I should?

COOK. Not at all, but to walk in fair and easy and they will not question you. (COOK *goes off*.)

((SIMON *is going towards door; the men at it fall back.* WITCH *comes out in full dress.*)

WITCH. What is your business here?

SIMON. A cook. I am one of Fatach Mor's cooks.

WITCH. What is that in your hand?

SIMON. Three caraway cakes they are, I have to bring to the young queen of the feast.

WITCH. Take care is there honey on them?

SIMON. Why wouldn't there be honey?

WITCH. The hall that is guarded with a swarm of very wicked bees.

SIMON. Do you say so?

WITCH. You can nearly hear their buzz. To go wild mad at the smell of honey they do. They will settle themselves down upon your hands and your eyes and your head.

SIMON. There is nothing I am in so great dread of as bees.

WITCH. It is best for you to wash the honey from off the cakes.

SIMON. I am loth to meddle with them.

WITCH. Go on so. There is one of the Blue Men after drowning himself in the stream, where he had hid a piece of a honeycomb within his cap. To crawl in they did under his steel suit.

SIMON. What way can I wipe it off?

WITCH. Here is a handkerchief; it was dipped in soapy water.

SIMON. That's it. (*He wipes off honey.*) Is there anything of the smell of it left on the cakes?

WITCH. I will bring you in now. The bees will take no notice of you at all. (*They go in.*)

(RURY *comes back, looks up at window.* MUIREANN *has come near it. Music is being played.* SIMON *hands her the cakes; she looks at them, then pushes them away.* SIMON *comes out from the door.*)

SIMON. I brought the cakes to her.

RURY. I saw that, and she would not take them. Did she say nothing?

SIMON. She did not, and no wonder. Believe me, it is a very strange company she is in.

RURY. Did she take notice of the honey-drops on the cakes?

SIMON. The honey-drops?

RURY. That were from her fingers she laid upon them?

SIMON. You had a right to tell me that sooner.

RURY. Why do you say that? What happened them?

SIMON. To wipe them off I did at the bidding of a queen-woman, that said I would be tackled and made an end of by a swarm of angry bees.

RURY. Will you never learn to know the Hag of Slaughter?

SIMON. For pity's sake! There is no beating that one for plans. It is a wonder that she, having hundreds of years, can go through the world as she does!

RURY. I will go in to Muireann myself.

SIMON. It's no use for you; it's not by weapons you'll reach to her, but by wit. If you wish to bring her down to where you are, give out mouth-music on the pipe.

RURY. That is a good thought. (*He plays Eileen Aroon on pipe.* MUIREANN *comes and stands at window, looks out, then turns to the door.*)

SIMON. There she is coming.

RURY. I will go meet her.

SIMON. Have a care!

RURY. I am done with carefulness. (*Goes towards door playing still.* TWO MEN *suddenly step behind and fling a cloak over his head, throw him down and drag him away.* SIMON *rushes to shadow at side.*)

MUIREANN (*coming out from door*). Rury! Rury! Where are you! (*She comes forward, her arms outstretched.*) Save me! Save me!

WITCH (*coming behind her and touching her arm*). Do you think to escape me so easy?

MUIREANN. I will escape! The King of Ireland's son is here. He will save me out of your hand.

WITCH. He will not. He never will stretch a hand to you again or look at you with love in his eyes.

MUIREANN. That is a lie! You cannot change him, you have no power over him! It is he will put you down and make an end of you when he will hear my story!

WITCH. You will have no voice from this out to tell a story, or to give out any news good or bad.

MUIREANN. Oh! What is it——Let me go! Rury!

WITCH. Did you think to make little of me that have worked spells from the early days of the world? (*She holds up a disguise with cat's head and paws.*)

MUIREANN. What are you doing?

WITCH. I put that shape on you through the power of earth that holds and that nourishes all shapes of beasts and of men!

(WITCH *is about to strike her with one of the three rods, but* MUIREANNN *rushes away from her through the gateway.* WITCH *follows her and a cry is heard outside. The men who took* RURY *away drag him back again, leaving him on the ground.*)

RURY (*starting up and throwing off cloak from his head*). Where is she? Where is my darling and my love?

SIMON (*coming forward*). Where is she indeed?

RURY. Did she come out the door?

SIMON. She did so.

RURY. Which side did she go? (MUIREANN, *disguised as a cat, creeps in at gate and goes to hide in shadow.*)

SIMON. It's best for you go seek her outside the gate.

RURY. You are certain she has gone out?

SIMON. She came down out of the house anyway. You can look around and see is she in this yard.

RURY. She might be hiding in the wood without.

SIMON. Come on so. The supper is over, those giants will be scattering themselves in search of her. Come on.

RURY. I will find her if I have to go back to the Garden on the Edge of the World every step of the way. (*Goes towards gate.*)

MUIREANN (*rushing up to him*). Miau! Miau!

RURY (*shaking her off*). Hoosh! Hoosh! Get away out of that! I am in no humour for cats!

Curtain.

ACT III

SCENE I. *The Garden. The tree is withered.* MUIREANN *and* GARDENER. *She has taken off cat's head and paws and holds them in her hands.*

MUIREANN. That is my story so far, and that is the cruelty was put upon me by the Witch.

GARDENER. Death and defeat on her! But what way now does it chance you to speak natural?

MUIREANN. There comes around from Heaven one day in the week, and one hour in that day, when there sounds through the air the Bell of the Saints out in Ireland, that has power to break for me the Witch's knot. And for that relief I give thanks to the King of Sunday.

GARDENER. The Lord be praised for that much of reprieve.

MUIREANN. Listen and you will hear that sweet, holy sound!

(*A distant peal of bells heard.*)

GARDENER (*taking off hat*). That it might go on for ever!

MUIREANN. But oh! What do you say hearing my case? Every time that hour comes around, the man that is my darling is not at hand!

GARDENER. The grasshoppers are hundreds of years old and have heard a great deal of talk, and they never knew so great a pity!

MUIREANN. O Gardener! what shall I do at all, at all?

GARDENER (*looking in the well*). Did you bring back the five little fishes itself safe and sound?

MUIREANN. My grief! When they saw me in the form of a cat they were in dread and affrighted. They went from me with a leap into a little freshwater stream. It is likely they are lost and swallowed up ere this by the beasts of the great ocean.

GARDENER. The poor little silvery things.

MUIREANN. Going from me, they left me as lonesome as that you never saw the like.

GARDENER. No wonder at all in that.

MUIREANN. It is my sorrow the Witch did not turn me to be a duck, the way I could sail along with them.

GARDENER. If Rury the King's son would but come!

MUIREANN. Oh! You have knowledge! Cannot you so much as rub me with a magic stone, or boil down an herb to take the enchantment from me?

GARDENER. So long as she owns those Three Rods of Mastery her power is stronger out and out than mine.

MUIREANN. Then I am lost and under disgrace for ever.

GARDENER. Bad cess to her, and that she may have her face to the storm whatever wind will blow!

MUIREANN. O Gardener! I that never drank out of a cup not having at the least a silver rim, look at me now the way I am!

GARDENER. The King's son to come he will relieve you.

MUIREANN. It is certain at one time he loved me—— Yet to know he was coming, I would go hide myself in the fold of a hill—

or my heart would break in me like a nut. It is bad the way I am! It is best for me waste and wither away!

GARDENER. He is the only one can save you.

MUIREANN. It would be better for me have gone to my death the time he gave me his love, than to be turned into a thing displeasing to him. Sorrow was never in it till now! I have a bad way in the day and in the night time. It is a bad case I to be that way. There is a road love leads to, and it is that brought me under disgrace. It was not right of the witch-woman! It would be better for me be under the sod than he to come meet me, and to see but the ugly grey face of a cat!

GARDENER. He would recognise you in spite of all, and would know it to be but spells.

MUIREANN. O Gardener! It is what happened. When I came before him and strove to call to him, I could give but the cry of the beast I am under the shape of. He was angry, he hooshed me off. O Rury, it was not from you I deserved it! I left a drop of my heart's blood in that place!

(PAMPOGUE *comes.*)

PAMPOGUE. God save all here except the cat!

GARDENER. It would be more fitting a young person to be kind.

PAMPOGUE. The next time the King of Ireland's son will come, it is to myself he will give his love.

MUIREANN. It is not the time to show me unkindness when my heart is closed up with trouble.

PAMPOGUE. They are saying the little fishes did not trust you.

GARDENER. That is no way to be talking.

MUIREANN. It is not the King of Ireland's son will forgive you for that treatment.

PAMPOGUE. What call have you to kings unless it might be the King Cat of the Western Island, that has you under his rule from this out?

MUIREANN. My thought is free to go where it likes, and to my own father that is a King.

PAMPOGUE. What way could you sit and eat at his table? A four-footed thing! It is a red mouse with the fur on it would be your choice dish.

GARDENER. That is beyond all measure!

PAMPOGUE. You have your own business to attend to. Herself sent this out for you to put up on the tree.

(*Gives him board with writing.*)

155

GARDENER (*putting it up*). What is it is written on it? The sight that is failing on me.

PAMPOGUE (*running off*). It is but to scare blackbirds.

MUIREANN (*looking at it*). It is an offer of a fourpenny bit to any one that will kill a cat.

GARDENER (*throwing it down and stamping on it*). That she may be seven hundred times worse this time next year! That she may never be cross until she meets with her death!

(SIMON *comes in.*)

MUIREANN. Oh! Is your master here?

SIMON. We are after climbing the wall.

MUIREANN. Where is he?

SIMON. We travelled far. He is washing the sweat from his flesh, and the dust.

MUIREANN. Oh, if he could see me while I am this way he would not turn from me!

GARDENER. Is it down at the stream to the west he is?

SIMON. I couldn't be rightly sure. It's best go seek him there.

GARDENER (*to* MUIREANN). Go search for him before the ringing of the bells will stop. (*She goes.*) That's right. It is Rury will take her case in hand.

SIMON. It would be best for him leave meddling with any haunted people at all.

GARDENER. A well-reared girl; a great beauty. It is well for him get her for a companion and a wife.

SIMON. It might. I would sooner a woman you would trust to go to the dairy to bring you in a drop of cream.

GARDENER. She that had a little blush upon her cheek was redder than the royal rose! It would make you sorry the way she is now, fretting and bare alone.

SIMON. It is the King's son I am in charge of.

GARDENER. She is as nice as you'd ask. A very mannerly little girl. They match one another as well as two ears of wheat.

SIMON. I never would like cats, if it was a whole fleet of them was in it.

GARDENER. You are talking like an innocent or a fool. You know well until this spell was put upon her she was an honest, proper woman. I never saw one so nice, or with such a coaxing way.

SIMON. I would sooner nearly to take the Witch's daughter that is natural, if she is cross itself. To go with a strange thing would put back your children.

GARDENER. She will be the same as before, and the enchantment taken off of her.

SIMON. I would not wish him to marry a cat-woman and she having a pound for every day of the year, or a divide of the three divides of the world, the same as Marcus Crassus or Pompey of the Plain.

GARDENER. He is in pieces about her. His soul is gone into her. You know that well.

SIMON. He is ignorant of what she is presently.

GARDENER. He is death down on her.

SIMON. The sickness of love is all one with madnesss that is put on us by the moon. He would be cured with one scrape of her paw. Crooked hooks on her hands, and maybe a poison-claw at the tip of her tail. A very troublesome life.

GARDENER. They are coming! She has found him!

SIMON. What way did she do that I wonder, and I after sending her west?

GARDENER. No, but it is Pampogue is with him.

(RURY and PAMPOGUE *come in.*)

RURY (*to* PAMPOGUE). Have you no news to give me?

PAMPOGUE. I have not, unless you will give it to me yourself.

RURY. It dreams to me that I saw her in the trees beyond and then she was gone like a little breeze of wind.

PAMPOGUE. She is gone out of this. You will not find her.

RURY. I will find her. I will ransack every corner of the earth. I will go following after her for ever.

PAMPOGUE. Why would you not stop with myself? I will give you all my riches and my estate. You will never know trouble any more.

RURY. From the west of the world to the freshness of the world I will search for her in every place!

PAMPOGUE. You will never find the woman will give you love the same as myself.

RURY (*calling out*). Muireann! Muireann!

PAMPOGUE. I gave up a great match for your sake. I took my seven oaths I would take no other man. (*Takes his hand.*)

RURY. Let go of me! I have it in my mind you did away with her yourself, or the Hag, your mother! I give you my word if you handle and hinder me I will strike off your head with my sword
(*She cries out and runs off.*)

(*To* GARDENER) It is you gave me a bad advice bidding me leave her in this place. Tell me, where is she now?

GARDENER (*tries to speak but cannot for a moment*). My tongue that is turned to stone when I strive to tell the secrets that are outside the world.

RURY (*to* SIMON). Did you see no sign of her?

SIMON. You will never come to her. You will never get her in hardness or in softness; without or within; on horseback or on foot. It is as good for you give up the search.

RURY. What was it happened when she came out the Giant's door? What did I bring her to, playing her little pipe? It is here beside the well I first saw her. The worst thing in the world to me now is to see my own shadow, and it alone!

GARDENER. It is in the well you will maybe see her shadow again.

RURY (*kneeling by it*). Come back to me, and it will be a garden again, and not a place of nettles and elder and corncrakes. My grief that I left you for one moment only! It is long to me the night is and the day! (MUIREANN *comes behind him and bends over his shoulder*). There is your very image down below——your shape and your features—— there is a mist of water between us—— And oh, I have a mind to throw myself in after you, and we will be a King and a Queen for ever in Land-Under-Wave, and I will forget father and country, and all that is before me and all that is behind! And if I would do that for the sake of your shadow, what would I do for yourself?

MUIREANN (*in a whisper*). Rury! (*The bells stop of a sudden.* WITCH *appears behind* MUIREANN *and drags her back behind trees, putting cat's head back on her.*)

RURY (*starting up*). Where are you? Muireann! (*A miau is heard.*) Where is she? I saw her in the well. I heard her voice. I am certain she was here. Where is she? (*Another miau from back.*) It was a vision. That cat broke it with her miauing. No, no, she was here—— I will go search. (WITCH *comes before him.*)

WITCH. Have you lost from your mind the man that is watching for you out in Ireland?

RURY. I will go back to him after I will come up with her.

WITCH. To-day that is Lady Day in Harvest, in the yellow moon of the badger. What day was it you set out from Ireland?

SIMON. This day year for the world!

RURY. That cannot be! We have not been travelling through the length of a year.

WITCH. You did not feel the time passing when you went stumbling on from the Wood of Wonders, or when you were in an enchanted sleep.

RURY. I will go. I must go back to my father.

SIMON. Where is the use going home to the very day, where you are without the apple for his cure?

RURY. I will go without it. I will confess my disgrace. I will not fail him where I gave my word. Let him put on me whatever punishment he will.

SIMON. Sick or sound he will make you welcome. It is likely he will smother you with kisses unless he will drown you in tears. (*To* GARDENER) And he to have gone out itself and he lying in his lone at Corcomroe, it is my own master that will get the sway!

RURY (*to Gardener*). Give me some swift way to go home.

SIMON. Let it be a safe way. I have no swim to cross the sea, unless I'd make a boat of my hat.

GARDENER. Herself that could put a swan-gander between your legs, or shape a flying ship out of two cross sticks.

WITCH (*to* GARDENER). Pull up for them two stalks of the Bohilaun, the horses of the Sheogue. (*He brings two stalks of yellow rag-weed and gives one to* RURY, *one to* SIMON.)

SIMON. Is it a yellow horse will be under me, and it having four green legs?

WITCH (*to* RURY). A golden saddle on his back and a silver bridle on his head, he will bring you coursing through the skies as swift as the sun and moon. (*Pushes them off.*)

PAMPOGUE (*coming and looking round*). It is you sent him away!

WITCH. If I did, it was to save you from refusal and from shame.

PAMPOGUE. You got your own share of the joy of the world, and now you begrudge me my own! The seven deaths upon you!

WITCH. Have a care! The senses are gone astray on you.

PAMPOGUE. That I may never see you again! It is ugly you are to me whatever shape you may put on! I tell you I will have that young man, by paying or by prayers! Let you give me up your treasure to buy him; you have the world to ramble, begging from door to door!

WITCH (*holding up rods*). If you let one more word out from your mouth I will strike you with these Rods!

PAMPOGUE (*snatching them*). It is long enough you have been spreading terror with these Rods and bringing myself no profit with them! That your luck may go backward from this out! (*Flings them away.*)

> (GARDENER *stoops swiftly and takes them.* WITCH *stumbles and sits down, her head in hands.*)

SCENE II. *The King's Court as before. The* KING *is propped up in his bed, looking from window.* SERVANTS *with him.*

KING (*to* SERVANT). Is there e'er a sign of him coming?

SERVANT. There is not.

KING. The delay is very heavy on me. It is a year since he went out, and a day.

SERVANT. It is a long time we are without tale or tidings of him.

KING. I am very sure he will come. If it was not for that I would die over.

SERVANT. It isn't easy bring yourself in the door to the very day of the month.

KING. He will come if he is on the ridge of the world. He not to be here by the heel of evening I will know he has found his harbour in Oilean-na-Marav, that is the Island of the Dead.

SERVANT. There is not one but wishes him to be back. No life in the place and no courage. No drinking or feasting or giving out rewards.

KING. What time is it now?

SERVANT (*looking out*). By the shadow under the yew tree it should be on the stroke of noon. (*Horn heard and bustle.*)

KING. There he is come! I knew well he would not fail. That sort is not in his breed, and he of the root-stock of kings.

SERVANT. I am well pleased he to have brought the cure.

KING. With or without the apple he will be welcome. Put now the chair here close beside me.

DOCTOR (*coming in*). I came in and the dust of the road upon me. I met with delays on my journey. I was in dread I might be late.

KING. Did he come with you? Rury my son?

DOCTOR. I came with myself only.

KING. Did you pass him on the way?

DOCTOR. I did not. Is it that he did not come?

KING. He not to be here, he is not living.

DOCTOR. I would sooner nearly that.

KING. Is it that you wish his death?

DOCTOR. Not at all, not at all. But I would not give an inch of my toe for a son that would forget his father.

KING. If he forgot me, my last end is come. It is likely death did not forget me.

DOCTOR. There is one did not forget you, and that man is myself. It is I will give you lengthening of life.

KING. You will try no more of your cures on me where the apple of healing did not come.

DOCTOR. The apple is here. (*Holds it up.*) It is I myself have brought it for your cure.

KING. The apple! Is that it in your hand?

DOCTOR. The golden apple from the Garden at the World's End.

KING. Give it here to me.

DOCTOR. Have a care. Do not be in so great a hurry.

KING (*taking a bite*). Why wouldn't I hurry and death being after my life like a hound after a hunted hare?

DOCTOR. It is to choke yourself you will.

KING (*coughing*). Cut it in small pieces, so.

DOCTOR (*cutting and giving him bits*). Fair and easy goes far in a day.

KING (*eating*). I would say it to be running through my veins—— It is going to the cockles of my heart—— (*Eats.*) I think I am out of the body and in the City of the Sun—— There is light going through me, and heat!

DOCTOR. That is the sap beginning to work. It is full up of the virtue of the Tree.

KING. Spring-time is come—— We are done with the nursing mother of the cold——

DOCTOR. Here is the heart of the apple, and the seeds——

KING. I feel in me the rising of the waves of Power.

DOCTOR. It is going through you the same as a flame.

KING (*sitting up. To* SERVANT). Go bid the cooks to put a tail end of beef to the fire, fat and tender. Let it be roasted rare.

SERVANT. It is long we did not hear an order the like of that. (*Goes.*)

KING. Bring here the barber. Let him put a face on me. Is there e'er a crumb left of the apple—or a pip——

(BARBER *comes with basin and soap, and begins to shave him.*)

DOCTOR. It is a world's wonder——He is gone backward in age——He looks elegant in the face——He shows out like a boy of fifteen years!

KING (*being shaved*). What way did you come to the apple?

DOCTOR. The voyage was very costly on me—but no matter. I came through it all in the end.

KING. No doubt but you saw great wonders.

DOCTOR. It is much that I escaped with my life——

KING. What sort is the Wood of Wonders? Is it as terrible as what they say?

DOCTOR. It is, to be sure.

KING. You should be a great warrior to get the better of the Hag of Slaughter—— Is it on a big tree the apple was?

DOCTOR. About the height of the house.

KING. What size was the Garden?

DOCTOR. Sizable enough—— Wait now and I'll tell you about the great fight I had with the great Giant, Fatach Mor.

KING. Is it that you fought with a giant?

DOCTOR. Wait till you hear——

KING. You had great courage.

DOCTOR. That was the fight! Blacker than a coal quenched in water he was, and having in every rib of hair the strength of a hundred men. It took me to tackle him!

KING. And did you put him down?

DOCTOR. He never was flogged before. He came at me as strong as the spring-tide! We made the hard soft and the soft into spring wells. The mountains that were far came and looked at us, and the mountains that were near moved away from us.

KING. That was a great battle!

DOCTOR. "Come on now," says he, "till I will put you under my long cold teeth." "Come on yourself," says I, "till I will make snuff of your bones!"

KING. Do you hear that! The bravery of him!

DOCTOR. We fought through three-quarters of the day till I put him down in the stones. He called out then for mercy. "It is much," says I, "if I give you your choice of two sods of earth to die on——"

KING. My grief I was not there to see the fight.

DOCTOR. With that I struck the head off him. It is much that I brought away my life, having laid the Giant dead!

KING. That is a great story. It will be told after the whole of us have left the world. And where at all at that time was Rury my son?

DOCTOR. You can ask some other person than myself. I never was one to be carrying stories.

KING. I leave my orders on you to tell out all that you heard.

DOCTOR. Ah! He's young! He's young!

KING. Mind yourself! I am getting back my strength! Speak out when I bid you.

DOCTOR. Oh, it's not much I heard. The people were saying he ran wild, rambling and courting—— He's young!

KING. Is it for rambling and courting he left me to go to my death?

DOCTOR. He maybe couldn't make his way home. They were

saying he had all his money spent, and that Simon the steward was tricking and telling lies on the road, striving to gather in more.

KING. He was maybe in need of it.

DOCTOR. So they were saying—— wild living. Giving out, the steward was, the King's son of Ireland was dead in the middle of a bog. Begging gold and silver he was for to furnish out the wake.

KING. Is it that he gave out I myself had no means to bury my son?

DOCTOR. It is but humbugging he was, to gain hand-money for himself and the young prince.

KING. That is queer humbugging to give out to the countries of the world that charity was needed to put a boarded coffin on the King of Ireland's son.

DOCTOR. Ah! the young do be apt to run random and they out foreign.

KING. I would sooner nearly he to be dead in earnest than to drag down my name the way he did! Let him keep out of this to his life's end!

(*A shout and music.*)

SERVANTS (*rushing in*). Prince Rury is at the door.

KING (*with a roar*). The young vagabond!

(RURY *and* SIMON *come in.*)

SIMON. Here we are now to the very year and a day!

RURY (*kneeling beside bed*). I ask your forgiveness, father.

KING. That is what you will not get.

RURY. It has failed me to bring the apple.

KING. So I see, and that you are come back empty.

RURY. My grief that it is so.

KING. Leaving me stretched on the bed, and dragging down my name by your doings! To go begging on the road, having scattered my gold and banished it! It is much that your head is not on the block!

RURY (*getting up*). That is the best sound I heard yet. The strength that has come into your voice.

KING. If I have strength, there is no debt on me to you. Ireland and the world waiting on you to bring me the cure, and you humbugging, and foxing death for your sport.

RURY. I never drew bridle or breath till I came back to you on this very day. I did all that a son can do.

KING. Tell out so the story of your doings.

RURY. Let the poets tell out stories of me in the time to come.

It is what I will never do myself, where you did not believe my first word.

SIMON. If he will not tell out his doings it is I myself will tell them out! He got the victory and the sway over the big Giant, Fatach Mor!

KING. You have that story robbed from the doctor.

SIMON. The doctor! Is it that he is in this place?

KING. Here he is beside me. It is through the courage and the kindness of that man I got the apple. He has put down the Giant and brought away the cure.

SIMON. I partly guessed it, and now I know it. It is the doctor, and no other, that was the thief!

DOCTOR. Stop your fool talk!

SIMON. Fool yourself! I am as good a story as you any day! To say he fought the Giant! A man that is no use at home or abroad—that is not worth an empty box of matches! Well, it is easier save yourself from a rogue than from a liary person. A man telling lies would disgust you!

DOCTOR. You are well able yourself to tell stories and lies.

SIMON. You tearing away our characters!

RURY. Come away out of this, where there is no welcome only for thieves.

KING. Whoever will say that, the head will be whipped off him!

RURY. I will not come back again till this flame of anger is burned out!

KING. You will not go out of this, so fiery and unruly as you are! It is in the prison you will be lodged and chained.

SIMON. Let the doctor be lodged there with us, and I'm content. I'll knock satisfaction out of him!

KING. The doctor! I would give him the kingdom as his reward, but that no man following his trade ever wore the crown of Ireland.

SIMON. And Rury to be thrown out and put back from what he has earned! I'm like the people that loses their mind and can't remember their memory.

DOCTOR. There is a plague of madness on him! Let him be tied by the five smalls!

KING. Bring them away! (*To the* GUARDS) Lodge Prince Rury and his comrade in the jail!

> (*Takes* DOCTOR'S *arm and goes out door.* SIMON *is dragged towards other door.*)

SIMON. Oh! that doctor! Give me the trumpets of the guard till I'll draw down a curse and a poem of vengeance! A mist of misfortune on you! Breaking and bruising on you! The curse of the weak on you, and of the strong! All the fevers ever you met with to be put running and racing through your blood! The curse of all you cured on you, and of all that you did not cure!

(*The cat* (MUIREANN), *which has come in, flies at* DOCTOR *and scratches him.* DOCTOR *calls out and rushes through door.*)

RURY. Any one would say that is the same cat was outside the Giant's castle the time I lost my secret love.

SIMON. Cat, is it? It is no cat she is! I will tell it out now she befriended us. It is the daughter of a King under spells she is. What do you say now, hearing that? (*Cat runs out.*)

RURY. A King's daughter—what is it? It could not be Muireann in that shape?

SIMON. The Witch that put it on her the way she would lose your love.

RURY. Oh, my love and my darling! —— Where is she—— Where is she gone?

SIMON. It is likely hiding from yourself she is. There is no woman would wish her bachelor to get a view of her, and she in a shape would not be pleasing to him.

RURY. My poor Muireann! My blossom of the branch!

GARDENER (*rushing in*). Where is the young queen?

RURY. She is but gone this very minute. O Gardener! did you hear what happened her?

GARDENER. I did, to be sure. It is that brought me here, to deliver her from the power of the Hag.

RURY. Can you do that?

GARDENER. Look at what I have in my hand. Her Three Rods of Magic and Mastery. It is with them I can take off the spell.

RURY. You can do that! I will go then and strike off the Witch's head.

GARDENER. She will be here within three minutes. It is easy to deal with her at this time. (*A miau heard outside door.*)

RURY. It is Muireann! (*Is going to door.*)

GARDENER. Stop where you are. It is I myself will bring her back. (*Goes out.*)

RURY. That Hag to come here, I'll put her in a way that she will enchant no more King's daughters!

SIMON. I'd ask no better than to be casting out to the wild dogs her three crooked bones. (*A low laugh heard.*)

RURY. That is my darling's little laugh!

SIMON. So it had a sweet sound.

(MUIREANN, *led by* GARDENER, *comes in wearing her fine clothes. She and* RURY *take hold of each other's hands*.)

RURY. Oh, Muireann! do I see you indeed? And what way did you come to me?

MUIREANN. The Giant that tied me in a bundle of green rushes and brought me here upon his shoulder. I was in dread I would scratch his face.

RURY. It was for my sake that trouble was put on you and that torment.

MUIREANN. And it was for your sake I parted with my little golden mitten!

RURY. Here I will put it on your hand.

(*Noise of people coming.* GIANT *and* WIFE *enter leading* WITCH *and* PAMPOGUE.)

SIMON. The Giant! Is it in pursuit of us he is?

WIFE. Not at all. It is time for him be getting wittier.

GIANT. It is a quiet Giant I am from this out.

WIFE. Just a common peaceable man. He wouldn't harm a child in a thousand years.

GIANT. To put myself under the King's protection I am come where the Grugach of the Humming is making threats, saying I have my contract with him broke.

RURY (*to* WITCH). This day will be the end of your plots and your enchantings, by whatever way you will be put to death.

SIMON. It would be right put her under the same shape she put on another.

GARDENER. Let the daughter be turned to a rat for her to be skivering with her claws.

WITCH. Do with me what you can do. But I ask mercy for the girl that is young.

WIFE. Give her here to me. We will want some one in the latter end of our days to mind us and to bring in a gallon of water, or a thing of the kind. I'll learn her to be a good slave and a good washerwoman.

GARDENER. She might get better senses yet. It is likely you will treat her better than the way she treated the young queen.

WITCH. If she must work out her punishment let it be a natural one. But let no enchanter ever give her long life, as there is little profit in it.

PAMPOGUE. You that are my mother, have been my enemy all through.

166

WITCH. In that I am your nearest friend. I gave you what I could, and little good it was to you.

RURY. You are right in asking no mercy for yourself.

WITCH. There is coming some change in the world, and why would I go on battling? I am tired remembering the string of years behind me, where I made no great hand of my life. (*She suddenly snatches the three rods from the* GARDENER.) I will leave my Three Rods of Mastery to no other one, or the joy of the seven spells! There——and there——and there—— (*She breaks them, tottering back to door.*) I that have been on the flood tide, I will not wait for the ebb, or live a woman without courage for ever! (*Goes.*)

GARDENER (*gathering up the pieces of rods and looking out after her*). With the breaking of the Rods her power is spent; all the years are come on her. There is nothing left of her on the flags but a little fistful of bones.

SIMON. Her like to be banished out of the world, they will be no miss. In one way or another she had us all but done away with.

(GUARDS *heard playing O'Donnell Abu outside.*)

GIANT. Is it that this is the King?

(KING, DOCTOR, *and* GUARDS *comes in.*)

KING. Are you here yet, my thief of a son?

RURY. Your son is here. It is on the other side of you is the thief.

KING. Have a care how you make little of the man that struck off Fatach Mor the Giant's head.

GIANT (*coming forward*). What is it he is saying he did?

DOCTOR. The Giant! (*Runs behind* KING.)

GIANT. Come out of that! (*Drags him forwards.*) Is it my own head that you struck off?

DOCTOR. Leave me! I never touched you, or harmed you at all.

GIANT (*shaking him*). Coming to look at the red of my tongue and to count the ticking of my pulse—— Telling me there was a worm within me, and it not being in it at all.

DOCTOR. Sure I had to tell you something.

GIANT. Promising me the golden apple for my cure, robbing it from the young King. Away with you, after leaving me no better than I was.

KING. Is it that you stole away the apple from my son?

DOCTOR. If I did, it was for your own healing.

KING. I know you now to be a very roguish man.

SIMON. Let him be put in the jail where we ourselves were to be lodged!

KING. I wouldn't darken the jail with him! Bring him away till such time as my mind is made up will I send him attending lepers as a present to the King of the Bogs and Marshes, or will I hang him from a bridge in Dublin!

RURY (*putting hand on sword*). Who are these strangers coming in?

GARDENER (*bringing in five young men*). With the breaking of the Witch's Rods the charm rose out of the fishes. Here they are now before you, the sons of the King of Spain.

MUIREANN. Oh! Is it that these are my dear brothers!

1ST BROTHER. We are in our own shape at last.

MUIREANN. But——You were not so big——You were my little comrades and playfellows, and we rising——You are grown to be tall young men.

1ST BROTHER. It is seven years since then.

MUIREANN. Oh, you can speak to me at last in your own voice!

BROTHER. The most thing we have to say to you is Good-bye.

MUIREANN. You must stop for my wedding feast. You will not refuse me that?

2ND BROTHER. We will not indeed. You are deserving of every good thing.

MUIREANN. You will be going home then to Spain, where our father is at the end of his days?

1ST BROTHER. Not a fear of us! We have no mind for kings' courts. Aren't we after wearing out enough of our young life, closed up under water in a pond?

ALL THE BROTHERS. There is another cause——

2ND BROTHER. Whisper—— There are too many fast days in it and Fridays. We are in dread we would be asked to eat fish.

1ST BROTHER. We have the Witch's treasure to spend. It is to the Eastern world we will face, to go leaping on Arabian horses and fighting with the armies of the Greeks! (*They leap with joy.*)

KING (*to* RURY). What way can I make up to you at all for giving in to the doctor's lies?

RURY. I will be well content to see you enjoying long life and good health.

KING. It is likely indeed, if signs are signs, it is long till you will be handling Ireland. It is best for me give up the kingdom to you now, as it is well you earned it. You are sixteen times better than the lad that went out. Bog and meadow, fire and water, I will bestow it all upon you.

RURY. I will not take it, where I am well able to go out and win a country for myself.

MUIREANN. Why would you do that, and the whole kingdom of
Spain being mine? (*He kisses her.*)

GIANT (*to* KING). To give me a gate-house or a thing of the sort,
I could be of use lighting lamps in the streets or putting up scollops
in the thatch. I am near tired telling lies.

SIMON. I am done with going to a foreign country. It is too long
I stood upon a sod of wandering. I don't know do they be talking
Irish out in Spain?

PAMPOGUE (*to* MUIREANN). Will you pardon and forgive me for
all I did?

SIMON (*to* PAMPOGUE). They are taken up with themselves. Who
knows but luck might turn to you? I might be looking for a companion for myself. It's a lonesome thing to be housekeeping alone!

Curtain.

THE JESTER

A PLAY IN THREE ACTS

FOR RICHARD

JANUARY, 1919
A. G.

THE JESTER

PERSONS
  THE FIVE PRINCES.
  THE FIVE WRENBOYS.
  THE GUARDIAN OF THE PRINCES AND GOVERNOR OF THE
    ISLAND.
  THE SERVANT.
  THE TWO DOWAGER MESSENGERS.
  THE OGRE.
  THE JESTER.
  THE SOLDIERS.
THE SCENE *is laid in The Island of Hy Brasil, that appears every
  seven years.*
TIME: *Out of mind.*

ACT I

SCENE. *A winter garden, with pots of flowering trees or fruit-
trees. There are books about and some benches with cushions on
them, and many cushions on the ground. The young* PRINCES *are
sitting or lying at their ease. One is playing "Home, Sweet Home"
on a harp. The* SERVANT—*an old man—is standing in the background.*

1ST PRINCE. Here, Gillie, will you please take off my shoe and
see what there is in it that is pressing on my heel.

SERVANT (*taking it off and examining it*). I see nothing.

1ST PRINCE. Oh, yes, there is something; I have felt it all the
morning. I have been thinking this long time of taking the shoe off,
but I waited for you.

SERVANT. All I can find is a grain of poppy seed.

1ST PRINCE. That is it of course—it was enough to hurt my skin.

2ND PRINCE. Gillie, there is a mayfly tickling my cheek. Will you
please brush it away.

SERVANT. I will and welcome. (*Fans it off.*)

3RD PRINCE. Just give me, please, that book that is near my
elbow. I cannot reach to it without taking my hand off my cheek.

SERVANT. I wouldn't wish you to do that. (*Gives him book.*)

4TH PRINCE. Gillie, I think, I am nearly sure, there is a feather in that cushion that has the quill in it yet. I feel something hard.

SERVANT. Give it to me till I will open it and make a search.

4TH PRINCE. No, wait a while till I am not lying on it. I will put up with discomfort till then.

5TH PRINCE. Would it give you too much trouble, Gillie, when you waken me in the morning, to come and call me three times, so that I can have the joy of dropping off again?

SERVANT. Why wouldn't I? And there is a thing I would wish to know. There will be a supper laid out here this evening for the Dowager Messengers that are coming to the Island, and I would wish to provide for yourselves whatever food would be pleasing to you.

1ST PRINCE. It is too warm for eating. All I will ask is a few grapes from Spain.

2ND PRINCE. A mouthful of jelly in a silver spoon . . . or in the shape of a little castle with towers. When will the Lady Messengers be here?

SERVANT. Not before the fall of day.

2ND PRINCE. The time passes so quietly and peaceably it does not feel like a year and a day since they came here before.

SERVANT. No wonder the time to pass easy and quiet where you are, with comfort all around you, and nothing to mark its course, and every season feeling the same as another, within the glass walls and the crystal roof of this place. And the old Queen, your godmother, sending her own Chamberlain to take charge of you, and to be your Guardian, and Governor of the Island. Sure, the wind itself must slacken coming to this sheltered place.

3RD PRINCE. That is a great thing. I would not wish the rough wind to be blowing upon me.

4TH PRINCE. Or the dust to be rising and coming in among us to spoil our suits.

5TH PRINCE. Or to be walking out on the hard roads, or climbing over stone walls, or tearing ourselves in hedges.

1ST PRINCE. That is the reason we were sent here by the Queen, our Godmother, in place of being sent to any school. To be kept safe and secure.

2ND PRINCE. Not to be running here and there like our own poor five first cousins, that used to be slipping out and rambling in their young youth, till they were swallowed up by the sea.

3RD PRINCE. It was maybe by some big fish of the sea.

2ND PRINCE. It might be they were brought away by sea-robbers coming in a ship.

3RD PRINCE. Foolish they were and very foolish not to stay in peace and comfort in the house where they were safe.

SERVANT. There is no fear of *ye* stirring from where you are, having every whole thing ye can wish.

4TH PRINCE. Here is the Guardian coming! (*They all rise.*)

GUARDIAN (*a very old man, much encumbered with wraps coming slowly in*). Are you all here, all the five of you?

ALL. We are here!

GUARDIAN (*standing, leaning on a stick, to address them*). It's a pity that these being holidays, your teachers and tutors are far away,

Gone off afloat in a cedar boat to a College of Learning out in Cathay.

1ST PRINCE. It's a pity indeed they're not here to-day.

GUARDIAN. For it's likely you looked in your almanacs, or judged by the shape of the lessening moon,

That your Godmother's Dowager Messengers are due to arrive this afternoon.

2ND PRINCE. We did and we think they'll be here very soon.

GUARDIAN. But I know they'll be glad that each royal lad, put under my rule in place of a school,

Can fashion his life without trouble or strife, and be shielded from care in a nice easy chair.

3RD PRINCE. As we always are and we always were.

GUARDIAN. It is part of my knowledge that lads in a college, and made play one and all with a bat and a ball,

Come often to harm with a knock on the arm, and their hands get as hard as the hands of a clown.

4TH PRINCE. But ours are as soft as thistledown.

GUARDIAN. And I've seen young princes not far from your age, go chasing beasts on a winter day,

And carted home with a broken bone, and a yard of a doctor's bill to pay;

Or going to sail in the teeth of a gale, when the waves were rising mountains high,

Or fall from a height that was near out of sight, robbing rooks from their nest in a poplar tree.

5TH PRINCE (*to another*). But that never happened to you or me.

GUARDIAN. Or travelling far to a distant war, with battles and banners filling their mind,

And creeping back like a crumpled sack, content if they'd left no limbs behind.

1ST PRINCE. But we'll have nothing to do with that, but stop at home with an easy mind.

GUARDIAN (*sitting down*). That's right. And now I would wish you to say over some of your tasks, to make ready for the Dowager Messengers, that they may bring back a good report to the Queen, your Godmother.

1ST PRINCE. We'll do that. We would wish to be a credit to you, sir, and to our teachers.

GUARDIAN. Say out now some little piece of Latin; that one that is my favourite.

1ST PRINCE.

>Aere sub gelido nullus rosa fundit odores,
>Ut placeat tellus, sole calesce Dei.

GUARDIAN. Say out the translation.

2ND PRINCE. Beneath a chilly blast the rose, loses its sweet, and scentless blows;

If you would have earth keep its charm, stop in the sunshine and keep warm.

GUARDIAN. Very good. Now your history book; you were learning of late some genealogies of kings, might suit your Godmother.

3RD PRINCE.

>William the First as the Conqueror known
>At the Battle of Hastings ascended the throne,
>His Acts were all made in the Norman tongue
>And at eight every evening the curfew was rung
>When each English subject by royal desire
>Extinguished his candle and put out his fire.
>He bridled the kingdom with forts round the Border
>And the Tower of London was built by his order.

2ND PRINCE.

>William called Rufus from having red hair,
>Of virtues possessed but a moderate share,
>But though he was one whom we covetous call,
>He built the famed structure called Westminster Hall.
>Walter Tyrrell his favourite, when hunting one day,
>Attempted a deer with an arrow to slay,
>But missing his aim, shot the King to the heart
>And the body was carried away in a cart.

GUARDIAN. That will do. You have that very well in your memory. Now let me hear the grammar lesson.

3RD PRINCE.

  A noun's the name of any thing
  As school or garden, hoop or swing.

GUARDIAN. Very good, go on.

4TH PRINCE.

  Adjectives tell the kind of noun
  As strong or pretty, white or brown.

5TH PRINCE.

  Conjunctions join the nouns together
  As men and children, wind or weather.

GUARDIAN. It will be very useful to you to have that so well grafted in your mind. . . . What noise is that outside?

SERVANT. It is some strolling people.

1ST PRINCE. Oh, Guardian, let them come in. We will do our work all the better if we have some amusement now.

GUARDIAN. Maybe so. I am well pleased when amusements come to our door, that you can see without going outside the walls.

  (*A* JESTER *enters in very ragged green clothes and broken shoes.*)

But this is a very ragged looking man. Do you know anything about him, Gillie?

SERVANT. I seen him one time before. . . . At the time of the earthquake out in Foreign. A mad jester he was. A tramp class of man. (*To* JESTER) Where is it you stop?

JESTER. Where do I stop? Where would I be but everywhere, like the bad weather. I stop in no place, but going through the whole roads of the world.

GUARDIAN. What brought you in here?

JESTER. Hearing questions going on, and answers. I am well able to give help in that. It's not long since I was giving instruction to the sons of the King of Babylon. Here now is a question. How many ladders would it take to reach to the moon?

1ST PRINCE. It should be a great many.

2ND PRINCE. I give it up.

JESTER. One . . . if it is long enough! Which is it easier to spell, ducks or geese?

3RD PRINCE. Ducks I suppose because it's shorter.

JESTER. Not at all but geese. Do you know why? Because it is spelled with *ees*. Tell me now, can you spell pup backwards?

4TH PRINCE. P-u-p. . . .

JESTER. Not at all.

4TH PRINCE. But it is.

JESTER. No, that is pup straight forwards. . . . Can you run back and forwards at the same time?

4TH PRINCE. Answer it yourself so.

JESTER. You would be as wise as myself then. But I'll show you some tricks. Look at these three straws on my hand. Will I be able to blow two of them away, and the other to stay in its place?

5TH PRINCE. They would all blow away.

JESTER. Look now. Puff! (*He has put his finger on the middle one.*) Now is it possible?

5TH PRINCE. It is easy when you know the way.

JESTER. That is so with all knowledge. Can you wag one ear and keep the other quiet?

1ST PRINCE. Nobody can do that.

JESTER (*wagging one ear with his finger*). There, now you see I have done it! There's more learning than is taught in books. Wait now and I'll give you out a song I'll engage you never heard. (*Sings or repeats*)

> It's I can rhyme you out the joy
> That's ready for a lively boy.
> Cuchulain flung a golden ball
> And followed it where it would fall,
> And when they counted him a child
> He took the flying swans alive.
> And Finn was given hares to mind
> Till he outran them and the wind;
> And he could swim and overtake
> The wild duck swimming on the lake.
> Osgar's young music was to thwack
> The enemy and drive him back. . . .

GUARDIAN. That's enough now. I have no fancy for that class of song. What other amusements are there?

SERVANT. There are the Wrenboys are come here at the end of their twelve days' funning.

JESTER. That's it! The Wrenboys; a rambling troop; rambling the world like myself. I will make place for them. The old must give way to the young.

(*He goes and sits down in a corner, munching a crust and dozing.*)

SERVANT. Come in here let ye, and show what ye can do!

(WRENBOYS *come in playing a fife. They are wearing little*

178

*masks and are dressed in ragged tunics; they carry drum
and fife, and stand in a line.)*
ALL FIVE WRENBOYS (*together*).

> The wren, the wren, the King of all birds,
> On Stephen's Day was caught in the furze.
> Although he's small his family's great,
> Rise up kind gentry and give us a treat!
> (*Rub-a-tub-tub-tub, on the drum.*)
>
> Down with the kettle and up with the pan
> And give us money to bury the wren!
> (*Rub-a-tub.*)
>
> We followed him twenty miles since morn,
> The Wrenboys are all tattered and torn
> From Kyle-na-Gno we started late
> And here we are at this grand gate!
> (*Rub-a-tub.*)
>
> He dipped his wing in a barrel of beer—
> We wish you all a Happy New Year!
> Give us now money to buy him a bier
> And if you don't, we'll bury him here!
> (*Rub-a-tub, and fife.*)

(PRINCES *laugh and clap hands.*)

1ST PRINCE. That is very good.

2ND PRINCE. We must give them some money to bury the wren!

GUARDIAN. Come on then and I will give you some. They will be
glad of it. Play now the harp as you go.

(PRINCES *go off playing, "Home, Sweet Home." The* WREN-
BOYS *sit down.*)

1ST WRENBOY. It is likely we'll get good treatment.

JESTER (*coming forward*). Ye should be tired.

2ND WRENBOY. We should be, but that we have our feet well
soled,—with the dust of the road!

3RD WRENBOY. If walking could tire us we might be tired. But
we're as well pleased to be moving, where we have no house or
home that you'll call a house or a home.

JESTER. That's not so with those young princes. Wouldn't you
be well pleased if ye could change places with them? (*He goes back
to his corner.*)

4TH WRENBOY. They are lovely kind young princes. I was near in dread they might set the dogs at us.

5TH WRENBOY. They would do that if they knew the Ogre had sent us to spy out the place for him.

1ST WRENBOY. It failed us to see what he wanted us to see. It is likely he will beat us, when we go back, with his cat-o'-nine-tails.

2ND WRENBOY. Wouldn't it be good if we could do as that Jester was saying and change places with those sons of kings! They that can lie in the sunshine on soft pillows.

3RD WRENBOY. They that can use food when they ask it, and not have to wait till they can find it, or steal it, or get it what way they can.

4TH WRENBOY. And not to be waiting till you'll hear a rabbit squealing, with the teeth of a weasel in his neck. And the weasel when you take it to be spitting poison at you, the same as a serpent.

5TH WRENBOY. It would be a nice thing to be eating sweet red apples in place of the green crabs.

1ST WRENBOY. Or to be maybe sucking marrow-bones.

2ND WRENBOY. It is likely they are as airy and as careless as the blackbird singing on the bush.

3RD WRENBOY. It's likely they go following after foxes on horses, having huntsmen and beagles at their feet.

4TH WRENBOY. Or go out sporting and fowling with their greyhound and with their gun.

5TH WRENBOY. Or matching fighting cocks.

1ST WRENBOY. It's likely they lead a gentleman's life, card-playing and eating and drinking, and racing with jockeys in speckled clothes.

2ND WRENBOY. Their brooches were shining like green fire, the same as a marten cat's eyes. They have everything finer than another.

3RD WRENBOY. Their faces as clean as a linen sheet. Their hair as if combed with a silver comb.

4TH WRENBOY. There is no one to so much as put a clean shirt on ourselves.

5TH WRENBOY (*rubbing his hand*). I never felt uneasy at the dirt that is gritted into me till I saw them so nice.

1ST WRENBOY. That music they were playing put me in mind of some far thing. It is dreamed to me, and it is never leaving my mind, that there is something I remember in the long ago . . .

music in a house that was as bright as the moon, or as the brightest night of stars.

5TH WRENBOY. Whisht! They are coming!

(*The* PRINCES *comes back.*)

1ST PRINCE. Here are coppers for you.

2ND PRINCE. And white money.

3RD PRINCE. And here is a piece of gold.

3RD WRENBOY. We are thankful to you! We'll bury the Wren in grand style now!

4TH PRINCE. Have you far to go?

1ST WRENBOY. Not very far if it was a straight road. But it is through the forest we go, beyond the lake.

2ND WRENBOY. We will hardly be there before the moon rises.

1ST PRINCE. Are you afraid in the night time?

2ND WRENBOY. I am not. But I've seen a great deal of strange things at that time.

2ND PRINCE. What sort of things?

2ND WRENBOY. Fairies you'd see.

3RD PRINCE. Are there such things?

2ND WRENBOY. One night I was attending a pot-still, roasting oats for to make still-whiskey, and I seen hares coming out of the wood, by fours and by sixes, and they as thin as thin . . .

3RD WRENBOY. Hares are the biggest fairies of all.

4TH WRENBOY. And down by the sea *I* met a weasel bringing up a fish in his mouth from the tide. And I often seen seals there, seals that are enchanted and look like humans, and will hold up a hand the same as a Christian.

5TH WRENBOY. I that saw a hedgehog running up the side of a mountain as swift as a racehorse.

1ST WRENBOY. It's the moonlight is the only time!

1ST PRINCE. I never saw the moon but through a window.

1ST WRENBOY. That's the time to go ramble. (*He chants*)

> You'll see the crane in the water standing,
> And never landing a fish, for fright,
> For he can but shiver seeing in the river
> His shadow shaking in the bright moon light.

2ND WRENBOY.

> Or you may listen to the plover's whistle,
> When high above him the wild geese screech;
> Or the mallard flying, as the night is dying,
> His neck out-stretched towards the salt sea beach.

3RD WRENBOY.

> When dawn discloses the oak and shows us
> The wide sky whitening through the scanty ash,
> High in the beeches the furry creatures,
> Squirrel and marten lightly pass.

4TH WRENBOY.

> The badger scurries to find his burrow
> The rabbit hurries to hide underground.

5TH WRENBOY.

> The pigeon rouses the thrush that drowses,
> The woods awaken and the world goes round!

1ST WRENBOY. Come now, it's time to be taking the road. Thank you, noble Gentlemen! That you may be doing the same thing this day fifty years!

(*They go off playing fife and beating drum.*)

1ST PRINCE. I would nearly wish to be in their place to go through the world at large.

2ND PRINCE. They can go visit strange cities, sailing in white-sailed ships.

3RD PRINCE. They have no lessons to learn.

4TH PRINCE. No hours to keep. No clocks to strike.

5TH PRINCE. No Lady Messengers coming to show off to.

1ST PRINCE. They should be as merry as midges.

2ND PRINCE. As free as the March wind.

3RD PRINCE. I don't know how we stopped so long shut up in this place.

4TH PRINCE. I would be nearly ready to change places with them if such a thing were possible.

JESTER (*who has had his back to them comes forward; the* PRINCES *stand on his right in a half circle*). And why wouldn't you change?

5TH PRINCE. It is a thing not possible.

JESTER. I never could know the meaning of that word "impossible." Where there's a will there's a way.

1ST PRINCE. It seems to me like the sound of a bell ringing a long way off, that I had leave at one time to go here and there.

JESTER. If you are in earnest wanting to come to that freedom again you will get it.

2ND PRINCE. No, we would be followed and brought back through kindness.

JESTER. If you have the strong wish to make the change you can make it.

1ST PRINCE. I think I was never so much in earnest in all my life.
   (*The* JESTER *takes his pipe and plays a note on it. The* WREN-
    BOYS *come back beating their drum. They stand in a half
    circle on* JESTER'S *left.*)
JESTER (*to* ALL).

> If it's true ye wish to change,
> Some to have a wider range,
> Some to have an easy life,
> Some to rove into the wild,
> If you do it, do it fast,
> Do it while you have the chance.

WRENBOYS (*together*). We will change! We will!
JESTER (*to* PRINCES).

> If you wish to leave your ease
> And live wild and free like these
> Like the fawn free and wild,
> Not closed in as is a child,
> Take your chance as it has come,
> Let you run and run and run,
> Where you'll get your joy and fun!

2ND PRINCE. They will know us, they will know us!
JESTER. Change your clothes, change your clothes!
3RD PRINCE. They will know us every place.
JESTER. Put their masks upon your face.
  (WRENBOYS *give them the masks.*)

> You never will be missed
> For I will throw a dust
> Before every body's eye
> That wants to look or pry
> To see *if* you are here,—
> And if you should appear
> To be someway strange or queer
> They will think themselves are blind
> Or confused in the mind!

  (*Throws a handful of dust over all the boys.*)

> Dust of Mullein, work your spell;
> Keep the double secret well!

5TH PRINCE (*to a* WRENBOY).

> Give me here your coat now fast
> I don't want to be the last.

  (*They all rapidly change coats and caps.*)
JESTER. That will do, that is enough.

1ST WRENBOY. But my hands are very rough.

JESTER.

> Never mind; never mind,
> The truth is hard to find!

GUARDIAN (*off stage*). Gillie, do as you are told, shut the door, it's getting cold.

1ST PRINCE. Oh, I'm in dread! What will be said!

2ND PRINCE. I'd sooner stay in my old way!

JESTER.

> Never mind; never mind,
> The truth is hard to find!
> Keep steady. Are you ready?

1ST WRENBOY. I'll be ashamed if I am blamed.

2ND WRENBOY. I have no grace or lovely face!

JESTER (*to* PRINCES). Too late, too late! Go out the gate!

> (*The* PRINCES *have taken up fife and drum. They march out playing.*)

Curtain.

ACT II

SCENE I. *A front scene. A poor hut or tent, the* PRINCES *are coming in slowly, some limping. They are in Wrenboys' clothes and the masks are in their hands.*

1ST PRINCE. This should be the hut where the Wrenboys told us to come.

2ND PRINCE. It is a poor looking place.

3RD PRINCE. It is good to have any place to sit down in for a while. My back is aching.

4TH PRINCE. My feet are all scratched and torn. There are blisters rising.

5TH PRINCE. I thought we would never come to the end of the road. The stones by the lake were so hard and so sharp.

1ST PRINCE. It was a root of a tree I fell over that made these bruises on my knees. I was watching a hawk that was still and quiet up in the air, and when it made a swoop all of a sudden I stumbled and fell.

2ND PRINCE. It was in slipping where the rocks are high I gave this twist to my arm. I can hardly move it.

3RD PRINCE. But wasn't the sight of the sunset splendid over the lake? And the hills so blue!

4TH PRINCE. I like the tall trees best. I tried to climb up one of them, but it was so smooth I did but slip and fall.

1ST PRINCE. I would wish to walk as far as the hills, and to have a view of the ocean that is beyond.

5TH PRINCE. I am hungry. I wonder where we will get our supper.

4TH PRINCE. Not in this place anyway, it must be making ready in some big guesthouse.

3RD PRINCE. What will they give us, I wonder?

2ND PRINCE. I wish we had in our hand what they have ready for us at home.

1ST PRINCE. What use would it be to us? Do you remember what we asked to be given, some jellies and a few grapes? It is not that much would satisfy me now.

2ND PRINCE. Indeed it would not. I never felt so sharp a hunger in my longest memory.

3RD PRINCE. It is roasted meat I would wish for.

4TH PRINCE. There were pigeons in the tall trees. They will maybe give us a pigeon pie.

5TH PRINCE. I would be content with a plate of minced turkey with poached eggs.

1ST PRINCE. I would sooner have a roasted chicken, with bread sauce.

2ND PRINCE. Be quiet. . . . I think I hear someone coming! (*Looks out.*)

3RD PRINCE (*looking out*). I see him. He is not a right man . . . he is very strange looking. . . .

4TH PRINCE (*looking out*). Oh! It is an Ogre! A Grugach!

(ALL *shrink back and hurriedly put on masks.*)

OGRE (*coming in: he wears a frightful mask, has red hair and a cloak of rough skins and carries a whip with many lashes*). What makes ye late to-night, ye young schemers? What was it delayed ye? Lagging along the road.

1ST PRINCE. We came as fast as we could. It was getting dusk in the wood.

OGRE. Dusk, good morrow to you! I'll dusk ye! I had a mind to go after ye and to change myself into the form of a wolf, and catch a hold of ye with my long sharp teeth!

2ND PRINCE. We did not know there was any great hurry.

OGRE. There is always hurry when you are on my messages. What did I bring you away from your own house for and put ye on the shaughraun for and keep ye wandering, if it was not to be serviceable and helpful to myself. Show me now what ye have in your pocket or your bag.

3RD PRINCE. This is all we got in the bag. (*Holds it out.*) It is but very little.

OGRE (*turning it out and counting it*). Coppers! Silver! What is this? A piece of gold! Is that what ye call little? What notions we have! Take care did ye keep any of it back! If ye did I'll skin ye with the lash of my cat-o'-nine-tails. (*Shakes it.*)

4TH PRINCE. That is all we got. It should maybe pay for our supper in some place.

OGRE. What supper? To go buy supper with my money! It will go to add to my store of treasure in the cave that is under ground.

5TH PRINCE. We are hungry, very hungry. When will the supper be ready?

OGRE. It will be ready whenever ye will ready it for yourselves. Ye should know that by this time.

1ST PRINCE. We would make it ready if we were acquainted with the way.

OGRE. Is it gone cracked ye are? What is it ye are thinking to get for your supper? What ailed ye that ye didn't climb a tree and suck a few pigeon's eggs?

2ND PRINCE. We were thinking of a pigeon pie.

OGRE. A what! ! !

2ND PRINCE. A pigeon pie.

OGRE. Hurry on then making your pigeon pie! There are pigeons enough there in the corner, that a hawk that is my carrier brought me in a while ago. And there's a pike that was in the lake these hundred years, an otter is after leaving at my door.

3RD PRINCE (*taking a pigeon*). I don't think this is a right pigeon.

4TH PRINCE. Pigeons in a pie are not the pigeons that have feathers.

5TH PRINCE (*to* OGRE). Please, sir, where can we find pigeons without feathers, that are trussed on a silver skewer?

OGRE. Aye? What's that?

1ST PRINCE. Never mind. You'll anger him. Maybe we can pull the feathers off these. I have read of plucking a pigeon in our books. (*They begin to pluck.*)

2ND PRINCE. It is very hard work.

3RD PRINCE. I never knew feathers could stick in so hard.

4TH PRINCE. The more we pull out the more there would seem to be left.

5TH PRINCE. It will be a feather pie we will be getting in the end.

1ST PRINCE (*throwing it down*). It is no use. We might work at it to-day and to-morrow and be no nearer to a finish.

2ND PRINCE. The pike might be better.

3RD PRINCE. It has no feathers anyway.

4TH PRINCE (*touching it*). It is raw and bleeding!

5TH PRINCE. We might roast it.

1ST PRINCE. The fire is black out.

2ND PRINCE. I wonder what way can we kindle it?

3RD PRINCE. Better ask him. (*Points to* OGRE.)

2ND PRINCE. Please, sir, what way can we kindle the fire?

OGRE. What!

4TH PRINCE. We would wish to light the fire.

OGRE. Well, do so.

5TH PRINCE. If we had a box of matches. . . .

OGRE. Matches! What are you talking about? Matches won't be invented for the next seven hundred years.

1ST PRINCE. What can we do then, we are starving with hunger.

OGRE. Let ye blow a breath upon a coal under the ashes, and bring in small sticks from the wood.

2ND PRINCE (*blowing*). The ashes are choking me.

OGRE. Very good. Then you'll put no delay on me, waiting till you'll cook your supper.

3RD PRINCE. Where can we get it then?

OGRE. You'll go without it, as you were too helpless to catch it, or to dress it, there's no one will force you to eat it.

4TH PRINCE. If there is nothing for us to eat we had best pass the time in sleep.

5TH PRINCE. I am all covered with ashes and dirt. (*To* OGRE) Please, where can I find a towel and a piece of soap?

OGRE. Soap! Is it bewitched ye are or demented in the head? Did ever anyone hear of soap unless of a Saturday night? Letting on to be as dainty and as useless as those young princes beyond, that are kept closed up in a tower of glass. Come on now. If there is no food that suits you, leave it. It is time for us to get to work.

1ST PRINCE. But it is bed-time.

OGRE. Your bed-time is the time when I have no more use for you. Don't you know I have made a plan? What was it I sent you for, spying out that place of the young princes? Wasn't it to see where is it that treasure is kept, the golden-handled sword of Justice that is used by the Guardian when he turns Judge.

2ND PRINCE. That is kept in the Courthouse.

OGRE. That's right . . . in what part of it?

3RD PRINCE. What do you want it for?

OGRE. I have it in my mind this long time to get and to keep it in my cave under ground, along with the rest of my treasures that are in charge of my two enchanted cats. I have had near enough of grubbing for gold with a pick in the clefts and crannies of the earth. It is time for me to find some rest, and get into my hand what is ready worked and smelted and purified. We are going to that Courthouse to-night. If we cannot get in at the door, I will put ye in at the window and ye can open the door to myself. I will find out where the sword is, and away with us, and it in my hand.

4TH PRINCE. But that would be stealing.

OGRE. What else would it be?

4TH PRINCE. But that is wrong. It is against the law.

OGRE. The law! That is the Judge's trade. Breaking it is mine.

5TH PRINCE. Ask him for it and maybe he will give it to you, he is so kind.

OGRE. I'll take no charity! What I get I'll earn by taking it. I would feel no pleasure it being given to me, any more than a huntsman would take pleasure being made a present of a dead fox, in place of getting a run across country after it. Come on now! We'll have the moon wasted. We'll hardly get there before the dawn of day.

1ST PRINCE. Whatever time you get there the Guardian will be awake. There is a cock of Denmark perched on the curtain rod of his bed, specially to waken him if there is any stir.

OGRE. There is, is there? What a fool you think me to be. Do you see that pot?

2ND PRINCE. We do see it.

OGRE. Look what there is in it.

3RD PRINCE. Nothing but a few bare bones.

OGRRE. Well, that is all that is left of the Judge's cock of Denmark, that was brought to me awhile ago by a fox that is my messenger, and that I have boiled and ate and devoured.

ALL THE PRINCES. O! O! O!

OGRE (*cracking his whip*). He was boiled in the little pot. Come on now and lead the way, or I give you my word it is in the big pot your own bones will be making broth for my breakfast in the morning! (*Cracks whip.*) Now, right about face! Quick march!

Curtain.

188

SCENE II. *The Winter Garden. The* SERVANT *settling benches and a table.*

GUARDIAN (*coming in*). Are the Dowager Messengers come? They are late.

SERVANT. They are come. They are at the looking-glasses settling themselves.

GUARDIAN. As soon as they are ready you will call in the Princes for their examination before them, and their tasks.

SERVANT. I will.

GUARDIAN. The Messengers will have a good report to bring back of them. They have come to be good scholars, in poetry, in music, in languages, in history, in numbers and all sorts. The old Queen-Godmother will be well satisfied with their report.

SERVANT. She might and she might not.

GUARDIAN. They would be hard to please if they are not well pleased with the lads, as to learning and as to manners and behaviour.

SERVANT. Maybe so. Maybe so. There are strange things in the world.

GUARDIAN. You're in bad humour, my poor Gillie. Have you been quarrelling with the cook, or did you get up on the wrong side of your bed?

SERVANT. There is times when it is hard not to be in a bad humour.

GUARDIAN. What are you grumbling and hinting at?

SERVANT. There's times when it's hard to believe that witchcraft is gone out of the world.

GUARDIAN. That is a thing that has been done away with in this Island through my government, and through enlightenment and through learning.

SERVANT. Maybe so. Maybe so.

GUARDIAN. I suppose a three-legged chicken has come out of the shell, or a magpie has come before you in your path? Or maybe some token in the stars?

SERVANT. It would take more than that to put me astray.

GUARDIAN. Whatever it is you had best tell it out.

SERVANT. To see lads of princes, sons of kings, and the makings of kings, that were mannerly and well behaved and as civil as a child a few hours ago, to be sitting in a corner at one time as if in dread of the light, and tricking and fooling and grabbing at other times.

GUARDIAN. Oh, is that all! The poor lads. They're out of their habits because of their Godmother's Messengers coming. They are making merry and funning, thinking there might be messages for them or presents.

SERVANT. Funning is natural. But blowing their nose with their fingers is not natural.

GUARDIAN. High spirits. Just to torment you in their joy.

SERVANT. To get a bit of chalk, and to make marks in the Hall of dancing, and to go playing hop-scotch.

GUARDIAN. High spirits, high spirits! I never saw boys better behaved or more gentle or with more sweetness of speech. I am thinking there is not one among them but will earn the name of Honey-mouth.

SERVANT. Have it your own way. But is it a natural thing, I am asking, for the finger nails to make great growth in one day?

GUARDIAN. Stop, stop, be quiet. Here now are the Dowager Messengers. (*Two old ladies in travelling costume appear; bowing low to them.*) You are welcome for the sake of her that sent you, and for your own sakes.

1ST DOWAGER MESSENGER. We are come from the Court of the Godmother Queen, for news of the Princes now in your charge;

She hopes they have manners, are minded well, and never let run at large;

For she never has yet got over the fret, of their five little cousins were swept away.

GUARDIAN. Let your mind be at ease, for you'll be well pleased with the youngsters you're going to see to-day.

They're learning the laws to speak and to pause—may be orators then, or Parliament men.

2ND DOWAGER MESSENGER. Are they shielded from harm?

GUARDIAN.

In my sheltering arm;

Do their work and their play in a mannerly way

And go holding their nose, and tipped on their toes,

If they pass through a street, that they'll not soil their feet.

2ND DOWAGER MESSENGER. And next to good manners and next to good looks . . .

GUARDIAN.

I know what you'll say . . . she asks news of the cooks;

I'm with her in putting them equal to books;

There's some rule by coaxing and some rule by beating,

But my principle is, tempt them on with good eating.

When everything's said, isn't Sparta as dead
As many a place never heard of black bread?
And as to a lad who a tartlet refuses,—
If Cato stewed parsnips he hated the Muses!

1ST DOWAGER MESSENGER. And at meals are they taught to behave as they ought?

GUARDIAN.

You'll be well satisfied and the Queen will have pride,
You will see every Prince use a fork with his mince,
And eating his peas like Alcibiades,
Who would sooner go mute than play on the flute
Lest it made him grimace and contorted his face.

1ST DOWAGER MESSENGER. Oh, all that you say delights us to-day!

We'll have good news to bring of these sons of a king.

SERVANT. Here they are now coming.

(WRENBOYS *in Princes' clothes come in awkwardly.*)

GUARDIAN.

Now put out a chair.
Where these ladies may hear.
Come over, my boys ... (Now what is that noise?)
Come here, take your places, and show us your faces,
And say out your task as these ladies will ask.
I would wish them to know how you say *Parlezvous,*
And I'd like you to speak in original Greek
And make numeration, and add up valuation;
But to lead you with ease and on by degrees
In case you are shy in the visitors' eye
I will let you recite, as you easily might,
The kings of that Island that no longer are silent
But ask recognition and to take a position—
(Though if stories are true they ran about blue,
While we in Hy-Brasil wore our silks to a frazzle—)
So the rhymes you may say that I heard you to-day;
And the opening will fall on the youngest of all.

SERVANT. Let you stand up now and do as you are bid. (*Touches* 5TH WRENBOY.)

GUARDIAN. Go on, my child, say out your lesson. William the First as the Conqueror known. ... (BOY *puts finger in mouth and hangs his head.*)

Ah, he is shy. Don't be affrighted, go on now; don't you remember it?

5TH WRENBOY. I do not.

GUARDIAN. Try it again now. You said it off quite well this morning.

5TH WRENBOY. It fails me.

GUARDIAN. Now I will give you a start; "William the First as the Conqueror known,

At the Battle of Hastings ascended the throne . . ." Say that now.

5TH WRENBOY (*nudging* 4TH). Let you word it.

4TH WRENBOY (*to* GUARDIAN). Let you word it again, sir.

GUARDIAN. "William the First as the Conqueror known."

4TH WRENBOY. William the First as the congereel known. . . .

GUARDIAN. What is that? You would not do it to vex me! Gillie is maybe right. There is something strange. . . . (*To another.*) You may try now. Go on to the next verse. "William called Rufus from having red hair." . . . (*He does not answer.*) Say it anyone who knows. . . .

3RD WRENBOY (*putting up his hand*). I know a man that has red hair!

ALL THE WRENBOYS (*cheerfully*). So do I! So do I!

2ND WRENBOY. He lives in the wood beyond! He is no way good! He is an Ogre, a Grugach. . . .

1ST WRENBOY. He can turn himself into the shape of a beast, or he can change his face at any time; sometimes he'll be that wicked you would think he was a wolf; he would skin you with his cat-o'-nine-tails!

GUARDIAN. What gibberish are you talking?

2ND WRENBOY. He goes working underground to get gold!

3RD WRENBOY. It is minded by enchanted cats!

4TH WRENBOY. They would tear in bits anyone that would find it!

GUARDIAN. Now take care, lads, this is carrying a joke too far. I was wrong to begin with that silly history. Tell me out now the parts of speech.

"A noun's the name of anything
As school or garden, hoop or swing."

5TH WRENBOY. An owl's the name of anything. . . .

GUARDIAN. A *noun*.

5TH WRENBOY. An *owl*.

GUARDIAN. Don't pretend you don't know it.

5TH WRENBOY. I do know it. I know an owl that sits in the cleft of the hollow sycamore and eats its fill of mice, till it can hardly put a stir out of itself.

GUARDIAN. I do wish you would stop talking nonsense.

1ST WRENBOY. It is not, but sense. It devoured ere yesterday a whole fleet of young rats.

2ND WRENBOY. It's as wise as King Solomon.

GUARDIAN. Gillie was right. There is surely something gone wrong in their heads.

2ND WRENBOY. Go out yourself and you'll see are we wrong in the head! Inside in the old sycamore he is sitting through the daylight.

1ST DOWAGER MESSENGER. There is something gone wrong in *somebody's* head.

2ND DOWAGER MESSENGER (*tapping her forehead*). The poor Guardian; he is too long past his youth. It is well we came to look how things were going before it is too late.

1ST DOWAGER MESSENGER. Ask them to say something they *do* know.

GUARDIAN. Here, you're good at arithmetic, say now your numbers.

1ST WRENBOY. Twelve coppers make a shilling. I never handled more than that.

GUARDIAN (*angrily*). Well, do as the lady said, tell us something you *do* know.

2ND WRENBOY (*standing up, excited*). I know the way to make bird-lime, steeping willow rods in the stream. . . .

3RD WRENBOY. I know how to use my fists; I knocked a tinker bigger than myself.

4TH WRENBOY. I am the best at wrestling. I knocked *him*self. (*Pointing at* 3RD.)

5TH WRENBOY. I that can skin a fawn after catching him running!

2ND DOWAGER MESSENGER. Where now did you get that learning?

5TH WRENBOY. Here and there, rambling the woods, sleeping out at night. I would never starve in any place where grass grows!

1ST DOWAGER MESSENGER. This is worse than neglect. The poor old Guardian the Queen put her trust in must be in his dotage.

GUARDIAN (*hastily*). Here, there is at least one thing you will not fail in. Take the harp (*hands it to the* 1ST WRENBOY) and draw out of it sweet sounds. (*To* DOWAGER MESSENGERS) He can play a tune so sweet it has been known to send all the hearers into a sound sleep. Here now, touch the strings with all your skill.

(1ST WRENBOY *bangs harp making a crash.*)

2ND DOWAGER MESSENGER (*with hands to ears*). Mercy! Our poor ears!

1ST DOWAGER MESSENGER. That is the poorest music we have ever heard.

2ND DOWAGER MESSENGER. That sound would send no one into their sleep. It would be more likely to send them into Bedlam.

1ST DOWAGER MESSENGER. Whatever they knew last year, they have forgotten it all now.

GUARDIAN (*weeping into his handkerchief*). I don't know what has come upon them! At noon they were the most charming lads in the whole world. Their memory seems to have left them!

2ND DOWAGER MESSENGER. It is as if another memory had come to them. They did not learn those wild tricks shut up in the garden.

SERVANT (*to* BOYS). Can't ye behave nice and not ugly? (*To* GUARDIAN) You would not believe me a while ago. I said and I say still there is enchantment on them, and spells.

GUARDIAN. Oh, I would be sorry to think such a thing. But they never went on this way in their greenest youth.

2ND DOWAGER MESSENGER. If there is a spell upon them what way can it be taken off?

SERVANT. It is what I always heard, that to make a rod of iron red in the fire, and to burn the enchantment out of them is the only way.

GUARDIAN. Oh, boys, do you hear that! You would not like to be burned with a red hot rod! Say out now what at all is the matter with you? What is it you feel within you that is putting you from your gentle ways?

1ST WRENBOY. The thing that I feel in me is hunger. The thing I would wish to feel inside me is a good fistful of food.

1ST DOWAGER MESSENGER. They have been starved and stinted! It would kill their Godmother on the moment if she was aware of that!

GUARDIAN. It is a part of their playgame. They have everything they ask.

2ND WRENBOY. I did not eat a farthing's worth since yesterday.

3RD WRENBOY. My teeth are rusty with the want of food!

4TH WRENBOY. I want some dinner!

5TH WRENBOY. We want something to eat!

GUARDIAN. Give them whatever you have ready for them, Gillie.

SERVANT (*giving the plates*). Here is the supper ye gave orders for this morning.

1ST WRENBOY. What is it at all?

SERVANT. It is your choice thing. Jellies and grapes from Spain.

2ND WRENBOY (*pushing away grapes*). Berries! I thought to get better than berries from the bush.

3RD WRENBOY. There's not much satisfaction in berries!

4TH WRENBOY. If it was a pig's foot now; or as much as a potato with a bit of dripping.

5TH WRENBOY (*looking at jelly*). What now is this? It has like the appearance of frog spawn.

1ST WRENBOY. Or the leavings of a fallen star.

5TH WRENBOY. Shivering it is and shaking. It's not natural! (*Drops his plate.*)

4TH WRENBOY. There is nothing here to satisfy our need.

2ND DOWAGER MESSENGER. I am nearly sorry for them poor youngsters. When they were but little toddlers they never behaved like that at home.

3RD WRENBOY. It's the starvingest place ever I was in!

1ST DOWAGER MESSENGER. There must be something in what they say. They would not ask for food if they were not in need of it. And the Guardian making so much talk about his table and his cooks. We cannot go home and report that they have no learning and no food.

2ND DOWAGER MESSENGER. As to learning I don't mind. But as to food, I would not wish to leave them without it for the night. They might be as small as cats in the morning.

GUARDIAN. They are dreaming when they say they are in want of food.

1ST DOWAGER MESSENGER. It is a dream that will waken up their Godmother.

SERVANT. Look ma'am, at the table behind you, and you will see is this a scarce house! That is what is set out for yourselves, ma'am, lobsters from Aughanish! A fat turkey from the barley gardens! A spiced and larded sucking pig! Cakes and sweets and all sorts! It is not the want of provision was ever brought against us up to this!

2ND DOWAGER MESSENGER. If all this is for us, we would sooner give it up to those poor children. (*To* WRENBOYS) Here, my dears, we will not eat while you are in want of food. We will give it all to you.

1ST WRENBOY. Is it that we can have what is on that table?

2ND DOWAGER MESSENGER. You may, and welcome.

1ST WRENBOY (*with a shout*). Do you hear that news! Come on now. Take your chance! I'll have the first start! Skib scab! Hip, hip, hooray!

>(*They rush at table and upset it flinging themselves on the food.*)

Curtain.

Act III

SCENE. *The Hall of Justice. It is nearly dawn. The last of the* PRINCES *is getting in through the window. They are wearing their masks.*

OGRE (*outside door to left*). Open now the door for myself.

1ST PRINCE. No, we will get rid of him now. Let the Grugach stay outside.

2ND PRINCE. That will be best. He cannot break the bars of this door, or get round over the high wall to the door on the other side.

3RD PRINCE. I am sore with the blows he put on us, driving us before him through the wood.

4TH PRINCE. Let us call to the Guardian, and let him deal with him. He can bring his foot soldiers and his guns.

5TH PRINCE. A villain that Ogre is and a thief, wanting to steal away the golden-handled sword. But we would not tell him where it was, and he never will find it under the step of the Judge's chair. (*Lifts top of step, takes out sword and puts it back again.*)

OGRE (*outside*). Are ye going to open the door?

1ST PRINCE. It is a great thing to have that strong door between us.

2ND PRINCE. Take care would he break it in.

3RD PRINCE. No fear. It would make too much noise. It would bring every person in the house running.

4TH PRINCE. Let us go quick and call the Guardian.

5TH PRINCE. What will he say seeing us in these clothes? He will be vexed with us.

1ST PRINCE. It was folly of us running away. But he will forgive us, knowing it will teach us better sense.

2ND PRINCE. Come to him then, I don't mind what he will do to us so long as we are safe from the terrible Grugach of an Ogre. (ALL *go to right door, it opens and* OGRE *bursts in.*)

OGRE. Ye thought to deceive me did ye? Ye thought to bar me out and keep me out? And I after minding you and caring you these seven years!

3RD PRINCE. What way did you get in?

OGRE. It's easy for me to get in any place. If I had a mind I could turn into a house fly and come through the lockhole of the door. It's much if I don't change the whole lot of ye into small birds, and myself to a hawk going through you! Or, into frightened mice, and I myself into a starving cat! It's much if I don't skin you with this whip, and grind your bones as fine as rape seed!

4TH PRINCE. I will call for help! (*Tries to shout.*)

OGRE (*putting hand over his mouth and lifting whip*). Shout now and welcome, and it is bare bones will be left of you! If it wasn't that I need you to search out the golden-handled sword for me I'd throttle the whole of ye as easy as I'd squeeze an egg! Come on now! Show me where the treasure is hid.

5TH PRINCE. How would we know?

OGRE. Didn't I send ye spying it out, and if it fails ye to make it out, I'll boil and bake you!

1ST PRINCE (*looking about and pointing to end of room*). It might be there.

OGRE. What way would it be on the bare floor? Search it out.

2ND PRINCE (*looking under a bench*). It might be here.

OGRE. It is not there.

3RD PRINCE (*looking up chimney*). This would be a good hiding-place.

OGRE (*looks up*). There is nothing in it, only an old nest of a jackdaw,—a bundle of bare twigs. Trying to deceive me you are and to lead me astray.

4TH PRINCE. It might be on the shelf.

OGRE. Stop your chat unless you have something worth saying.

5TH PRINCE (*sitting down on step under which sword is hidden*). Are you certain there is any treasure at all?

OGRE. You are humbugging and making a fool of me! (*Lashes whip and seizes him.*) Get up now out of that! (*Drags him up and taps board.*) There is a hollow sort of a sound. . . . That is a sort of place where a treasure might be hid. (*Drags up board.*) I see something shining. (*Pulls out sword.*) Oh, it is a lovely sword! And the handle of pure gold. The best I ever seen!

1ST PRINCE (*to the others*). I'll make a run now and call out and awaken all in the house! (*Is going towards door.*)

OGRE (*seizing him*). You'd make your escape would you?

1ST PRINCE (*calling out*). Ring the big bell, ring the bell! I forgot it till now.

(*They pull a bell-rope and bell is heard clanging.*)

OGRE (*rushing at them as they ring it*). I'll stop that!

(*Voices are heard at door to right. OGRE rushes to the other door.*)

2ND PRINCE. I'll get the sword from him. (*Snatches it away as OGRE is rushing at him. SERVANT and GUARDIAN come in.*)

GUARDIAN. What is going on! (*Blows a whistle.*) Here, soldiers of the guard!

(*Feet are heard marching and bugle blowing at left door. OGRE rapidly slips off his mask, and appears as a harmless old man.*)

GUARDIAN. Thieves! Robbers! Burglars! Here, soldiers, surround the place; who are these ruffians? Murder! Robbery! Fire!

(*TWO SOLDIERS come in.*)

SERVANT. They are the very same youngsters were at our door this morning, doing their play; those Wrenboys!

GUARDIAN. They are thieves. There is one of them bringing away my gold-handled sword. (*He and SERVANT seize sword.*)

OGRE (*coming forward and bowing low*). It is time for you to come, your honour my lordship! I am proud to see you coming! It was I myself that rang the bell and that called and awakened you, where I would not like to see the place robbed and left bare by these scum of the world!

ALL THE PRINCES. Oh! Oh! Oh!

GUARDIAN. What have you to do with it? Where do you come from?

OGRE. An honest poor man I am. . . .

SERVANT. You have a queer wild sort of a dress.

OGRE. Making a living I do be, dressing up as a hobgoblin and a bogey man to get an odd copper from a mother here and there, would be wishful to frighten a stubborn child from bawling or from tricks. Passing the door I was, and hearing a noise I looked in, and these young villains were after rising a board and taking out that sword you seen in their hands. It is then that I made a clamour with the bell.

(*The PRINCES laugh.*)

GUARDIAN. Who are they at all?

OGRE. It is I myself say it; they are the terror of the whole district.

1ST PRINCE. You may save your breath and stop that talk. This gentleman knows us well. He knows us and will recognise us.

GUARDIAN. I do recognise you. I saw you but yesterday.

2ND PRINCE. There now, what do you say?

GUARDIAN. You are those vagabond Wrenboys that came tricking and begging to my gate.

PRINCES. Oh! Oh! Oh!

OGRE. That's it! Spying round they were! Thinking to do a robbery! Robbery they're after doing!

3RD PRINCE. We were doing no such thing!

GUARDIAN. You were! I stopped you making off with my sword of Justice.

OGRE. If it wasn't for me hindering them they would have it swept.

GUARDIAN. That was very honest of you.

4TH PRINCE (*rushing at* OGRE). It is you that are a rogue and a thief!

OTHER PRINCES. Throw him down while we have the chance. (*They surround him.*)

GUARDIAN. Silence! Don't make that disturbance! I felt a suspicion yesterday the first time I saw your faces there was villainy hidden beneath the dust that was on your cheeks.

4TH PRINCE. Listen to us, listen!

GUARDIAN. And whatever I thought then, you are seventeen times more wicked looking now! And the very scum of the roads!

5TH PRINCE. Oh, have you forgotten your nurslings!

GUARDIAN. It is well you reminded me of them. (*To* SERVANT) Go now and bring the young Princes here till they will see justice done! They are maybe gone a bit wild and foolish since yesterday, put out by those Dowager Messengers. But whatever they were at their worst, they are King George compared with these!

1ST PRINCE. You *must* listen!

GUARDIAN. Must! What is that language! That is a word was never said to me since I was made the Queen's Chamberlain. Here! Put a gag upon their mouths! (SOLDIERS *do so, tying a handkerchief on mouth of each.*) Tie their hands behind them with ropes. (*This is done.*) Rapscallions! Do they think to terrify and command me! I that am not only Governor of the Island but am Supreme Judge whenever I come into this Court.

OGRE. That is very good and very right! Keep the gag in their mouth! You wouldn't like to be listening to the things they were saying a while ago! They were giving out great impudence and very disrespectful talk!

GUARDIAN. Give me here my Judge's wig and my gown! (*Puts them on.*) Where now are the young Princes?

SERVANT. They are coming now.

GUARDIAN. It will be a great help in their education seeing justice done by me, as straight as was ever done by Aristides. Give me here that book of punishments and rewards. I'll see what is bad enough for these lads! (*He consults book.*)

SERVANT. Here now are the Princes.

(WRENBOYS *come in wearing Princes' clothes.*)

1ST WRENBOY (*to another*). Do you see who it is that is in it?

2ND WRENBOY. It is the young Princes in our clothes!

3RD WRENBOY. What in the world wide brought them here? Believe me it was through some villainy of the Grugach.

4TH WRENBOY. What at all has happened?

5TH WRENBOY. Go ask them what it was brought them, or what they came doing.

1ST WRENBOY (*to* PRINCES). What is it brought you here so soon?

(PRINCES *shake their heads.*)

2ND WRENBOY (*coming back*). There is a gag on their mouths!

3RD WRENBOY (*going and looking*). Their hands are tied with a rope.

4TH WRENBOY. They had not the wit to stand against the Grugach; it is not long till they were brought to trouble.

5TH WRENBOY. It was seventeen times worse for them to be under him than for ourselves that was used to him, and to his cruelty and his ways.

1ST WRENBOY. It was bad enough for ourselves. We were not built for roguery.

(*The* DOWAGER MESSENGERS *rushing in.*)

DOWAGER MESSENGERS (*together*). What is going on? What has happened?

GUARDIAN. What you see before you has happened. Those young thieves came to try and to rob the house. They were found by myself in the very act of bringing away my golden-handled sword! They were stopped by this honest man. (*Points to* OGRE.)

1ST DOWAGER MESSENGER. There would seem to be a great deal of wickedness around this place!

GUARDIAN. I'll put a stop to it! I'll use my rights as Judge! To have that sort of villainy running through the Island, it would come through walls of glass or of marble, and lead away the best.

2ND DOWAGER MESSENGER. There must be something gone wrong in the stars, our own young princes having gone wild out of measure, and these young vagabonds doing no less than house-breaking! It is hard to live!

OGRE. Indeed, ma'am, it would be a great blessing to the world if all the boys in it could be born grown up.

GUARDIAN (*sighing*). I, myself, am beginning to have that same opinion.

1ST DOWAGER MESSENGER. And so am I myself. Young men have strength and beauty, and old men have knowledge and wisdom, but as to boys! After what we saw a while ago in the supper-room!

SERVANT. The Court is about to sit! Take your places!

(WRENBOYS *make for the dock and* PRINCES *the jury-box*.)

GUARDIAN. What do you mean prisoners, going up there, that is the place for honourable men! For a jury! It is here in the criminals' dock your place is.

SERVANT (*to* WRENBOYS). Oh, that is the wrong place you're in. That is for the wicked and the poor that are brought to be tried and condemned.

1ST WRENBOY. It is a place the like of that I was put one time I was charged before a magistrate for snaring rabbits.

SERVANT. Silence in the Court! The Judge is about to speak!

GUARDIAN (*reading out of book*).

It's laid down in a clause of the Cretian laws,
That were put through a filter by Solon,
That for theft the first time, though a capital crime
A criminal may keep his poll on.
Though (*consults another book*) some jurists believe
That a wretch who can thieve,
Has earned a full stop, not a colon.

OGRE. That was said by a better than Solon.

GUARDIAN.

And the books says in sum, to cut off the left thumb,
May be penalty enough for a warning;
Though (*looks at another book*) the commentors say
That one let off that way
Will be thieving again before morning.

OGRE. So he will, and the jury suborning.

GUARDIAN.

> For the second offence, as the crime's more immense,
> Take the thumb off the *right* hand instead;
> And the third time he'll steal, without any appeal,
> The hangman's to whip off his head.

OGRE.

> Very right to do so, for a thief as we know,
> Isn't likely to steal when he's dead.

2ND DOWAGER MESSENGER.

> You won't order the worst, as this crime is the first,
> It's a pity if they have to swing.

GUARDIAN.

> In the Commentors' sense, a *primal* offence
> Is as much an impossible thing
> As a stream without source, a blow struck without force,
> Or leaves without roots in the spring.

OGRE. Or a catapult wanting a sling.

GUARDIAN.

> But although this case is proved on its face
> To be what is called *a priori*
> I cannot refuse to consider the views
> Of the amiable lady before me. (*Bows to* 2ND DOWAGER
>   MESSENGER.)
> In compliance to her I am ready to err
> On the side that she leans to, of mercy,
> For she has a kind tongue, and the prisoners are young;
> But that they may not live to curse me,
> I give out my decree, the *left* thumb shall be
> Kept in Court till the next time they'll come.
> And now if you please let whoever agrees
> With my pledge turn down his own thumb.

1ST DOWAGER MESSENGER. It is very just and right. (*Turns down hers.*)

OGRE. You're letting them off too easy. They're a bad example to the world. But to take the thumb off them is better than nothing! (*Turns down both his thumbs.*)

GUARDIAN (*to* WRENBOYS). Well, my dear pupils, I don't see you turn down your thumbs.

1ST WRENBOYS. We cannot do it. (*They cover their faces with their hands.*)

OGRE. Get on so. I never saw the work I'd sooner do than checking youngsters!

GUARDIAN. Where is the Executioner?

SERVANT. I sent seeking him a while ago, thinking he might be needed.

GUARDIAN. Bring him in.

SERVANT. He is not in it. There was so little business for him this long time under your own peaceable rule, that he is after leaving us, and taking a job in a slaughter house out in foreign.

2ND DOWAGER MESSENGER. Maybe that is a token we should let them off.

OGRE (*briskly*). I am willing to be useful; give me here a knife or a hatchet!

SERVANT (*to* OGRE). You need not be pushing yourself forward. (*To* GUARDIAN) There is a stranger of an Executioner chanced to be passing the road, just as I sent out, and he looking for work. He said he would do the job for a fourpenny bit and his dinner, that he is sitting down to now.

GUARDIAN (*sitting up straight and taking up sword*).
Bring him in quick. It often seems a curious thing that I,
Who in my ordinary clothes would hardly hurt a fly,
Hold to the rigour of the law when I put on gown and wig,
As if for mere humanity I didn't care a fig.
For once I'm seated on the bench I do not shrink or flinch
From the reddest laws of Draco, or the practice of Judge Lynch.

SERVANT (*at door*). Here he is now.

(JESTER *comes in, disguised as Executioner, a long cloak with hood over his head.*)

GUARDIAN. Here is the sword (*hands it to him and reads*), "In case of the first act of theft the left thumb is to be struck off." There are the criminals before you. That is what you have to do.

JESTER (*taking the sword*). Stretch out your hands! There is hurry on me. I was sitting at the dinner I engaged for. I was called away from the first mouthful, and I would wish to go back to the second mouthful that is getting cold.

GUARDIAN (*relenting*). Maybe now the fright would be enough to keep them from crimes from this out. They are but young.

JESTER (*to* PRINCES). Don't be keeping me waiting! Put out now your hands. (*They shake their heads.*)

SERVANT. They cannot do that, being bound.

JESTER. If you will not stretch out your hands when I ask you, I will strike off your heads without asking! (*Flourishes sword.*)

GUARDIAN (*standing up*). I did not empower you to go so far as that! It is without my authority!

JESTER. You have given over the power of the law to the power of the sword. It must take its way!

GUARDIAN. I will not give in to that! I have all authority here!

JESTER. If you grow wicked with the Judge's wig on your head, so do I with this sword in my hand! You called me in to do a certain business and I am going to do it! I am not going to get a bad name put on me for breach of contract! If a labourer is given piece work cutting thistles with a hook he is given leave to do it, or a rat catcher doing away with vermin in the same way! He is not bid after his trouble to let them go loose out of his bag! And why would an Executioner that is higher again in the profession be checked. Isn't my pride in my work the same as theirs? And along with that, let me tell you I belong to a Trades Union!

(GUARDIAN *moans and covers his face*.)

(*To the* PRINCES) Kneel down now! Where you kept me so long waiting and that the Judge attempted to interfere with me, I have my mind made up to make an end of you! (*Holds up sword*.)

1ST WRENBOY (*rushing forward and putting his arms about* PRINCE). You must not touch him! These lads never did any harm!

2ND WRENBOY (*protecting a* PRINCE). It is we ourselves are to be punished if anyone must be punished.

3RD WRENBOY. They are innocent whoever is to blame.

JESTER. Take their place so! Someone must be put an end to.

(*All the* WRENBOYS *kneel*.)

1ST WRENBOY. Here we are so. We changed places with them for our own pleasure, thinking to lead a prince's life, and if there is anyone must suffer by reason of that change let it be ourselves.

JESTER. I'll take off their gags so and let them free.

(*He cuts cords of gags and hands, then throws some dust over* ALL BOYS as before saying)

Dust of Mullein leave the eyes
You made fail to recognise
Princes in their poor disguise;
Princes all, had men clear eyes!

(*The* PRINCES *throw off their masks*.)

1ST PRINCE. It is all a mistake! Oh, Guardian, don't you know now that we are your nurslings and your wards! Look at the royal mark upon our arm, that we brought with us into the world. (*They turn up sleeves and show their arms*.)

2ND DOWAGER MESSENGER. I am satisfied without looking at

the royal sign. I have been looking at their finger nails. Those other nails (*pointing to* WRENBOYS) have never been touched with a soapy brush.

2ND PRINCE. It is strange you did not recognise us. It was that Jester yesterday when we changed our coats that threw a dust of disguise between you and us.

1ST DOWAGER MESSENGER. Was it that these lads robbed you of your clothes?

3RD PRINCE. Not at all.

4TH PRINCE. We ourselves that were discontented and wishful to change places with them.

GUARDIAN. A very foolish thing, and that I have never read of in any of my histories.

5TH PRINCE. We were the first to wish the change. It is we should be blamed.

5TH WRENBOY. No, but put the blame on us! The Wrenboys you seen yesterday.

GUARDIAN. Ah, be quiet, how do I know who you are, or if ever I saw you before! My poor head is going round and round.

1ST WRENBOY. Now do you know us! (ALL *recite "The Wren, the Wren, the King of All Birds." Give first verse.*)

GUARDIAN (*stopping his ears*). Oh, stop it! That makes my poor head worse again.

2ND WRENBOY (*pulling up sleeve*). If you had chanced to see our right arm you would recognise us. We were not without bringing a mark into the world with us, if it is not royal itself.

(WRENBOYS *strip their arms.*)

1ST DOWAGER MESSENGER. What is he talking about? (*Seizes arm and looks at it.*)

2ND DOWAGER MESSENGER. It is the same mark as is on the princes, the sign and token of a King!

1ST DOWAGER MESSENGER. It is certain these must be their five little royal cousins, that were stolen away from the coast.

1ST WRENBOY. If we were brought away it was by that Grugach that has kept us in his service through the years.

2ND DOWAGER MESSENGER. It is no wonder they took to one another. It was easy to know by the way they behaved they had in them royal blood.

(*The* BOYS *turn to each other, the* OGRE *is slipping out.*)

JESTER (*throwing off his cloak and showing his green ragged clothes*). Stop where you are!

OGRE. Do your best! You cannot hinder me! I have spells could change the whole of ye to a cairn of grey stones! (*Makes signs with his hands.*)

JESTER (*in a terrible voice*). Are you thinking to try your spells against *mine*?

OGRE (*trembling and falling on his knees*). Oh, spare me! Hold your hand! Do not use against me your spells of life and death! I know you now! I know you well through your ragged dress! What are my spells beside yours? You the great Master of all magic and all enchantments, Manannan, Son of the Sea!

JESTER. Yes, I am Manannan, that men are apt to call a Jester and a Fool, and a Disturber, and a Mischief-maker, upsetting the order of the world and making confusion in its order and its ways. (*Recites or sings*)

> For when I see a master
> Hold back his hireling's fee
> I shake my pepper castor
> Into his sweetened tea!
>
> And when I see a plan make
> The Birds that watch us frown,
> I come and toss the pancake
> And turn it upside down!
>
> In this I follow after
> Lycurgus who was wise;
> To the little god of laughter
> I make my sacrifice!

And now here is my word of command! Everyone into his right place!

OGRE. Spare me! Let me go this time!

JESTER. Go out now! I will not bring a blemish on this sword by striking off your ugly head. But as you have been through seven years an enemy to these young boys, keeping them in ignorance and dirt, they that are sons of a king, I cross and command you to go groping through holes and dirt and darkness through three times seven years in the shape of a rat, with every boy, high or low, gentle or simple, your pursuer and your enemy. And along with that I would recommend you to keep out of the way of your own enchanted cats!

(OGRE *gives a squeal and creeps away on all fours.*)

GUARDIAN. I think I will give up business and go back to my old trade of Chamberlain and of shutting out draughts from the Court.

The weight of years is coming on me, and it is time for me to set my mind to some quiet path.

1ST DOWAGER MESSENGER. Come home with us so, and help us to attend to our cats, that they will be able to destroy the rats of the world.

2ND DOWAGER MESSENGER (*to* PRINCES). It is best for you come to your Godmother's Court, as your Guardian is showing the way.

1ST PRINCE. We may come and give news of our doings at the end of a year and a day.

But now we will go with our comrades to learn their work and their play.

2ND PRINCE. For lying on silken cushions, or stretched on a feathery bed.

We would long again for the path by the lake, and the wild swans overhead.

3RD PRINCE. Till we'll harden our bodies with wrestling and get courage to stand in a fight.

4TH PRINCE. And not to be blind in the woods or in dread of the darkness of night.

1ST WRENBOY. And we who are ignorant blockheads, and never were reared to know

The art of the languaged poets, it's along with you we will go.

5TH PRINCE. Come show us the wisdom of woods, and the way to outrun the wild deer,

Till we'll harden our minds with courage, and be masters of hardship and fear.

2ND WRENBOY. But you are candles of knowledge, and we'll give you no ease or peace,

Till you'll learn us manners and music, and news of the Wars of Greece.

1ST PRINCE. Come on, we will help one another, and going together we'll find,

Joy with those great companions, Earth, Water, Fire, and Wind. (*They join hands.*)

JESTER. It's likely you'll do great actions, for there is an ancient word,

That comradeship is better than the parting of the sword,

And that if ever two natures should join and grow into one,

They will do more together than the world has ever done.

So now I've ended my business, and I'll go, for my road is long,

But be sure the Jester will find you out, if ever things go wrong!

(*He goes off singing*)

And so I follow after
Lycurgus who was wise;
To the little god of laughter
I pay my sacrifice!

Curtain.

THE DRAGON

THE DRAGON

PERSONS
THE KING.
THE QUEEN.
THE PRINCESS NUALA.
THE DALL GLIC. *The blind Wise Man.*
THE NURSE.
THE PRINCE OF THE MARSHES.
MANUS. *King of Sorcha.*
FINTAN. *The astrologer.*
TAIG.
SIBBY. *Taig's mother.*
GATEKEEPER.
TWO AUNTS *of the Prince of the Marshes.*
FOREIGN MEN *bringing in food.*
THE DRAGON.

ACT I

SCENE. *A room in the King's house at Burren. Large window at back with deep window seat. Doors right and left. A small table and some chairs.*

DALL GLIC (*coming in with tray, which he puts on table. Goes back to door*). You can come in, King. There is no one here.

KING (*coming in*). That's very good. I was in dread the Queen might be in it.

DALL GLIC. It is a good thought I had bringing it in here, and she gone to give learning to the Princess. She is not likely to come this side. It would be a great pity to annoy her.

KING (*hastily swallowing a mouthful*). Look out now the door and keep a good watch. The time she will draw upon me is when I am eating my little bite.

DALL GLIC. I'll do that. What I wouldn't see with my one eye, there's no other would see with three.

KING. A month to-day since I wed with her, and well pleased I

am to be back in my own place. I give you word my teeth are rust-
ing with the want of meat. On the journey I got no fair play. She
wouldn't be willing to see me nourish myself, unless maybe with
the marrow bone of a wren.

DALL GLIC. Sure she lays down she is but thinking of the good
of your health.

KING. Maybe so. She is apt to be paying too much attention to
what will be for mine and for the world's good. I kept my health
fair enough, and the first wife not begrudging me my enough. I
don't know what in the world led me not to stop as I was.

DALL GLIC. It is what you were saying, it was for the good of
the Princess Nuala, and of yourself.

KING. That is what herself laid down. It would be a great ease to
my mind, she was saying, to have in the house with the young girl,
a far-off cousin of the King of Alban, and that had been conversation woman in his Court.

DALL GLIC. So it might be too. She is a great manager of people.

KING. She is that . . . I think I hear her coming . . . Throw a
cloth over the plates.

QUEEN (*coming in*). I was in search of you.

KING. I thought you were in Nuala's sunny parlour, learning her
to play music and to go through books.

QUEEN. That is what I thought to do. But I hadn't hardly started
to teach her the principles of conversation and the branches of
relationships and kindred of the big people of the earth, when she
plucked off the coverings I had put over the cages, and set open
their doors, till the fiery birds of Sabes and the canaries of the
eastern world were screeching around my head, giving out every
class of cry and call.

KING. So they would too.

QUEEN. The royal eagles stirred up till I must quit the place with
their squawking, and the enchanted swans raising up their heads
and pecking at the beadwork on my gown.

KING. Ah, she has a wish for the birds of the air, that are by
nature light and airy the same as herself.

QUEEN. It is time for her to turn her mind to good sense. What's
that? (*Whipping cloth from tray.*) Is it that you are eating again,
and it is but one half-hour since your breakfast?

KING. Ah, that wasn't a breakfast you'd call a breakfast.

QUEEN. Very healthy food, oaten meal flummery with whey, and
a griddle cake; dandelion tea and sorrel from the field.

KING. My old fathers ate their enough of wild herbs and the like in the early time of the world. I'm thinking that it is in my nature to require a good share of nourishment as if to make up for the hardships they went through.

QUEEN. What now have you within that pastry wall?

KING. It is but a little leveret pie.

QUEEN (*poking with fork*). Leveret! What's this in it? The thickness of a blanket of beef; calves' sweetbreads; cocks' combs; balls mixed with livers and with spice. You to so much as taste of it, you'll be crippled and crappled with the gout, and roaring out in your pain.

KING. I tell you my generations have enough done of fasting and for making little of the juicy meats of the world.

QUEEN. And the waste of it! Goose eggs and jellies. . . . That much would furnish out a dinner for the whole of the King of Alban's Court.

KING. Ah, I wouldn't wish to be using anything at all, only for to gather strength for to steer the business of the whole of the kingdom!

QUEEN. Have you enough ate now, my dear? Are you satisfied?

KING. I am not. I would wish for a little taste of that saffron cake having in it raisins of the sun.

QUEEN. Saffron! Are you raving? You to have within you any of the four-and-twenty sicknesses of the race, it would throw it out in red blisters on your skin.

KING. Let me just taste one little slab of that venison ham.

QUEEN (*poking with a fork*). It would take seven chewings! Sudden death it would be! Leave it alone now and rise up. To keep in health every man should quit the table before he is satisfied —there are some would walk to the door and back with every bite.

KING. Is it that I am to eat my meal standing, the same as a crane in a shallow, or moving from tuft to thistle like you'd see a jennet on the high road?

QUEEN. Well, at the least, let you drink down a share of this tansy juice. I was telling you it would be answerable to your health.

KING. You are doing entirely too much for me.

QUEEN. Sure I am here to be comfortable to you. This house before I came into it was but a ship without a rudder! Here now, take the spoon in your hand.

DALL GLIC. Leave it there, Queen, and I'll engage he'll swallow it down bye-and-bye.

QUEEN. Is it that *you* are meddling, Dall Glic? It is time some person took you in hand. I wonder now could that dark eye of yours be cured?

DALL GLIC. It is given in that it can not, by doctors and by druids.

QUEEN. That is a pity now, it gives you a sort of a one-sided look. It might not be so hard a thing to put out the sight of the other.

DALL GLIC. I'd sooner leave them the way they are.

QUEEN. I'll put a knot on my handkerchief till such time as I can give my mind to it. . . . Now, my dear (*to* KING), make no more delay. It is right to drink it down after your meal. The stomach to be bare empty, the medicine might prey upon the body till it would be wore away and consumed.

KING. Time enough. Let it settle now for a minute.

QUEEN. Here, now, I'll hold your nose the way you will not get the taste of it.

(*She holds spoon to his mouth. A ball flies in at window; he starts and medicine is spilled.*)

PRINCESS (*coming in with* NURSE). Is it true what they are telling me?

QUEEN. Do you see that you near hit the King with your ball, and, what is worse again, you have his medicine spilled from the spoon.

PRINCESS (*patting him*). Poor old King.

QUEEN. Have you your lessons learned?

PRINCESS (*throwing books in the air*). Neither line nor letter of them! Poem book! Brehon Laws! I have done with books! I am seventeen years old to-day!

QUEEN. There is no one would think it and you so flighty as you are.

PRINCESS (*to* KING.) Is it true that the cook is gone away?

KING (*aghast*). What's that you're saying?

QUEEN. Don't be annoying the King's mind with such things. He should be hidden from every trouble and care.

PRINCESS. Was it you sent him away?

QUEEN. Not at all. If he went it was through foolishness and pride.

PRINCESS. It is said in the house that you annoyed him.

QUEEN. I never annoyed any person in my life, unless it might be for their own good. But it fails some to recognise their best friend. Just teaching him I was to pickle onion thinnings as it was done at the King of Alban's Court.

PRINCESS. Didn't he know that before?

QUEEN. Whether or no, he gave me very little thanks, but turned around and asked his wages. Hurrying him and harrying him he said I was, and away with him, himself and his four-and-twenty apprentices.

KING. That is bad news, and pitiful news.

QUEEN. Do not be troubling yourself at all. It will be easy find another.

KING. It might not be easy to find so good a one. A great pity! A dinner or a supper not to be rightly dressed is apt to give no pleasure in the eating or in the bye-and-bye.

QUEEN. I have taken it in hand. I have a good headpiece! I put out a call with running lads, and with the army captains through the whole of the five provinces; and along with that, I have it put up on tablets at the post office.

PRINCESS. I am sorry the old one to be gone. To remember him is nearly the farthest spot in my memory.

QUEEN (*sharply*). If you want the house to be under your hand only, it is best for you to settle into one of your own.

PRINCESS. Give me the little rush cabin by the stream and I'll be content.

QUEEN. If you mind yourself and profit by my instruction it is maybe not a cabin you will be moving to but a palace.

PRINCESS. I'm tired of palaces. There are too many people in them.

QUEEN. That is talking folly. When you settle yourself it must be in the station where you were born.

PRINCESS. I have no mind to settle myself yet awhile.

NURSE. Ah, you will not be saying that the time Mr. Right will come down the chimney, and will give you the marks and tokens of a king.

QUEEN. There might have some come looking for her before this, if it was not for you petting and pampering her the way you do, and encouraging her flightiness and follies. It is likely she will get no offers till such time as I will have taught her the manners and the right customs of courts.

NURSE. Sure I am acquainted with courts myself. Wasn't it I fostered comely Manus that is presently King of Sorcha, since his father went out of the world? And as to lovers coming to look for her! They do be coming up to this as plenty as the eye could hold them, and she refusing them, and they laying the blame upon the King!

KING. That is so, they laying the blame upon myself. There was the uncle of the King of Leinster; he never sent me another car-load of asparagus from the time you banished him away.

PRINCESS. He was a widower man.

KING. As to the heir of Orkney, since the time you sent him to the right about, I never got so much as a conger eel from his hand.

PRINCESS. As dull as a fish he was. He had a fish's eyes.

KING. That wasn't so with the champion of the merings of Ulster.

PRINCESS. A freckled man. He had hair the colour of a fox.

KING. I wish he didn't stop sending me his tribute of heather beer.

QUEEN. It is a poor daughter that will not wish to be helpful to her father.

PRINCESS. If I am to wed for the furnishing of my father's table, it's as good for you to wrap me in a speckled fawnskin and roast me!

(*Runs out, tossing her ball.*)

QUEEN. She is no way fit for marriage unless with a herd to the birds of the air, till she has a couple of years schooling.

KING. It would be hard to put her back to that.

QUEEN. I must take it in hand. She is getting entirely too much of her own way.

NURSE. Leave her alone, and in the end it will be a good way.

QUEEN. To keep rules and hours she must learn, and to give in to order and good sense. (*To* KING.) There is a pigeon messenger I brought from Alban I am about to let loose on this day with news of myself and of yourself. I will send with it a message to a friend I have, bidding her to make ready for Nuala a place in her garden of learning and her school.

KING. That is going too fast. There is no hurry.

QUEEN. She is seventeen years. There is no day to be lost. I will go write the letter.

NURSE. Oh, you wouldn't send away the poor child!

DALL GLIC. It would be a great hardship to send her so far. Our poor little Princess Nu!

QUEEN (*sharply*). What are you saying?

(DALL GLIC *is silent.*)

KING. I would not wish her to be sent out of this.

QUEEN. There is no other way to set her mind to sense and learning. It will be for her own good.

NURSE. Where's the use troubling her with lessons and with

books that maybe she will never be in need of at all. Speak up for
her, King.

KING. Let her stop for this year as she is.

QUEEN. You are all too soft and too easy. She will turn on you
and will blame you for it, and another year or two years slipped by.

NURSE. That she may!

DALL GLIC. Who knows what might take place within the twelvemonth that is coming?

KING. Ah, don't be talking about it. Maybe it never might come
to pass.

DALL GLIC. It will come to pass, if there is truth in the clouds of
the sky.

KING. It will not be for a year, anyway. There'll be many an ebb-
ing and flowing of the tide within a year.

QUEEN. What at all are you talking about?

KING. Ah, where's the use of talking too much.

QUEEN. Making riddles you are, and striving to keep the meaning
from your comrade, that is myself.

KING. It's best not be thinking about the thing you would not
wish, and maybe it might never come around at all. To strive to
forget a threat yourself, it might maybe be forgotten by the universe.

QUEEN. Is it true something was threatened?

KING. How would I know is anything true, and the world so full
of lies as it is?

NURSE. That is so. He might have been wrong in his foretelling.
What is he in the finish but an old prophecy?

DALL GLIC. Is it of Fintan you are saying that?

QUEEN. And who, will you tell me, is Fintan?

DALL GLIC. Anyone that never heard tell of Fintan never heard
anything at all.

QUEEN. His name was not up on the tablets of big men at the
King of Alban's Court, or of Britain.

NURSE. Ah, sure in those countries they are without religion or
belief.

QUEEN. Is it that there was a prophecy?

KING. Don't mind it. What are prophecies? Don't we hear them
every day of the week? And if one comes true there may be seven
blind and come to nothing.

QUEEN (*to* DALL GLIC). I must get to the root of this, and the
handle. Who, now, is Fintan?

DALL GLIC. He is an astrologer, and understanding the nature of the stars.

NURSE. He wore out in his lifetime three eagles and three palm trees and three earthen dykes. It is down in a cleft of the rocks beyond he has his dwelling presently, the way he can be watching the stars through the daytime.

DALL GLIC. He prophesied in a prophecy, and it is written in clean letters in the King's yewtree box.

KING. It is best to keep it out of sight. It being to be, it will be; and, if not, where's the use troubling our mind?

QUEEN. Sound it out to me.

DALL GLIC (*looking from window and drawing curtain*). There is no story in the world is worse to me or more pitiful; I wouldn't wish any person to hear.

NURSE. Oh, take care it would come to the ears of my darling Nu!

DALL GLIC. It is said by himself and the heavens that in a year from this day the King's daughter will be brought away and devoured by a scaly Green Dragon that will come from the North of the World.

QUEEN. A Dragon! I thought you were talking of some danger. I wouldn't give in to dragons. I never saw one. I'm not in dread of beasts unless it might be a mouse in the night-time!

KING. Put it out of mind. It is likely anyway that the world will soon be ended the way it is.

QUEEN. I will send and search out this astrologer and will question him.

DALL GLIC. You have not far to search. He is outside at the kitchen door at this minute, and as if questioning after something, and it a half-score and seven years since I knew him to come out of his cave.

KING. Do not! He might waken up the Dragon and put him in mind of the girl, for to make his own foretelling come true.

NURSE. Ah, such a thing cannot be! The poor innocent child! (*Weeps.*)

QUEEN. Where's the use of crying and roaring? The thing must be stopped and put an end to. I don't say I give in to your story, but that would be an unnatural death. I would be scandalized being stepmother to a girl that would be swallowed by a sea-serpent!

NURSE. Ochone! Don't be talking of it at all!

QUEEN. At the King of Alban's Court, one of the royal family to die over, it will be naturally on a pillow, and the dead-bells ringing, and a burying with white candles, and crêpe on the knocker of the door, and a flagstone put over the grave. What way could we put a stone or so much as a rose-bush over Nuala and she in the inside of a water-worm might be ploughing its way down to the north of the world?

NURSE. Och! that is what is killing me entirely! O save her, save her.

KING. I tell you, it being to be, it will be.

QUEEN. You may be right, so, when you would not go to the expense of paying her charges at the Royal school. But wait, now, there is a plan coming into my mind.

NURSE. There must surely be some way!

QUEEN. It is likely a king's daughter the beast—if there is a beast —will come questing after, and not after a king's wife.

DALL GLIC. That is according to custom.

QUEEN. That's what I am saying. What we have to do is to join Nuala with a man of a husband, and she will be safe from the danger ahead of her. In all the inventions made by poets, for to put terror on children or to knock laughter out of fools, did any of you ever hear of a Dragon swallowing the wedding-ring?

ALL. We never did.

QUEEN. It's easy enough so. There must be no delay till Nuala will be married and wed with someone that will bring her away out of this, and let the Dragon go hungry home!

NURSE. That she may! Isn't it a pity now she being so hard to please!

QUEEN. Young people are apt to be selfish and to have no thought but for themselves. She must not be hard to please when it will be to save and to serve her family and to keep up respect for their name. Here she is coming.

NURSE. Ah, you would not tell her! You would not put the dear child under the shadow of such a terror and such a threat!

KING. She must not be told. I never could bear up against it.

(NUALA *comes in.*)

QUEEN. Look now at your father the way he is.

PRINCESS (*touching his hand*). What is fretting you?

QUEEN. His heart as weighty as that the chair near broke under him.

PRINCESS. I never saw you this way before.

QUEEN. And all on the head of yourself!

PRINCESS. I am sorry, and very sorry, for that.

QUEEN. He is loth to say it to you, but he is tired and wore out waiting for you to settle with some match. See what a troubled look he has on his face.

PRINCESS (*to* KING). Is it that you want me to leave you? (*He gives a sob.*) (*To* DALL GLIC.) Is it the Queen urged him to this?

DALL GLIC. If she did, it was surely for your good.

NURSE. Oh, my child and my darling, let you strive to take a liking to some good man that will come!

PRINCESS. Are you going against me with the rest?

NURSE. You know well I would never do that!

PRINCESS. Do you, father, urge me to go?

KING. They are in too big a hurry. Why wouldn't they wait a while, for a quarter, or three-quarters of a year.

PRINCESS. Is that all the delay I am given, and the term is set for me, like a servant that would be banished from the house?

KING. That's not it. That's not right. I would never give in to let you go . . . if it wasn't . . .

PRINCESS. I know. (*Stands up.*) For my own good!

(*Trumpet outside.*)

GATEKEEPER (*coming in*). There is company at the door.

QUEEN. Who is it?

GATEKEEPER. Servants, and a company of women, and one that would seem to be a Prince, and young.

PRINCESS. Then he is come asking me in marriage.

DALL GLIC. Who is he at all?

GATEKEEPER. They were saying he is the son of the King of the Marshes.

KING. Go bring him in.

(GATEKEEPER *goes.*)

DALL GLIC. That's right! He has great riches and treasure. There are some say he is the first match in Ireland.

NURSE. He is not. If his father has a copper crown, and our own King a silver one, it is the King of Sorcha has a crown of gold! The young King of Sorcha that is the first match.

DALL GLIC. If he is, this one is apt to be the second first.

QUEEN. Do you hear, Nuala, what luck is flowing to you?

DALL GLIC. Do not now be turning your back on him as you did to so many.

PRINCESS. No; whoever he is, it is likely I will not turn away from this one.

QUEEN. Go now and ready yourself to meet him.

PRINCESS. Am I not nice enough the way I am?

QUEEN. You are not. The King of Alban's daughter has hair as smooth as if a cow had licked it.

(PRINCESS *goes.*)

GATEKEEPER. Here is the Prince of the Marshes!

(*Enter* PRINCE, *very young and timid, an old lady on each side slightly in advance of him.*)

KING. A great welcome before you. . . . And who may these be?

PRINCE. Seven aunts I have . . .

FIRST AUNT (*interrupting*). If he has, there are but two of us have come along with him.

SECOND AUNT. For to care him and be company for him on his journey, it being the first time he ever quitted home.

QUEEN. This is a great honour. Will you take a chair?

FIRST AUNT. Leave that for the Prince of the Marshes. It is away from the draught of the window.

SECOND AUNT. We ourselves are in charge of his health. I have here his eel-skin boots for the days that will be wet under foot.

FIRST AUNT. And I have here my little bag of cures, with a cure in it that would rise the body out of the grave as whole and as sound as the time you were born.

(*Lays it down.*)

KING (*to* PRINCE). It is many a day your father and myself were together in our early time. What way is he? He was farther out in age than myself.

PRINCE. He is . . .

FIRST AUNT (*interrupting*). He is only middling these last years. The doctors have taken him in hand.

KING. He was more for fowling, and I was more for horses—before I increased so much in girth. Is it for horses you are, Prince?

PRINCE. I didn't go up on one up to this.

FIRST AUNT. Kings and princes are getting scarce. They are the most class is wearing away, and it is right for them keep in mind their safety.

SECOND AUNT. The Prince has no need to go upon a horse, where he has always a coach at his command.

KING. It is fowling that suits you so?

PRINCE. I would be well pleased . . .

FIRST AUNT. There is great danger going out fowling with a gun that might turn on you after and take your life.

SECOND AUNT. Why would the Prince go into danger, having servants that will go following after birds?

QUEEN. He is likely waiting till his enemies will make an attack upon the country to defend it.

FIRST AUNT. There is a good dyke around about the marshes, and a sort of quaking bog. It is not likely war will come till such time as it will be made by the birds of the air.

KING. Well, we must strive to knock out some sport or some pleasure.

PRINCE. It was not on pleasure I was sent.

FIRST AUNT. That's so, but on business.

SECOND AUNT. Very weighty business.

KING. Let the lad tell it out himself.

PRINCE. I hope there is no harm in me coming hither. I would be loth to push on you . . .

FIRST AUNT. We thought it was right, as he was come to sensible years . . .

KING. Stop a minute, ma'am, give him his time.

PRINCE. My father . . . and his counsellors . . . and my seven aunts . . . that said it would be right for me to join with a wife.

QUEEN. They showed good sense in that.

PRINCE (*rapidly*). They bade me come and take a look at your young lady of a Princess to see would she be likely to be pleasing to them.

FIRST AUNT. That's it, and that is what brought ourselves along with him—to see would we be satisfied.

KING. I don't know. The girl is young—she's young.

FIRST AUNT. It is what we were saying, that might be no drawback. It might be easier train her in our own ways, and to do everything that is right.

KING. Sure we are all wishful to do the thing that is right, but it's sometimes hard to know.

SECOND AUNT. Not in our place. What the King of the Marshes would not know, his counsellors and ourselves would know.

QUEEN. It will be very answerable to the Princess to be under such good guidance.

FIRST AUNT. For low people and for middling people it is well enough to follow their own opinion and their will. But for the Prince's wife to have any choice or any will of her own, the people would not believe her to be a *real* princess.

(PRINCESS *comes to door, listening unseen.*)

KING. Ah, you must not be too strict with a girl that has life in her.

222

PRINCE. My seven aunts that were saying they have a great distrust of any person that is lively.

FIRST AUNT. We would rather than the greatest beauty in the world get him a wife who would be content to stop in her home.

(PRINCESS *comes in very stately and with a fine dress. She curtseys.* AUNTS *curtsey and sit down again.* PRINCE *bows uneasily and sidles away.*)

FIRST AUNT. Will you sit, now, between the two of us?

PRINCESS. It is more fitting for a young girl to stay in her standing in the presence of a king's kindred and his son, since he is come so far to look for me.

SECOND AUNT. That is a very nice thought.

PRINCESS. My far-off grandmother, the old people were telling me, never sat at the table to put a bit in her mouth till such time as her lord had risen up satisfied. She was that obedient to him that if he had bidden her, she would have laid down her hand upon red coals.

(PRINCE *looks bored and fidgets.*)

FIRST AUNT. Very good indeed.

PRINCESS. That was a habit with my grandmother. I would wish to follow in her ways.

KING. This is some new talk.

QUEEN. Stop; she is speaking fair and good.

PRINCESS. A little verse, made by some good wife, I used to be learning. "I always should: Be very good: At home should mind: My husband kind: Abroad obey: What people say."

FIRST AUNT (*getting up*). To travel the world, I never thought to find such good sense before me. Do you hear that, Prince?

PRINCE. Sure I often heard yourselves shaping that sort.

SECOND AUNT. I'll engage the royal family will make no objection to this young lady taking charge of your house.

PRINCESS. I can do that! (*Counts on fingers.*) To send linen to the washing-tub on Monday, and dry it on Tuesday, and to mangle it Wednesday, and starch it Thursday, and iron it Friday, and fold it in the press against Sunday!

SECOND AUNT. Indeed there is little to learn you! And on Sundays, now, you will go driving in a painted coach, and your dress sewed with gold and with pearls, and the poor of the world envying you on the road.

QUEEN (*claps hands*). There is no one but must envy her, and all that is before her for her lifetime!

FIRST AUNT. Here is the golden arm-ring the Prince brought for to slip over your hand.

SECOND AUNT. It was put on all our generations of queens at the time of the making of their match.

PRINCESS (*drawing back her hand*). Mine is not made yet.

FIRST AUNT. Didn't you hear me saying, and the Prince saying, there is nothing could be laid down against it.

PRINCESS. There is one thing against it.

QUEEN. Oh, there can be nothing worth while!

PRINCESS. A thing you would think a great drawback and all your kindred would think it.

QUEEN (*rapidly*). There is nothing, but maybe that she is not so tall as you might think, through the length of the heels of her shoes.

SECOND AUNT. We would put up with that much.

PRINCESS (*rapidly*). It is that there was a spell put upon me—by a water-witch that was of my kindred. At some hours of the day I am as you see me, but at others I am changed into a sea-filly from the Country-under-Wave. And when I smell salt on the west wind I must race and race and race. And when I hear the call of the gulls or the sea-eagles over my head, I must leap up to meet them till I can hardly tell what is my right element, is it the high air or is it the loosened spring-tide!

QUEEN. Stop your nonsense talk. She is gone wild and raving with the great luck that is come to her!

(PRINCE *has stood up, and is watching her eagerly*.)

PRINCESS. I feel a wind at this very time that is blowing from the wilderness of the sea, and I am changing with it. . . . There. (*Pulls down her hair*.) Let my mane go free! I will race you, Prince, I will race you! The wind of March will not overtake me, Prince, and I running on the top of the white waves!

(*Runs out;* PRINCE *entranced, rushes to door*.)

AUNTS (*catching hold of him*). Are you going mad wild like herself?

PRINCE. Oh, I will go after her!

FIRST AUNT (*clutching him*). Do not! She will drag you to destruction.

PRINCE (*struggling to door*). What matter! Let me go or she will escape me! (*Shaking himself free*.) I will never stop till I come to her.

(*He rushes out,* SECOND AUNT *still holding on to him*.)

FIRST AUNT. What at all has come upon him? I never knew him this way before!

(*She trots after him.*)

PRINCESS (*comes leaping in by window*). They are gone running the road to Muckanish! But they won't find me!

QUEEN. You have a right to be ashamed of yourself and your play-game. It's easy for you to go joking, having neither cark nor care: that is no way to treat the second best match in Ireland!

KING. You were saying you had your mind made up to take him.

PRINCESS. It failed me to do it! Himself and his counsellors and his seven aunts!

QUEEN. He will give out that you are crazed and mad.

PRINCESS. He will be thankful to his life's end to have got free of me!

KING. I don't know. It seemed to me he was better pleased with you in the finish than in the commencement. But I'm in dread his father may not be well pleased.

PRINCESS (*patting him*). Which now of the two of you is the most to be pitied? He to have such a timid son or you to have such an unruly daughter?

QUEEN. It is likely he will make an attack on you. There was a war made by the King of Britain on the head of a terrier pup that was sent to him and that made away on the road following hares. It's best for you to make ready to put yourself at the head of your troop.

KING. It's long since I went into my battle dress. I'm in dread it would not close upon my chest.

QUEEN. Ah, it might, so soon as you would go through a few hardships in the fight.

KING. If the rest of Adam's race was of my opinion there'd be no fighting in the world at all.

QUEEN. It is this child's stubbornness is leading you into it. Go out, Nuala, after the Prince. Tell him you are sorry you made a fool of him.

PRINCESS. He was that before—thinking to put me sitting and sewing in a cushioned chair, listening to stories of kings making a slaughter of one another.

QUEEN. Tell him you have changed your mind, that you were but funning; that you will wed with him yet.

PRINCESS. I would sooner wed with the King of Poison! I to have to go to his kingdom, I'd sooner go earning my wages footing turf, with a skirt of heavy flannel and a dress of the grey frieze! Himself and his bogs and his frogs!

QUEEN. I tell you it is time for you to take a husband.

PRINCESS. You said that before! And I was giving in a while ago, and I felt the blood of my heart to be rising against it! And I will not give it to you again! It is my own business and I will take my own way.

QUEEN (*to* KING). This is all one with the raving of a hag against heaven!

KING. What the Queen is saying is right. Try now and come around to it.

PRINCESS. She has set you against me with her talk!

QUEEN (*to* KING). It is best for you to lay orders on her.

PRINCESS. The King is not under your orders!

QUEEN. You are striving to make him give in to your own!

KING. I will take orders from no one at all!

QUEEN. Bid her go bring back the Prince.

PRINCESS. I say that I will not!

QUEEN. She is standing up against you! Will you give in to that?

KING. I am bothered with the whole of you! I will give in to nothing at all!

QUEEN. Make her do your bidding so.

KING. Can't you do as you are told?

PRINCESS. This concerns myself.

KING. It does, and the whole of us.

PRINCESS. Do you think you can force me to wed?

KING. I do think it, and I will do it.

PRINCESS. It will fail you!

KING. It will not! I was too easy with you up to this.

PRINCESS. Will you turn me out of the house?

KING. I will give you my word, it is little but I will!

PRINCESS. Then I have no home and no father! It is to my mother you must give an account. You know well it is with the first wife you will go at the Judgment!

QUEEN. Is it you that would make threats to the King? And put insults upon myself? Now she is daring and defying you! Let you put an end to it!

KING. I will do that! (*Stands up.*) I swear by the oath my people swear by, the seven things common to us all; by sun and moon; sea and dew; wind and water; the hours of the day and night, I will give you in marriage and in wedlock to the first man that will come into the house!

PRINCESS (*shrinking as from a blow*). It is the Queen has done this.

QUEEN. I will give you out the reason, and see will you put blame on me or praise!

NURSE. Oh, let you stop and not draw it down upon her!

QUEEN. It is right for me to tell it; it is true telling! You not to be married and wed by this day twelvemonth, there will be a terrible thing happen you . . .

NURSE. Be quiet! Don't you see Fintan himself looking in the window!

KING. Fintan! What is it brings you here on this day?

FINTAN (*a very old man in strange clothes at window*). What brings me is to put my curse upon the whole tribe of kitchen boys that are gone and vanished out of this, without bringing me my request, that was a bit of rendered lard that would limber the swivel of my spy-glass, that is clogged with the dripping of the cave.

NURSE. And you have no bad news?

QUEEN. Nothing to say on the head of the Princess, this being, as it is, her birthday?

FINTAN. What birthday? This is not a birthday that signifies. It is the next will be the birthday will be concerned with the great story that is foretold.

QUEEN. It is right for her to know it.

KING. It is not! It is not!

PRINCESS. Whatever the story is, let me know it, and not be treated as a child that is without courage or sense.

FINTAN. It's long till I'll come out from my cleft again, and getting no peace or quiet on the ridge of the earth. It is laid down by the stars that cannot lie, that on this day twelvemonth, you yourself will be ate and devoured by a scaly Green Dragon from the North!

Curtain.

ACT II

SCENE. *The Same*. PRINCESS *and* NURSE.

NURSE. Cheer up now, my honey bird, and don't be fretting.

PRINCESS. It is not easy to quit fretting, and the terrible story you are after telling me of all that is before and all that is behind me.

227

NURSE. They had no right at all to go make you aware of it. The Queen has too much talk. An unlucky stepmother she is to you!

PRINCESS. It is well for me she is here. It is well I am told the truth, where the whole of you were treating me like a child without sense, so giddy I was and contrary, and petted and humoured by the whole of you. What memory would there be left of me and my little life gone by, but of a headstrong, unruly child with no thought but for myself.

NURSE. No, but the best in the world you are; there is no one seeing you pass by but would love you.

PRINCESS. That is not so. I was wild and taking my own way, mocking and humbugging.

NURSE. I never will give in that there is no way to save you from that Dragon that is foretold to be your destruction. I would give the four divisions of the world, and Ireland along with them, if I could see you pelting your ball in at the window the same as an hour ago!

PRINCESS. Maybe you will, so long as it will hurt nobody.

NURSE. Ah, sure it's no wonder there to be the tracks of tears upon your face, and that great terror before you.

PRINCESS. I will wipe them away! I will not give in to danger or to dragons! No one will see a dark face on me. I am a king's daughter of Ireland, I did not come out of a herd's hut like Deirdre that went sighing and lamenting till she was put to death, the world being sick and tired of her complaints, and her finger at her eye dripping tears!

NURSE. That's right, now. You had always great courage.

PRINCESS. There is like a change within me. You never will hear a cross word from me again. I would wish to be pleasant and peaceable until such time . . .

(*Puts handkerchief to eyes and goes.*)

DALL GLIC (*coming in*). The King is greatly put out with all he went through, and the way the passion rose in him a while ago.

NURSE. That he may be twenty times worse before he is better! Showing such fury towards the innocent child the way he did!

DALL GLIC. The Queen has brought him to the grass plot for to give him his exercise, walking his seven steps east and west.

NURSE. Hasn't she great power over him to make him do that much?

DALL GLIC. I tell you I am in dread of her myself. Some plan she has for making my two eyes equal. I vexed her someway, and she got queer and humpy, and put a lip on herself, and said she would take me in hand. I declare I never will have a minute's ease thinking of it.

NURSE. The King should have done his seven steps, for I hear her coming.

(DALL GLIC *goes to recess of window.*)

QUEEN (*coming in*). Did you, Nurse, ever at any time turn and dress a dinner?

NURSE (*very stiff*). Indeed I never did. Any house I ever was in there was a good kitchen and well attended, the Lord be praised!

QUEEN. Ah, but just to be kind and to oblige the King.

NURSE. 'Troth, the same King will wait long till he'll see any dish I will ready for him! I am not one that was reared between the flags and the oven in the corner of the one room! To be a nurse to King's children is my trade, and not to go stirring mashes, for hens or for humans!

QUEEN. I heard a crafty woman lay down one time there was no way to hold a man, only by food and flattery.

NURSE. Sure any mother of children walking the road could tell you that much.

QUEEN. I went maybe too far urging him not to lessen so much food the way he did. I only thought to befriend him. But now he is someway upset and nothing will rightly smooth him but to be thinking upon his next meal; and what it will be I don't know, unless the berries of the bush.

DALL GLIC (*leaning out of the window*). Here! Hi! Come this way!

QUEEN. Who are you calling to?

DALL GLIC. It is someone with the appearance of a cook.

QUEEN. Are you saying it is a cook? That now will put the King in great humour!

(MANUS *appears at the window.*)

NURSE (*looking at him*). I wouldn't hardly think he'd suit. He has a sort of innocent look. I wouldn't say him to be a country lad. I don't know is he fitted to go readying meals for a royal family, and the King so wrathful if they do not please him as he is. And as to the Princess Nu! There to be the size of a hayseed of fat overhead on her broth, she'd fall in a dead faint.

MANUS. I'll go on so.

QUEEN. No, no. Bring him in till I'll take a look at him!

MANUS (*coming inside*). I am a lad in search of a master.

MANUS (*inside*). I am a lad in search of a master.

QUEEN. And I myself that am wanting a cook.

MANUS. I got word of that and I going the road.

QUEEN. You would seem to be but a young lad.

MANUS. I am not very far in age to-day. But I'll be a day older to-morrow.

QUEEN. In what country were you born and reared?

MANUS. I came from over, and I am coming hither.

QUEEN. What wages now would you be asking?

MANUS. Nothing at all unless what you think I will have earned at the time I will be leaving your service.

QUEEN. That is very right and fair. I hope you will not be asking too much help. The last cook had a whole fleet of scullions that were no use but to chatter and consume.

MANUS. I am asking no help at all but the help of the ten I bring with me.

(*Holds up fingers.*)

QUEEN. That will be a great saving in the house! Can I depend upon you now not to be turning to your own use the King's ale and his wine?

MANUS. If you take me to be a thief I will go upon my road. It was no easier for me to come than to go out again.

QUEEN (*holding him*). No, now, don't be so proud and thinking so much of yourself. If I give you trial here I would wish you to be ready to turn your hand to this and that, and not be saying it is or is not your business.

MANUS. My business is to do as the King wishes.

QUEEN. That's right. That is the way the servants were in the palace of the King of Alban.

MANUS. That's the way I was myself in the King's house of Sorcha.

QUEEN. Are you saying it is from that place you are come? Sure that should be a great household! The King of Sorcha, they were telling me, has seven castles on land and seven on the sea, and provision for a year and a day in every one of them.

MANUS. That might be. I never was in more than one of them at the one time.

QUEEN. Anyone that has been in that place would surely be fitting here. Keep him, Nurse! Don't let him make away from us till I will go call the King!

(*Goes out.*)

NURSE. Sure it was I myself that fostered the young King of Sorcha and reared him in my lap! What way is he at all? My lovely child! Give me news of him!

230

MANUS. I will do that . . .

NURSE. To hear of him would delight me!

MANUS. It is I that can tell you. . . .

NURSE. It is himself should be a grand king!

MANUS. Listen till you hear! . . .

NURSE. His father was good and his mother was good, and it's likely, himself will be the best of all!

MANUS. Be quiet now and hearken! . . .

NURSE. I remember well the first day I saw him in the cradle, two and a score of years back! Oh! it is glad, and very glad, I'll be to get word of him!

MANUS. He is come to sensible years. . . .

NURSE. A golden cradle it was and it standing on four golden balls the very round of the sun!

MANUS. He is out of his cradle now. (*Shakes her shoulder.*) Let you hearken! He is in need of your help.

NURSE. He'll get it, he'll get it. I doted down on that child! The best to laugh and to roar!

MANUS (*putting hand on her mouth*). Will you be silent, you hag of a nurse? Can't you see that I myself am Manus, the new King of Sorcha?

NURSE (*starting back*). Do you say that? And how's every bit of you? Sure I'd know you in any place. Stand back till I'll get the full of my eyes of you! Like the father you are, and you need never be sorry to be that! Well, I said to myself and you looking in at the window, I would not believe but there's some drop of kings' blood in that lad!

MANUS. That was not what you said to me!

NURSE. And wasn't the journey long on you from Sorcha, that is at the rising of the sun? Is it your foot-soldiers and your bullies you brought with you, or did you come with your hound and your deer-hound and with your horn?

MANUS. There was no one knew of my journey. I came bare alone. I threw a shell in the sea and made a boat of it, and took the track of the wild duck across the mountains of the waves.

NURSE. And where in the world wide did you get that dress of a cook?

MANUS. It was at a tailor's place near Oughtmana. There was no one in the house but the mother. I left my own clothes in her charge and my purse of gold; I brought nothing but my own blue sword. (*Throws open blouse and shows it.*) She gave me this suit, where a cook from this house had thrown it down in payment for a drink of milk. I have no mind any person should know I am a king. I am letting on to be a cook.

NURSE. I would sooner you to come as a champion seeking battle, or a horseman that had gone astray, or so far as a poet making praises or curses according to his treatment on the road. It would be a bad day I would see your father's son taken for a kitchen boy.

MANUS. I was through the world last night in a dream. It was dreamed to me that the King's daughter in this house is in a great danger.

NURSE. So she is, at the end of a twelve-month.

MANUS. My warning was for this day. Seeing her under trouble in my dream, my heart was hot to come to her help. I am here to save her, to meet every troublesome thing that will come at her.

NURSE. Oh, my heavy blessing on you doing that!

MANUS. I was not willing to come as a king, that she would feel tied and bound to live for if I live, or to die with if I should die. I am come as a poor unknown man, that may slip away after the fight, to my own kingdom or across the borders of the world, and no thanks given him and no more about him, but a memory of the shadow of a cook!

NURSE. I would not think that to be right, and you the last of your race. It is best for you to tell the King.

MANUS. I lay my orders on you to tell no one at all.

NURSE. Give me leave but to *whisper* it to the Princess Nu. It's ye would be the finest two the world ever saw. You will not find her equal in all Ireland!

MANUS. I lay it as crosses and as spells on you to say no word to her or to any other that will make known my race or my name. Give me now your oath.

NURSE (*kneeling*). I do, I do. But they will know you by your high looks.

MANUS. Did you yourself know me a while ago?

NURSE (*getting up*). Oh, they're coming! Oh, my poor child, what way will you that never handled a spit be able to make out a dinner for the King?

MANUS. This silver whistle, that was her pipe of music, was given to me by a queen among the Sidhe that is my godmother. At the sound of it there will come through the air any earthly thing I wish for, at my command.

NURSE. Let it be a dinner so.

MANUS. So it will come, on a green tablecloth carried by four

232

swans as white as snow. The freshest of every meat, the oldest of every drink, nuts from the trees in Adam's Paradise!

(KING, QUEEN, PRINCESS, DALL GLIC *come in.* PRINCESS *sits on window sill.*)

QUEEN (*to* KING). Here now, my dear. Wasn't I telling you I would take all trouble from your mind, and that I would not be without finding a cook for you?

KING. He came in a good hour. The want of a right dinner has downed kingdoms before this.

QUEEN. Travelling he is in search of service from the kings of the earth. His wages are in no way out of measure.

KING. Is he a good hand at his trade?

QUEEN. Honest he is, I believe, and ready to give a hand here and there.

KING. What way does he handle flesh, I'd wish to know? And all that comes up from the tide? Bream, now; that is a fish is very pleasant to me—stewed or fried with butter till the bones of it melt in your mouth. There is nothing in sea or strand but is the better of a quality cook—only oysters, that are best left alone, being as they are all gravy and fat.

QUEEN. I didn't question him yet about cookery.

KING. It's seldom I met a woman with right respect for food, but for show and silly dishes and trash that would leave you in the finish as dwindled as a badger on St. Bridget's day.

QUEEN. If this youth of a young man was able to give satisfaction at the King of Sorcha's Court, I am sure that he will make a dinner to please yourself.

MANUS. I will do more than that. I will dress a dinner that will please *my*self.

PRINCESS (*clapping hands*). Very well said!

KING. Sound out now some good dishes such as you used to be giving in Sorcha, and the Queen will put them down in a line of writing, that I can be thinking about them till such time as you will have them readied.

QUEEN. There are sheeps' trotters below; you might know some tasty way to dress them.

MANUS. I do surely. I'll put the trotters within a fowl, and the fowl within a goose, and the goose in a suckling pig, and the suckling pig in a fat lamb, and the lamb in a calf, and the calf in a Maderalla. . .

KING. What now is a Maderalla?

MANUS. He is a beast that saves the cook trouble, swallowing all those meats one after another—in Sorcha.

KING. That should be a very pretty dish. Let you go make a start with it the way we will not be famished before nightfall. Bring him, Dall Glic, to the larder.

DALL GLIC. I'm in dread it's as good for him to stop where he is.

KING. What are you saying?

DALL GLIC. Those lads of apprentices that left nothing in it only bare hooks.

NURSE. It is the Queen would give no leave for more provision to come in, saying there was no one to prepare it.

MANUS. If that is so, I will be forced to lay my orders on the Hawk of the Grey Rock and the Brown Otter of the Stream to bring in meat at my bidding.

KING. Hurry on so.

QUEEN. I myself will go and give you instructions what way to use the kitchen.

MANUS. Not at all! What I do I'd as lief do in your own royal parlour! (*Blows whistle; two dark-skinned men come in with vessels.*) Give me here those pots and pans!

QUEEN. What now is about to take place?

DALL GLIC. I not to be blind, I would say those to be very foreign-looking men.

KING. It would seem as if the world was grown to be very queer.

QUEEN. So it is, and the mastery being given to a cook.

MANUS. So it should be too! It is the King of Shades and Shadows would have rule over the world if it wasn't for the cooks!

KING. There's some sense in that now.

(*Strange men are moving and arranging baskets and vessels.*)

MANUS. There was respect for cooks in the early days of the world. What way did the Sons of Tuireann get their death but going questing after a cooking spit at the bidding of Lugh of the Long Hand! And if a spit was worthy of the death of heroes, what should the man be worth that is skilled in turning it? What is the difference between man and beast? Beast and bird devour what they find and have no power to change it. But we are Druids of those mysteries, having magic and virtue to turn hard grain to tender cakes, and the very skin of a grunting pig to crackling causing quarrels among champions, and it singing upon the coals. A cook! If I am I am not without good generations before me! Who was the first old father of us, roasting and reddening the fruits of the earth from hard to soft, from bitter to kind, till they are fit for

234

a lady's platter? What is it leaves us in the hard cold of Christmas but the robbery from earth of warmth for the kitchen fire of (*takes off cap*) the first and foremost of all master cooks—the Sun!

PRINCESS. You are surely not ashamed of your trade!

MANUS. To work now, to work. I'll engage to turn out a dinner fit for Pharaoh of Egypt or Pharamond King of the Franks! Here, Queen, is a silver-breast phœnix—draw out the feathers—they are pure silver—fair and clean. (QUEEN *plucks eagerly*.) King, take your golden sceptre and stir this pot.

(*Gives him one.*)

KING (*interested*). What now is in it?

MANUS. A broth that will rise over the side and be consumed and spilt if you stop stirring it for one minute only! (KING *stirs furiously*.) Princess (*She is looking on and he goes over to her.*) there are honey cakes to roll out, but I will not ask you to do it in dread that you might spoil the whiteness . . .

PRINCESS. I have no mind to do it.

MANUS. Of the flour!

PRINCESS. Give them here.

(*Rolls them out indignantly.*)

MANUS. That is right. Take care, King, would the froth swell over the brim.

PRINCESS. It seems to me you are doing but little yourself.

MANUS. I will turn now and . . . . boil these eggs.

(*Takes some on a plate; they roll off.*)

PRINCESS. You have broken them.

MANUS (*disconcerted*). It was to show you a good trick, how to make them sit up on the narrow end.

PRINCESS. That is an old trick in the world.

MANUS. Every trick is an old one, but with a change of players, a change of dress, it comes out as new as before. Princess (*speaks low*), I have a message to give you and a pardon to ask.

PRINCESS. Give me out the message.

MANUS. Take courage and keep courage through this day. Do not let your heart fail. There is help beside you.

PRINCESS. It has been a troublesome day indeed. But there is a worse one and a great danger before me in the far away.

MANUS. That danger will come to-day, the message said in the dream. Princess, I have a pardon to ask you. I have been playing vanities. I think I have wronged you doing this. It was surely through no want of respect.

GATEKEEPER (*coming in*). There is word come from Ballyvelehan

235

there is a coach and horses facing for this place over from Ought-mana.

QUEEN. Who would that be?

GATEKEEPER. Up on the hill a woman was, brought word it must be some high gentleman. She could see all colours in the coach, and flowers on the horse's heads.

(*Goes out.*)

DALL GLIC. That is good hearing. I was in dread some man we would have no welcome for would be the first to come in this day.

QUEEN. Not a fear of it. I had orders given to the Gateman who he would and would not keep out. I did that the very minute after the King making his proclamation and his law.

KING. Pup, pup. You need not be drawing that down.

QUEEN. It is well you have myself to care you and to turn all to good. I gave orders to the Gateman, I say, no one to be let in to the door unless carriage company, no other ones, even if they should wipe their feet upon the mat. I notched that in his mind, telling him the King was after promising the Princess Nu in marriage to the first man that would come into the house.

MANUS. The King gave out that word?

QUEEN. I am after saying that he did.

DALL GLIC. Come along, lad. Don't be putting ears on yourself.

MANUS. I ask the King did he give out that promise as the Queen says?

KING. I have but a poor memory.

NURSE. The King did say it within the hour, and swore to it by the oath of his people, taking contracts of the sun and moon of the air!

DALL GLIC. What is it to you if he did? Come on, now.

MANUS. No. This is a matter that concerns myself.

QUEEN. How do you make that out?

MANUS. You, that called me in, know well that I was the first to come into the house.

QUEEN. Ha, ha! You have the impudence! It is a *man* the King said. He was not talking about cooks.

MANUS (*to the* KING). I am before you as a serving lad, and you are a King in Ireland. Because you are a King and I your hired servant you will not refuse me justice. You gave your word.

KING. If I did it was in haste and in vexation, and striving to save her from destruction.

MANUS. I call you to keep to your word and to give your daughter to no other one.

QUEEN. Speak out now, Dall Glic, and give your opinion and your advice.

DALL GLIC. I would say that this lad going away would be no great loss.

MANUS. I did not ask such a thing, but as it has come to me I will hold to my right.

QUEEN. It would be right to throw him to the hounds in the kennel!

MANUS (*to* KING). I leave it to the judgment of your blind wise man.

QUEEN (*to* DALL GLIC). Take care would you offend myself or the King!

MANUS. I put it on you to split justice as it is measured outside the world.

DALL GLIC. It is hard for me to speak. He has laid it hard on me. My good eye may go asleep, but my blind eye never sleeps. In the place where it is waking, an honourable man, king or beggar, is held to his word.

KING. Is it that I must give my daughter to a lad that owns neither clod nor furrow? Whose estate is but a shovel for the ashes and a tongs for the red coals.

QUEEN. It is likely he is urged by the sting of greed—it is but riches he is looking for.

KING. I will not begrudge him his own asking of silver and of gold!

MANUS. Throw it out to the beggars on the road! I would not take a copper half-penny! I'll take nothing but what has come to me from your own word!

(KING *bows his head.*)

PRINCESS (*coming forword*). Then this battle is not between you and an old king that is feeble, but between yourself and myself.

MANUS. I am sorry, Princess, if it must be a battle.

PRINCESS. You can never bring me away against my will.

MANUS. I said no word of doing that.

PRINCESS. You think, so, I will go with you of myself? The day I will do that will be the day you empty the ocean!

MANUS. I will not wait longer than to-day.

PRINCESS. Many a man waited seven years for a king's daughter!

MANUS. And another seven—and seven generations of hags. But that is not my nature. I will not kneel to any woman, high or low, or crave kindness that she cannot give.

PRINCESS. Then I can go free!

MANUS. For this day I take you in my charge. I cross and claim you to myself, unless a better man will come.

PRINCESS. I would think it easier to find a better man than one that would be worse to me!

MANUS. If one should come that you think to be a better man, I will give you your own way.

PRINCESS. It is you being in the world at all that is my grief.

MANUS. Time makes all things clear. You did not go far out in the world yet, my poor little Princess.

PRINCESS. I would be well pleased to drive you out through the same world!

MANUS. With or without your goodwill, I will not go out of this place till I have carried out the business I came to do.

DALL GLIC. Is it the falling of hailstones I hear or the rumbling of thunder, or is it the trots of horses upon the road?

QUEEN (*looking out*). It is the big man that is coming—Prince or Lord or whoever he may be. (*To* DALL GLIC.) Go now to the door to welcome him. This is some man worth while. (*To* MANUS.) Let you get out of this.

MANUS. No, whoever he is I'll stop and face him. Let him know we are players in the one game!

KING. And what sort of a fool will you make of me, to have given in to take the like of you for a son-in-law? They will be putting ridicule on me in the songs.

QUEEN. If he must stop here we might put some face on him. . . . If I had but a decent suit. . . . Give me your cloak, Dall Glic. (*He gives it.*) Here now . . . (*To* MANUS.) Put this around you. . . . (MANUS *takes it awkwardly.*) It will cover up your kitchen suit.

MANUS. Is it this way?

QUEEN. You have no right handling of it—stupid clown! This way!

MANUS (*flinging it off*). No, I'll change no more suits! It is time for me to stop fooling and give you what you did not ask yet, my name. I will tell out all the truth.

GATEKEEPER (*at door*). The King of Sorcha! (TAIG *comes in.*)

KING AND QUEEN. The King of Sorcha! (*They rush forward to greet him.*)

NURSE (*To* MANUS). Did ever anyone hear the like!

MANUS. It seems as if there will be a judgment between the man and the clothes!

QUEEN (*To* TAIG). There is someone here that you know, King. This young man is giving out that he was your cook.

TAIG. He was not. I never laid an eye on him till this minute.

QUEEN. I was sure he was nothing but a liar when he said he would tell the truth! Now, King, will you turn him out the door?

KING. And what about the great dinner he has me promised?

MANUS. Be easy King. Whether or no you keep your word to me I'll hold to mine! (*Blows whistle.*) In with the dishes! Take your places! Let the music play out!

(*Music plays, the strange men wheel in tables and dishes.*)

Curtain.

ACT III

SCENE: *Same. Table cleared of all but vessels of fruits, cocoa-nuts, etc.* QUEEN *and* TAIG *sitting in front,* NURSE *and* DALL GLIC *standing in background.*

QUEEN. Now, King, the dinner being at an end, and the music, we have time and quiet to be talking.

TAIG. It is with the King's daughter I am come to talk.

QUEEN. Go, Dall Glic, call the Princess. She will be here on the minute, but it is best for you to tell me out if it is to ask her in marriage you are come.

TAIG. It is so, where I was after being told she would be given as a wife to the first man that would come into the house.

QUEEN. And who in the world wide gave that out?

TAIG. It was the Gateman said it to a hawker bringing lobsters from the strand, and that got no leave to cross the threshold by reason of the oath given out by the King. The half of the kingdom she will get, they were telling me, and the king living, and the whole of it after he will be dead.

NURSE. There did another come in before you. Let me tell you that much!

TAIG. There did not. The lobster man that set a watch upon the door.

QUEEN. A great honour you did us, coming asking for her, and you being King of Sorcha!

TAIG. Look at my ring and my crown. They will bear witness that I am. And my kind coat of cotton and my golden shirt! And under that again there's a stiff pocket. (*Slaps it.*) Is there e'er a looking-glass in any place? (*Gets up.*)

DALL GLIC. There is the shining silver basin of the swans in the garden without.

TAIG. That will do. I would wish to look tasty when I come looking for a lady of a wife. (*He and* DALL GLIC *go outside window but in sight.*)

(PRINCESS *comes in very proud and sad.*)

QUEEN. You should be proud this day, Nuala, and so grand a man coming asking you in marriage as the King of Sorcha.

NURSE. Grand, indeed! As grand as hands and pins can make him.

PRINCESS. Are you not satisfied to have urged me to one man and promised me to another since sunrise?

QUEEN. What way could I know there was this match on the way, and a better match beyond measure? This is no black stranger going the road, but a man having a copper crown over his gateway and a silver crown over his palace door! I tell you he has means to hang a pearl of gold upon every rib of your hair! There is no one ahead of him in all Ireland, with his chain and his ring and his suit of the dearest silk!

PRINCESS. If it was a suit I was to wed with he might do well enough.

QUEEN. Equal in blood to ourselves! Brought up to good behaviour and courage and mannerly ways.

PRINCESS. In my opinion he is not.

QUEEN. You are talking foolishness. A King of Sorcha must be mannerly, seeing it is he himself sets the tune for manners.

PRINCESS. He gave out a laugh when old Michelin slipped on the threshold. He kicked at the dog under the table that came looking for bones.

QUEEN. I tell you what might be ugly behaviour in a common man is suitable and right in a king. But you are so hard to please and so pettish, I am seven times tired of yourself and your ways.

PRINCESS. If no one could force me to give in to the man that made a claim to me to-day, according to my father's bond, that bond is there yet to protect me from any other one.

QUEEN. Leave me alone! Myself and the Dall Glic will take means to rid you of that lad from the oven. I'll send in now to you the King of Sorcha. Let you show civility to him, and the wedding-day will be to-morrow.

PRINCESS. I will not see him, I will have nothing to do with him; I tell you if he had the rents of the whole world I would not go with him by day or by night, on foot or on horseback, in light or in darkness, in company or alone!

(QUEEN *has gone while she cries this out.*)

NURSE. The luck of the seven Saturdays on himself and on the Queen!

PRINCESS. Oh, Muime, do not let him come near me! Have you no way to help me?

NURSE. It's myself that could help you if I was not under bonds not to speak!

PRINCESS. What is it you know? Why won't you say one word?

NURSE. He put me under spells. . . . There now, my tongue turned with the word to be dumb.

TAIG (*at the window*). Not a fear of me, Queen. It won't be long till I bring the Princess around.

PRINCESS. I will not stay! Keep him here till I will hide myself out of sight! (*Goes.*)

TAIG (*coming in*). They told me the Princess was in it.

NURSE. She has good sense, she is in some other place.

TAIG (*sitting down*). Go call her to me.

NURSE. Who is it I will call her for?

TAIG. For myself. You know who I am.

NURSE. My grief that I do not!

TAIG. I am the King of Sorcha.

NURSE. If you say that lie again there will blisters rise up on your face.

TAIG. Take care what you are saying, you hag!

NURSE. I know well what I am saying. I have good judgment between the noble and the mean blood of the world.

TAIG. The Kings of Sorcha have high, noble blood.

NURSE. If they have, there is not so much of it in you as would redden a rib of scutch-grass.

TAIG. You are crazed with folly and age.

NURSE. No, but I have my wits good enough. You ought to be as slippery as a living eel, I'll get satisfaction on you yet! I'll show out who you are!

TAIG. Who am I so?

NURSE. That is what I have to get knowledge of, if I must ask it at the mouth of cold hell!

TAIG. Do your best! I dare you!

NURSE. I will save my darling from you as sure as there's rocks on the strand! A girl that refused sons of the kings of the world!

TAIG. And I will drag your darling from you as sure as there's foxes in Oughtmana!

NURSE. Oughtmana . . . Is that now your living place?

TAIG. It is not. . . . I told you I came from the far-off kingdom of Sorcha. Look at my cloak that has on it the sign of the risen sun!

NURSE. Cloaks and suits and fringes. You have a great deal of talk of them. . . . Have you e'er a needle around you, or a shears?

TAIG (*his hand goes to breast of coat, but he withdraws it quickly*). Here . . . no . . . What are you talking about? I know nothing at all of such things.

NURSE. In my opinion you do. Hearken now. I know where is the real King of Sorcha!

TAIG. Bring him before me now till I'll down him!

NURSE. Say that the time you will come face to face with him! Well, I'm under bonds to tell out nothing about him, but I have liberty to make known all I will find out about yourself.

TAIG. Hurry on so. Little I care when once I'm wed with the King's daughter!

NURSE. That will never be!

TAIG. The Queen is befriending me and in dread of losing me. I will threaten her if there is any delay I'll go look for another girl of a wife.

NURSE. I will make no delay. I'll have my story and my testimony before the white dawn of the morrow.

TAIG. Do so and welcome! Before the yellow light of this evening I'll be the King's son-in-law! Bring your news, then, and little thanks you'll get for it! The King and Queen must keep up my name then for their own credit's sake. (*Makes a face at her as* KING *comes in with* DALL GLIC, *and servants with cushions.* NURSE *goes out, shaking her fist.*) (*Rises.*) I was just asking to see you, King, to say there is a hurry on me. . . .

KING (*sitting down on window seat while* SERVANT *arranges cushions about him.*) Keep your business a while. It's a poor thing to be going through business the very minute the dinner is ended.

TAIG. I wouldn't but that it is pressing.

KING. Go now to the Queen, in her parlour, and be chatting and whistling to the birds. I give you my word since I rose up from the table I am going here and there, up and down, craving and striving to find a place where I'll get leave to lay my head on the cushions for one little minute.

(TAIG *goes reluctantly.*)

DALL GLIC (*taking cushions from servants*). Let you go now and leave the King to his rest.

(*They go out.*)

KING. I don't know in the world why anyone would consent to be a king, and never to be left to himself, but to be worried and wearied and interfered with from dark to daybreak and from morning to the fall of night.

DALL GLIC. I will be going out now. I have but one word only to say . . .

KING. Let it be a short word! I would be better pleased to hear the sound of breezes in the sycamores, and the humming of bees in the hive and the crooning and sleepy sounds of the sea!

DALL GLIC. There is one thing only could cause me to annoy you.

KING. It should be a queer big thing that wouldn't wait till I have my rest taken.

DALL GLIC. So it is a big matter, and a weighty one.

KING. Not to be left in quiet and all I am after using! Food that was easy to eat! Drink that was easy to drink! That's the dinner that *was* a dinner. That cook now is a wonder!

DALL GLIC. That is now the very one I am wishful to speak about.

KING. I give you my word, I'd sooner have one goose dressed by him than seven dressed by any other one!

DALL GLIC. The Queen that was urging me for to put my mind to make out some way to get quit of him.

KING. Isn't it a hard thing the very minute I find a lad can dress a dinner to my liking, I must be made an attack on to get quit of him?

DALL GLIC. It is on the head of the Princess Nu.

KING. Tell me this, Dall Glic. Supposing, now, he was . . . in spite of me . . . to wed with her . . . against my will . . . and it might be unknownst to me.

DALL GLIC. Such a thing must not happen.

KING. To be sure, it must not happen. Why would it happen? But supposing—I only said supposing it did. Would you say would that lad grow too high in himself to go into the kitchen . . . it might be only an odd time . . . to oblige me . . . and dress a dinner the same as he did to-day?

243

DALL GLIC. I am sure and certain that he would not. It is the way, it is, with the common sort, the lower orders. He'd be wishful to sit on a chair at his ease and to leave his hand idle till he'd grow to be bulky and wishful for sleep.

KING. That is a pity, a great pity, and a great loss to the world. A big misfortune he to have got it in his head to take a liking to the girl. I tell you he was a great lad behind the saucepans!

DALL GLIC. Since he did get it in his head, it is what we have to do now, to make an end of him.

KING. To gaol him now, and settle up ovens and spits and all sorts in the cell, wouldn't he, to shorten the day, be apt to start cooking?

DALL GLIC. In my belief he will do nothing at all, but to hold you to the promise you made, and to force you to send away the King of Sorcha.

KING. To have the misfortune of a cook for a son-in-law, and without the good luck of profiting by what he can do in his trade! That is a hard thing for a father to put up with, let alone a king!

DALL GLIC. If you will but listen to the advice I have to give . . .

KING. I know it without you telling me. You are asking me to make away with the lad! And who knows but the girl might turn on me after, women are so queer, and say I had a right to have asked leave from herself?

DALL GLIC. There will be no one suspect you of doing it, and you to take my plan. Bid them heat the big oven outside on the lawn that is for roasting a bullock in its full bulk.

KING. Don't be talking of roasted meat! I think I can eat no more for a twelvemonth!

DALL GLIC. There will be nothing roasted that any person will have occasion to eat. When the oven door will be open, give orders to your bullies and your foot-soldiers to give a tip to him that will push him in. When evening comes, news will go out that he left the meat to burn and made off on his rambles, and no more about him.

KING. What way can I send orders when I'm near crazed in my wits with the want of rest. A little minute of sleep might soothe and settle my brain.

(*Lies down.*)

DALL GLIC. The least little word to give leave . . . or a sign . . . such as to nod the head.

KING. I give you my word, my head is tired nodding! Be off now and close the door after you and give out that anyone that comes to this side of the house at all in the next half-hour, his neck will be on the block before morning!

DALL GLIC (*hurriedly*). I'm going! I'm going.

(*Goes.*)

KING (*locking door and drawing window curtains*). That you may never come back till I ask you! (*Lies down and settles himself on pillows.*) I'll be lying here in my lone listening to the pigeons seeking their meal. "Coo-coo," they're saying, "Coo-coo."

(*Closes eyes.*)

NURSE (*at door*). Who is it locked the door? (*Shakes it.*) Who is it is in it? What is going on within? Is it that some bad work is after being done in this place? Hi! Hi! Hi!

KING (*sitting up*). Get away out of that, you torment of a nurse! Be off before I'll have the life of you!

NURSE. The Lord be praised, it is the King's own voice! There's time yet!

KING. There's time, is there? There's time for everyone to give out their chat and their gab, and to do their business and take their ease and have a comfortable life, only the King! The beasts of the field have leave to lay themselves down in the meadow and to stretch their limbs on the green grass in the heat of the day, without being pestered and plagued and tormented and called to and wakened and worried, till a man is no less than wore out!

NURSE. Up or down, I'll say what I have to say, if it costs me my life. It is that I have to tell you of a plot that is made and a plan!

KING. I won't listen! I heard enough of plots and plans within the last three minutes!

NURSE. You didn't hear this one. No one knows of it only myself.

KING. I was told it by the Dall Glic.

NURSE. You were not! I am only after making it out on the moment!

KING. A plot against the lad of the saucepans?

NURSE. That's it! That's it! Open now the door!

KING (*putting a cushion over each ear and settling himself to sleep*). Tell away and welcome!

(*Shuts eyes.*)

NURSE. That's right! You're listening. Give heed now. That schemer came a while ago letting on to be the King of Sorcha is no such thing! What do you say? . . . Maybe you knew it before? I wonder the Dall Glic not to have seen that for himself with his one eye. . . . Maybe you don't believe it? Well, I'll tell it out and prove it. I have got sure word by running messenger that came cross-cutting over the ridge of the hill. . . . That carrion that came in a coach, pressing to bring away the Princess before nightfall, giving himself out to be some great one, is no other than Taig the Tailor, that should be called Taig the Twister, down from his mother's house from Oughtmana, that stole grand clothes which were left in the mother's charge, he being out at the time cutting cloth and shaping lies, and has himself dressed out in them the way you'd take him to be King! (KING *has slumbered peacefully all through.*) Now, what do you say? Now, will you open the door?

QUEEN (*outside*). What call have you to shouting and disturbing the King?

NURSE. I have good right and good reason to disturb him!

QUEEN. Go away and let me open the door.

NURSE. I will go and welcome now; I have told out my whole story to the King.

QUEEN (*shaking door*). Open the door, my dear! It is I myself that is here! (KING *looks up, listens, shakes his head and sinks back.*) Are you there at all, or what is it ails you?

NURSE. He is there, and is after conversing with myself.

QUEEN (*shaking again*). Let me in, my dear King! Open! Open! Open! unless that the falling sickness is come upon you, or that you are maybe lying dead upon the floor!

NURSE. Not a dead in the world.

QUEEN. Go, Nurse, I tell you, bring the smith from the anvil till he will break asunder the lock of the door!

(KING, *annoyed, waddles to door and opens it suddenly.* QUEEN *stumbles in.*)

KING. What at all has taken place that you come bawling and disturbing my rest?

QUEEN. Oh! Are you sound and well? I was in dread there did something come upon you, when you gave no answer at all.

KING. Am I bound to answer every call and clamour the same as a hall-porter at the door?

QUEEN. It is business that cannot wait. Here now is a request I have written to the bully of the King of Alban, bidding him to strike the head off whatever man will put the letter in his hand. Write your name and sign to it, in three royal words.

KING. I wouldn't sign a letter out of my right hour if it was to make the rivers run gold. There is nothing comes of signing letters but more trouble in the end.

QUEEN. Give me, so, to bind it a drop of your own blood as a token and a seal. You will not refuse, and I telling you the messenger, will go with it, and that will lose his head through it, is no less than that troublesome cook!

KING (*with a roar*). Anyone to say that word again I will not leave a head on any neck in the kingdom! I declare on my oath it would be best for me to take the world for my pillow and put that lad upon the throne!

(QUEEN *goes back frightened to door.*)

GATEMAN (*coming in*). There is a man coming in that will take no denial. It is Fintan the Astrologer.

(FINTAN *enters with* DALL GLIC, NURSE, PRINCESS, TAIG, MANUS *and* PRINCE OF THE MARSHES *crowding after him.*)

KING. Another disturbance! The whole world would seem to be on the move!

QUEEN. Fintan! What brings him here again?

FINTAN. A great deceit! A terrible deception!

KING. What at all is it?

FINTAN. Long and all as I'm in the world, such a thing never happened in my lifetime!

QUEEN. What is it has happened?

FINTAN. It is not any fault of myself or any miscounting of my own! I am certain sure of that much. Is it that the stars of heaven are gone astray, they that are all one with a clock—unless it might be on a stormy night when they are wild-looking around the moon.

KING. Go on with your story and stop your raving.

FINTAN. The first time ever I came to this place I made a prophecy.

DALL GLIC. You did, about the child was in the cradle.

FINTAN. And that was but new in the world. It is what I said, that she was born under a certain star, and that in a score of years all but two, whatever acting was going on in that star at the time she was born, she would get her crosses in the same way.

DALL GLIC. The cross you foretold to her was to be ate by a Dragon. You laid down it would come upon a twelvemonth from this very day.

FINTAN. That's it. That was according to my reckoning. There was no mistake in that. And I thought better of the Seven Stars than they make a fool of me, after all the respect I had showed them, giving my life to watching themselves and the plans they have laid down for men and for mortals.

KING. It seems as if I myself was the best prophet and that there is no Dragon at all.

FINTAN. What a bad opinion you have of me that I would be so far out as that! It would be a deception and a disappointment out of measure, there to come no Dragon, and I after foretelling and prophesying him.

KING. Troth, it would be no disappointment at all to ourselves.

FINTAN. It would be better, I tell you, a score of king's daughters to be ate and devoured, than the high stars in their courses to be proved wrong. But it must be right, it surely must be right. I gave the prophecy according to her birth hour, that was one hour before the falling back of the sun.

DALL GLIC. It was not, but an hour before the rising of the sun.

FINTAN. Not at all! It was the Nurse herself told me it was at evening she was born.

QUEEN. There is the Nurse now. Let you ask her account.

FINTAN (*to* NURSE). It was yourself laid down it was evening!

NURSE. Sure I wasn't in the place at all till Samhuin time, when she was near three months in the world.

FINTAN. Then it was some other hag the very spit of you! I wish she didn't tell a lie.

NURSE. Sure that one was banished out of this on the head of telling lies. An hour ere sunrise, and before the crowing of the cocks. The Dall Glic will tell you that much.

DALL GLIC. That is so. I have it marked upon the genealogies in the chest.

FINTAN. That is great news! It was a heavy wrong was done me! It had me greatly upset. Twelve hours out in laying down the birthtime! That clears the character of myself and of the carwheel of the stars. I knew I could make no mistake in my office and in my billet!

KING. Will you stop praising yourself and give out some sense?

FINTAN. Knowledge is surely the greatest thing in the world! And truth! Twelve hours with the planets is equal to twelve months on earth. I am well satisfied now.

QUEEN. So the Dragon is not coming, and the girl is in no danger at all?

FINTAN. Not coming! Heaven help your poor head! Didn't I get word within the last half-hour he is after leaving his den in the Kingdoms of the Cold, and is at this minute ploughing his way to Ireland, the same as I foretold him, but that I made a miscount of a year?

NURSE (*putting her arm round* PRINCESS). Och! do not listen or give heed to him at all!

QUEEN. When is he coming so?

248

FINTAN. Amn't I tired telling you this day in the place of this day twelvemonth. But as to the minute, there's too much lies in this place for me to be rightly sure.

KING. The curse of the seven elements upon him!

FINTAN. Little he'll care for your cursing. The whole world wouldn't stop him coming to your own grand gate.

PRINCESS (*coming forward*). Then I am to die to-night?

FINTAN. You are, without he will be turned back by someone having a stronger star than your own, and I know of no star is better, unless it might be the sun.

QUEEN. If you had minded me, and given in to ring the wedding bells, you would be safe out of this before now.

FINTAN. That Dragon not to find her before him, he will ravage and destroy the whole district with the poisonous spittle of his jaw, till the want will be so great the father will disown his son and will not let him in the door. Well, good-bye to ye! Ye'll maybe believe me to have foreknowledge another time, and I proved to be right. I have knocked great comfort out of that!

(*Goes.*)

KING. Oh, my poor child! My poor little Nu! I thought it never would come to pass, I to be sending you to the slaughter. And I too bulky to go out and face him, having led an easy life!

PRINCESS. Do not be fretting.

KING. The world is gone to and fro! I'll never ask satisfaction again either in bed or board, but to be wasting away with watercresses and rising up of a morning before the sun rises in Babylon! (*Weeps.*) Oh, we might make out a way to baffle him yet! Is there no meal will serve him only flesh and blood? Try him with Grecian wine, and with what was left of the big dinner a while ago!

GATEMAN (*coming in*). There is some strange thing in the ocean from Aran out. At first it was but like a bird's shadow on the sea, and now you would nearly say it to be the big island would have left its moorings, and it steering its course towards Aughanish!

DALL GLIC. I'm in dread it should be the Dragon that has cleared the ocean at a leap!

KING (*holding* PRINCESS). I will not give you up! Let him devour myself along with you!

DALL GLIC (*to* PRINCESS). It is best for me to put you in a hiding-hole under the ground, that has seven locked doors and seven locks on the farthest door. It might fail him to make you out.

NURSE. Oh, it would be hard for her to go where she cannot hear the voice of a friend or see the light of day!

PRINCESS. Would you wish me to save myself and let all the district perish? You heard what Fintan said. It is not right for destruction to be put on a whole province, and the women and the children that I know.

QUEEN. There is maybe time yet for you to wed.

PRINCESS. So long as I am living I have a choice. I will not be saved in that way. It is alone I will be in my death.

MANUS (*coming to* KING). I am going out from you, King. I might not be coming in to you again. I would wish to set you free from the promise you made me a while ago, and the bond.

KING. What does it signify now? What does anything signify, and the world turning here and there!

MANUS. And another thing. I would wish to ask pardon of the King's daughter. I ought not to have laid any claim to her, being a stranger in this place and without treasure or attendance. And yet . . . and yet . . . (*stoops and kisses hem of her dress*), she was dear to me. It is a man who never may look on her again is saying that.
(*Turns to door.*)

TAIG. He is going to run from the Dragon! It is kind father for a scullion to be timid!

QUEEN. It is in his blood. He is maybe not to blame for what is according to his nature.

MANUS. That is so. I am doing what is according to my nature.
(*Goes,* NURSE *goes after him.*)

QUEEN (*to* DALL GLIC). Go throw a dishcloth after him that the little lads may be mocking him along the road!

DALL GLIC. I will not. I have meddled enough at your bidding. I am done with living under dread. Let you blind me entirely! I am free of you. It might be best for me the two eyes to be withered, and I seeing nothing but the ever-living laws!

PRINCE OF MARSHES (*coming to* PRINCESS). It is my grief that with all the teachers I had there was not one to learn me the handling of weapons or of arms. But for all that I will not run away, but will strive to strike one blow in your defence against that wicked beast.

PRINCESS. It is a good friend that would rid us of him. But it grieves me that you should go into such danger.

PRINCE OF MARSHES (*to* DALL GLIC). Give me some sword or casting spears.
(DALL GLIC *gives him spears.*)

PRINCESS. I am sorry I made fun of you a while ago. I think you are a good kind man.

PRINCE OF MARSHES (*kissing her hand*). Having that word of praise I will bring a good heart into the fight.

(*Goes.*)

(TAIG *is slipping out after him.*)

QUEEN. See now the King of Sorcha slipping away into the fight. Stop here now! (*Pulls him back.*) You have a life that is precious to many besides yourself. Do not go without being well armed— and with a troop of good fighting men at your back.

TAIG. I am greatly obliged to you. I think I'll be best with myself.

QUEEN. You have no suit or armour upon you.

TAIG. That is what I was thinking.

QUEEN. Here anyway is a sword.

TAIG (*taking it*). That's a nice belt now. Well worked, silver thread and gold.

QUEEN. The King's own guard will go out with you.

TAIG. I wouldn't ask one of them! What would you think of me wanting help! A Dragon! Little I'd think of him. I'll knock the life out of him. I'll give him cruelty!

QUEEN. You have great courage indeed!

TAIG. I'll cut him crossways and lengthways the same as a yard of frieze! I'll make garters of his body! I'll smooth him with a smoothing iron! Not a fear of me! I never lost a bet yet that I wasn't able to pay it!

GATEMAN (*as he rushes in*, TAIG *slips away*). The Dragon! The Dragon! I seen it coming and its mouth open and a fiery flame from it! And nine miles of the sea is dry with all it drank of it! The whole country is gathering the same as of a fair day for to see him devour the Princess.

(PRINCESS *trembles and sinks into a chair.* KING, QUEEN *and* DALL GLIC *look from window. They turn to her as they speak.*)

QUEEN. There is a terrible splashing in the sea! It is like as if the Dragon's tail had beaten it into suds of soap!

DALL GLIC. He is near as big as a whale!

KING. He is, and bigger!

QUEEN. I see him! I see him! He would seem to have seven heads!

DALL GLIC. I see but one.

QUEEN. You would see more if you had your two eyes! He has six heads at the least!

KING. He has but one. He is twisting and turning it around.

DALL GLIC. He is coming up towards the flaggy shore!

KING. I hear him! He is snoring like a flock of pigs!

QUEEN. He is rearing his head in the air! He has teeth as long as a tongs!

DALL GLIC. No, but his tail he is rearing up! It would take a ladder forty feet long to get to the tip of it!

QUEEN. There is the King of Sorcha going out the gate for to make an end of him.

DALL GLIC. So he is, too. That is great bravery.

KING. He is going to one side. He is come to a stop.

DALL GLIC. It seems to me he is ready to fall in his standing. He is gone into a little thicket of furze. He is not coming out, but is lying crouched up in it the same as a hare in a tuft. I can see his shoulders narrowed up.

QUEEN. He maybe got a weakness.

KING. He did, maybe, of courage. Shaking and shivering, he is like a hen in thunder. In my opinion, he is hiding from the fight.

QUEEN. There is the Prince of the Marshes going out now, and his coach after him! And his two aunts sitting in it and screeching to him not to run into danger!

KING. He will not do much. He has not pith or power to handle arms. That sort brings a bad name on kings.

DALL GLIC. He is gone away from the coach. He is facing to the flaggy shore!

QUEEN. Oh, the Dragon has put up his head and is spitting at him!

KING. He has cast a spear into its jaw! Good man!

(PRINCESS *goes over to window.*)

DALL GLIC. He is casting another! His hand shook . . . it did not go straight. He is gone on again! He has cast another spear! It should hit the beast . . . it let a roar!

PRINCESS. Good little Prince! What way is the battle now?

DALL GLIC. It will kill him with its fiery breath! He is running now . . . he is stumbling . . . the Dragon is after him! He is up again! The two Aunts have pushed him into the coach and have closed the iron door.

KING. It will fail the beast to swallow him coach and all. It is gone back to refresh itself in the sea. You can hear it puffing and plunging!

QUEEN. There is nothing to stop it now. (*To* PRINCESS) If you have e'er a prayer, now is the time to say it.

DALL GLIC. Stop a minute . . . there is another champion going out.

KING. A man wearing a saffron suit . . . who is he at all? He has the look of one used to giving orders.

PRINCESS (*looking out*). Oh! he is but going to his death. It would be better for me to throw myself into the tide and make an end of it.

(*Is rushing to door*.)

KING (*holding her*). He is drawing his sword. Himself and the Dragon are thrusting at one another on the flags!

PRINCESS. Oh, close the curtains! Shut out the sound of the battle.

(DALL GLIC *closes curtains*.)

KING. Strike up now a tune of music that will deafen the sound!

(ORCHESTRA *plays*. PRINCESS *is kneeling by* KING. *Music changes from discord to victory.* TWO AUNTS *and* GATEMAN *rush in. Noise of cheering heard without as the* GATEMAN *silences music*.)

GATEMAN. Great news and wonderful news and a great story!

FIRST AUNT. The fight is ended!

SECOND AUNT. The Dragon is brought to his last goal!

GATEMAN. That young fighting man that has him flogged! Made at him like a wave breaking on the strand! They crashed at one another like two days of judgment! Like the battle of the cold with the heat!

FIRST AUNT. You'd say he was going through dragons all his life!

SECOND AUNT. It can hardly put a stir out of itself!

GATEMAN. That champion has it baffled and mastered! It is after being chased over seven acres of ground!

FIRST AUNT. Drove it to its knees on the flaggy shore and made an end of it!

KING. God bless that man to-day and to-morrow!

SECOND AUNT. He has put it in a way it will eat no more kings' daughters!

PRINCESS. And the stranger that mastered it—is he safe?

FIRST AUNT. What signifies if he is or is not, so long as we have our own young prince to bring home!

GATEKEEPER. He is not safe. No sooner had he the beast killed and conquered than he fell dead, and the life went out of him.

PRINCESS. Oh, that is not right! He to be dead and I living after him!

KING. He was surely noble and high-blooded. There are some that will be sorry for his death.

PRINCESS. And who should be more sorry than I myself am sorry? Who should keen him unless myself? There is a man that gave his life for me, and he young and all his days before him, and shut his eyes on the white world for my sake!

QUEEN. Indeed he was a man you might have been content to wed with, hard and all as you are to please.

PRINCESS. I never will wed with any man so long as my life will last, that was bought for me with a life was more worthy by far than my own! He is gone out of my reach; let him wait for me to give him my thanks on the other side. Bring me now his sword and his shield till I will put them before me and cry my eyes down with grief!

GATEMAN. Here is his cap for you, anyway, and his cleaver and his bunch of skivers. For the champion you are crying was no other than that lad of a cook!

QUEEN. That is not true! It is not possible!

GATEMAN. Sure I seen him myself going out the gate a while ago. He put off his cook's apparel and threw it along with these behind the turfstack. I gathered them up presently and I coming in the door.

KING. The world is gone beyond me entirely! But what I was saying all through, there was something beyond the common in that boy!

QUEEN (*to* PRINCESS, *who is clinging to chair*). Let you be comforted now, knowing he cannot come back to lay claim to you in marriage, as it is likely he would, and he living.

PRINCESS. It is he saved me after my unkindness! . . . Oh, I am ashamed . . . ashamed!

QUEEN. It is a queer thing a king's daughter to be crying after a man used to twisting the spit in place of weapons, and over skivers in the place of a sword!

PRINCESS (*gropes and totters*). What has happened? There is something gone astray! I have no respect for myself. . . . I cannot live! I am ashamed? Where is Nurse? Muime! Come to me Muime! . . . My grief! The man that died for me, whether he is of the noble or the simple of the world, it is to him I have given the love of my soul!

(DALL GLIC *supports her and lays her on window seat*.)

NURSE (*rushing in*). What is it, honey? What at all are they after doing to you?

QUEEN. Throw over her a skillet of water. She is gone into a faint.

DALL GLIC (*who is bending over her*). She is in no faint. She is gone out.

NURSE. Oh, my child and my darling! What call had I to leave you among them at all?

KING. Raise her up. It is impossible she can be gone.

DALL GLIC. Gone out and spent, as sudden as a candle in a blast of wind.

KING. Who would think grief would do away with her so sudden, there to be seven of the like of him dead?

NURSE (*rises*). What did you do to her at all, at all? Or was it through the fright and terror of the beast?

QUEEN. She died of the heartbreak, being told that the strange champion that had put down the Dragon was killed dead.

NURSE. Killed, is it? Who now put that lie out of his mouth? (*Shouts in her ear.*) What would ail him to be dead? It is myself can tell you the true story. No man in Ireland ever was half as good as him! It was himself mastered the beast and dragged the heart out of him and forced down a squirrel's heart in its place, and slapped a bridle on him. And he himself did but stagger and go to his knees in the heat and drunkenness of the battle, and rose up after as good as ever he was! It is out putting ointments on him that I was up to this, and healing up his cuts and wounds! Oh, what ails you, honey, that you will not waken?

QUEEN. She thought it to be a champion and a high up man that had died for her sake. It is what broke her down in the latter end, hearing him to be no big man at all, but a clown!

NURSE. Oh, my darling! And I not here to tell you! You are a motherless child, and the curse of your mother will be on me! It was no clown fought for you, but a king, having generations of kings behind him, the young King of Sorcha, Manus, son of Solas son of Lugh.

KING. I would believe that now sooner than many a thing I would hear.

NURSE (*keening*). Oh, my child, and my share! I thought it was you would be closing my eyes, and now I am closing your own! You to be brought away in your young youth! Your hand that was whiter than the snow of one night, and the colour of the foxglove on your cheek.

(*A great shouting outside and burst of music. A march played.* MANUS *comes in, followed by* FINTAN *and* PRINCE OF THE MARSHES. *Shouts and music continue. He leads the Dragon by a bridle. The others are in front of* PRINCESS, *huddled from Dragon.* QUEEN *gets up on a chair.*)

MANUS. Where is the Princess Nu? I have brought this beast to bow itself at her feet.

(*All are silent.* MANUS *flings bridle to* FINTAN's *hand. Dragon backs out. All go aside from* PRINCESS.)

NURSE. She is here dead before you.

MANUS. That cannot be! She was well and living half an hour ago.

NURSE (*rises*). Oh, if she could but waken and hear your voice! She died with the fret of losing you, that is heaven's truth! It is tormented she was with these giving out you were done away with, and mocking at your weapons that they laid down to be the cleaver and the spit, till the heart broke in her like a nut.

MANUS (*kneeling beside her*). Then it is myself have brought the death darkness upon you at the very time I thought to have saved you!

NURSE. There is no blame upon you, but some that had too much talk!

(*Goes on keening*).

MANUS. What call had I to come humbugging and letting on as I did, teasing and tormenting her, and not coming as a King should that is come to ask for a Queen! Oh, come back for one minute only till I will ask your pardon!

DALL GLIC. She cannot come to you or answer you at all for ever.

MANUS. Then I myself will go follow you and will ask for your forgiveness wherever you are gone, on the Plain of Wonder or in the Many-Coloured Land! That is all I can do . . . . to go after you and tell you it was no want of respect that brought me in that dress, but hurry and folly and taking my own way. For it is what I have to say to you, that I gave you my heart's love, what I never gave to any other, since first I saw you before me in my sleep! Here, now, is a short road to reach you!

(*Takes sword.*)

PRINCE OF MARSHES (*catching his hand*). Go easy now, go easy.

MANUS. Take off your hand! I say I will die with her!

PRINCE OF MARSHES. That will not raise her up again. But I, now, if I have no skill in killing beasts or men, have maybe the means of bringing her back to life.

NURSE. Oh, my blessing on you! What is it you have at all?

PRINCE OF MARSHES (*taking bag from his* AUNT). These three

leaves from the Tree of Power that grows by the Well of Healing. Here they are now for you, tied with a thread of the wool of the sheep of the Land of Promise. There is power in them to bring one person only back to life.

FIRST AUNT. Give them back to me! You have your own life to think of as well as any other one!

SECOND AUNT. Do not spend and squander that cure on any person but yourself!

PRINCE OF MARSHES (*giving the leaves*). And if I have given her my love that it is likely I will give to no other woman for ever, indeed and indeed, I would not ask her or wish her to wed with a very frightened man, and that is what I was a while ago. But you yourself have earned her, being brave.

MANUS (*taking leaves*). I never will forget it to you. You will be a brave man yet.

PRINCE OF MARSHES. Give me in place of it your sword; for I am going my lone through the world for a twelvemonth and a day, till I will learn to fight with my own hand.

(MANUS *gives him sword. He throws off cloak and outer coat and fastens it on.*)

NURSE. Stand back, now. Let the whole of ye stand back. (*She lays a leaf on the* PRINCESS'S *mouth and one on each of her hands.*) I call on you by the power of the Seven Belts of the Heavens, of the Twelve Winds of the World, of the Three Waters of the Sea!

(PRINCESS *stirs slightly.*)

KING. That is a wonder of wonders! She is stirring!

MANUS. Oh, my share of the world! Are you come back to me?

PRINCESS. It was a hard fight he wrestled with. . . . I thought I heard his voice. . . . Is he come from danger?

NURSE. He did. Here he is. He that saved you and that killed the Dragon, and that let on to be a serving boy, and he no less than one of the world's kings!

MANUS. Here I am, my dear, beside you, to be your comrade and your company for ever.

PRINCESS. You! . . . Yes, it is yourself. Forgive me. I am sorry that I spoke unkindly to you a while ago; I am ashamed that it failed me to know you to be a king.

(*She stands up, helped by* NURSE.)

MANUS. It was my own fault and my folly. What way could you know it? There is nothing to forgive.

PRINCESS. But . . . if I did not recognise you as a king . . . anyway

257

... the time you dropped the eggs ... I was nearly certain that you were no cook!

(*They embrace.*)

QUEEN. There now I have everything brought about very well in the finish!

(*A scream at door.* TAIG *rushes in, followed by* SIBBY, *in country dress. He kneels at the* QUEEN'S *feet, holding on to her skirt.*)

SIBBY. Bad luck and bad cess to you! Torment and vexation on you! (*Seizes him by back of neck and shakes him.*) You dirty little scum and leavings! You puny shrimp you! You miserable ninth part of a man!

QUEEN. Is it King or the Dragon Killer he is letting on to be yet, or do you know what he is at all?

SIBBY. It's myself knows that, and does know it! He being Taig the tailor, my own son and my misfortune, that stole away from me a while ago, bringing with him the grand clothes of that young champion (*points to* MANUS) and his gold! To borrow a team of horses from the plough he did, and to bring away the magistrate's coach! But I followed him! I came tracking him on the road! Put off now those shoes that are too narrow for you, you red thief, you! For, believe me, you'll go facing home on shank's mare!

TAIG (*whimpering*). It's a very unkind thing you to go screeching that out before the King, that will maybe strike my head off!

SIBBY. Did ever you know of anyone making a quarrel in a whisper? To wed with the King's daughter, you would? To go vanquish the water-worm you would? I'll engage you ran before you went anear him!

TAIG. If I didn't I'd be tore with his claws and scorched with his fiery breath. It is likely I'd be going home dead!

SIBBY. Strip off now that cloak and that bodycoat and come along with me, or I'll make split marrow of you! What call have you to a suit that is worth more than the whole of the County Mayo? You're tricky and too much tricks in you, and you were born for tricks! It would be right you to be turned into the shape of a limping foxy cat!

TAIG (*weeping as he takes off clothes*). Sure I thought it no harm to try to go better myself.

PRINCE OF MARSHES (*giving his cloak and coat*). Here, I bestow these to you. If you were a while ago a tailor among kings, from this out you will be a king among tailors.

SIBBY (*curtseying*). Well, then, my thousand blessings on you!

258

He'll be as proud as the world of that. Now, Taig, you'll be as dressed up as the best of them! Come on now to Oughtmana, as it is long till you'll quit it.

(*They go towards door.*)

DRAGON (*putting his head in at window*). Manus, King of Sorcha, I am starved with the want of food. Give me a bit to eat.

FINTAN. He is not put down! He will devour the whole of us! I'd sooner face a bullet and ten guns!

DRAGON. It is not mannerly to eat without being invited. Is it any harm to ask where will I find a meal will suit me?

PRINCESS. Oh, does he ask to make a meal of me, after all?

DRAGON. I am hungry and dancing with the hunger! It was you, Manus, stopped me from the one meal. Let you set before me another.

KING. There is reason in that. Drive up now for him a bullock from the meadow.

DRAGON. Manus, it is not bullocks I am craving, since the time you changed the heart within me for the heart of a little squirrel of the wood.

MANUS (*taking a cocoa-nut from table*). Here is a nut from the island of Lanka, that is called Adam's Paradise. Milk there is in it and a kernel as white as snow.

(*He throws it out.* DRAGON *is heard crunching.*)

DRAGON (*putting head in again*). More! Give me more of them! Give them out to me by the dozen and by the score!

MANUS. You must go seek them in the east of the world, where you can gather them in bushels on the strand.

DRAGON. So I will go there! I'll make no delay! I give you my word, I'd sooner one of them than to be cracking the skulls of kings' daughters, and the blood running down my jaws. Blood! Ugh! It would disgust me! I'm in dread it would cause vomiting. That and to have the plaits of hair tickling and tormenting my gullet!

PRINCESS (*claps hands*). That is good hearing, and a great change of heart.

DRAGON. But if it's a tame dragon I am from this out, I'm thinking it's best for me to make away before you know it, or it's likely ye'll be yoking me to harrow the clods, or to be dragging the water-car from the spring well. So good-bye the whole of ye, and get to your supper. Much good may it do you! I give you my word there is nothing in the universe I despise, only the flesh-eaters of Adam's race!

Curtain.

ARISTOTLE'S BELLOWS

ARISTOTLE'S BELLOWS

PERSONS
    THE MOTHER
    CELIA. *Her Daughter*
    CONAN. *Her Stepson*
    TIMOTHY. *Her Serving Man*
    ROCK. *A Neighbour*
    FLANNERY. *His Herd*
    TWO CATS

ACT I

SCENE: *A Room in an old half-ruined castle.*

MOTHER. Look out the door, Celia, and see is your uncle coming.

CELIA (*who is lying on the ground, a bunch of ribbons in her hand, and playing with a pigeon, looks towards door without getting up*). I see no sign of him.

MOTHER. What time were you telling me it was a while ago?

CELIA. It is not five minutes hardly since I was telling you it was ten o'clock by the sun.

MOTHER. So you did, if I could but have kept it in mind. What at all ails him that he does not come in to the breakfast?

CELIA. He went out last night and the full moon shining. It is likely he passed the whole night abroad, drowsing or rummaging, whatever he does be looking for in the rath.

MOTHER. I'm in dread he'll go crazy with digging in it.

CELIA. He was crazy with crossness before that.

MOTHER. If he is it's on account of his learning. Them that have too much of it are seven times crosser than them that never saw a book.

CELIA. It is better to be tied to any thorny bush than to be with a cross man. He to know the seventy-two languages he couldn't be more crabbed than what he is.

MOTHER. It is natural to people do be so clever to be fiery a little, and not have a long patience.

CELIA. It's a pity he wouldn't stop in that school he had down in the North, and not to come back here in the latter end of life.

MOTHER. Ah, he was maybe tired with enlightening his scholars and he took a notion to acquaint ourselves with knowledge and learning. I was trying to reckon a while ago the number of the years he was away, according to the buttons of my gown (*fingers bodice*) —but they went astray on me at the gathers of the neck.

CELIA. If the hour would come he'd go out of this, I'd sing, I'd play on all the melodeons that ever was known! (*Sings.*) (*Air*, "*Shule Aroon.*")

> "I would not wish him any ill,
>   But were he swept to some far hill
>   It's then I'd laugh and laugh my fill,
>   Coo, Coo, my birdeen bán astore.

> "I wish I was a linnet free
>   To rock and rustle on the tree
>   With none to haste or hustle me,
>   Coo, Coo, my birdeen bán astore! "

MOTHER. Did you make ready now what will please him for his breakfast?

CELIA (*laughing*). I'm doing every whole thing, but you know well to please him is not possible.

MOTHER. It is going astray on me what sort of egg best suits him, a pullet's egg or the egg of a duck.

CELIA. I'd go search out if it would satisfy him the egg of an eagle having eyes as big as the moon, and feathers of pure gold.

MOTHER. Look out again would you see him.

CELIA (*sitting up reluctantly*). I wonder will the rosy ribbon or the pale put the best appearance on my party dress to-night? (*Looks out.*) He is coming down the path from the rath, and he having his little old book in his hand, that he gives out fell down before him from the skies.

MOTHER. So there is a little book, whatever language he does be wording out of it.

CELIA. If you listen you'll hear it now, or hear his own talk, for he's mouthing and muttering as he travels the path.

CONAN (*comes in: the book in his hand open, he is not looking at it*). "Life is the flame of the heart . . . that heat is of the nature of the stars." . . . It is Aristotle had knowledge to turn that flame here and there. . . . What way now did he do that?

264

MOTHER. Ah, I'm well pleased to see you coming in, Conan. I was getting uneasy thinking you were gone astray on us.

CONAN (*dropping his book and picking it up again*). I never knew the like of you, Maryanne, under the canopy of heaven. To be questioning me with your talk, and I striving to keep my mind upon all the wisdom of the ancient world. (*Sits down beside fire.*)

MOTHER. So you would be too. It is well able you are to do that.

CONAN (*to* CELIA). Have you e'er a meal to leave down to me?

CELIA. It will be ready within three minutes of time.

CONAN. Wasting the morning on me! What good are you if you cannot so much as boil the breakfast? Hurry on now.

CELIA. Ah, hurry didn't save the hare. (*Sings ironically as she prepares breakfast.*) (*Air,* "Mo Bhuachailin Buidhe.")

"Come in the evening or come in the morning,
   Come when you're looked for or come without warning;
   Kisses and welcome you'll find here before you
   And the oftner you come here the more I'll adore you."

CONAN. Give me up the tea-pot.

CELIA. Best leave it on the coals awhile.

CONAN. Give me up those eggs so. (*Seizes them.*)

CELIA. You can take the tea-pot too if you are calling for it. (*Goes on singing mischievously as she turns a cake.*)

"I'll pull you sweet flowers to wear if you'll choose them,
   Or after you've kissed them they'll lie on my bosom."

CONAN (*breaking eggs*). They're raw and running!

CELIA. There's no one can say which is best, hurry or delay.

CONAN. You had them boiled in cold water.

CELIA. That's where you're wrong.

CONAN. The young people that's in the world now, if you had book truth they wouldn't believe it. (*Flings eggs into the fire and pours out tea.*)

MOTHER. I hope now that is pleasing to you?

CONAN (*threatening* CELIA *with spoon*). My seven curses on yourself and your fair-haired tea. (*Puts back tea-pot.*)

CELIA (*laughing*). It was hurry left it so weak on you!

MOTHER. Ah, don't be putting reproaches on him. Crossness is a thing born with us. It do run in the blood. Strive now to let him have a quiet life.

CONAN. I am not asking a quiet life! But to come live with your own family, you might as well take your coffin on your back!

CELIA (*sings*).

"We'll look on the stars and we'll list to the river
'Till you ask of your darling what gift you can give her."

CONAN. That girl is a disgrace sitting on the floor the way she is! If I had her for a while I'd put betterment on her. No one that was under me ever grew slack!

CELIA. *You* would never be satisfied and you to see me working from dark to dark as hard as a pismire in the tufts.

MOTHER. Leave her now, she's a quiet little girl and comely.

CONAN. Comely! I'd sooner her to be like the ugliest sod of turf that is pockmarked in the bog, and a handy housekeeper, and her pigeon doing something for the world if it was but scaring its comrades on a stick in a barley garden!

CELIA. Ah, do you hear him! (*Stroking pigeon.*) (*Sings.*)

"But when your friend is forced to flee
You'll spread your white wings on the sea
And fly and follow after me—
Go-dé tu Mavourneen slán!"

MOTHER. I wonder you to be going into the rath the way you do, Conan. It is a very haunted place.

CONAN. Don't be bothering me. I have my reason for that.

MOTHER. I often heard there is many a one lost his wits in it.

CONAN. It's likely they hadn't much to lose. Without the education anyone is no good.

MOTHER. Ah, indeed you were always a tip-top scholar. I didn't ever know how good you were till I had my memory lost.

CONAN. Indeed, it is a strange thing any wits at all to be found in *this* family.

MOTHER. Ah, sure we are as is alloted to us at the time God made the world.

CONAN. Now *I* to make the world—

Mother. You are not saying you would make a better hand of it?

CONAN. I am certain sure I could.

MOTHER. Ah, don't be talking that way!

CONAN. I'd make changes you'd wonder at.

CELIA. It's likely you'd make the world in one day in place of six.

MOTHER. It's best make changes little by little the same as you'd put clothes upon a growing child, and to knock every day out of

266

what God will give you, and to live as long as we can, and die when we can't help it.

CONAN. And the first thing I'd do would be to give you back your memory and your sense. (*Sings.*) (*Air, "The Bells of Shandon."*)

> "My brain grows rusty, my mind is dusty,
> The time I'm dwelling with the likes of ye,
> While my spirit ranges through all the changes
> Could turn the world to felicity!
> When Aristotle . . ."

MOTHER. It is like a dream to me I heard that name. Aristotle of the books.

CONAN (*eagerly*). What did you hear about him?

MOTHER. I don't know was it about him or was it some other one. My memory to be as good as it is bad I might maybe bring it to mind.

CONAN. Hurry on now and remember!

MOTHER. Ah, it's hard remember anything and the weather so uncertain as what it is.

CONAN. Is it of late you heard it?

MOTHER. It was maybe ere yesterday or some day of the sort; I don't know. Since the age tampered with me the thing I'd hear to-day I wouldn't think of to-morrow.

CONAN. Try now and tell me was it that Aristotle, the time he walked Ireland, had come to this place.

MOTHER. It might be that, unless it might be some other thing.

CONAN. And that he left some great treasure hid—it might be in the rath without.

MOTHER. And what good would it do you a pot of gold to be hid in the rath where you would never come near to it, it being guarded by enchanted cats and they having fiery eyes?

CONAN. Did I say anything about a pot of gold? This was better again than gold. This was an enchantment would raise you up if you were gasping from death. Give attention now . . . Aristotle.

MOTHER. It's Harry he used to be called.

CONAN. Listen now. (*Sings.*) (*Air, "Bells of Shandon."*)

> "Once Aristotle hid in a bottle
> Or some other vessel of security
> A spell had power bring sweet from sour
> Or bring blossoms blooming on the blasted tree."

MOTHER (*repeating last line*). "Or bring blossoms blooming on the blasted tree."

CONAN. Is that now what you heard . . . that Aristotle has hid some secret spell?

MOTHER. I won't say what I don't know. My memory is too weak for me to be telling lies.

CONAN. You could strengthen it if you took it in hand, putting a knot in the corner of your shawl to keep such and such a thing in mind.

MOTHER. If I did I should put another knot in the other corner to remember what was the first one for.

CONAN. You'd remember it well enough if it was a pound of tea!

MOTHER. Ah, maybe it's best be as I am and not to be running carrying lies here and there, putting trouble on people's mind.

CONAN. Isn't it terrible to be seeing all this folly around me and not to have a way to better it!

MOTHER. Ah, dear, it's best leave the time under the mercy of the Man that is over us all.

CONAN (*jumping up furious*). Where's the use of old people being in the world at all if they cannot keep a memory of things gone by! (*Sings.*) (*Air, "O the time I've lost in wooing."*)

> "O the time I've lost pursuing
> And feeling nothing doing,
> The lure that led me from my bed
> Has left me sad and rueing!
> Success seemed very near me!
> High hope was there to cheer me!
> I asked my book where would I look
> And all it did was fleer me! "

MOTHER. What is it ails you?

CONAN. That secret to be in the world, and I all to have laid my hand on it, and it to have gone astray on me!

MOTHER. So it would go too.

CONAN. A secret that could change the world! I'd make it as good a world to live in as it was in the time of the Greeks. I don't see much goodness in the trace of the people in it now. To change everything to its contrary the way the book said it would! There would be great satisfaction doing that. Was there ever in the world a family was so little use to a man? (*Sings in dejection.*) (*Air, "My Molly O."*)

268

"There is a rose in Ireland, I thought it would be mine
But now that it is hid from me I must forever pine.
Till death shall come and comfort me for to the grave I'll go
And all for the sake of Aristotle's secret O!"

CELIA. I wonder you wouldn't ask Timothy that is older again
than what my mother is.

CONAN. Timothy! He has the hearing lost.

CELIA. Well there is no harm to try him.

CONAN (*going to door*). Timothy! ... There, he's as deaf as a
beetle.

MOTHER. It might be best for him. The thing the ear will not
hear will not put trouble on the heart.

CELIA (*who has gone out comes pushing him in*). Here he is now
for you.

CONAN. Did ever you hear of Aristotle?

TIMOTHY. Aye?

CONAN. Aristotle!

TIMOTHY. Ere a bottle? I might ...

CONAN. Aristotle.... That had some power?

TIMOTHY. I never seen no flower.

CONAN. Something he hid near this place.

TIMOTHY. I never went near no race.

CONAN. Has the whole world its mind made up to annoy me!

CELIA. Raise your voice into his ear.

CONAN (*chanting*).

"Aristotle in the hour
He left Ireland left a power
In a gift Eolus gave
Could all Ireland change and save!"

TIMOTHY. Would it now?

CONAN. You said you had heard of a bottle.

TIMOTHY. A charmed bottle. It is Biddy Early put a cure in it
and bestowed it in her will to her son.

CONAN. Aristotle that left one in the same way.

TIMOTHY. It is what I am thinking that my old generations used
to be talking about a bellows.

CONAN. A bellows! There's no sense in that!

TIMOTHY. Have it your own way so, and give me leave to go
feeding the little chickens and the hens, for if I cannot hear what
they say and they cannot understand what I say, they put no re-

proach on me after, no more than I would put it on themselves. (*Goes.*)

CELIA. Let you be satisfied now and not torment yourself, for if you got the world wide you couldn't discover it. You might as well think to throw your hat to hit the stars.

CONAN. You have me tormented among the whole of ye. To be without ye would be no harm at all. (*Sits down and weeps.*) Of all the families anyone would wish to live away from I am full sure my family is the worst.

MOTHER. Ah, dear, you're worn out and contrary with the want of sleep. Come now into the room and stretch yourself on the bed. To go sleeping out in the grass has no right rest in it at all! (*Takes his arm.*)

CONAN. Where's the use of lying on my bed where it is convenient to the yard, that I'd be afflicted by the turkeys yelping and the pullets praising themselves after laying an egg! and the cackling and hissing of the geese.

MOTHER. Lie down so on the settle, and I'll let no one disturb you. You're destroyed, avic, with the want of sleep.

CONAN. There'll be no peace in this kitchen no more than on the common highway with the people running in and out.

MOTHER. I'll go sit in the little gap without, and the whole place will be as quiet as St. Colman's wilderness of stones.

CONAN. The boards are too hard.

MOTHER. I'll put a pillow in under you.

CONAN. Now it's too narrow. Leave me now it'll be best.

MOTHER. Sleep and good dreams to you. (*Goes singing sleepy song.*)

CONAN. The most troublesome family ever I knew in all my born days! Why it is that people cannot have behaviour now the same as in ancient Greece. (*Sits up.*) I'll not give them the satisfaction of going asleep. I'll drink a sup of the tea that is black with standing and with strength. (*Drinks and lies down.*) I'll engage that'll keep me waking. (*Music heard.*) Is it to annoy me they are playing tunes of music? I'll let on to be asleep! (*Shuts eyes.*)

(*Two large Cats with fiery eyes look over top of settle.*)

1ST CAT.   See the fool that crossed our path
           Rummaging within the rath.

           Coveting a spell is bound
           Agelong in our haunted ground.

Hid that none disturb its peace
By a Druid out from Greece.

Spies and robbers have no call
Rooting in our ancient wall.

Man or mortal what is he
Matched against the mighty Sidhe?

2ND CAT.   Bid our riders of the night
Daze and craze him with affright,

Leave him fainting and forlorn
Hanging on the moon's young horn.

Let the death-bands turn him pale
Through the venom of our tail.

Let him learn to love our law
With the sharpness of our claw.

Let our King-cat's fiery flash
Turn him to a heap of ash.

1ST CAT.   Punishment enough he'll find
In his cross and cranky mind.

Ha, ha, ha, and ho, ho, ho,
He'd a sharper penance know,

We'd have better sport today
If he got his will and way,

Found the spell that lies unknown
Underneath his own hearthstone.

(*They disappear saying together:*)

Men and mortals what are ye
Matched against the mighty Sidhe?

CONAN (*looking out timidly*). Are they gone? Here, Puss, puss! Come hither now poor Puss! They're not in it. . . . Here now! here's milk for ye. And a drop of cream. . . . (*Gets up, peeps under settle and around.*) They are gone! And that they may never come back! I wouldn't wish to be brought riding a thorny bush in the night time into the cold that is behind the sun! What now did they say? They spoke clear and plain. The hidden spell that I was seeking, they said it to be in the hiding hole under the hearth. (*Pokes, sneezes.*) Bad cess to Celia leaving that much ashes to be choking me. Well, the luck has come to me at last!

(*Sings as he searches.*)

"Proudly the note of the trumpet is sounding,
Loudly the war cries rise on the gale;
Fleetly the steed by Lough Swilly is bounding
To join the thick squadrons in Saimear's green vale.
On every mountaineer, strangers to flight and fear;
Rush to the standard of dauntless Red Hugh
Bonnaught and gallowglass, throng from each mountain
 pass.
On for old Erin, O'Donnall Abu."

(*Pokes at hearthstone.*) Sure enough, it's loose! It's moving! Wait till I'l get a wedge under it!

(*Takes fork from table.*) It's coming!

(*Door suddenly opens and he drops fork and springs back.*)

MOTHER (*coming in with* ROCK *and* FLANNERY). Here now, come in the two of ye. Here now, Conan, is two of the neighbours, James Rock of Lis Crohan and Fardy Flannery the rambling herd, that are come to get a light for the pipe and they walking the road from the Fair.

CONAN. That's the way you make a fool of me promising me peace and quiet for to sleep!

MOTHER. Ah, so I believe I did. But it slipped away from me, and I listening to the blackbird on the bush.

CONAN (*to* ROCK). I wonder James Rock, that you wouldn't have on you so much as a half-penny box of matches!

ROCK (*trying to get to hearth*). So I have matches. But why would I spend one when I can get for nothing a light from a sod?

FLANNERY. Sure, I could give you a match I have this long time, waiting till I'll get as much tobacco as will fill a pipe.

MOTHER. It's the poor man does be generous. It's gone from my mind, Fardy, what was it brought you to be a servant of poverty?

FLANNERY. Since the day I lost on the road my forty pound that I had to stock my little farm of land, all has wore away from me and left me bare owning nothing unless daylight and the run of water. It was that put me on the Shaughrann.

(*Sings "The Bard of Armagh."*)

"Oh, list to the lay of a poor Irish harper,
And scorn not the strains of his old withered hand,
But remember the fingers could once move sharper
To raise the merry strains of his dear native land;
It was long before the shamrock our dear isle's loved
    emblem
Was crushed in its beauty 'neath the Saxon Lion's paw
I was called by the colleens of the village and valley
Bold Phelim Brady, the bard of Armagh."

ROCK. Bad management! Look what I brought from the Fair through minding my own property—£20 for a milch cow, and thirty for a score of lambs!

MOTHER. £20 for a cow! Isn't that terrible money!

CONAN. Let you whist now! You are putting a headache on me with all your little newses and country chat!

(MOTHER *goes, the others are following.*)

ROCK (*turning from door*). It might be better for yourself, Conan Creevey, if you had minded business would bring profit to your hand in place of your foreign learning, that never put a penny piece in anyone's pocket that ever I heard. No earthly profit unless to addle the brain and leave the pocket empty.

CONAN. You think yourself a great sort! Let me tell you that my learning has power to do more than that!

ROCK. It's an empty mouth that has big talk.

CONAN. What would you say hearing I had power put in my hand that could change the entire world? And that's what you never will have power to do.

ROCK. What power is that?

CONAN. Aristotle in the hour
    He left Ireland left a power. . . .

ROCK. Foolishness! I never would believe in poetry or in dreams or images, but in ready money down. (*Jingles bag.*)

CONAN. I tell you you'll see me getting the victory over all Ireland!

ROCK. You have but a cracked headpiece thinking that will come to you.

CONAN. I tell you it will! No end at all in the world to what I am about to bring in!

ROCK. It's easy praise yourself!

CONAN. And so I am praising myself, and so will you all be praising me when you will see all that I will do!

ROCK. It is what I think you got demented in the head and in the mind.

CONAN. It is soon the wheel will be turned and the whole of the nation will be changed for the best. (*Sings*.)

"Dear Harp of my country, in darkness I found thee,
The cold chain of silence had hung o'er thee long,
When proudly, my own Irish Harp, I unbound thee,
And gave all thy chords to light, freedom and song,
The warm lay of love and the light note of gladness
Have waken'd thy fondest, thy liveliest thrill;
But so oft hast thou echo'd the deep sigh of sadness,
That ev'n in thy mirth it will steal from thee still."

FLANNERY. That's a great thought if it is but a vanity or a dream.

ROCK (*sneeringly*). Well now and what would *you* do?

FLANNERY. I would wish a great lake of milk, the same as blessed St. Bridget, to be sharing with the family of Heaven. I would wish vessels full of alms that would save every sorrowful man. Do that now, Conan, and you'll have the world of prayers down on you!

ROCK. It's what I'd do, to turn the whole of Galway Bay to dry land, and I to have it for myself, the red land, the green land, the fallow and the lea! The want of land is a great stoppage to a man having means to lay out in stock.

(*Sings*) (*Air*, "*I wish I had the shepherd's lamb.*")

"I wish I had both mill and kiln,
I wish I had of land my fill;
I wish I had both mill and kiln,
And all would follow after! "

FLANNERY. Ah, the land, the land, the rotten land, and what will you have in the end but the breadth of your back of it? Let you now soften the heart in that one (*points to* ROCK) till he would restore to me the thing he is aware of.

CONAN. It was not for that the spell was promised, to be changing a few neighbours or a thing of the kind, or to be doing wonders in this broken little place. A town of dead factions! To change any of the dwellers in this place would be to make it better, for it would be impossible to make it worse. The time you wouldn't be meddling with them you wouldn't know them to be bad, but the time you'd have to do business with them that's the time you'd know it!

ROCK. I suppose it is what you are asking to do, to make yourself rich?

CONAN. I do not! I would be loth to take any profit, and Aristotle after laying down that *to* pleasure or *to* profit every wealthy man is a slave!

FLANNERY. What would you do, so?

CONAN. I will change all into the similitude of ancient Greece! There is no man at all can understand argument but it is from Greece he is. I know well what I'm doing. I'm not like a potato having eyes this way and that. People were harmless long ago and why wouldn't they be made harmless again? Aristotle said, "Fair play is more beautiful than the morning and the evening star!"

"Be friendly with one another," he said, "and let the lawyers starve!" I'll turn the captains of soldiers to be as peaceable as children picking strawberries in the grass. I've a mind to change the tongue of the people to the language of the Greeks, that no farmer will be grumbling over a halfpenny Independent, but be following the plough in full content, giving out Homer and the praises of the ancient world!

FLANNERY. If you make the farmers content you will make the world content.

ROCK. You will, when you'll bring the sun from Greece to ripen our little lock of oats!

CONAN. So I will drag Ireland from its moorings till I'll bring it to the middling sea that has no ebb or flood!

ROCK. You will do well to put a change on the college that harboured you, and that left you so much of folly.

CONAN. I'll do that! I'll be in College Green before the dawn is white—no but before the night is grey! It is to Dublin I will bring my spell, for I ever and always heard it said what Dublin will do to-day Ireland will do to-morrow! (*Sings*)

> "Let Erin remember the days of old
> Ere her faithless sons betrayed her—
> When Malachy wore the collar of gold
> Which he won from her proud invader—
> When her kings with standards of green unfurl'd,
> Led the Red-Branch knights to danger;
> Ere the emerald gem of the western world
> Was set in the crown of a stranger."

ROCK. And maybe you'll tell us now by what means you will do all this?

CONAN. Go out of the house and I will tell you in the by and bye.

275

ROCK. That is what I was thinking. You are talking nothing but lies.

CONAN. I tell you that power is not far from where you stand! But I will let no one see it only myself.

FLANNERY. There might be some truth in it. There are some say enchantments never went out of Ireland.

CONAN. It is a spell, I say, that will change anything to its contrary. To turn it upon a snail, there is hardly a greyhound but it would overtake; but a hare it would turn to be the slowest thing in the universe; too slow to go to a funeral.

ROCK. I'll believe it when I'll see it.

CONAN. You could see it if I let you look in this hiding hole.

ROCK. Good-morrow to you!

CONAN. Then you will see it, for I'll raise up the stone. (*Kneels.*)

ROCK. It to be anything it is likely a pot of sovereigns.

FLANNERY. It might be the harp of Angus.

ROCK. I see no trace of it.

CONAN. There is something hard! It should likely be a silver trumpet or a hunting-horn of gold!

ROCK. Give me a hold of it.

CONAN. Leave go! (*Lifts out bellows.*)

ROCK. Ha! Ha! Ha! after all your chat, nothing but a little old bellows! . . .

CONAN. There is seven rings on it. . . . They should signify the seven blasts. . . .

ROCK. If there was seventy times seven what use would it be but to redden the coals?

CONAN. Every one of these blasts has power to make some change.

ROCK. Make one so, and I'll plough the world for you.

CONAN. Is it that I would spend one of my seven blasts convincing the like of ye?

ROCK. It is likely the case there is no power in it at all.

CONAN. I'm very sure there is surely. The world will be a new world before to-morrow's Angelus bell.

FLANNERY. I never could believe in a bellows.

ROCK. Here now is a fair offer. I'll loan you this bag of notes to pay your charges to Dublin if you will change that little pigeon in the crib into a crow.

CONAN. I will do no such folly.

ROCK. You wouldn't because you'd be afeared to try.

CONAN. Hold it up to me. I'll show you am I afeared!

ROCK. There it is now. (*Holds up cage.*)

CONAN. Have a care! (*Blows.*)

ROCK (*dropping it with a shriek*). It has me bit with its hard beak, it is turned to be an old black crow.

FLANNERY. As black as the bottom of the pot.

CROW. Caw! Caw! Caw!

(CATS *reappear and look over back of settle.*)
(*Music from behind.*) ("*O'Donnall Abu.*")

Curtain.

ACT II

(CONAN *alone holding up bellows, singing*)

CONAN.
> "And doth not a meeting like this make amends
> For all the long years I've been wandering away
> Deceived for a moment it's now in my hands—
> I breathe the fresh air of life's morning again!"

CELIA (*comes in having listened amused at door; claps hands*). Very good! It is you yourself should be going to the dance house to-night in place of myself. It is long since I heard you rise so happy a tune!

CONAN (*putting bellows behind him*). What brings you here? Is there no work for you out in the garden—the cabbages to be cutting for the cow. . . .

CELIA. I wouldn't wish to roughen my hands before evening. Music there will be for the dancing!

(*She lilts* MISS McLEOD'S *Reel.*)

CONAN. Let you go ready yourself for it so.

CELIA. Is it at this time of the day? You should be forgetting the hours of the clock the same as the poor mother.

CONAN. It is a strange thing since I came to this house I never can get one minute's ease and quiet to myself.

CELIA. It was hearing you singing brought me in.

CONAN. I'd sooner have you without! Be going now.

277

CELIA. I will and welcome. It is to bring out my little pigeon I will, where there is a few grains of barley fell from a car going the road.

CONAN. Hurry on so!

CELIA (*taking up cage*). He is not in his crib. (*Looking here and there.*) Where now can he have gone?

CONAN. He should have gone out the door.

CELIA. He did not. He could not have come out unknown to me. Coo, coo,—coo—coo.

CONAN. Never mind him now. You are putting my mind astray with your Coo, coo—

CELIA. He might be in under the settle. (*Stoops.*) Where are you my little bird. (*Sings.*) (*Air, "Shule Aroon."*)

> "But now my love has gone to France
> His own fair fortune to advance;
> If he come back again 'tis but a chance;
> Os go dé tu Mavourneen slán!"

CONAN (*pulling her away*). What way would he be in it? Let you put a stop to that humming. (*Seizes her.*) Come here to the light . . . is it you sewed this button on my coat?

CELIA. It was not. It is likely it was some tailor down in the North.

CONAN. It is getting loose on the sleeve.

CELIA. Ah, it will last a good while yet. Coo, coo!

CONAN (*getting before her*). It would be no great load on you to get a needle and put a stitch would tighten it.

CELIA. I'll do it in the by and bye. There, I twisted the thread around it. That'll hold good enough for a while.

CONAN. "Anything worth doing at all is worth doing well."

CELIA. Aren't you getting very dainty in your dress?

CONAN. Any man would like to have a decent appearance on his suit.

CELIA. Isn't it the same to-day as it was yesterday?

CONAN. Have you ne'er a needle?

CELIA. I don't know where is it gone.

CONAN. You haven't a stim of sense. Can't you keep in mind "Everything in its right place."

CELIA. Sure, there's no hurry—the day is long.

CONAN. Anything has to be done, the quickest to do it is the best.

CELIA. I'm not working by the hour or the day.

CONAN. Look now at Penelope of the Greeks, and all her riches, and her man not at hand to urge her, how well she sat at the loom from morn till night till she'd have the makings of a suit of frieze.

CELIA. Ah, that was in the ancient days, when you wouldn't buy it made and ready in the shops.

CONAN. Will you so much as go to find a towel would take the dust off of the panes of glass?

CELIA. I wonder at you craving to disturb the spider and it after making its web.

CONAN. Well, go sit idle outside. I wouldn't wish to be looking at you! Aristotle that said a lazy body is all one with a lazy mind. You'll be begging your bread through the world's streets before your poll will be grey.

(*Sings*)

> "You'll dye your petticoat, you'll dye it red,
> And through the world you'll beg your bread;
> And you not hearkening to e'er a word I said,
> It's then you'll know it to be true!"

CELIA (*sings*)

> "Come here my little birdeen! Coo!"

CONAN (*putting his hand on her mouth*). Be going out now in place of calling that bird that is as lazy and as useless as yourself.

CELIA. My little dove! Where are you at all!

CONAN. A cat to have ate it would be no great loss!

CELIA. Did you yourself do away with him?

CONAN. I did not.

CELIA (*wildly breaking free throws herself down*). There is no place for him to be only in under the settle!

CONAN (*dragging at her*). It is not there.

CELIA (*who has put in her hand*). O what is that? It has hurt me!

CONAN. A nail sticking up out of the floor.

CELIA (*jumping up with a cry*). It's a crow! A great big wicked black crow!

CONAN. If it is let you leave it there.

CELIA (*weeping*). I'm certain sure it has my pigeon killed and ate!

CONAN. To be so doleful after a pigeon! You haven't a stim of sense!

CELIA. It was you gave it leave to do that!

CONAN. Stop your whimpering and blubbering! What way can I settle the world and I being harassed and hampered with such a contrary class! I give you my word I have a mind to change myself into a ravenous beast will kill and devour ye all! That much would be no sin when it would be according to my nature. (*Sings or chants*)

> "On Clontarf he like a lion fell,
>   Thousands plunged in their own gore;
>   I to be such a lion now
>   I'd ask for nothing more!"

CELIA (*sitting down miserable*). You are a very wicked man!

CONAN. Get up out of that or I'll make you!

CELIA. I will not! I'm certain you did this cruel thing!

CONAN (*taking up bellows*). I'd hardly begrudge one of my six blasts to be quit of your slowness and your sluggish ways! Rise up now before I'll make you that you'll want shoes that will never wear out, you being ever on the trot and on the run from morning to the fall of night! Start up now! I'm on the bounds of doing it!

CELIA. What are your raving about?

CONAN. To get quit of you I cannot, but to change your nature I might! I give you warning . . . one, two, three!

(*Blows.*) (*Sings: "With a Chirrup."*) (*Air, "Garryowen."*)

> "Let you rise and go light like a bird of the air
>   That goes high in its flight ever seeking its share;
>   Let you never go easy or pine for a rest
>   Till you'll be a world's wonder and work with the best!
>   With a chirrup, a chirrup, a chirrup,
>   A chirrup, a chirrup, a chirrup,
>   A chirrup, a chirrup, a chirrup, a chirrup,
>   A chirrup, a chirrup, a chirrup, a chirrup!"

CELIA (*staring and standing up*). What is that? Is it the wind or is it a wisp of flame that is going athrough my bones!

(ROCK *and* FLANNERY *come in.*)

(CELIA *rushes out.*)

ROCK (*out of breath*). We went looking for a car to bring you to the train!

FLANNERY. There was not one to be found.

ROCK. But those that are too costly!

FLANNERY. Till we went to the Doctor of the Union.

ROCK. For to ask a lift for you on the ambulance. . . .

FLANNERY. But when he heard what we had to tell—

ROCK. He said he would bring you and glad to do it on his own car, and no need to hansel him.

FLANNERY. And welcome, if it was as far as the grave!

ROCK. All he is sorry for he hasn't a horse that would rise you up through the sky—

CONAN. Let him give me the lift so—it will be a help to me. It wasn't only with his own hand Alexander won the world!

FLANNERY. Unless you might give him, he was saying, a blast of the bellows, that would change his dispensary into a racing stable, and all that come to be cured into jockeys and into grooms!

CONAN. What chatterers ye are! I gave ye no leave to speak of that.

ROCK. Ah, it costs nothing to be giving out newses.

FLANNERY. The world and all will be coming to the door to throw up their hats for you, and you making your start, cars and ass cars, jennets and traps. (*Sings*)

"O Bay of Dublin, how my heart your troublin',
 Your beauty haunts me like a fever dream;
 Like frozen fountains that the sun set bubblin'
 My heart's blood warms when I but hear your name!"

CONAN. It's my death I'll come to in Dublin. That news to get there ahead of me I'll be pressed in the throng as thin as a griddle.

FLANNERY. So you might be, too. All I have that might protect you I offer free, and that's this good umbrella that was given to me in a rainstorm by a priest. (*Holds it out.*)

ROCK. And what do you say to me giving you the loan of your charges for the road?

CONAN. Come in here, Maryanne! and give a glass to these honest men till they'll wish me good luck upon my journey, as it's much I'll need it, with the weight of all I have to do.

MOTHER (*coming in*). So I will, so I will and welcome . . . but that I disremember where did I put the key of the chest.

CONAN. I'll engage you do! There it is before you in the lock since ere yesterday. (MOTHER *puts bottle and glasses on table.*)

FLANNERY (*lifting glass*). That you may bring great good to Ireland and to the world!

ROCK. Here's your good health!

CONAN. I'm obliged to you!

ROCK AND FLANNERY (*sing*) (*Air*, "*The Cruiskeen lán.*")

"Gramachree ma cruiskeen Slainte geal mavourneen,
Gramachree a cool-in bawn, bawn, bán-bán-bán,
Oh, Gra-ma-chree a cool-in bawn."

(*They nod as they finish and take out their pipes and sit down. A banging is heard.*)

CONAN. What disturbance is that?

(CELIA *comes in, her hair screwed up tight, skirt tucked up, is carrying a pail, brush, cloth, etc., lets them drop and proceeds to fasten up skirt.*)

MOTHER. Ah, Celia, what is on you? I never saw you that way before.

CONAN. Ha! Very good! I think that you will say there is a great change come upon her, and a right change.

CELIA. Look now at the floor the way it is.

MOTHER. I see no other way but the way it is always.

CELIA. There's a bit of soot after falling down the chimney. (*Picks up tongs.*)

MOTHER. Ah, leave it now, dear, a while.

CELIA. Anything has to be done, the quickest way to do it is the best. (*Having taken up soot, flings down tongs.*)

CONAN. Listen to that! Now am I able to work wonders?

ROCK. It is that you have spent on her a blast?

CONAN. If I did it was well spent.

FLANNERY. I'm in dread you have been robbing the poor.

ROCK. It is myself you have robbed doing that. You have no call to be using those blasts for your own profit!

CONAN. I have every right to bring order in my own dwelling before I can do any other thing!

CELIA. All the dust of the world's roads is gathered in this kitchen. The whole place ate with filth and dirt.

(*Begins to sweep.*)

CONAN. Ah, you needn't hardly go as far as that.

CELIA. Anything that is worth doing is worth doing well. (*To* ROCK) Look now at the marks of your boots upon the ground. Get up out of that till I'll bustle it with the broom!

ROCK (*getting up*). There is a change indeed and a queer change. Where she used to be singing she is screeching the same as a slate where you'd be casting sums!

CELIA (*to* FLANNERY). What's that I see in under your chair? Rise up. (*He gets up.*) It's a pin! (*Sticks it in her dress.*) Everything in its right place! (*Goes on flicking at the furniture.*)

MOTHER. Leave now knocking the furniture to flitters.

CELIA. I will not, till I'll free it from the dust and dander of the year.

MOTHER. That'll do now. I see no dust.

CELIA. You'll see it presently. (*Sweeps up a cloud.*)

MOTHER. Let you speak to her, Conan.

CONAN. Leave now buzzing and banging about the room the same as a fly without a head!

CELIA. Never put off till to-morrow what you can do to-day.

CONAN. I tell you I have things to settle and to say before the car will come that is to bring me on my road to Dublin.

CELIA (*stopping short*). Is it that you are going to Dublin?

CONAN. I am, and within the hour.

CELIA. Pull off those boots from your feet!

CONAN. I will not! Let you leave my boots alone!

CELIA. You are not going out of the house with that slovenly appearance on you! To have it said out in Dublin that you are a class of man never has clean boots but of a Sunday!

CONAN. They'll do well enough without you meddling!

CELIA. Clean them yourself so! (*Gives him a rag and blacking and goes on dusting.*)

(*Sings*) (*Air, "City of Sligo."*)

> "We may tramp the earth
> For all that we're worth,
> But what odds where you and I go,
> We never shall meet
> A spot so sweet
> As the beautiful city of Sligo."

CONAN. What ailed me that I didn't leave her as she was before.

CELIA (*stopping work*). What way are they now?

CONAN (*having cleaned his boots, putting them on hurriedly*). They're very good. (*Wipes his brow, drawing hand across leaving mark of blacking.*)

CELIA. The time I told you to put black on your shoes I didn't bid you rub it upon your brow!

CONAN. I didn't put it in any wrong place.

CELIA. I ask the whole of you, is it black his face is or white?

ALL. It is black indeed.

CELIA. Would you put a reproach on the whole of the barony, going up among big citizens with a face on you the like of that?

CONAN. I'll do well enough. There will be the black of the smoke from the engine on it any way, and I after journeying in the train.

CELIA. You will not go be a disgrace to me.

CONAN. If it is black it is yourself forced me to it.

CELIA. If I did I'll make up for it, putting a clean face upon you now. (*Dips towel in pail and sings "With a fillip"—air, "Garry-owen"—as she washes him.*)

"Bring to mind how the thrush gathers twigs for his nest
And the honey bee toils without ever a rest
And the fishes swim ever to keep themselves clean,
And you'll praise me for making you fit to be seen!
With a fillip, a fillip, a fillip.
A fillip, a fillip, a fillip.
A fillip, a fillip, a fillip, a fillip,
A fillip, a fillip, a fillip, a fillip! "

CONAN. Let me go, will you! Let you stop! The soap that is going into my eye!

CELIA. My grief you are! Let you be willing to suffer, so long as you will be tasty and decent and be a credit to ourselves.

CONAN. The suds are in my mouth!

CELIA. One minute now and you'll be as clean as a bishop!

CONAN. Let me go, can't you!

CELIA. Only one thing wanting now.

CONAN. I'm good enough, I tell you!

CELIA. To cut the wisp from the back of your poll.

CONAN. You will not cut it!

CELIA. And you'll go into the grandeurs of Dublin and you being as neat as an egg.

CONAN (*with a roar*). Leave meddling with my hair. I that can change the world with one turn of my hand!

CELIA. Wait till I'll find the scissors! That's not the way to be going showing off in the town, if you were all the saints and Druids of the universe!

CONAN (*breaking free and rushing out*). My seven thousand curses on the minute when I didn't leave you as you were. (*Goes.*)

CELIA (*looking at* MOTHER). There's meal on your dress from the cake you're after putting in the oven—where now did that bellows fall from? (*Taking up bellows.*) It comes as handy as a gimlet. There (*blows the meal off*), that now will make a big difference in you.

ROCK (*seizing bellows*). Leave now that down out of your hand. Let you go looking for a scissors!

(CELIA *goes off singing "The Beautiful City of Sligo."*)

MOTHER (*sitting down*). I'm thinking it's seven years to-day, James Rock, since you took a lend of my clock.

ROCK. You're raving! What call would I have to ask a lend of your clock?

MOTHER. The way you would rise in time for the fair of Feakle in the morning.

ROCK. Did I now?

MOTHER. You did, and that's my truth. I was standing here, and you were standing there, and Celia that was but ten years was sucking the sugar off a spoon I was after putting in a bag that had come from the shop, for to put a grain into my tea.

ROCK (*sneering*). Well now, didn't your memory get very sharp!

MOTHER. You thought I had it forgot, but I remember it as clear as pictures. The time it stood at was seven minutes after four o'clock, and I never saw it from that day till now. This very day of the month it was, the year of the black sheep having twins.

ROCK. It was but an old clock anyway.

MOTHER. If it was it is seven years older since I laid an eye on it. And it's kind father for you robbing me, where it's often you robbed your own mother, and you stealing away to go cardplaying the half crowns she had hid in the churn.

ROCK. Didn't you get very wicked and hurtful, you that was a nice class of a woman without no harm!

FLANNERY. Ah, Ma'am, you that was easy-minded, it is not kind for you to be a scold.

MOTHER. And another thing, it was the same day where Michael Flannery (*turns to him*) came in an' told me of you being grown so covetous you had made away with your dog, by reason you begrudged it its diet.

ROCK (*to* FLANNERY). You had a great deal to say about me!

MOTHER. And more than that again, he said you had it buried secretly, and had it personated, creeping around the haggard in the half dark and you barking, the way the neighbours would think it to be living yet and as wicked as it was before.

ROCK (*to* FLANNERY). I'll bring you into the Courts for telling lies!

MOTHER (*coming near* ROCK *and speaking into his ear*). And there's another thing I know, and that I made a promise to her that was your wife not to tell, but death has that promise broke.

ROCK. Stop, can't you!

MOTHER. I know by sure witness that it was you found the forty

285

pound *he* (*points to* FLANNERY *who nods*) lost on the road, and kept it for your own profit. Bring me now, I dare you, into the Courts!

ROCK (*fearfully*). That one would remember the world! It is as if she went to the grinding young!

(CONAN'S *voice heard. Singing:* "*Let me be merry*" *in a melancholy voice.*)

> "If sadly thinking with spirits sinking
> Could more than drinking my cares compose,
> A cure for to-morrow from sighs I'd borrow,
> And hope to-morrow would end my woes.
> But as in wailing there's nought availing,
> And Death unfailing will strike the blow,
> Then for that reason and for a season,
> Let us be merry before we go! "

MOTHER. It is Conan will near lose his wits with joy when he knows what is come back to me!

CONAN (*peeping in*). Is Celia gone?

FLANNERY. She is, Conan.

CONAN. It's a queer thing with women. If you'll turn them from one road it's likely they'll go into another that is worse again.

ROCK. That is so indeed. There is Celia's mother that is running telling lies, and leaving a heavy word upon a neighbour.

MOTHER. I'll give my promise not to tell it out in Court if he will give to poor Michael Flannery what is due to him, and that is the whole of what he has in his bag!

CONAN (*laughing scornfully*). Sure *she* has no memory at all. It fails her to remember that two and two makes four.

MOTHER. You think that? Well, listen now to me. Two and two is it? No, nine times two that is eighteen and nine times three twenty-seven, nine times four thirty-six, nine times five forty-five, nine times six fifty-four, nine times seven sixty-three, nine times eight seventy-two, nine times nine eighty-one. . . . Yes and eleven times, and any times that you will put before me!

CONAN. That's enough, that's enough!

MOTHER. Ha, ha! You giving out that I can keep no knowledge in mind and no learning, when I should sit on the chapel roof to have enough of slates for all I can cast up of sums! Multiplication, Addition, Subtraction, and the rule of three!

CONAN. Whist your tongue!

MOTHER. Is it the verses of Raftery's talk into the Bush you would wish me to give out, or the three hundred and sixty-nine verses of the Contention of the Bards—(*Repeats verse of "The Talk with the Bush" in Irish*)

"Céad agus míle roimh am na h-Airce
Tús agus crothugadh m'aois agus mo dhata
Thá me o shoin im' shuidhe san áit so
Agus is iomdha sgéal a bhféadain trácht air."

Or I'll English it if that will please you:

"A hundred years and a thousand before the time of the Ark
Was the beginning and creation of my age and my date;
I am from that time sitting in this place,
And it's many a story I am able to give news of."

CONAN (*puting hands to ears and walking away*). I am thinking your mind got unsettled with the weight of years.

MOTHER (*following him*). No, but your own that got scattered from the time you ran barefoot carying worms in a tin can for that Professor of a Collegian that went fishing in the stream, and that you followed after till you got to think yourself a lamp of light for the universe!

CONAN. Will you stop deafening the whole world with your babble!

MOTHER. There was always a bad drop in you that attached to you out of the grandfather. What did your languages do for you but to sharpen your tongue, till the scrape of it would take the skin off, the same as a cat! My blessing on you, Conan, but my curse upon your mouth!

CONAN. Oh, will you stop your chat!

MOTHER. Every word you speak having in it the sting of a bee that was made out of the curses of a saint!

CONAN. Stop your gibberish!

MOTHER. Are you satisfied now?

CONAN. I'm not satisfied!

MOTHER. And never will be, for you were ever and always a fault-finder and full of crossness from the day that you were small suited.

CONAN. You remember that, too?

MOTHER. I do well!

CONAN. Where is the bellows? Was it you (*to* FLANNERY) that blew a blast on her?

FLANNERY. It was not.

CONAN. Or you?

ROCK. It's long sorry I'd be to do such a thing!

CONAN. It is certain someone did it on her. Where now is it?

MOTHER (*seizing him*). And I remember the day you threw out your mug of milk into the street, by reason, says you, you didn't like the colour of the cow that gave it!

CONAN. Will you stop ripping up little annoyances, till I'll find the bellows!

ROCK. It's what I'm thinking her memory will soon be back at the far side of Solomon's Temple.

MOTHER (*repeats in Irish*). Agus is iomdha sgéal a bhféadain trácht air!

CONAN (*shouting*). Is it that you'll drive the seven senses out of me!

MOTHER. Is it that you begrudge me my recollection? Ha, I have it in spite of you. (*Sings*)

"Oft in the stilly night
    Ere slumber's chain hath bound me
    Fond memory brings the light
    Of other days around me.
    The smiles, the tears, of childhood's years,
    The words of love then spoken—
    The eyes that shone, now dimmed and gone,
    The cheerful hearts now broken.

    Thus in the still night—
    Ere slumber's chain hath bound me
    Fond memory brings the light
    Of other days around me!"

CELIA (*bursting in*). Where is Conan?

CONAN. What do you want of me?

CELIA. I have got the hair brush.

CONAN. Let you not come near me!

CELIA. And the comb!

CONAN. Get away from me!

CELIA. And the scissors.

CONAN. Will you drive me out of the house or will I drive you out of it!

CELIA. Ah, be easy!

CONAN. I will not be easy!

CELIA (*pushing him back in a chair*). It will delight the world to see the way I'll send you out!

CONAN. Is the universe gone distracted mad!

CELIA. Be quiet now!

CONAN. Leave your hold of me!

CELIA. One stir, and the scissors will run into you!
(*Sings* "*With a snippet, a snippet, a snippet.*")

Curtain.

ACT III

SCENE. *The* TWO CATS *are looking over the settle. Music behind
scene:* "*O Johnny, I hardly knew you!*"

1ST CAT. We did well leaving the bellows for that foolish Human
to see what he can do. There is great sport before us and behind.

2ND CAT. The best I ever saw since the Jesters went out from
Tara.

1ST CAT. They to be giving themselves high notions and to be
looking down on Cats!

2ND CAT. Ha, Ha, Ha, the folly and the craziness of men! To
see him changing them from one thing to the next, as if they
wouldn't be a two-legged laughing stock whatever way they would
change.

1ST CAT. There's apt to be more changes yet till they will hardly
know one another, or every other one, to be himself! (*Sings*)

"Where are your eyes that looked so mild,
　　Hurroo! Hurroo!
Where are your eyes that looked so mild
When my poor heart you first beguiled,
Why did you run from me and the child?
　　O Johnny, I hardly knew you!

"With drums and guns and guns and drums,
　　The enemy nearly slew you!
My darling dear you look so queer,
　　O Johnny, I hardly knew you!

"Where are the legs with which you run,
When you went to carry a gun.
Indeed your dancing days are done,
　　O Johnny, I hardly knew you! "

(TIMOTHY *and* MOTHER *come in from opposite doors.* CATS *disappear—music still heard faintly.*)

MOTHER (*looking at litttle bellows in her hand*). Do you know *That* what it is, Timothy?

TIMOTHY. Is it now a hand-bellows? It's long since I seen the like of that.

MOTHER. It is, but *what* bellows?

TIMOTHY. Not a bellows? I'd nearly say it to be one.

MOTHER. There has strange things come to pass.

TIMOTHY. That's what we've all been praying for this long time!

MOTHER. Ah, can't you give attention and strive to listen to me. It is all coming back to my mind. All the things I am remembering have my mind tattered and tossed.

TIMOTHY (*who has been trying to hear the music, sings a verse*).

"You haven't an arm and you haven't a leg,
　　Hurroo! Hurroo!
You're a yellow noseless chickenless egg,
You'll have to put up with a bowl to beg.
　　O Johnny, I hardly knew you! (*Music ceases.*)

MOTHER. Will you give attention, I say! It will be worth while for you to go chat with me now I can be telling you all that happened in my years gone by. What was it Conan was questioning me about a while ago? What was it now. . . .

"Aristotle in the hour
He left Ireland left a power! . . .

TIMOTHY. That now is a very nice sort of a little prayer.

MOTHER (*calling out*). That's it! Aristotle's Bellows! I know now what has happened. This that is in my hand has in it the power to make changes. Changes! Didn't great changes come in the house to-day! (*Shouts*) Did you see any great change in Celia?

TIMOTHY. Why wouldn't I, and she at this minute fighting and barging at some poor travelling man, saying he laid a finger mark of bacon-grease upon the lintel of the door. Driving him off with a broken-toothed rake she is, she that was so gentle that she wouldn't hardly pluck the feathers of a dead duck!

MOTHER. It was surely a blast of this worked that change in her, as the blast she blew upon me worked a change in myself. O! all the thoughts and memories that are thronging in my mind and in my head! Rushing up within me the same as chaff from the flail! Songs and stories and the newses I heard through the whole course of my lifetime! And I having no person to tell them out to! Do you hear me what I'm saying, Timothy? (*Shouts in his ear.*) What is come back to me is what I lost so long ago, my MEMORY.

TIMOTHY. So it is a very good song.

(*Sings*)

> "By Memory inspired, and love of glory fired,
> The deeds of men I love to dwell upon,
> And the sympathetic glow of my spirit must bestow
> On the memory of Mitchell that is gone, boys, gone—
> The memory of Mitchell that is gone! "

MOTHER. Thoughts crowding on one another, mixing themselves up with one another for the want of sifting and settling! They'll have me distracted and I not able to speak them out to some person! Conan as surly as a bramble bush, and Celia wrapped up in her bucket and her broom! And yourself not able to hear one word I say. (*Sobs, and bellows falls from her hands.*)

TIMOTHY. I'll lay it down now out of your way, ma'am, the way you can cry your fill whatever ails you.

MOTHER (*snatching it back*). Stop! I'll not part with it! I know now what I can do! Now! (*Points it at him.*) I'll make a companion to be listening to me through the long winter nights and the long summer days, and the world to be without any end at all, no more than the round of the full moon! You that have no hearing, this will bring back your hearing, the way you'll be a listener and a benefit to myself for ever. I wouldn't feel the weeks long that time!

(*Blows.* TIMOTHY *turns away and gropes toward wall.*)
(*She sings: Air,* "*Eileen Aroon.*")

> "What if the days go wrong,
> When you can hear!
> What if the evening's long,
> You being near,
> I'll tell my troubles out,
> Put darkness to the rout
> And to the roundabout!
> Having your ear! "

(ROCK *at door: sneezes.* MOTHER *drops bellows and goes.* TIMOTHY *gives a cry, claps hands to ears and rushes out as if terrified.*)

ROCK (*coming in seizes bellows*). Well now, didn't this turn to

291

be very lucky and very good! The very thing I came looking for to be left there under my hands! (*Puts it hurriedly under coat.*)

FLANNERY (*coming in*). What are you doing here, James Rock?

ROCK. What are you doing yourself?

FLANNERY. What is that under your coat?

ROCK. What's that to you?

FLANNERY. I'll know that when I see it.

ROCK. What call have you to be questioning me?

FLANNERY. Open now your coat!

ROCK. Stand out of my way!

FLANNERY (*suddenly tearing open coat and seizing bellows*). Did you think it was unknownst to me you stole the bellows?

ROCK. Ah, what steal?

FLANNERY. Put it back in the place it was!

ROCK. I will within three minutes.

FLANNERY. You'll put it back here and now.

ROCK (*coaxingly*). Look at here now, Michael Flannery, we'll make a league between us. Did you ever see such folly as we're after seeing to-day? Sitting there for an hour and a half till that one settled the world upside down!

FLANNERY. If I did see folly, what I see now is treachery.

ROCK. Didn't you take notice of the way that foolish old man is wasting and losing what was given him for to benefit mankind? A blast he has lost turning a pigeon to a crow, as if there wasn't enough in it before of that tribe picking the spuds out of the ridges. And another blast he has lost turning poor Celia, that was harmless, to be a holy terror of cleanness and a scold.

FLANNERY. Indeed, he'd as well have left her as she was. There was something very pleasing in her little sleepy ways.

(*Sings*)

> "But sad it is to see you so
> And to think of you now as an object of woe;
> Your Peggy'll still keep an eye on her beau.
> O Johnny, I hardly knew you!"

ROCK. Bringing back to the memory of his mother every old grief and rancour. She that has a right to be making her peace with the grave!

FLANNERY. Indeed it seems he doesn't mind what he'll get so long as it's something that he wants.

ROCK. Three blasts gone! And the world didn't begin to be cured.

FLANNERY. Sure enough he gave the bellows no fair play.

ROCK. He has us made a fool of. He using it the way he did, he has us robbed.

FLANNERY. There's power in the four blasts left would bring peace and piety and prosperity and plenty to every one of the four provinces of Ireland.

ROCK. That's it. There's no doubt but I'll make a better use of it than him, because I am a better man than himself.

FLANNERY. I don't know. You might not get so much respect in Dublin.

ROCK. Dublin, where are you! What would I'd do going to Dublin? Did you never hear said the skin to be nearer than the shirt?

FLANNERY. What do you mean saying that?

ROCK. The first one I have to do good to is myself.

FLANNERY. Is it that you would grab the benefit of the bellows?

ROCK. In troth I will. I've got a hold of it, and by cripes I'll knock a good turn out of it.

FLANNERY. To rob the country and the poor for your own profit? You are a class of man that is gathering all for himself.

ROCK. It is not worth while we to fall out of friendship. I will use but the one blast.

FLANNERY. You have no right or call to meddle with it.

ROCK. The first thing I will meddle with is my own rick of turf. And I'll give you leave to go do the same with your own umbrella, or whatever property you may own.

FLANNERY. Sooner than be covetous like yourself I'd live and die in a ditch, and be buried from the Poorhouse!

ROCK. Turf being black and light in the hand, and gold being shiny and weighty, there will be no delay in turning every sod into a solid brick of gold. I give you leave to do the same thing, and we'll be two rich men inside a half an hour!

FLANNERY. You are no less than a thief! (*Snatches at bellows.*)

ROCK. Thief yourself. Leave your hand off it!

FLANNERY. Give it up here for the man that owns it!

ROCK. You may set your coffin making for I'll beat you to the ground.

FLANNERY (*as he clutches*). Ah, you have given it a shove. It has blown a blast on yourself!

ROCK. Yourself that blew it on me! Bad cess to you! But I'll do the same bad turn upon you! (*Blows.*)

293

FLANNERY. There is some footstep without. Heave it in under the ashes.

ROCK. Whist your tongue! (*Flings bellows behind hearth.*)

(CONAN *comes in.*)

CONAN. With all the chattering of women I have the train near lost. The car is coming for me and I'll make no delay now but to set out.

(*Sings.*)

"Oh the French are on the sea,
        Says the Sean Van Vocht,
Oh the French are on the sea,
        Says the Sean Van Vocht,
Oh the French are in the bay,
        They'll be here without delay,
        And the Orange will decay,
        Says the Sean Van Vocht! "

Here now is my little pack. You were saying, Thomas Flannery, you would be lending me the loan of your umbrella.

FLANNERY. Ah, what umbrella? There's no fear of rain.

CONAN (*taking it*). You to have proffered it I would not refuse it.

FLANNERY (*seizing it*). I don't know. I have to mind my own property. It might not serve it to be loaning it to this one and that. It might leave the ribs of it bare.

CONAN. That's the way with the whole of ye. I to give you my heart's blood you'd turn me upside down for a pint of porter!

FLANNERY. I see no sense or charity in lending to another anything that might be of profit to myself.

CONAN. Let you keep it so! That your ribs may be as bare as its own ribs that are bursting out through the cloth!

ROCK. Do not give heed to him, Conan. There is in this bag (*takes it out*) what will bring you every whole thing you might be wanting in the town. (*Takes out notes and gold and gives them.*)

CONAN. It is only a small share I'll ask the lend of.

ROCK. The lend of! No, but a free gift!

CONAN. Well now, aren't you turned to be very kind? (*Takes notes.*)

ROCK. Put that back in the bag. Here it is, the whole of it. Five and fifty pounds. Take it and welcome! It is yourself will make a good use of it laying it out upon the needy and the poor. Changing all for their benefit and their good! Oh, since St. Bridget spread her cloak upon the Curragh this is the most day and the happiest day ever came to Ireland.

CONAN (*giving bag to* FLANNERY). Take it you, as is your due by what the mother said a while ago about the robbery he did on you in the time past.

FLANNERY. Give it here to me. I'll engage I'll keep a good grip on it from this out. It's long before any other one will get a one look at it!

CONAN. There would seem to be a great change—and a sudden change come upon the two of ye. . . . (*With a roar.*) Where now is the bellows?

FLANNERY (*sulkily*). What way would I know?

CONAN (*shaking him*). I know well what happened! It is *ye* have stolen two of my blasts! Putting changes on yourselves ye would— much good may it do ye—Thieving with your covetousness the last two nearly I had left!

ROCK (*sulkily*). Leave your hand off me! I never stole no blast!

CONAN. There's a bad class going through the world. The most people you will give to will be the first to cry you down. This was a wrong out of measure! Thieves ye are and pickpockets! Ye that were not worth changing from one to another, no more than you'd change a pinch of dust off the road into a puff of ashes. Stealing away my lovely blasts, bad luck to ye, the same as Prometheus stole the makings of a fire from the ancient gods!

FLANNERY. That is enough of keening and lamenting after a few blasts of barren wind—I'll be going where I have my own business to attend.

CONAN. Where, so, is the bellows?

FLANNERY. How would I know?

CONAN. The two of ye won't quit this till I'll find it! There is another two blasts in it that will bring sense and knowledge into Ireland yet!

ROCK. Indeed they might bring comfort yet to many a sore heart!

CONAN (*searching*). Where now is it? I couldn't find it if the earth rose up and swallowed it. Where now did I lay it down?

ROCK. There's too much changes in this place for me to know where anything is gone.

CONAN (*at door*). Where are you Maryanne! Celia! Timothy! Let ye come hither and search out my little bellows!

(TIMOTHY *comes in followed by* MOTHER.)

CONAN. Hearken now, Timothy!

TIMOTHY (*stopping his ears*). Speak easy, speak easy!

CONAN. Take down now your fingers from your ears the way you will hear my voice!

TIMOTHY. Have a care now with your screeching would you split the drum of my ear?

CONAN. Is it that you have got your hearing?

TIMOTHY. My hearing is it? As good as that I can hear a lie, and it forming in the mind.

CONAN. Is that the truth you're saying?

TIMOTHY. Hear, is it! I can hear every whisper in this parish and the seven parishes are nearest. And the little midges roaring in the air.—Let ye whist now with your sneezing in the draught!

CONAN. This is surely the work of the bellows. Another blast gone!

ROCK. So it would be too. Mostly the whole of them gone and spent. It's hard know in the morning what way will it be with you at night. (*Sings.*)

> "I saw from the beach when the morning was shining
>   A bark o'er the waters move gloriously on—
> I came when the sun o'er the beach was declining,
>   The bark was still there, but the waters were gone."

TIMOTHY. It is yourself brought the misfortune on me, calling your Druid spells into the house.

CONAN. It is not upon you I ever turned it.

TIMOTHY. You have a great wrong done to me!

MOTHER. It is glad you should be and happy.

TIMOTHY. Happy, is it? Give me a hareskin cap for to put over my ears, having wool in it very thick! (*Sings.*)

> "Silent, O Moyle, be the roar of thy water,
>   Break not ye breezes your chain of repose,
> While murmuring mournfully Lir's lonely daughter
>   Tells to the night-star her tale of woes.
>
> When shall the swan, her death-note singing,
>   Sleep with wings in darkness furl'd?
> When will heaven its sweet bells ringing
>   Call my spirit from this stormy world?"

MOTHER. Come with me now and I'll be chatting to you.

TIMOTHY. Why would I be listening to your blather when I have the voices of the four winds to be listening to? The night wind, the east wind, the black wind and the wind from the south!

CONAN. Such a thing I never saw before in all my natural life.

TIMOTHY. To be hearing, without understanding it, the language of the tribes of the birds! (*Puts hands over ears again.*) There's too many sounds in the world! The sounds of the earth are terrible! The roots squeezing and jostling one another through the clefts, and the crashing of the acorn from the oak. The cry of the little birdeen in under the silence of the hawk!

CONAN (*to* MOTHER). As it was you let it loose upon him, let you bring him away to some hole or cave of the earth.

TIMOTHY. It is my desire to go cast myself in the ocean where there'll be but one sound of its waves, the fishes in its meadows being dumb! (*Goes to corner and hides his head in a sack.*)

MOTHER. Even so there might likely be a mermaid playing reels on her silver comb, and yourself craving after the world you left.

(*Sings: Air, "Spailpín Fánach."*)

"You think to go from every woe to peace in the wide ocean,
But you will find your foolish mind repent its foolish notion.
When dog-fish dash and mermaids splash their finny tails to find
you,
I'll make a bet that you'll regret the world you left behind you!"

CELIA (*clattering in with broom, etc*). What are ye doing, coming in this room again after I having it settled so nice? I'll allow no one in the place again, only carriage company that will have no speck of dust upon the sole of their shoe!

MOTHER. Oh, Celia, there has strange things happened!

CELIA. What I see strange is that some person has meddled with that hill of ashes on the hearth and set it flying athrough the air. Is it hens ye are wishful to be, that would be searching and scratching in the dust for grains? And this thrown down in the midst! (*Holds up bellows.*)

CONAN. Give me my bellows!

MOTHER. No, but give it to me!

ROCK AND FLANNERY. Give it to myself!

TIMOTHY (*looking up, with hands on ears*). My curse upon it and its work. Little I care if it goes up with the clouds.

CELIA. What in the world wide makes the whole of ye so eager to get hold of such a thing?

CONAN. It has but the one blast left! (*Sings.*)

" 'Tis the last Rose of Summer
Left blooming alone,
All her lovely companions
Are faded and gone.
No flower of her kindred,
No rosebud is nigh,
To reflect back her blushes
Or give sigh for sigh! "

CELIA. What are you fretting about blasts and about roses?
ROCK. It has a charm on it—
FLANNERY. To change the world—
MOTHER. That changed myself—
CONAN. For the worse—
MOTHER. And Timothy—
CONAN. For the worse—
ROCK. Myself and Flannery—
CONAN. For the worse, for the worse—
MOTHER. Conan that changed yourself with it—
CONAN. For the very worst!
CELIA (to CONAN). Is it riddles, or is it that you put a spell and a change upon me?
CONAN. If I did, it was for your own good!
CELIA. Do you call it for my good to set me running till I have my toes going through my shoes? (Holds them out.)
CONAN. I didn't think to go that length.
CELIA. To roughen my hands with soap and scalding water till they're near as knotted and as ugly as your own!
CONAN. Ah, leave me alone. I tell you it is not by my own fault. My plan and my purpose that went astray and that broke down.
CELIA. I will not leave you till you'll change me back to what I was. What way can these hands go to the dance house to-night? Change me back, I say!
ROCK. And me—
TIMOTHY. And myself, that I'll have quiet in my head again.
CONAN. I cannot undo what has been done. There is no back way.
TIMOTHY. Is there no way at all to come out of it safe and sane?
CONAN (shakes head). Let ye make the best of it.
FLANNERY (sings). (Air, "I saw from the Beach.")

"Ne'er tell me of glories serenely adorning
The close of our day, the calm eve of our night.
Give me back, give me back the wild freshness of morning,
Her clouds and her tears are worth evening's best light."

MOTHER (*who has bellows in her hand*). Stop! Stop—my mind is travelling backward . . . so far I can hardly reach to it . . . but I'll come to it . . . the way I'll be changed to what I was before, and the town and the country wishing me well, I having got my enough of unfriendly looks and hards words!

TIMOTHY. Hurry on Ma'am, and remember, and take the spell off the whole of us.

MOTHER. I am going back, back, to the longest thing that is in my mind and my memory! . . . I myself a child in my mother's arms the very day I was christened. . . .

CONAN. Ah, stop your raving!

MOTHER. Songs and storytelling, and my old generations laying down news of this spell that is now come to pass. . . .

ROCK. Did they tell what way to undo the charm?

MOTHER. You have but to turn the bellows the same as the smith would turn the anvil, or St. Patrick turned the stone for fine weather . . . and to blow a blast . . . and a twist will come inside in it and the charm will fall off with that blast, and undo the work that has been done!

ALL. Turn it so!

(CATS *look over, playing on fiddles* "O Johnny, I hardly knew you," *while mother blows on each.*)

TIMOTHY. Ha! (*Takes hands from ears and puts one behind his ear.*)

ROCK. Ha! Where now is my bag? (*Turns out his pockets, unhappy to find them empty.*)

FLANNERY. Ha! (*Smiles and holds out umbrella to* CONAN *who takes it.*)

MOTHER (*to* CELIA). Let you blow a blast on me. (CELIA *does so.*) Now it's much if I can remember to blow a blast backward upon yourself!

CELIA. Stop a minute! Leave what is in me of life and of courage till I will blow the last blast is in the bellows upon Conan.

CONAN. Stop that! Do you think to change and to crow over me. You will not or I'll lay my curse upon you, unless you would change me into an eagle would be turning his back upon the whole of ye, and facing to his perch upon the right hand of the master of the gods!

CELIA. Is it to waste the last blast you would? Not at all. As we burned the candle we'll burn the inch! I'll not make two halves of it, I'll give it to you entirely!

CONAN. You will not, you unlucky witch of illwill!

(*Protects himself with umbrella.*)

CELIA (*having got him to a corner*). Let you take things quiet and easy from this out, and be as content as you have been contrary from the very day and hour of your birth!

(*She blows upon him and he sits down smiling.* MOTHER *blows on* CELIA, *and she sits down in first attitude.*)

CELIA (*taking up pigeon*). Oh, there you are come back my little dove and my darling!

(*Sings:* "*Shule Aroon.*")

> "Come sit and settle on my knee
> And I'll tell you and you'll tell me
> A tale of what will never be,
> Go-dé-tóu-Mavourneen slan! "

CONAN (*lighting pipe*). So the dove is there, too. Aristotle said there is nothing at the end but what there used to be at the beginning. Well now, what a pleasant day we had together, and what good neighbours we all are, and what a comfortable family entirely.

ROCK. You would seem to have done with your complaints about the universe, and your great plan to change it overthrown.

CONAN. Not a complaint! What call have I to go complaining? The world is a very good world, the best nearly I ever knew.

(*Sings.*)

> "O, a little cock sparrow he sat on a tree,
> O, a little cock sparrow he sat on a tree,
> O, a little cock sparrow he sat on a tree,
> And he was as happy as happy could be,
> With a chirrup, a chirrup, a chirrup!
>
> "A chirrup, a chirrup, a chirrup!
> A chirrup, a chirrup, a chirrup!
> A chirrup, a chirrup, a chirrup!
> A chirrup, a chirrup, a——! "

Curtain.

THE STORY BROUGHT BY BRIGIT

THE STORY BROUGHT BY BRIGIT

PERSONS

JOEL. *A Boy from the Mountains.*
DANIEL. *A Tramp.*
MARCUS. *A Sergeant of Pilate's Guard.*
SILAS. *A Scribe in Caiaphas's Employment.*
PILATE. *The Roman Governor.*
JUDAS ISCARIOT.
ST. JOHN.
ST. BRIGIT.
1ST WOMAN.
2ND WOMAN.
3RD WOMAN.
1ST MAN.
2ND MAN.
1ST SOLDIER.
2ND SOLDIER.
3RD SOLDIER.
A YOUNG SCRIBE.
AN EGYPTIAN NURSE.
THE MOTHER.
THE CHRIST.
A CROWD.

ACT I

SCENE: *Outside the Gate of Jerusalem. Before the curtain goes up voices are heard singing:*

> *Bring every bough of the budding willow;*
> *Strew every branch on the stony street.*
> *He that has made the stones his pillow*
> *Ready the road before his feet!*

As the curtain rises, the three WOMEN *are seen strewing green branches as they go off.* DANIEL *is sitting at the Gate.* JOEL *is looking down the road, shading his eyes with his hand.*

JOEL. I think the time will never come when I will see him!
DANIEL. He should be near at hand. I could see the dust rising

when I was on the height above. There would seem to be a great throng of people following after him.

JOEL. He is worthy of it. The whole of the country is for him.

DANIEL. Ah, it's easy gather a crowd. There are always fools knocking about that would follow after anyone's whistle.

JOEL. They are no fools that follow after this man. They are saying up in the mountains it is himself has come to raise up the ruin of our people.

DANIEL. I've seen them come and seen them go. A great cry at the beginning for anyone with a big voice, and its likely all turning against him at the latter end.

JOEL. They will never turn against *him*. He is the leader we have been waiting for this long time. He will be our Prince and Captain, the same as Judas Maccabæus that rose up and fought for his nation.

DANIEL. Little he'll lead you to that will be of any use.

JOEL. Every use! To put out the Roman strangers and to take off their yoke. Haven't they enough of countries in their hand without coming ploughing through the sea for to meddle with our own?

DANIEL. And what call has this man preaching on the road to go meddle with them?

JOEL (*coming nearer*). Where was his birthplace? Isn't it fore-told in the prophecies? "But thou Bethlehem, though thou be little among the thousands of Judea, yet out of thee shall come a ruler in Israel! He will deliver you from your enemies. He will go through them, as a young lion among the flocks of sheep!" To give us our freedom.

DANIEL. Ah, freedom never put a penny in anyone's pocket. What is wanted is to do away with the rich, and to give their goods to the poor.

JOEL. "Instead of a bondwoman our country will become a free woman!"

DANIEL. Freedom how are you! The rich will be stiff and cove-tous, and the grabbers will grab all the same as at this day. But I'll give in that this Nazarene gave a good advice when he said, "If any man take away your coat let him have your cloak also." That hits at the wealthy ones that own a coat and a cloak along with it.

JOEL. Maybe so. They are saying it is the moneyed people are keeping up the foreign Government.

DANIEL. You would like to be listening to his talk, they were telling me, of the wealthy man that was sent to the flames of hell.

That's the chat! Let him frighten them with fire to their heels till they'll divide with us the riches they own.

JOEL. Ah, be quiet. You only want to grab for yourself. Little you care for the country or the nation.

DANIEL. It is you rebels are destroying us with all your foolish talk. I don't know what put it in your head at all.

JOEL. I heard rebellion talked ever and always and I a child, in the high mountains and on the low ground. Our country a ruin, our people scattered—

DANIEL. Sure enough the country is in tatters. It is hardly worth begging around for your bite, let alone striving to find the price of a drink.

JOEL. There can be no content until we send the foreign devils back to their own place in the North, or wherever Rome may be. They thinking it is crucifying the half of us will bring the rest of us kissing their hand. We'll put trembling in their heart yet!

DANIEL. You'll put yourselves in jeopardy, that's sure enough. And you never will have strength to stand against them.

JOEL. He that is in the prophecy, "a leader and commander of the people," will be well able to banish the whole drift of them.

(*The* WOMEN *come back.*)

1ST WOMAN (*to* JOEL). It will not be long now till you will see him. There was a sound brought upon the wind a while ago, like the noise of the little bees at their harvesting.

(BRIGIT *comes in from the gate. She wears a long cloak, and carries a staff. There is dust on her.*)

ST. BRIGIT. God save all here!

THE WOMEN. God save you kindly.

ST. BRIGIT. I am a stranger and astray in this place. All the people in the houses and in the street are running to and fro, as if preparing for the marriage or the crowning of a king. I could get no answer from them, or no word.

1ST WOMAN. You should be a stranger indeed, and not to know this is the day of preparation for the great feast of the Passover.

ST. BRIGIT. I am come from the West, from the edge of the great ocean. I have crossed land and sea; I have seen many a rising and setting of the sun.

2ND WOMAN. Oh, wasn't the journey long on you!

ST. BRIGIT. Winter came on me and the heat of summer, and winter again, till I hardly knew the seasons of the year, through the way they change according as I travel.

3RD WOMAN. It should be to look for some friend or some one of your kindred you are come?

ST. BRIGIT. It was in a dream or a vision of the night I saw a Young Man having wounds on him. And I knew him to be One I had helped and had fostered, and he a Child in his mother's arms. And it was showed me in my dream there would trouble come on him but in the end he would put gladness in the heart of His friends. And it was showed to me that the place where I would find him would be in this country of Judea, a long, long way to the east.

2ND WOMAN. And was it in your own country you had fostered him?

ST. BRIGIT. There came to my own country about thirty years ago a Young Woman that was seeking shelter and a hiding place for her Child. There was some wicked king looking for his life, some cruel man, one Herod.

JOEL. That is it. A cruel man he was, and left a bad name after him.

1ST WOMAN. It's likely enough he would have made away with the child. There was great talk of it at the time.

3RD WOMAN. And what way could a young child and his mother go travel beyond the waves of the sea?

ST. BRIGIT. It might be that an angel opened a path before them. A shining Messenger, and a Young Woman, and a Baby on her arm, and they so beautiful that all the people were crowding on them to see the beautiful people that were passing by.

2ND WOMAN. Thirty years ago. He should be a grown man now and in his bloom. Do you think could it be the Man we are waiting for to-day?

ST. BRIGIT. It may be so, but up to this time it has failed me to get any tidings of that Mother and that Child.

JOEL. It is he has power to free and to deliver his people. There will be a great welcome before him, and he coming into Jerusalem. You might hear the shouting a while ago, if you were outside of the city.

ST. BRIGIT. I thought to find him in the House of God that is there, for surely God Himself had a hand in him. And so I went into the Temple.

JOEL. You did not find him there.

ST. BRIGIT. It had more the look of a fair or a market than of a place of prayer. Cattle and sheep were in it, sellers and buyers, money-lenders calling out and cheating, barging and bargaining. No place for anyone that would come without money in the hand.

So I left it and came away. It had not the appearance of the Gate of Heaven.

1ST WOMAN. That is what our Master said a while ago—"My House should be called the house of prayer, but ye have made it a den of thieves." And whatever it was then, it is seven times worse at this time of the preparation for the Feast.

3RD WOMAN. Sit down now and put off from you the weight of the journey, and you will see him when he comes to this place. (BRIGIT *sits down.*)

2ND WOMAN. He is coming nearer.

JOEL. No, he has stopped again. There are people around Him in droves. They are pressing on Him. There is one brought in a bed.

1ST WOMAN. They have brought him to our Lord for his healing. The shadows are beginning to lengthen, and they will never give him leave to pass the road.

3RD WOMAN. No doubt at all but he is a great Saint. I saw a lame man going to him on crutches, and after he had laid a hand on him he walked away cured, leaving the sticks after him.

1ST WOMAN. There was a man that had the eyesight lost—stone dark he was—brought to him, and going away he was as well able to find his way as any other person. He is not like the scribes and Pharisees that don't care if you died on the side of the road.

3RD WOMAN (*to* BRIGIT). Come hither where the road rises, and you might chance to get a sight of him.

ST. BRIGIT. If I see him you are speaking of, and that he is the same I fostered, it is a great story I will have to bring back to the West. I always knew when I looked at that child that he had on him the blessing of Heaven.

(*She and the three* WOMEN *go down the road.*)

DANIEL (*who has been looking in at the gate*). There are two I see coming have no good will, it is likely, towards that man that is walking the road.

JOEL (*looking in at the gate*). One of them would seem to be a Roman.

DANIEL. He is Marcus, that is Sergeant of the Guard to Pilate the Governor, and that was reared in his house, and is the keeper of his secrets and his keys. Come here, out of their way. (*They move aside.*) The other is Silas, a very crabbed man of the sect of the Pharisees, that is a scribe in the pay of Caiaphas, the High Priest, and that some give out is his spy. I see him going here and everywhere. Picking up news he is to bring his master. Come on now, I'd as lief get out of this.

307

(*As they go from the gate,* MARCUS, *an old man in soldier's dress, comes on, followed quickly by* SILAS, *who is middle-aged and fat.*)

SILAS. A fine day, Marcus, to be taking the air outside the gate. There is too much of noise and of dust within in the city.

MARCUS (*sitting down on the seat* DANIEL *has left*). I was looking at the throng in the streets for a while, flocking about, having carcasses of beasts in their hands. An outlandish sort of a sight.

SILAS. Making ready they are for the Passover.

MARCUS. Pilate himself was taking a view of them for a while from the steps of his palace. He laid down it was as laughable a thing as ever he saw in a circus.

SILAS. We'll get some ease from the cattle after this week. It is our great Feast of the year.

MARCUS. I wonder you yourself would be free to come out here, and you in Caiaphas's household. Your mind should be running on the killing of the lambs for your big day.

SILAS. That is not my work. I have plenty of time to go abroad in the air.

MARCUS. You'd want it. Well, it's not altogether for pleasuring I am here myself, but to see what way is order kept, and nothing taking place that would annoy the over-Government. You yourself should be able to tell me that much.

SILAS (*looking round*). Don't be talking here. You wouldn't know who might be listening.

MARCUS. Little I care what is heard of anything I have to say. The Roman Power is safe, whatever illwishers may do or think. What is this I am told about some new preacher or prophet that is risen up—one that they call the Nazarene?

SILAS. That is the very one is now coming up the road. It is likely you were not without hearing that much within the Governor's house.

MARCUS. I heard some talk that all your common people were cracked after him, and making much of him wherever he goes.

SILAS. There are some without sense that will run after anyone that is new and would loosen the commands of the law. An ignorant man! Paying no respect to learning! Would make nothing of breaking the ten commandments. You'll see Caiaphas will whip them in on the Feast days and bring them back to their duties.

MARCUS. There were some complaints made to us. But we are not here to protect your Jewish law but our own.

SILAS. That is where you make a great mistake. You have a right to join with us on the side of keeping law and order. This man is disorderly and a vagabond, a cause of all mischief, a rascally rambler of the roads. Owing no respect to the religion was laid down for us by Moses. It is that vexes my heart! Our religion is not like your own that is slipping like a wall where it wasn't built solid —with all your heathenish gods!

MARCUS. There are some are saying this man you are running down is a messenger sent from your own Jewish God.

SILAS. That is blasphemy. He that goes eating and drinking with a low class that do not so much as wash their hands!

MARCUS. What have we to do with that? It is nothing that will bring our Government into danger.

SILAS. To keep the people within the four corners of the law of Moses will check the coming in of this mischief, and will give strength to your hands as well as to our own.

MARCUS. A good deal of your law could be broken without bringing any danger to the Empire of Rome.

SILAS (angrily). It's danger to the whole world the way he is going on! Making little of Solomon's Temple, saying that God does not dwell in houses made with hands! Breaking the Sabbath the way he does! He goes so far as to do his cures on that day the same as any other day.

MARCUS. No harm at all in that. I remember well that Sabbath day out in the villages when my own collar-bone was broken with the upsetting of the car upon the stones, and your Jewish doctor made an oath he would not put a hand to it until after the setting of the sun. We brought him to reason with a little prod of a sword. I laughed my fill, sore and all as I was, when he said it was forbidden by your law to so much as thread a needle on the Seventh Day. We paid him off, saying it was against our own law to give him any fee on the days that were under our own gods, and that was every day of the year!

SILAS. You will maybe think worse of him upsetting the customs of the State under a colour of charity. That is his aim and drift. What he calls the law of love, that he preaches, would leave the lawyers to starve, and the soldiers that idle they would run riot through the streets having no way to earn their pay! I don't like the way you are talking. To make little of what I am telling you is to make little of myself. If you have Pilate the Governor's ear, you have no right to be putting insults on my master's Scribe!

MARCUS. That's the way with you. You are always calling out against the Roman Government, and the minute you have a quarrel with some one of your own people you come calling and craving for our help. Is it that he has an armed troop at his back?

SILAS. He has not, but a poor sort—tax-gatherers, process servers, fisher boys. He has put some sort of a spell on them. Is it that class you wish to see get the upper hand?

MARCUS. It is laid down that he bade them pay their tax to Cæsar.

SILAS. If he did I'll go bail it was through cunning, the way your Romans would not meddle with him, but leave him to nourish war and sedition. I saw a lad here at the gate this very minute that I have information is a noted rebel in his talk. A heady youngster from the hillsides, sworn to free the country from your rule.

MARCUS. Let him try that and welcome. Pilate is for policy and for patience. To tell the clean truth, a little Rising now and then is no harm at all. It gives us an excuse to get rid of disturbers and to bring more of our armies in. A Rising too is very apt to lead to splits, and splits are a great help when you want to keep a country down.

SILAS. All right so. Let him stir up discontent and turn the head of the ignorant women and men that believe him to be a messenger from heaven.

MARCUS. Be easy now. Pilate will keep an eye on him. He will do nothing to weaken your law, so long as it will help to keep the people quiet in his hand.

SILAS. Here they are coming. No, it is but one of his faction I have my eye on, one Iscariot. A class of a man I am told that would be wishing to do well for himself.

(JUDAS *comes from the road*.)

SILAS. Here now, what is this delay?

JUDAS. The people that are thronging him. He can hardly walk the road.

SILAS. Stop a minute.

JUDAS (*going on*). There is hurry on me.

SILAS. I bade you come and see me this morning.

JUDAS. I made no promise.

(*The* WOMEN *come back*.)

SILAS. Your Master will blame you if you refuse a piece of money for the bag.

1ST WOMAN. Indeed it is little our Master ever loses on himself.

2ND WOMAN. He is content with a wisp of rushes for his bed.

SILAS (*flinging a piece of silver to* JUDAS *as he goes*). It will fill someone's mouth anyway.

310

(JUDAS *takes it up and goes.*)
(*A great shout heard. People come on and stand at the road-side.* ST. BRIGIT *with them and* JOEL.)

1ST WOMAN. Blessed be he that cometh in the name of the Lord!

2ND WOMAN. Blessed be the Kingdom of our Father David!

JOEL. Blessed is the King of Israel!

(*The* WOMEN *strew more branches.*)

1ST WOMAN (*sings*)

> O blossomed branch and O apple flower!
> O sun in harvest, O blessed face!
> O golden spear in the hand of power!
> O harp that sounds in the Court of Grace!
> Lift up the gates of the golden city,
> Welcome the King of Glory in!
> Mind without malice, heart of pity.
> Lord that will master death and sin!

(CHRIST *appears. He is followed by* ST. JOHN *and a crowd. The* WOMEN *stand aside.*)

1ST WOMAN. May God enable you!

3RD WOMAN. All the luck in the world to you!

1ST WOMAN. The blessing of the Sun and Moon upon you!

JOEL. Surely his equal never walked on land or grass!

2ND WOMAN. God bless every hair of his head!

ST. BRIGIT. Why would we not shout for him that is more than any earthly King!

MARCUS (*to* SILAS). He has a great gathering of people sure enough.

SILAS. That I may live to see a bigger crowd gathered to see him made an end of!

MARCUS. No doubt but he has got them in his hand.

(*The women and others kneel before* CHRIST. *He lifts his hand in blessing. Others press round Him.*)

SILAS. What are they but fools that do not stand up and question him. Here now is a Scribe of our Court (*he takes the arm of a young man he has been whispering with*) who will stand up to him and will be well able to entangle him in his talk!

(SILAS *pushes forward the young man.*)

YOUNG SCRIBE (*going up to* CHRIST *confidently*). Tell me now, which is the first commandment of all?

CHRIST. The first of all the commandments is this: "The Lord our God is one Lord. And thou shalt love the Lord thy God with all thy heart and all thy soul and with all thy mind and with all thy strength." This is the first commandment. And the second is like, namely, "Thou shalt love thy neighbour as thyself." There is none other commandment greater than these.

YOUNG SCRIBE (*as if abashed, and moving back a step*). Well, Master, thou hast said the truth, for there is one God and none other but He. And to love Him with all the heart and with all the understanding, and to love his neighbour as himself, is more than all burnt offerings and sacrifies.

CHRIST (*raising his hand to bless him*). Thou art not far from the Kingdom of God. (*The young man goes and kneels among his followers.*)

MARCUS (*to* SILAS). You had best leave him alone unless you can do better yourself.

SILAS. So I will do better. I'll question him—or anyway that follower of his that is his nearest friend. (*Goes to* ST. JOHN.) Tell me now why is it that Master of yours that is preaching against evil doers sits down to eat with publicans and sinners?

CHRIST (*turning to look at him*). They that be whole need not a physician, but they that are sick. Go and learn what this meaneth, "I will have mercy and not sacrifice, for I am not come to call the righteous but sinners to repentance." (SILAS *turns away muttering, but at a laugh from* MARCUS *turns back again angrily.*)

SILAS. Why do your disciples transgress the tradition of the elders, not washing their hands?

CHRIST. Why do ye also transgress the counsel of God by your tradition? Ye hypocrites! Well did Esaias prophesy of you, saying, "This people draweth nigh to me with their mouth and honoureth me with their lips, but their heart is far from me!" Woe unto you Scribes and Pharisees, hypocrites! For ye shut up the kingdom of Heaven against men; for ye neither go in yourselves neither suffer ye them that are entering to go in. Ye pay tithes of mint and anise and cummin, and have omitted the weightier matters of the law, judgment, mercy and faith; these ought ye to have done, and not to leave the other undone. Ye bind heavy burdens and heavy to be borne and lay them on men's shoulders, but ye yourselves will not lift them with one of your fingers. (SILAS *slinks away.* CHRIST *goes on toward the Gate, and stops for a moment outside it.*) O Jerusalem, Jerusalem, thou that killeth the prophets and stonest them that are sent to thee! How often would I have gathered thee to me as a hen gathereth her chickens under her wing, and ye would not.

If thou hadst known, even thou, at least in this thy day, the things that belong to thy peace! But now they are hid from thine eyes. Behold your house is left unto you desolate! (*He goes in through the Gate.* SILAS *takes up a stone to fling at him, but* BRIGIT *stops him.*)

ST. BRIGIT. This is surely a man from beyond the world.

ST. JOHN. He is the Christ of God.

SILAS. He is no better than a blasphemer, breaking through the commands of the law!

ST. JOHN. The law was given by Moses, but grace and truth came by Jesus Christ. (*Goes on.*)

JOEL. He is surely the man that will deliver Israel. He is well fitted to be our King. He teaches with authority and not as do the Scribes.

(*They all follow him through the Gate, except* MARCUS *and* SILAS.)

SILAS. He must be put down. If we let him alone there is not a man but will believe in him. You must give a hand to it. Where you made your mind up to take and to keep this country ye must take the burden of governing it.

MARCUS. You have your own Courts and your Judges.

SILAS. There is no satisfaction in that. He must be put down by Roman Law.

MARCUS. You are making little of your own laws. I see no sense in that.

SILAS. There is sense and good sense in it and good reason.

MARCUS. Running down the Court of your own High Priest! You should be satisfied with that.

SILAS. I cannot be satisfied.

MARCUS. It can judge and give sentence.

SILAS. There is one thing it cannot give.

MARCUS. What thing is that?

SILAS. The penalty of death.

MARCUS. He has done nothing worthy of death.

SILAS. If we show you that he has, will you come to our aid?

MARCUS. Well, I'm not saying but we might.

SILAS. I'll hold you to that word.

MARCUS. There's no hurry. You know well you cannot bring him before us while the city is given over to your Feast. There would be an uproar of the people. Wait till he'll do something out of the way.

SILAS. He cannot be left at large misleading them as he is. He must be taken before the Feast will begin.

313

MARCUS. It's best wait a while. Pilate himself will be glad to get a little reprieve on the Feast days, and not to be attending his Court.

SILAS. There can be no delay. We must take him by craft. If we can but get someone to spy on him and get him in a snare when he is away from the throng. And here is the very one coming back I had in my mind——

MARCUS. That surly fellow who was carrying the bag?

SILAS. I was trying my hand on him yesterday. He is coveting a plot of land that has a price on it of thirty pieces of silver. I nearly had him gained, but he turned around in the finish and left me there! That's the trouble in this country! Anyone that has the name of a disturber or a rebel is as safe among them as your Cæsar on his golden throne. There is no one will harm the smallest rib of his hair.

MARCUS. Well, that is your own business.

SILAS. Just leave me with him for two minutes of time. I could maybe come around him saying it will be best for his Master's own safety to keep him gaoled for a while, and out of reach of those fierce sects that will be coming through these days from the North.

MARCUS. That'll do. I'll go on to the head of the road.

SILAS. I'll be able to do with a little coaxing and humouring.

(MARCUS *goes as* JUDAS *comes on from the Gate, walking quickly.*)

SILAS (*catching hold of his arm*). Stop a minute!

JUDAS. Let go my arm!

SILAS. What a hurry you are in. Are you forgetting what we were talking about yesterday—the price of that little field outside the walls.

JUDAS (*shaking himself free and looking at him*). Was it *you* betrayed me?

SILAS. What are you saying?

JUDAS. If it was I give you my word you'll be sorry for it.

SILAS. There was nothing to betray.

JUDAS. What was it made my comrades put me out of their company? Giving hard looks at me—turning me back this very minute from the Temple gate. What way could they know I had lent an ear to you, and you asking me to whisper one little word as to where our Master would be in the night time?

SILAS. If I did I made a good offer with it. A nice thing a little garden of land to have and to own. Money may be spent or be stolen, but the land cannot run away——

JUDAS (*with a harsh laugh*). You are wasting all that talk! I'll take your silver and your job! There is a devil come into me since yesterday, and little I care where he'll lead me. If they turn their back on me I'll make them repent it! If they reproach me with being a thief I'll be worse again than a thief! That's it. Give me money in my hand! If I liked it well up to this it will be my darling from this out, and my weapon. I'll make them know I can bring down the whole of them in giving up their Master!

SILAS. That's right. I was nearly in dread you had not that much courage.

JUDAS. I have courage! And I will face him, and will go up to him, and salute him, and betray him into your hand!

(*Shouting is heard inside the Gate.*)

SILAS. Here is the money. Thirty pieces of silver. (*He gives it in a heavy leather purse.*)

JUDAS. Give it here to me! (*Turns to go.*) And I thought ere yesterday I never would go against him, but would be his well-wisher to the world's end! (*He goes off as* MARCUS *returns.*)

DANIEL (*running out from the Gate, money clutched in his hand*). That's the way to serve them!

SILAS. What has happened?

JOEL (*coming after him*). It is begun and well begun!

SILAS. Speak plain, can't you!

JOEL. Those big men and those sons of pride in the Temple that are content to be under the foreigners and have struck no blow for freedom, he has brought down their pride!

SILAS. What are you talking about?

JOEL. He gave them a great overthrow! That's how we'll see the Romans running before him in the same way!

DANIEL. He made great havoc among them! Look at what I gathered on the ground—a full handful of copper and of silver—my grief that it is not gold! You never saw such a welter as was in it!

JOEL. The day is not far off when the strangers will be stretched without anyone to cry after them! And we ourselves lighting a bonfire that will reach as high as the stars of heaven! (*Runs on.*)

SILAS (*to* DANIEL). Where now did you steal that much?

DANIEL. Would you call it stealing to pick up what was thrown down upon the floor? Would you wish golden coins to run into mouseholes, or down the steps into the street?

SILAS (*seizing him*). What are you raving about?

DANIEL. Up the Nazarene! He was ever and always for the poor against the rich! Hadn't I the luck that I followed him inside the gate and as far as the Temple?

SILAS. The Temple!

DANIEL. In with him, and he had the traders cleared out of the place on the minute, before the crack of his whip!

SILAS. He never dared do that much!

DANIEL. That's my darling! Cattle-dealers, money-lenders, merchants and moneyed people, the whole fleet of them, and he driving them before him with his scourge! Bullocks having flesh piled up on them! Heifers and horned cattle running to and fro! Tables falling, stalls broken; gold and silver rolling there and hither! My grief I had not a bit of wax spread upon the sole of my shoe before I was driven out the door by the weight of the crowd.

SILAS. What ailed him to go meddle with the stalls that are owned by Caiaphas? He will go stark mad.

DANIEL. I wouldn't miss for seven years of life the fun I had viewing the bankers, fat and frightened as they were, making their escape with their lives! And the pigeons that are reared by Annas flying in their circles above in the high air, and his profits going with them into the clouds! You couldn't but laugh seeing that. Wait till I'll go shout it down the road!

SILAS. Get out of that! (*Pushes him. He stumbles, and his handful of money is scattered.*)

DANIEL. O you have my handful of silver scattered! Wait till I'll gather it up!

SILAS (*pushing him on*). Get out of this. Look now, go before me to the Chief Priest's house, and I'll put you in the way of a job will bring the double of that into your hand.

DANIEL. I'd sooner have my own. My grief I didn't spend it and enjoy it in the commencement! (*Goes.*)

SILAS (*to* MARCUS). Now will you believe me telling you this Nazarene is a danger?

MARCUS. Indeed he would seem to be a very turbulent fellow.

SILAS. Will you give him leave to go stir up the whole country, making his attack on the wealthy and the well-to-do?

MARCUS. He had best be silenced for a while. Pilate would not give a clipping of his nail for that thing you call "religion." But to turn around upon property, that is a thing that might spread.

SILAS. Maybe *now* you will let your soldiers lend a hand to put him down?

MARCUS. But when will you get a hold of him? The Head Government would sooner not meddle with him in the daytime.

SILAS. Never fear. He will be gaoled before morning. We will take him this very night!

Curtain.

ACT II

SCENE. *An open place in the City. In the centre the steps of* PILATE'S *Palace. A street goes right and left. It is early morning. There are lighted lamps by the Palace door.* 1ST WOMAN *is sitting on the steps.*

1ST WOMAN (*sings*)

> There in the night, his comrades leaving,
> No shadow near him but his own,
> The winds around him keening, grieving,
> He fought his battle out alone.

> A traitor's kiss the traitor's token;
> My grief that such a thing could be!
> The strings of every harp are broken,
> The leaves are withered on every tree.

> My bitter shame, my lasting sorrow,
> The crowds that sent his name so high
> Failed and forsook him on the morrow,
> And he must go alone to die!

(*She gets up and goes out to the left, singing lower to herself. The two other women come in from the right, one hurrying after the other.*)

2ND WOMAN. Is it true what they are saying that he is taken?

3RD WOMAN. That is what they were telling me down the road. My heart started with trouble hearing that.

2ND WOMAN. It must surely be a lie. It is impossible his enemies would dare it, and all the whole country shouting for him yesterday.

3RD WOMAN. That is the very thing put anger on them. It would wound your heart to think anyone would lay a hand on him, and he the best man that ever walked the road.

2ND WOMAN. Och! This is a heavy day surely, and the darkest May morning that ever came upon the world!

(ST. BRIGIT *comes on.* IST WOMAN *comes from the other side.*)

3RD WOMAN. Here is that Saint of the Gael coming, that some call the fostermother of Christ. She might have some tidings. (*To* ST. BRIGIT) Where were you through the night time?

ST. BRIGIT. I was with the Mother of our Lord.

IST WOMAN. And what way is she? This trouble must lie very heavy on her.

ST. BRIGIT. It is as if it was foreshowed to her from the beginning. It is a long time there has been a shadow across her heart.

(*The dawn begins to break.* JOEL *comes on, looking downcast.*)

2ND WOMAN. It is hard to know what is happening. There is no stir yet on this side of Pilate's house.

JOEL. It is on the other side the stir is, where Annas the High Priest has his Court.

2ND WOMAN. Annas! And for what reason is that old man holding his Court in the night time?

JOEL. For a bad reason, and a very bad cause.

3RD WOMAN. Is it true that they have taken our Master?

JOEL. They have taken him indeed, and by treachery.

IST WOMAN. By treachery. That story is the breaking of my heart to me. And indeed I never heard the like in all my years gone by.

2ND WOMAN. It is a pity for anyone that was against him. There is not a better man to help the poor on this side of the world. Not on this side of the world.

3RD WOMAN. Who is there that could show him illwill? A man without blemish. There was no friend or no stranger he would refuse. Look at the Woman of Samaria, how she brought the whole district to believe on him.

JOEL. It was no stranger did it.

2ND WOMAN. Some very bitter enemy it should be, having a black, cruel heart.

JOEL. Ah, leave talking. It was one of the twelve were nearest him. One of his comrades and his friends.

2ND WOMAN. Which of them was it, I wonder. It cannot have been John—or Peter.

318

JOEL. I will not blacken my mouth with that name that will be under a curse for ever!

(*The dawn brightens.*)

1ST WOMAN. He should be a long time before Annas.

JOEL. No, but they brought him to Caiaphas with the crowing of the cock—That there may be a curse upon this day for ever!

ST. BRIGIT. But he is not judged yet, or condemned.

JOEL. He is as good as judged. They are all his sworn enemies, Scribes and Pharisees, priests and people of note. The best of them is as thorny as a briar.

3RD WOMAN. They will need some excuse against him.

JOEL. What excuse does the wolf make when he grips the lamb by the throat?

2ND WOMAN. He is white and innocent as a lamb.

ST. BRIGIT. He is the Lamb of God.

JOEL. It is a lion he would be if he had but time to raise the country. He had but to call to us that knew him to be the man we were promised through the ages, "To stand for an ensign of the people; to assemble the outcasts of Israel; to gather together the dispersed of Judah." He had but to give us the wind of the word! We would have put fire to every Roman house if he had made but a sign with his hand!

1ST WOMAN. It is likely he was our Redeemer indeed that was foretold, that would make the lame to leap like a deer and the blind to see.

JOEL. He had but to make his call, "Awake, awake! Put on thy beautiful garments, O Jerusalem! Shake thyself from the dust, loose the bands of thy neck, O captive daughter of Zion!" Oh, if I could see her free, and the Roman eagles gone, I think I would be content to lose my soul!

2ND WOMAN. Maybe he had not the chance, and he brought away in the darkness. A great pity there was no friend within call.

JOEL. I myself was not far from him at that time, when he was taken and after he was taken.

3RD WOMAN. Oh, were you there! And what way at all did it come about?

JOEL. I went after him, thinking to get some word or some sign to bring back to the mountains. But when I reached to the olive trees of the garden he was lost to me in the shadows, and I could hear no word. And then I saw his friends.

ST. BRIGIT. The Twelve?

JOEL. Themselves—or the most of them. But I was no wiser than before, and I might as well have been deaf and blind, for there had fallen upon them a passion of sleep.

ST. BRIGIT. Oh! How could they sleep and he in danger!

2ND WOMAN. It is likely they did not know of that. And they should be tired and worn out following him as they did on the road through the whole length of the day.

ST. BRIGIT. And was our Lord himself asleep?

JOEL. Tired and all as he was, I think he had never closed an eye. When I went farther I could hear his voice as if praying for a while. It would seem as if there was some hard thing before him.

ST. BRIGIT. It was surely made known to him what was about to take place.

JOEL. The last word I heard him say was "Father if it be possible let this cup pass from me; nevertheless not as I will but as thou wilt!"

ST. BRIGIT. It was to his Father indeed he was calling. For if he calls himself the Son of Man it is certain he is the Son of the living God.

JOEL. I heard then the soldiers coming, and the Chief Priest's men. And I was in dread they would find me there, and I slipped away and rambled the streets for a while. And then I saw lights in a big house, and some stir, and people moving about at the door. I asked no question, but I heard them saying it was Jesus of Nazarene had been brought to be judged. And I slipped in unknownst among the crowd.

2ND WOMAN. Did you do that? And what way was he?

JOEL. Someway tired he looked, with weakness and the want of sleep. Annas was saying it was known he kept company with rebels and with lawbreakers, and was trying to pick out of him the names of his followers and of his friends.

3RD WOMAN. He would never give them up.

JOEL. You may say that indeed. He is the good tree that never would let fall any branch. With all the power Annas has, and his threats, it failed him to get one word out of his mouth.

1ST WOMAN. He never preached hurt or harm to anyone.

JOEL. If he did not itself they would likely put a twist on his words. If they are looking for the truth, it is for a truth would suit themselves. Annas had that thought in his mind asking him what he had taught. But he gave a right answer—he spoke very stiff. Not to ask him what he had taught, but to ask them that had heard him.

3RD WOMAN. That was very fair and very good.

JOEL. One of the soldiers said that was no answer to give the High Priest, and hit him a blow in the face.

ST. BRIGIT. Oh! Did they strike him indeed!

JOEL. They did so. And with that Annas sent him on to the Court of Caiaphas.

3RD WOMAN. He is great with Caiaphas that is joined and wedded with his daughter. I'm in dread he will find no better treatment there.

JOEL. And what happened after I don't know, for the soldiers would let no one go into that Court without them having leave.

1ST WOMAN. A great wonder he did not call down fire from Heaven to destroy the whole of them.

ST. BRIGIT. What he is come for is not to destroy the world, but that the world through him should be saved.

2ND WOMAN. Oh, they will send him to his death! Is there no door of hope?

(DANIEL *comes on.*)

JOEL (*standing up*). What at all are we doing here, prating and chattering, and the man that came to save us being like a bird in the fowler's net!

DANIEL. And what are you thinking to do?

JOEL. To do in this very hour what was foretold to us through the years past. To rise up and throw out the Romans and their friends that are about to send him to the slaughter! (*He cries out, as* SILAS *comes in and stands behind a pillar*) Who will come to the help of the Country and of the Nazarene?

(*A crowd gathers from both sides.*)

DANIEL. Well, I'll give my help to whoever will give me the price of a drop to keep up my courage!

JOEL. Let alone talking of prices or profit! (*Goes up a step.*) The man, Jesus of Nazareth that is come to be our leader and will be our King——

CROWD. So he will! He is well worthy!

1ST MAN. He has the prayers of the poor of the world!

JOEL. He is brought to prison! His enemies are judging him. They are putting insults on him! I saw a soldier hitting him a clout on the face——

(*A murmur of anger from the crowd.*)

1ST MAN. We'll drag him out of their hands!

2ND MAN. We'll pull down the Court!

3RD MAN. Town and country will come to his aid!

321

(SILAS, *who has been whispering with* DANIEL, *and has put something in his hand, comes in front of the pillar.*)

JOEL. Once we get him out of their hands he will be safe!

1ST MAN. Not a door but will be open to him!

2ND MAN. Their best won't find him!

1ST MAN. Come on now till we'll save him!

JOEL. We'll fall on the guard as they are bringing him out of the Court, till he will slip away through us!

1ST MAN. Everyone of us will do away with one of the soldiers!

2ND MAN. We'll banish them!

3RD MAN. The curse of the weak on them!

1ST MAN. And the curse of the strong!

JOEL. We'll put fire to their barracks that are empty! They'll find nothing but ashes when they'll go look for their catapults and their swords!

CROWD. Come on! Come on! Away with Cæsar! We'll have a King of our own.

SILAS (*coming forward*). Hearken now to me. What everyone of you will have is a rope around your neck, and a death by stoning or by the sword.

JOEL (*turning to him*). Even so! If we are killed itself, to die for our country is a good death to die!

SILAS. If it is death you are craving you'll get it, and go fatten the foxes in the fields!

JOEL. We're not so easy put down! We'll give Rome her wages for the bones she has left bleaching through the world!

SILAS. And what have ye in your hands to go battle with Rome that has conquered Gaul and the most of the countries of the known world? Maybe a stump of a stick you might go cut in the garden above!

JOEL. Every gap will be made easy to us! God is stronger than the Romans!

SILAS (*to the crowd, holding up tablets*). What have ye to say? I am writing on my tablets the name of such of you as are ready to follow this mountainy lad that never walked the streets of a town till yesterday! Is it along with him ye are going like conies into a snare or a trap?

1ST MAN. Maybe the right time didn't come yet.

JOEL. Do not renage now! Come on and put them to the rout!

2ND MAN. Sure enough we might find ourselves taken and tormented in a gaol.

3RD MAN. I've no mind to put myself in a sharp-toothed trap.

1ST MAN. In my opinion we can serve the country better living than dead.

JOEL. What did the prophets say? "Turn ye to the stronghold ye prisoners of hope! For now I will break the yoke from off thee and will break thy bonds in sunder." That saying must come true!

2ND MAN. The time didn't come yet. We'll wait for another chance. (*Goes.*)

JOEL. Are you all forsaking him?

3RD MAN. I wouldn't wish to go against the neighbours. (*Goes.*)

JOEL. Oh! If I was up on the hillsides, I wouldn't be without help this day! (*All have gone but* SILAS.)

SILAS. You were I suppose a close friend of the Nazarene?

JOEL. I never saw him till yesterday, but I know him to be the man is come to save us.

SILAS. You thought him to be like yourself—a red enemy to the Romans?

JOEL. There is no good man but is that.

SILAS. To be sure, to be sure. I am saying nothing against it. Wouldn't we all be well pleased having the country in our own hands?

JOEL. I see yourself very thick with the foreigners.

SILAS. Getting what I can by civility. I do more for the country that way than you rebels by showing your ill-will.

JOEL. It was by your help our leader was taken.

SILAS. Your leader is he? Well, there are as great fools to-day as ever there were in the world.

JOEL. In or out of prison my heart is with the man that is being tried for his life.

SILAS. And you thought him to be for upsetting the Government? Well, let me tell you he was deceiving you.

JOEL. No one but a fool or a woman would say such a thing as that!

SILAS. No one but a cracked mountainy youngster would be ignorant that he bade the people pay tribute to Cæsar. All the world knows that. And more again, there is a story going that he did miracles, bringing the money for tribute up from the depths of the sea sooner than let the Government be at the loss of it.

JOEL. There must be some answer to that.

SILAS (*interrupting*). Blind as you are can't you see that when he thought himself strong enough to make an attack, what he attacked was not the palace of Pilate or his Court. No, but the Temple of the Jews, our own Temple and the glory of our nation.

Threaten he did to knock the whole of it within three days. Could he do that without the foreign soldiers' help? To knock down our laws along with it, and our customs. What had he in mind doing that but to put Judea entirely into the hand of Rome, the same as a bird's nest?

JOEL (*passionately*). I would as soon believe the sun to be failing in the sky!

(*He goes away sorrowfully, as* MARCUS *comes out from the door.*)

MARCUS. Well, Silas, I was looking for you in the Court of Caiaphas, and the trial of the Nazarene going on.

SILAS. I have my own work to do among the people. There was danger they would make some attempt to rescue him. But it's likely now that unless an odd woman or a cripple there is no one will put out any cry for him at all. What way is the trial going? What happened with Caiaphas?

MARCUS (*with a laugh*). What you might know would happen! With all your bragging of your Jewish law it would seem not to be able to deal with one poor prophet of the roads, but to send him from Caiaphas to the Court of Pilate to settle the case! Rousing him from his sleep and his slumber to put on his judgment robes, and go question the prisoner, that they brought in by the side door, unknown to the people of the city. I wonder he brought his life so far, for if your old Annas is cranky and crabbed enough, I give you my word the son-in-law is worse again.

SILAS. That is not the way to be speaking of the High Priests.

MARCUS. All the talk you had of your laws, from Moses down, and the danger of a man doing cures by the roadside, and that he would pull down the whole Empire, and that all we had to do was to get a hold of him and bring him before your judges!

SILAS. And what complaint have you to make of being asked to do that much?

MARCUS. That much! Dragging our soldiers out on a job that is no profit to us, and will bring us into discredit with the people! And when we have done all that, and delivered him into your Court that is swarming with Scribes and lawyers—what happens?

SILAS. To question him I suppose they did; and to bring witnesses.

MARCUS. That's it! Witnesses! Isn't that the first thing if a man is to be found guilty, to have the witnesses ready against him?

SILAS. So they had them ready. They were gathering them this week past.

MARCUS. Then they are bad harvesters. It's the Judges in Rome that would laugh their fill if they could be here to-day! Witnesses! A whole fleet of them, paid and unpaid, coming in pairs and in threes and alone, to work malice on him. And whatever way they came it was easy seen after a few questions that there was no two or no three of them that could agree together.

SILAS. I had a right to have been there myself. Bad management.

MARCUS. They brought in two together at the last, that said the prisoner had given out in their hearing he would pull down the Temple stone by stone. Is that sort of talk enough to call together the High Court in the night time?

SILAS. He said it sure enough.

MARCUS. A pity you were not there to swear to that, for the two that told it could not agree upon the words. After that, Caiaphas took in hand himself to catechize the Nazarene.

SILAS. It was time for him. Why couldn't he do it at the first.

MARCUS. Little he got by it. No answer at all, until at the last the question was put in the name of the living God.

SILAS. He answered that?

MARCUS. It was put to him straight and fair—"Are you the Son of God?" He said to that, "If I tell you ye will not believe"; and then, "ye say that I am." And he said the Son of Man would sit in the hereafter on the right hand of the power of God. And whether he meant himself, or some one of the everliving Gods, I cannot tell.

SILAS. That was rank blasphemy. There is no need of other witnesses. That is worthy of death.

MARCUS. So they are saying in the Court, the whole of them. It was the first thing they could catch a hold of. And as to Caiaphas, he made the most of it, showing off as if on a stage, tearing his clothes as if raging mad. He has a bitter and a hasty nature sure enough.

SILAS. It is no wonder he should be in a passion.

MARCUS. As to the rest of them, soldiers and lookers on, they began to spit at the prisoner, and to strike at him, and buffet him, and to cover his eyes, and say, "Prophesy now which of us hit that stroke?" The whole of the assembly ran wild with spite and malice, that nearly seemed to come from some sort of fear or fright.

SILAS. Our Judges are not so easy frightened, whatever fear there might be on that author of mischief, the Nazarene, finding himself in their hand.

MARCUS. He was indeed like a bird of the high air cast down

among wild cats of the clefts. They lost no time making their attack on him.

SILAS. That's right. Give him cruelty till you'll put sense in him. That's the way to tame him and to bring him down.

MARCUS. I don't know. I give you my word you would wonder at him, facing the whole of them as he did, without fear or flinching, without any frown on his face, but as if he was not in the one world with them at all.

SILAS. It seems like as if he had put some spell upon yourself, or some craziness.

MARCUS. To look at him, and to see his courage, and never a friend to help, you would nearly say him to be the only man in the place you would call a man, whether he is or is not of the gods.

SILAS. It will be a poor story if Pilate your master leans to his side as you yourself are seeming to do.

MARCUS. Pilate won't take that much notice of him. He is easy-minded. He will maybe give him up to the priests that are calling for his death, to humour them, even if he finds no cause against him. And if he does that, it will not be for the sake of the Roman Empire, but that you are welcome to do away with as many of your own nation as is pleasing to you.

SILAS. So it will please the people and satisfy them.

MARCUS. I saw no sign of that yesterday, when the whole full of the road was shouting for him.

SILAS. You may believe me telling you they will have another shout and another story to-day.

MARCUS. So they might. This shouting of crowds is but the cackling of ganders and their flock, or the howling of wild dogs after their prey. And I wouldn't wonder at all if Pilate gets vexed with them making their clamour around his house, after spoiling his sleep on him, and will let off the Nazarene in the finish, that gave him no annoyance at all.

(*He goes as* JOEL *comes back and is walking across gloomily.*)

SILAS. Come hither now! Did you hear that your leader that is going to rise against Rome is after being brought before Pilate?

JOEL. That is you own doing, and your own fault. Recognizing the foreign Courts.

SILAS. You'll see now is he in with the foreign Government! Like master, like man, and Pilate's trusted man was here on the minute, and if you heard him putting a good name on the Nazarene, and saying he was the best man in the Court, you would maybe believe he had some settlement made with them.

JOEL. That he had betrayed the country? I would never believe that.

SILAS. Wait a while and maybe you'll see Pilate is on his side, and will make excuses for him.

JOEL. If Pilate does that and had any treaty with him, I will never believe again in anyone at all, man, priest or God, in or out of the world.

(*He goes off.* SILAS *goes over to meet* DANIEL, *who comes on.*)

SILAS. Did you do the work I bade you?

DANIEL (*drunkenly*). I did. I went into the drinking houses, and gave a glass—and the promise of another—to every man that would come into the Square and call out against the Nazarene.

SILAS. Very good. His own followers are affrighted and scattered here and there. That will do. (*Is going.*)

DANIEL. I have all the money spent. I am wanting more.

SILAS. You'll not get it till this day's work is done, or you'll be lying in a ditch, and no use to anyone.

DANIEL. I am use! And great use! If you have the people threatened, I have them coaxed!

SILAS (*giving him some money*). Go on then—put hurry on you. Make no delay. There is some stir in the Governor's house. It is likely the trial is at an end. (*Pushes him off, and goes in at door.*)

DANIEL (*shouting*). Come on, lads! Let ye shout against the Nazarene till your throat is dry. (*Crowd begins to gather.*) And believe me you won't be drouthy to-night! Come on, now! Come on, here! Down with the Nazarene! Up Pilate!

SILAS (*coming from the door*). Bid them to call for Pilate to come out the door! Let him see they are against the prisoner! (*The* WOMEN *come on.*)

DANIEL. Let ye shout now! Make a call for Pilate!

1ST MAN. What is it we want with him?

DANIEL. Little I care! Let him come out till we'll get a view of him. Pilate! Pilate!

CROWD. Pilate! Pilate! Come out and speak to us! Pilate!

SILAS. Take care is he shielding the Nazerene that is your enemy!

1ST WOMAN. He is no enemy but our friend!

SILAS (*pushing her away*). Raising riots he is! Pulling down the country!

3RD WOMAN. He is worthy to be our King!

SILAS (*to the crowd*). Be said and led by those that have knowledge and that you know. He is bringing trouble on you. He will wreck and destroy the city along with the Temple. He will bring the soldiers on you!

(*Groans from the crowd.*)

SILAS. No peace and comfort in your lives! Starvation in place of plenty! Rid yourselves of him or the whole of ye will be driven in chains (*groans*). Let this man die, and save the whole nation. Tell out that now to Pilate!

CROWD. Pilate! Pilate! Come out, Pilate!

PILATE (*coming out on the steps, holds up his hand for silence*). What is this uproar?

CROWD. Down with the Nazerene!

PILATE (*holding up his hand again*). Be silent! (*The crowd obeys.*) This man was brought to me as one that is perverting the nation, and leading the people astray.

CROWD. That's right! So he is leading us astray!

PILATE. A ringleader, a pestilent fellow, and a mover of sedition —forbidding to give tribute to Cæsar——

CROWD. So he is against Cæsar!

PILATE. That is what was laid down. But it is not the manner of the Romans to deliver any man to die before that he which is accused have the accuser face to face, and have licence to answer for himself concerning the crime laid against him.

SILAS. So they did face him! The witnesses laid their clear case before Caiaphas!

CROWD. That's it! That's it! Their clear case!

PILATE. Their witness did not agree, and therefore it did not stand.

SILAS. If he was not a malefactor we would not have sent him to you!

CROWD. That's the chat!

PILATE. They had certain questions against him of their own superstition. But I, as a Roman Governor, have nothing against him.

1ST MAN. He is giving us no clear answer!

SILAS. Never fear he will give in to us when he'll see we will not give in to him. (*To* PILATE) Is it nothing to you that he gave himself out to be a King?

PILATE. I questioned him as to that. His answer was, "My Kingdom is not of this world."

1ST WOMAN. That is so. He is the King of Heaven.

PILATE. My jurisdiction does not go outside this world and this Empire of Rome. I asked him again, "Art thou a King?" and he said, "To that end was I born, and to this end came I into the world that I should bear witness to the truth."

1ST WOMAN. That is so. He came to bear witness to the truth.

PILATE. What is truth? (*He turns to go.*)

1ST MAN. Will you let him make his escape!

2ND MAN. Little he cares for ourselves!

3RD MAN. Or for our Priests! Up Caiaphas!

PILATE (*turning back*). Am I a Jew? It is best for me to send him back to your own judgment seat, and let you judge him by your own laws.

SILAS. It is for his death we make our call. You know well it is not lawful for us to put any man to death.

CROWD. He is deserving of death!

PILATE. Have your own way, then. I will not refuse the Chief Priests and the people. I am willing to do what is pleasing to them. I will go back and give judgment against him.

CROWD. That's right! (*They cheer.*)

1ST MAN. Come back, let ye, to the door of the Court!

2ND MAN. Hurry on till we'll see him condemned! (*They all run off.*)

(PILATE *turns to go.* MARCUS *meets him inside the doorway.*)

MARCUS. Here is the Egyptian Nurse with a message. (*He goes back.*)

EGYPTIAN (*pushing past him*). Pilate, Pilate, your wife is calling for you.

PILATE. Tell her I cannot come. I am going to the Hall of Judgment.

EGYPTIAN. She bade me give you a message.

PILATE. It must wait.

EGYPTIAN. It is not an idle matter makes her call to you.

PILATE. My own business is not idle, a matter of a man's life.

EGYPTIAN. Her business also is concerned with life and death.

PILATE. I have but to give sentence. There will be little delay in that.

EGYPTIAN (*seizing his arm*). Hearken Pilate. She had a vision of the night.

PILATE. What has that to do with life or death?

EGYPTIAN. She cried out in her sleep—a sharp cry that wakened me. I asked her what ailed her. She was pale and trembling. She called for you, "Pilate, come!" and then, "Where is he? Where is my husband? There is some great danger before him."

PILATE. A foolish dream. What way could I be in danger in my own Judgment Hall?

EGYPTIAN. She was as if shivering. She held my hands. She said, "Shadow-shapes gathered around me calling out a warning—a warning against the shedding of innocent blood." She asked me then were you sleeping yet, and if you had any heavy business before you. I told her they had wakened you at the parting of night and day to go judge some disturber, some lawbreaker that was accused by the Jews. She cried out again——

PILATE. That could lead me into no danger. It is but a wandering Nazarene that has given offence to some of these Jewish bigots. That is folly.

EGYPTIAN. You would think it no folly if you had seen the way she was, as if remembering some dreadful thing. "I see it—I see it, as it was in the dream," she said. "I saw him sending a just man to his death. I saw blood—dropping, dropping—I saw as if in a mirror Pilate sent back to Italy—to Rome."

PILATE. To Italy! That is good. Oh that I could be there at this time! That I could see the gardens by the Tiber, and feel the peace that is in the heart of Rome! To be rid of these ugly scolding priests, and their God that sends but his harsh threatenings and has no human form!

EGYPTIAN. In Rome she saw you, and beyond Rome, and sent on again—on again—without rest. And all the time she saw you trying to wipe away some blood that was on your hands. And you were as if in disgrace, and she could not reach to you.

PILATE. And then—what did she see?

EGYPTIAN. Far away, westward—in the country of the Gauls— she saw you. (*She covers her eyes with her hand.*)

PILATE. What did she see?

EGYPTIAN. She saw you in the single shirt of linen that was your shroud. She saw blood again upon your hands——. And this time it was your own life blood. And it was by yourself it was shed.

PILATE (*in a whisper*). That was the end?

EGYPTIAN. She rose up then, and she called out, as if she was but just on the moment awake: "Tell him to have nothing to do with that just man, for I have suffered many things in my dream because of him!"

(*She goes back into the Palace. PILATE leans for a moment against the door. The people come running back.*)

1ST MAN. There is Pilate. He never went to the Court at all.

2ND MAN. He was but mocking us!

3RD MAN. Making little of us! Ridiculing us!

CROWD. Hurry on with the judgment! No delay!

SILAS. That is not the way to treat our nation!

PILATE (*coming forward slowly*). I would need more evidence that he has broken the law before I would condemn him.

SILAS. He stirred up the people, urging them to destruction!

DANIEL. Through the whole country!

1ST MAN. Through every district—beginning from Galilee!

PILATE. From Galilee! Is he a Galilean?

1ST MAN. He is that!

2ND MAN. So he is! A Galilean!

PILATE. Then I am free of him! He belongs to Herod's jurisdiction, not mine. I will send him to Herod's Court! (*He goes back into the Palace.*)

1ST MAN. Come and see him with Herod!

2ND MAN. Come on to Herod's Court!

3RD MAN. He will get no mercy there! (*They all go off, except the* WOMEN *and* DANIEL.)

1ST WOMAN. From one Judge to another, and every one worse than another.

3RD WOMAN. He will find no escape. Herod that struck the head off John the Baptist will not spare him that is a greater prophet again.

JUDAS (*coming in has heard the last words*). What are you saying? Is it that he is sent to Herod?

1ST WOMAN. You are one of his followers. It is often I took notice of you in his company. To know of his life being in danger must put a great weight upon your heart.

JUDAS. They will but banish him. Or maybe gaol him for a while.

1ST WOMAN. It is his death his enemies are calling for. A bad crowd against him, and a careless Pilate. They are very bitter. It will be hard for him to make his escape.

3RD WOMAN. Twelve friends that we thought would die for him, and one of them betrayed him.

2ND WOMAN. There could hardly be a greater treachery than that. To betray his Master!

1ST WOMAN. If ever it is known who it is, there will be a cruel end before him.

JUDAS (*going on*). Why wouldn't he get the better of them if he has power from Heaven? Wouldn't he be able to throw a mist of darkness around him, and to slip away?

3RD WOMAN. He will never make his escape that way. You might

331

remember him saying, "He that findeth his life will lose it, but he that loses it will find it."

JUDAS. Or to call down fire from Heaven.

2ND WOMAN. It is on whoever betrayed him that should fall.

(JUDAS *goes on.*)

DANIEL (*still rather drunken, catching hold of him as he passes*). You did that night work well surely. I am a good man myself to do a job of the sort, but you are a better.

JUDAS. Leave go of me!

DANIEL. To bring the soldiers up so nice and so quiet through the darkness, where there was no one to call out, or to make any disturbance at all.

JUDAS. Let me go, I say! (*The* WOMEN *have gathered around them.*)

DANIEL. Sure you need not mind me knowing it. Don't be so stiff now. I earn my money fair and honest calling Hi! for one, and Down with another, according as I am paid. Why wouldn't I earn my little supper shouting with my voice as good as labouring with my hands? Do not be so unfriendly now. Aren't we on the one side? The two of us are covetous for money. You are a big man, and I am a small man that drank away my means, and must go forage along the roads. And I don't begrudge you your reward. If all I got out of it is these coppers, and they gave you silver on this job, there's not the black of my nail between us. For if I have the corner boys all bought, you have your Master sold!

3RD WOMAN. Oh, isn't he the terrible type of a ruffian?

1ST WOMAN. The worst man you could think of wouldn't do a thing like that!

(*They all shrink from him.* ST. JOHN *and* ST. BRIGIT *come in.*)

ST. JOHN. Judas, is *that* your Master? (*He goes on.* DANIEL *slinks away.*)

2ND WOMAN. It is best for you hide your head for ever. To take money for betraying him! That is the worst of all.

JUDAS (*holding out the purse*). I wish to God you would take the money, and know how little I covet it! I bestow it to you as a free gift!

2ND WOMAN. Do you think I would touch it with my hand! It is a crooked and a very crooked way you got it!

JUDAS (*to* 1ST WOMAN). Can't you bring it away, and divide it on the poor.

1ST WOMAN. There is no beggar going the road would touch it, or no leper, knowing it to be the price of blood!

ST. BRIGIT. Go and repent. Go bring it to the priests in your temple as an offering for sin. (*He steals away, the* WOMEN *follow whispering.* MARCUS *comes out from the door, and* SILAS *from the street.*)

SILAS. What happened since with the prisoner?

MARCUS (*with a scornful laugh*). The same as would happen a ball you would strike against a wall with your stick. Back again he comes to us, from the *third* of your Jewish big men.

SILAS. And did Herod do nothing at all?

MARCUS. To all the questions he put out of his mouth he got no answer. He bade him then do some miracle before him; but the Nazarene never stirred hand or foot, and said no word.

SILAS. Herod is not used to be made little of that way.

MARCUS. If he wanted talk he heard enough of it from the Chief Priests and the Scribes, that called the prisoner all the names, one worse than another, and accused him of this and that. And when it was said he had claimed to be a King, Herod put on him in mockery the purple dress of a King, and ridiculed him, and gave him to be handled by the soldiers, and made a speedy riddance of him, sending him back here to us again.

(JOEL *comes in, but stops, seeing them.*)

SILAS. Pilate has nothing to do now but to condemn him.

MARCUS. I don't know in the world wide what happened Pilate. He would seem as if unwilling to see him again, or to go against him. I never knew him to be this way before.

(*He goes on.*)

SILAS (*to* JOEL). Did you hear that? Now will you believe me saying he had his terms made with the foreign Government?

JOEL. I would never believe it unless from himself—or it might be from Pilate himself.

CROWD (*coming back from one side, as the* WOMEN *come from the other*). Pilate! Pilate!

MARCUS (*coming out*). Make way there!

(PILATE *comes out.*)

1ST MAN. Here he is! Up Pilate!

2ND MAN. Put down the Nazarene!

DANIEL. Down with him! Up the Empire! Up Cæsar!

PILATE (*holds up his hand impatiently, and speaks petulantly*). When ye brought this man to me I told you I found no fault in him touching those things whereof ye accuse him.

CROWD. Boo-oo! Boo-ooo!

PILATE. No, nor yet Herod—for I sent you to him, and you see

333

he found nothing worthy of death in him. I will therefore chastise him—and release him.

SILAS. You will let him go free!

CROWD. To let him off! Boo-ooo!

PILATE. Why, what evil has he done? I tell you again, I find no fault in him.

CROWD. Away with him! He is worthy of death!

PILATE. Listen! It is a custom that at the Feast I release one prisoner to you——

CROWD. Barabbas! Give us out Barabbas!

PILATE. Barabbas! That is a robber?

CROWD. Give us Barabbas!

JOEL. I would nearly sooner have Barabbas that we knew from the first to be a rogue!

PILATE. What will ye then that I do to him whom ye call the King of the Jews?

CROWD. Crucify him! Let him be crucified! (SOLDIERS *bring* CHRIST *to the door.*)

JOEL. Crucify him!

(PILATE *leads Him on to steps. He wears a crown of thorns and a purple robe.*)

PILATE. Behold the Man!

CROWD. Crucify him!

PILATE. Take ye him and crucify him, for I find no fault in him.

SILAS. We have a law, and by our law he ought to die, because he made himself the Son of God!

PILATE (*to* CHRIST). Speakest thou not? Knowest thou not that I have power to crucify thee, and power to release thee?

CHRIST. Thou couldst have no power at all against me except it were given thee by God. Therefore he that delivered me unto thee hath the greater sin.

(PILATE *hesitates.*)

PILATE (*making a last cry to the people*). Shall I crucify your King?

DANIEL. We have no king but Cæsar!

SILAS (*to* PILATE, *coming in front of the crowd*). Whoever makes himself a king speaks against Cæsar. If you let this man go you are not Cæsar's friend.

(PILATE *bows his head. The* EGYPTIAN *comes out swiftly with a silver jug and basin. She splashes water over* PILATE'S *hands. He shakes the water off, rinsing his hands.*)

PILATE. I am innocent of the blood of this just person! See ye to it!

CROWD. Let him be crucified!

(*The* SOLDIERS *seize* CHRIST.)

Curtain.

ACT III

SCENE. *A roadside, the road rising in rough steps on one side; on the other, a little booth with wine and fruit, where some* SOLDIERS *are drinking.*

1ST SOLDIER (*shading his eyes, and looking up the hill.*) They are just putting up the Cross for the Nazarene.

2ND SOLDIER (*coming in from the road, throws down a hammer and some nails he is carrying, and a coil of rope, and takes some wine*). He fell carrying it. He is on the road yet. He has great courage, but his body is weak after all he went through.

3RD SOLDIER. I never heard yet for what crime he was sent to his death. He was not a thief, like the other two, or a murderer the same as Barabbas.

1ST SOLDIER. These Jewish priests that were jealous of him, they are saying. In dread more respect would be paid to him than to themselves through the feast days. They had it settled in their minds to get quit of him.

3RD SOLDIER. I wonder at Pilate giving in to them, for it was easy seen he didn't like the job.

1ST SOLDIER. There are some women making their way to the Cross that has been put up for him on the height. It's best drive them back from it. There is no use having crying and bawling going on with the sound of the hammering of the nails.

3RD SOLDIER (*goes up a step and shouts*). Send down those women out of that! They have no call to be getting into the way of our work!

2ND SOLDIER. There was a Woman following after him on the road, and that helped him up when he fell. They were saying it was his Mother.

3RD SOLDIER. I would nearly pity any mother of a son that would see him sent to such a hard death.

(*The* WOMEN *come down the steps.*)

1ST SOLDIER. Come on, now! There is no place for you there above!

1ST WOMAN. May we stop here, sir, by the side of the road?

1ST SOLDIER. I wonder what at all brings you looking at such an ugly sight?

1ST WOMAN. He is our Master and our Lord.

1ST SOLDIER. Well, keep yourselves quiet and behave yourselves, or it will be worse for you. (*To the other* SOLDIERS) Come on now to hurry them that are on the road.

(*They go off.*)

1ST WOMAN (*sitting down*). If it is long the night was, the day is longer again.

3RD WOMAN. It is a pitiful story the way he is. The reach of his hand was always good to the poor.

1ST WOMAN. He never put grief on his Mother, or on any child at all.

2ND WOMAN. Why at all does he not save himself? If he would but lift his hand there is not one of them but would fall dead.

1ST WOMAN. He is maybe weary of serving the world, with the bad treatment and the abuse he was given.

1ST WOMAN. He is the just Prince of patience. He gives kindness for hatred. (*She sings*)

> He shows no malice, but love and pity,
> Forgives them all with his failing breath;
> The foreign soldiers that spoil our city,
> That flog and drag him to shameful death.

(ST. BRIGIT *comes in from down the road.*)

> They bruised his brow with their crown of briars;
> They mocked him with every ugly thing;
> He that could shrivel them all with fire
> He held his silence, and he a King!

> I call and cry to the King of Graces,
> To scourge and scatter by land and sea,
> To bring disgrace on their wicked faces;
> To smite and shrivel that crooked tree!

2ND WOMAN. If the world was talking, the relics of the old religion would be in you yet.

336

ST. BRIGIT. He used to be saying, the Disciple was telling me, "Love your enemies; bless them that curse you; pray for them which despitefully use you."

3RD WOMAN. It will be hard for him to say that to-day.

ST. BRIGIT. He will say it to the last. He is clean gold. Surely, there will never be any man east or west will refuse to forgive another, where our Lord gave forgiveness to his enemies.

2ND WOMAN. You did well coming here to see him with your own eyes. For this is a story will have seven shapes put on it.

1ST WOMAN. Indeed it is a heart-broken story you will have to bring back to Ireland.

ST. BRIGIT. No; but a great story and a great praise I will bring with me. I have heard him myself, and know that this is indeed the Christ, the Saviour of the world.

1ST WOMAN. You would never think they would get leave to strike and scourge him the way they did.

ST. BRIGIT. I heard some saying it was written in the old prophecies, "A man of sorrows and acquainted with grief."

3RD WOMAN. I don't know what was it brought him into this world at all. Great courage he had coming to such an unruly place. He behaved well facing it when he knew what was before him.

2ND WOMAN. The worst at all is to think of the poor Mother. Why wouldn't they leave him to the death that is allotted by nature? It is too soon his candle to be spent.

1ST WOMAN. No smile and no laughter will be upon her lips for ever.

ST. BRIGIT. Never fear there will be joy in her heart in the years to come, knowing that he has visited and redeemed his people.

(*She goes back by the road.*)

3RD WOMAN. Her darling to be taken from her that is comely without and within. And he young, that I thought his keeners would not yet be born.

2ND WOMAN. That is the best (*laughs to herself*). Isn't it happy for him to go out of our sight, while he is in his bloom, and the ugliness of the body in age never to be remembered against him.

1ST WOMAN (*singing*).

The first great joy that Mary had, it was the joy of one,
To see her own son Jesus to suck at her breastbone;

337

2ND WOMAN.

The next great joy that Mary had it was the joy of two
To see her own son Jesus to make the lame to go!

3RD WOMAN.

The third great joy that Mary had, it was the joy of three
To see her own son Jesus to make the blind to see!

(*The* CROWD *rushes on from the road,* DANIEL *among them.*)

1ST MAN. Hurry on till we'll get a good place!

DANIEL. You'll get no good view here, but higher up.

2ND MAN (*turning back from the steps*). The soldiers will let us go no farther.

1ST SOLDIER (*coming with others down the steps*). Let you keep back! Stop where you are. There is no leave to pass.

DANIEL (*sitting down*). I'll stop where I am, so. There's as good a chance of luck turning to you, and you sitting at your ease, as if you were thrusting after it.

2ND SOLDIER. What do you want coming here at all?

DANIEL. I have all my money spent, giving drinks to this one and that one, and little thanks for it. Where will I get my night's lodging and my bite? There is always a chance of some profit turning up in a crowd.

(*Slow music and drums heard in the distance.*)

1ST SOLDIER. Here he is coming.

2ND SOLDIER. He is not, only the thieves.

1ST SOLDIER. No, they were brought by the other road a while ago.

DANIEL. That's a pity. When we come out to see a show, the more of it we can see the better.

(SILAS *and* MARCUS *come on from the road. The crowd draw back.*)

MARCUS. A strange thing your Hebrew people thronging to see a man crucified. Why wouldn't they keep him for a circus and throw him to the wild beasts? That now is sport worth losing a day on.

SILAS. That sort of a death is not suitable to our law.

MARCUS. It is suitable enough for Octavius Cæsar. Ye are a gloomy race, and have no right notion of taking your pleasure.

SILAS. It is pleasure enough to see our enemy put down.

MARCUS. Those two thieves, now, would have made a good fight with a lion or a thing of the kind. They had the appearance of being used to violence.

SILAS. We are satisfied with our own customs, and have no need of yours.

MARCUS. You are getting very impudent since you got your own way this morning.

SILAS. You that were mocking at our Judges! I tell you I myself picked the fun of the world out of your own Pilate, the way he went swaying from side to side.

MARCUS. Have a care now! I'd as lief give you up to the captain beyond for throwing contempt on the Government, as I'd throw an empty oyster shell into the waves!

SILAS. Let you stop putting insults on me!

MARCUS. Gabbing as if you were some great grandee, with all your gibberish about your laws! I've a mind to lodge you in a cell to learn you respect for Roman law!

(*Pushes him. He stumbles and is caught by* JOEL *who comes in.* MARCUS *goes on up the steps.*)

JOEL. My bitter curse on you, where you deceived me a while ago, making me call out against the best man the world ever saw! You have a great wrong done me! If he was not a rebel itself, his name will surely be written in the book of the people! His friendship would be better to me than all the world's gold.

SILAS. Leave handling me! What have I to do with you? You are no use to me now.

JOEL. My bitter shame! I cried out, "Crucify him!" That you may come to the same death yourself for that wicked deed!

IST SOLDIER (*coming down steps seizes* SILAS). Here you, Jew, what are you brawling about? First with the Sergeant of Pilate's guard, and now with this vagabond!

SILAS. Take your hand off me!

IST SOLDIER. We'll put you in a safe place till we'll have time to listen to you. (SOLDIERS *drag* SILAS *off up the steps.*)

(*A shout from the crowd—"Here he is coming!"*)

JOEL. Oh, shining God! Why couldn't we fight and beat them all! Oh, let me hide myself! His eye to fall on me my heart would break like a nut! (*He goes over to the* WOMEN, *who have stood up.*)

IST WOMAN. You were shouting for him but yesterday.

JOEL. That's the way of it! All the generations looking for him and praying for him. We wanted him, and we got him, and what we did with him was to kill him. And that is the way it will be ever and always, so long as leaves grow upon the trees!

3RD WOMAN. He is the Lord we looked for sure enough.

JOEL. If he is or is not the Christ I cannot tell. But whether or no, he is the only whole gentleman in the world! (*He kneels. The tramp of feet is heard to the right. The* WOMEN *look down the road. They beat their hands, and cry out.*)

1ST WOMAN. Oh, my grief! To see him bound with the narrow ropes of hemp! The marks of the thorns on his brow!

2ND WOMAN. My heart is withered like the withering of the trees! (*They hide their faces in their hands and kneel.*)

> (CHRIST *appears. He is still wearing the crown of thorns and the purple robe. A* SOLDIER *carries the inscription, "I.N.R.I."—Jesus of Nazareth the King of the Jews—The* MOTHER *and* ST. JOHN *are following him, and* ST. BRIGIT. *She comes over to the* WOMEN. *The* SOLDIERS *stop to take wine from the booth. The procession stops.*)

CHRIST (*turning to the* WOMEN). Daughters of Jerusalem, weep not for me, but weep for yourselves and for your children.

1ST WOMAN. You to be gone, who have we to go to? You have the words of eternal life!

CHRIST. I will not leave you comfortless. I will come to you.

1ST WOMAN. Have you any word to leave with us at all?

CHRIST. A new commandment I give you, that ye love one another as I have loved you. By this shall all men know that ye are my disciples if you have love one to another.

1ST WOMAN. We will keep that word in our heart till our life's end.

CHRIST (*going on a step farther*). Father, the hour is come! Now I am no more in the world, and I come to Thee. Holy Father, keep through thine own name those thou hast given me, that they may be one as we are one!

MARCUS (*coming back*). Move on, there! What is this delay for?

2ND SOLDIER (*putting his hand on* CHRIST'S *shoulder, and pushing him*). You have no leave to stop!

3RD SOLDIER. If you are the King of the Jews save yourself!

2ND SOLDIER. He trusted in God. Let him deliver him now if he will have him.

1ST SOLDIER. He might want another touch of the scourge. (*Takes up the rope from the ground and threatens him.*)

3RD SOLDIER. Bare his shoulders for it! (*They drag off his robe roughly.*)

ST. JOHN (*calling out*). Is it nothing to you, all ye that pass by?

340

CHRIST. Father forgive them, for they know not what they do! (*He goes up the steps followed by the* MOTHER *and* ST. JOHN.)

1ST SOLDIER (*taking the robe*). It is a good coat. I will keep it for my share.

2ND SOLDIER. You will not! I earned it well myself!

1ST SOLDIER. I'll run my sword through it. I'll make two halves.

2ND SOLDIER. You'll spoil it splitting it. It is without any seam.

3RD SOLDIER. No, but keep it and divide it with the rest of the clothes.

2ND SOLDIER. The rest are no good. This is the only garment worth while.

1ST SOLDIER. If we had dice we'd play for it.

DANIEL. Here now, I have dice for games in my hand.

1ST SOLDIER. I'll engage you have, and for tricking. I know your sort.

2ND SOLDIER. Play for it. The highest wins. (*They go to table.*)

1ST SOLDIER (*throwing*). Six and deuce! Beat that if you can!

2ND SOLDIER (*throwing*). Four and three!

3RD SOLDIER. Deuce and ace. No luck. I'll try again.

1ST SOLDIER. You will not! It's my throw. (*Throws.*)

3RD SOLDIER. Your hurry didn't help you! It is but double three.

1ST SOLDIER. Give it now to me! (*Seizes box.*)

2ND SOLDIER (*snatching it from him*). No, it's my turn. (*Throws.*) Double six! I have it.

1ST SOLDIER. No, but nothing! They rolled off the board!

2ND SOLDIER. It was yourself that shook it! (*He seizes the robe and goes towards the steps.*)

1ST SOLDIER (*following him*). That's a lie!

3RD SOLDIER. It will be torn between you, and no use at all.

(1ST *and* 2ND SOLDIERS *go off dragging at it.*)

1ST WOMAN (*laying her hand on the arm of* 3RD SOLDIER, *and holding out a pitcher*). If ever you had kindness from a mother or a mother's son, will you bring this drink to our Lord?

3RD SOLDIER. What is it? To hasten his death?

1ST WOMAN. No, but there are sleepy herbs in it that might give a little ease from his pain. (*He takes it and goes.*)

2ND SOLDIER (*coming back*). It is here I left the hammer and the nails.

DANIEL. Here they are for you. (*He holds them out.*)

2ND SOLDIER (*takes them, hesitates and throws them down*). No, I will not. I cannot use them. There was never a man spoke like this man.

VOICE OF 1ST SOLDIER. Come on, bring the hammer. That is your job.

2ND SOLDIER. I will never lift a hand against him.

1ST SOLDIER (*coming to top of steps*). Hurry! Hurry! What ails you?

2ND SOLDIER (*to* DANIEL). Go you and drive in the nails in place of me. Here, I will give you the whole of my day's pay. (*Puts money in his hands.*)

DANIEL. Sitting still is the best. I was thinking I would not go empty out of this. Just to sit still and quiet, and profit will turn to you in the finish.

(*He goes off, taking the hammer and nails.*)

2ND SOLDIER (*calling after him*). That you may never have any quiet or any rest from wandering for ever for your share in this day's work! And as much of my curse as does not reach to you, may it reach to your tribe and to your children! (*Follows him.*)

(JUDAS *comes in from the road. He walks across shading his eyes, looking up the hill, goes out of sight a moment, and comes back with his hand over his eyes.*)

JOEL. That God may perish him!

1ST WOMAN. It is Judas that betrayed him.

2ND WOMAN. The black-hearted traitor!

3RD WOMAN. Let him go hide himself under some scalp of a rock, or in a hole in the earth, or in the thickness of the woods!

JUDAS (*putting his hands over his ears*). Oh! the sound of the hammering! What way can I ever shut it out!

JOEL. Reproach and withering on you!

1ST WOMAN. It will go hard with you on the Day of the Mountain!

3RD WOMAN. To bring him as you did to his death sod! Thursday sold to his enemies, and on Friday a sieve of holes with the nails!

ST. BRIGIT. Go ask his forgiveness even now. He never refused any.

JUDAS. What is your chattering to me? He looked at me a while ago as he passed the road. It is I myself that betrayed the Son of God!

(*He hides his face again.*)

1ST WOMAN. I declare I'd nearly pity him. It might be it was his lot, and that he had his treachery settled for him four thousand years before his birth.

JOEL. It is a heavy curse there will be on you, and a price on your head, the same as there would be upon a wolf. It is a lone shadow you will be, going through the world.

JUDAS. Ah, what are your words and your curses, and what need is there to ring the bell against me? My heart that is turned to a black coal within me. These feet that were washed by him! These lips that kissed him! A lone shadow! Yes, and a doleful shadow, a wretched ghost, beaten by the waves of the sea. It is all there before me—black, bitter waters—bitter, winter winds. Dogs tearing, hounds hunting, a rock frozen in the waves. A wave of ice and a wave of fire—that is the wages of the betrayal of the King!

ST. BRIGIT. He is a King who will seek and save those that are lost.

JUDAS. I am going to that death and that punishment whatever it may be. And all I bring with me is the knowledge that he is the Christ that was promised to Israel, and it is little profit it will be to me, and it is hard I earned it! (*He snatches up the rope and rushes out.*)

JOEL. That noosed rope is a fitting friend to him.

1ST WOMAN. May God have mercy on him!

ST. BRIGIT. He might find kindness yet for one good deed he did, laying a wide flagstone in a desolate boggy place, where it is a great comfort to them that pass the way.

3RD SOLDIER (*coming back with pitcher*). Here is the vessel. It is full yet. When he had tasted of it he would not drink. He is a brave man. He would not shun any of the pain.

(1ST WOMAN *takes it and he goes.*)

1ST WOMAN. I could cry tears down to think of him bearing all that, and no one next or near to aid him.

ST. BRIGIT. The people of Heaven are standing waiting for him. He has beside him the right hand angel of God.

(*A great shout and clamour is heard from the hill. Then silence. The day darkens.*)

1ST WOMAN. There is coming a heavy mist.

3RD WOMAN. The song of the birds has stopped.

1ST WOMAN. There is the blessed Mother coming down the hill.

ST. BRIGIT. And with her the disciple that he loved.

(*She goes to meet them.*)

2ND WOMAN. She got her own scourge this day.

1ST WOMAN. It's no wonder a broken heart to be with her. Let her keen him and cry her fill.

(*She chants, the others joining in the caoine.*)

O what is this woman crying,
Coming down from the hillside,
Och, och, agus, Och-uch-an!
"Go, call the three Maries,
Till they keen my white darling,
Och, Och, agus Ochone O!

"Where is my child that I carried
Through three-quarters of a year?
Och, och, agus, Och-uch-an!
Have you seen my bright darling,
That never angered his Mother?
Och, Och, agus Ochone O!"

We did see him, O poor Mother!
We saw your white darling,
Och, Och, agus Och-uch-an.
A tall young man on the hillside,
His enemies all around him
And He on the Tree of Passion.
Och, Och, agus, Ochone O!

(*There is another heavy shout from the hill. The darkness
increases.*)

3RD WOMAN. Here she is coming to us. (*They kneel and continue
the caoine.*)

Isn't it great the pity,
The Child she crooned in her arm,
Och, Och, agus, Och-uch-an!
The spear to be in his side,
The dust to be on his head!
Och, Och, agus Ochone-O!

(*As it ends, the* MOTHER, ST. JOHN, *and* ST. BRIGIT *come on.*)

1ST WOMAN. Och! He is surely gone from us!

ST. JOHN. "It is finished!" That is what he said. And then he
said, "Father, into thy hands I commit my spirit." And with that
the soul parted from the body.

(*He covers his face.*)

ST. BRIGIT. He is gone from the shadows of the world to be with
his Father in the Garden of Paradise.

JOEL. My bitter blame upon the place where he died! I thought
it had been he would have redeemed Israel!

St. Brigit. It is the whole of the Universe he has redeemed.

Joel. Dead or alive, he will always be my Master and my King!

1st Woman. There will be no candle wasted with him. It is the angels of God that will keep a watch over him.

(*The sky brightens.* John *is seen looking upwards.*)

St. John. Give over keening. Look at that brightness. Listen! Listen!

St. Brigit. It is like the far-off music of the Birds of the plains of Heaven.

St. John. Hush! He is speaking! (*He bends his head and listens intently.*)

2nd Woman. Oh! What word does he say!

St. John (*still listening and speaking slowly*). "I am He that liveth and was dead. And behold I am alive for evermore!"

1st Woman. O King of Glory! He has broken before us the battle of death!

3rd Woman. Hush! Listen!

St. John. "Behold I stand at the door and knock. If any man hear my voice and open the door, I will come in to him, and will sup with him, and he with me."

1st Woman. Oh! Our white Lord!

St. John (*holding up his hand for silence, and as if hearing with greater difficulty*). "To him that overcometh and keepeth my words to the end, will I give to eat of the Tree of Life, which is in the midst of the Paradise of God——and I will give him the Morning Star——"

St. Brigit. That God may bring us to the same joy his blessed soul returned to!

The Women. O Blessed Christ!

Curtain.

345

DAVE

TO

A. E.

DAVE

PERSONS

    NICHOLAS O'CAHAN. *Elderly, very neatly dressed in old-fashioned clothes, with knee breeches.*

    KATE O'CAHAN. *His wife, a good deal younger. She is winding a ball of wool from skeins on the back of a chair. She walks back and forward to this.*

    TIMOTHY LOUGHLIN. *A serving man.*

    JOSEPHINE LOUGHLIN. *A young girl, his niece.*

    DAVE. *A youth in poor working clothes. Looks sullen and slouches. His hair hangs over his forehead.*

    TIME. *A hundred years ago.*

SCENE. *A room well furnished with old-fashioned things, a settle, a chest, an armchair, a turf basket. The door left opens into a little entry; door right leads to the kitchen.* TIMOTHY *is on his knees arranging the fire.*

TIMOTHY (*shouts*). Bring in, Dave, the turf! (*No answer.*) Come on, you lazy cur! Hurry now.

(DAVE *comes in with an armful.*)
Couldn't you come when I called you?

DAVE (*sullenly*). I could if I brought the turf wet.

TIMOTHY. Don't be giving impudence. You know well you were scheming or slouching around some hole or corner.

DAVE. Have it your own way so. (*He is putting the turf in the basket.*)

TIMOTHY. If I had my own way it's walking the road you would be—put out of this house.

DAVE. I wouldn't please you to go out, or it's out of the reach of your tongue I'd be gone before now.

TIMOTHY. I'll get quit of you in spite of yourself. Hurry on, now, go get another load of the turf. What, now, is keeping that little girl of mine so long in the village?

DAVE. There she is at the door. (JOSEPHINE *enters as he goes out.*)

JOSEPHINE. I left the message for the driver of the long car, that Nicholas O'Cahan and the Missis would be wanting a seat to the town when he'll be passing.

TIMOTHY. You took your time doing that. Idling in the shop I'll engage you were, and the dark of the evening coming on. Fingering ribbons and fooleries.

JOSEPHINE. You're out there. I was not in the shop at all.

TIMOTHY. What kept you so? Fooling and gabbing with idlers, the same as yourself. Here now is the Missis.

(KATE *comes in from the other door.*)

TIMOTHY (*getting up*). Josephine that is after bidding the car to wait for you and the Master, ma'am, to bring you to the town for the night.

KATE. I thought you were talking as if vexed with someone.

TIMOTHY. So I am vexed with that lad that's slow bringing in the turf. Come on, now—come, fill up the basket. (DAVE *comes in and begins putting in more sods.*) And I was telling this niece of mine she had too much time lost with chattering down in the village.

JOSEPHINE. Well, I was not chattering or saying any word at all —but listening.

TIMOTHY. That's it. To some person with as little sense as yourself.

JOSEPHINE. You're out again. It was to a holy man was preaching in the street.

KATE (*interested*). Was it a priest that was preaching—or a friar?

JOSEPHINE. I don't rightly know. He was a stranger—a sort of a missioner. Asking help he was for the people of Iar Connacht that are down under the fever and the famine.

TIMOTHY. What brought him questing here? All the help we have to give, it is for ourselves we should keep it as is right.

KATE. Tell me, now, Josephine, what account did he give?

JOSEPHINE. The fever is running through the country, he was saying. It is a terrible scourge. It is what he said, the people are dying in empty walls with no roof over them, or in a shed in the haggards, or out by the side of the road.

KATE. God help them, they are surely under great trouble.

(DAVE *has stopped filling basket, and is listening.*)

TIMOTHY. The right place for them is the poorhouse, that was built for the like of that class.

JOSEPHINE. It is what he was saying, the poorhouses are filled till there is no more room in them. The people are dying, he said, without help of priest or friar or anything at all.

KATE. That is a terrible story, if it is true.

JOSEPHINE. And worse again——

KATE. There could hardly be worse than that.

JOSEPHINE. The breath would hardly be gone out of them, he said, before they'd be put into the earth. No one to give them burial, but a bag made and the body put in it and thrown in a hole in the wild bog, and the shaking sod closing over their head. And he said "in Connemara over it is the dogs bring the bodies out of the houses, and ask no leave!"

KATE (*puts her hand over her eyes*). The poor creatures! What are we doing that we cannot come to their help! The Lord have mercy on them, and bring them to the comfort of Heaven!

TIMOTHY. I wouldn't believe a word of it. It's certain the half of them should be in gaol, as it's likely the gaol fever is rotting the most of them.

JOSEPHINE. I tell you the Missioner said it, and he rising up his hand.

TIMOTHY. Talk is easy. It's hard trust any of Adam's race.

DAVE (*comes a step forward, lets fall the sods of turf from his arm. To* JOSEPHINE). Where is that man was preaching? Is he in the street yet?

TIMOTHY (*taking hold of his arm*). Mind you own business. Have you the gap in the wall settled yet? Come on, now. There are things to make ready before the master will make his start.

(*Pushes* DAVE *before him out of door.* KATE *takes her skein of wool that is on the back of a chair, and begins winding it into a ball.*)

JOSEPHINE. I'm in dread, Ma'am, you'll get a wetting going to the town. There is rain overhead yet, and all that came down through the night and through the morning is lying in pools and in splashes on the road.

KATE. What is weather and a wetting beside what we are after hearing? That is as pitiful a story as any ever I heard.

JOSEPHINE. Ah, the weather might cheer up before you will make your start. It's myself would like to be going with you, and to see all the grandeur and the people of the town.

(*She goes into kitchen as* NICHOLAS *comes in.*)

NICHOLAS (*closes a book he has been reading as he comes in, keeping his finger in the place*). This is a great book I got from the pedlar. I nearly begrudge going to the town, and not to be reading it through from start to finish.

KATE. Indeed, I myself have not much heart to go there after all I have been hearing of the fever and the famine, but to stop and say a prayer for all that are under trouble.

NICHOLAS. Pup, pup, woman. You know your witness is required at the court-house along with my own in that case that concerns Thomas O'Cahan's right of way, and he my third cousin by the two great-grandfathers. Stop now interrupting me till you'll hear what this old poet says (*sits down in his armchair and reads*):

> *The Kingdom started up altogether,*
> *To put out the Danes who put trouble on Ireland;*
> *The Kennedys and the strength of the Lorcans,*
> *Morans and Brogans armed and dressed* (looks up)

—the whole of them were in the battle of Clontarf.

KATE. The poor men!

NICHOLAS. Don't be interrupting me!

> *They travelled from Munster as may be read,*
> *O'Sullivan out from the west of Ireland*— (excited)

Ha! Here it is put down clear and plain!

KATE. What is it?

NICHOLAS. The name I was in search of! And that I made sure should be in the poem. And that is my own name.

KATE. Is it Nicholas O'Cahan?

NICHOLAS. What about Nicholas? That is a name is well enough, but that likely may not have been in the world in those early times. Listen, now:

> *O'Donovan of the deer, O'Maher and O'Cahan.*

The Battle of Clontarf was not fought without them being in it!

KATE. That should be a long time ago.

NICHOLAS. Near to a thousand years!

KATE. And was he killed in it?

NICHOLAS. Killed or not killed what signifies? How do I know did ever he strike a blow, or get a blow? Battle or no battle he would be dead now anyway.

KATE. It is for the people dying of the hunger at this time I am fretting. You might have heard the Missioner down in the village?

NICHOLAS. Wait now till I'll see is it put down were there any more of my old fathers in the world at that time. O'Malley, O'Mara

—O'Shaughnessy. It is a great book. You would know, reading it, what people are worth nothing, and which of them are worth while.

KATE. We'd mostly know that living anear them.

NICHOLAS. Believe me, high blood and ancient blood is the best property at all to run in a family.—Do you know what I'm thinking?

KATE. I do not, without you'd tell me.

NICHOLAS. It is going through my mind that if the Lord had sent us a son we would find it hard to make our mind up what name to bestow on him, among all the big names in my family.

KATE (*coming back with her ball of wool, interested*). I used often to be thinking I would call him Patrick.

NICHOLAS. Not at all. It is well enough for people with no genealogy to go seeking a name among the saints. But where there is family, it is right to show respect to the family. I should have a good deal of quality belonging to me.

KATE. I was only saying——

NICHOLAS. Go easy, now! It is natural for you to be running down race. I am finding no fault with yourself. But it is the first time an O'Cahan ever joined with a Heniff! You'll be saying, I suppose, that lad Dave, that is a foundling is not far from being equal to myself!

KATE (*turning back to her chair*). You need not be running down my people. I never saw poverty out of my father or my mother. Everyone belonging to me came from the old stock of the parish, and my grandmother coming to Mass every Sunday on a pillion and a black mare!

NICHOLAS. Don't be talking. Where is Timothy? (*calls*) Timothy! I must tell him about the antiquity of the O'Cahans.

TIMOTHY (*coming in*). I sent the message, sir, to the driver of the long car——

NICHOLAS. Stop a minute and listen. (*Takes up book.*) Did you ever hear news of the families that drove out the Danes, the Lochlanach, from Ireland?

TIMOTHY. What way would I hear it, sir? I have not learning like yourself.

NICHOLAS. Long ago as it was, Timothy, near to a thousand years, they were not without one of my own race and name.

TIMOTHY. Why wouldn't there be one of them? It's easy know that out of yourself—or twenty-one of them! The O'Cahans are a great breed surely. It's the finest thing in the known world to have high generations behind you.

353

NICHOLAS. It is proud my third cousin Thomas O'Cahan will be to-morrow, hearing he had a far-off father living close on a thousand years ago. Hurry on, now, Kate, and make ready for the road.

KATE. I will, so soon as I'll have this ball of wool wound. I have but to put on my bonnet and my shawl. I hope no bad thing will happen the house, and we away from it through the whole of the night time.

NICHOLAS. Timothy Loughlin will be in charge, and the little girl Josephine, his niece, till such time as we'll come back to-morrow.

TIMOTHY. Believe me, sir, I'll take good care of all—only that lad——

NICHOLAS. Give me here my Sunday boots (*begins taking off the boots he is wearing*).

TIMOTHY (*bringing boots*). It is what I was saying, that lad Dave——I'd sooner you'd bring him along with you. It is hard for me keep control of him. He is a bad class of a scamp.

NICHOLAS. I have it in my mind you were making some report of him a while ago.

TIMOTHY. I give you my word, sir, in the twelve-month I lived with you, I had but the half of it peaceable, before that lad was brought in here. (*He kneels to lace NICHOLAS'S boots.*)

NICHOLAS. I have some memory it was yourself brought him in from where he was standing, a *spailpin* with his spade in his hand, seeking work at the Easter fair. Saying, you were, he would be easy brought on his back, having no kindred to be running to.

TIMOTHY. There is not a day but I'll hear some troublesome thing of him. Rambling and idling, card-playing up in the mountains—that's where he was through last night.

KATE. Ah, there's boys will do that sort of thing to the end of time.

TIMOTHY. He's tricky, and has too much tricks in him. He is a holy terror.

KATE. Well, he should be as God made him.

NICHOLAS. Do not be taking his side now. It was against my own judgment I brought him into the house. A lad whose race and kindred no one knows, and whose father and mother no one knows.

KATE. He is but a youth of a boy. It's a pity to put on him the sins of the generations before him.

NICHOLAS. He has no generations before him, bad or good, to give him that excuse.

TIMOTHY. That's it. A by-child reared in the workhouse. It's likely a tinker's brat.

NICHOLAS. That's a class I don't like, and I wouldn't like it, and I'm a man that couldn't like it.

KATE. He was maybe born into his troubles. It's easy be good having good means and a good way and plenty of riches.

NICHOLAS. Hurry on, now, Kate, and make ready. Give me here the key till I'll lock this book in the chest. (*Takes keys and puts one in the lock.*)

TIMOTHY. The vagabone! It's a skelping he should get to bridle him that would take the skin off him. He is bad out and out. He brought badness into the world with him, the same as you might bring a birthmark.

KATE (*going over to take last threads of the skein off the chair*). Maybe so, maybe so. I never got learning out of books. But it's often I heard said there is no child comes into the world but brings with him some grain of the wisdom of Heaven. It's the mother can know that, watching his little ways. The Spirit of God given in the beginning wasn't given to one or to two. I myself can tell that much if I never had a child of my own. (*Goes.*)

TIMOTHY (*as NICHOLAS is about to lock the chest*). There is Dave coming. Have a care, sir, where you would conceal your choice things——

(DAVE *comes in.*)

TIMOTHY. Where were you?

DAVE. Where you bade me go. Putting up the gap in the wall——

TIMOTHY. I'll believe that when I'll see myself is it done. It's likely you would make a poor job of it with the drowsiness is on you after being out rambling through the night time.

DAVE. I hear what you're saying.

NICHOLAS (*who is turning over the pages of his book, and putting a mark in*). Tut, tut, try and behave now.

TIMOTHY. You see the way he is, sir, a sullen miserable hound.

NICHOLAS. It is right you should learn behaviour. But I would not be hard on you, as I would on one who had a good rearing and a good name.

DAVE. What fault have you to find with my name? Anyway I got no other name. Dave, short and sharp like you would shout for a dog.

TIMOTHY. Have some shame on you! I tell you, you not to have come into the world would be no loss at all.

NICHOLAS. That's enough, Timothy. I don't know where are my glasses? (*He puts down the book and looks for them.*)

TIMOTHY. Hearken now. Your master is going away for one night—or two nights. I myself will be in charge of all here. I lay it on you that you will not be drinking or stealing, or be going to night sports or dance-houses with scamps and schemers, gambling or smoking or snuffing—fighting and quarrelling—bringing bad lads into the house on top of me.

DAVE (*with a bitter laugh*). Go on with your A.B.C. Put on me all the sins you can find to put on me, and I'll not deny them! Swearing big oaths and blasphemy! To laugh at my neighbour's downfall! To make nothing of breaking the Ten Commandments! I've a right to be put running with a price on my head, the same as a wild dog of the hills.

TIMOTHY. Oh, to listen to him! It is to the assizes he should be dragged by the hair of his head!

DAVE. Have a care now. I could put curses out of myself as quick as you!

NICHOLAS (*putting on his hat*). Leave off that uproar and go in there to the Missis. (*He goes. Calls out.*) Hurry now, Kate, or we'll miss the car. Dave will bring out all your little packages and wearables.

(KATE *comes out, followed by* DAVE, *with packages. She is dressed for the journey.*)

TIMOTHY. God speed you, sir, and come back to us safe and sain. I'll mind the house well. (*They go out.*) It's a pity you're not bringing that lad before the judge that might put the terror of the law on him!

(*He turns back as* JOSEPHINE *comes in, bringing a kettle in her hand.*)

JOSEPHINE. Oh, are they gone! (*Calls from door*) Oh, Ma'am, won't you stop a minute, and I'll have the tea wet for you! (*She turns round.*) She beckons she could not come back. (*She puts kettle down on hearth.*)

TIMOTHY (*looking from window*). They are going down the road in a hard trot. I was in dread the wet would come down again, and turn them back from making their start.

JOSEPHINE (*flinging herself into* NICHOLAS's *armchair*). My joy go with them in a bottle of moss. If they never come back they'll be no great loss! Here's his old book on the floor! (*Kicks it.*)

TIMOTHY (*giving it a kick, and then picking it up*). Himself and his ancient generations! And looking at myself over the top of it as

356

if I was dirt! If I didn't make up my mind to humour him I'd like well to face him on the head of that.

JOSEPHINE. He hasn't a great deal of sense. Will you look what they left after them? Their whole bunch of keys. Stuck in the lock-hole of the chest one of them is.

TIMOTHY. Do you say so! I never knew Nicholas O'Cahan leave that chest open till now.

JOSEPHINE (*opening it*). Well, we'll take a view of it. Here is a grand shawl I never saw. It would suit myself well. (*Puts it on, gets up on a chair to look at herself in the mirror.*) A great pity it to be lying there idle. (*Looks in chest again.*) And the silk skirt she put on at the time of the wedding at the Keanes. (*Slips it on.*) I would be well pleased to wear silk clothes, and to have a lady's life.

TIMOTHY (*who has taken the keys and opened the cupboard*). Here is where he keeps his cellar. (*Takes out a jar, pours some of its contents into a glass, and drinks it off. Pours some more into the glass and leaves it on the table.*) That's good stuff, and no mistake.

JOSEPHINE (*kneeling at the chest*). Linen sheets as white as if they were for her burying—and towels of the finest flax, fit for any bishop, or any big lord.

TIMOTHY (*stooping over chest*). Here is some weighty thing——

JOSEPHINE. A teapot—and a milk jug. Is it silver they are?

TIMOTHY (*examining*). White pewter they might be—no it's silver, sure enough.

JOSEPHINE (*putting her hand deeper in the chest*). There is some weighty thing here below—a stocking——

TIMOTHY. Give it here to me. (*Unrolls it.*) Why wouldn't it be weighty, and the foot of it being full of golden guineas! (*Shakes it.*)

JOSEPHINE. Gold! That is better again than silver.

TIMOTHY. What use is it to him where he has full and plenty? He cannot bring it with him to the tomb. (*Starts, and drops stocking.*) There is some noise!

JOSEPHINE (*getting up, goes to window*). It is but thunder. I was thinking it would be coming with the weight of blackness gathering overhead. There now is the rain pouring down.

TIMOTHY (*taking stocking again, and weighing it in his hand*). By cripes! if I got this I'd knock a good turn out of it.

DAVE (*comes in unheard, shakes the rain from his hat, claps his hands, and calls ironically*). God bless the work!

TIMOTHY (*hastily stuffing stocking into his pocket while JOSEPHINE shuts lid of chest*). What brings you snaking in here, idling and spying around?

357

DAVE. It's well for yourselves it is not Nicholas O'Cahan that came in and his Missis. (*He takes up the glass of whiskey, and drinks it off.*)

TIMOTHY. If they did itself what signifies? I'm not like yourself that no one would trust with a fourpenny bit without he'd keep his two eyes fixed on you through the hours of the day and night.

DAVE. You can save your chat. I know you well to be a class of a man that is gathering up for himself. You not to have crookedness in you, how would you go picturing it in every other one? I know well what happened the three lambs you told Nicholas O'Cahan were torn and ate with the fox!

TIMOTHY. You'll go bringing every lie and every bad story to him, I suppose?

DAVE. Why would I? It is not for him I ever said a prayer, or to please him I'll ever turn informer.

TIMOTHY. You'd best not. There's many a thing I can say about yourself.

DAVE. Do your best! There is no wrong thing ever I did since I came to the place but you have it told out ere this, and ten times as much told, and the most made of it, and the worst, the way I never got a penny in my hand for wages, but all stopped for fines or for punishment. I don't know at all what is it holds me back from doing every crime and every robbery, when there could not be put upon me a worse name for badness than what is put upon me now.

TIMOTHY. What could there be in you but badness, you that were left at the side of a ditch by vagabones of tinkers that were travelling the roads of the world since the day of the Crucifixion!

DAVE. Didn't I hear enough of that story the seventeen years I am in the world? In the poorhouse, in the street, in this house, nothing but the one bad word. I got no chance in any corner but what my two hands gave me and God! I don't know in the world wide what kept me back that I didn't kill and destroy the whole of ye, and bring down the roof over your head. I declare to my God it's often I'd have choked the breath out of yourself and your master if it wasn't there is a look of pity in the old woman's face, if she hasn't the courage to stretch a hand to me itself.

TIMOTHY. Why would any Christian stretch a hand to you or the like of you?

DAVE. What now is the worst thing and the most thing I could do to punish the world and the whole of ye?

JOSEPHINE. Ah, let you quieten down, and not be shouting to call in the country entirely.

358

DAVE. To put a wisp of lighted straw in among the lumber in the chest, and to put another in the thatch of the roof? To burn the house and all that's in it, and to leave the whole of ye without a roof over your head! That is what I owe to the world that gave me nothing only insult since ever I made my start upon its plains! (*He begins flinging things into the chest.*)

JOSEPHINE (*seizing his arm*). Stop, now—can't you only let on to have burned them, and we ourselves will share with you whatever it's worth while.

(TIMOTHY *hastily collects what things are best in the chest and puts them in the basket, from which he throws out the turf.*)

DAVE. Bring here and throw on them the vessel of sheep's fat was rendered for to dip the candles! That will make a bonefire will sparkle up to the rafters of the roof. I'll put fire to the house, and all that's in it—only that jar I'll bring out on the road till I'll call to some of the wild class—thieves and sheepstealers, and the worst of the world's rogues! (*To* TIMOTHY) It's yourself should come drink with me then! (*He seizes a handful of paper thrown out from the chest, and lights a twist of it at the fire.*)

JOSEPHINE. There is someone opening the door. Who could be coming in on this night of thunder and of rain?

DAVE (*going to door with the lighted wisp in his hand*). Come in, come in fellow law-breakers! There's a fire lighting will make you a ladder to the stars! There is whiskey before you in the jar!

(NICHOLAS *and* KATE O'CAHAN *come in, she shaking the rain from the umbrella she holds before her.* DAVE *falls back.*)

NICHOLAS. Dave! Leave down that wisp of fire in the hearth! Are you gone clean mad! (*Snatches wisp from him, and puts it out.*)

(TIMOTHY *rushes at* DAVE *from behind, gives him a violent blow, and strikes him down. He falls heavily with a cry, striking his head against a chair, and lies senseless.*)

KATE. Oh, is it killed he is!

TIMOTHY. Lift him up on the settle till I bind him to it. (*He and* NICHOLAS *lift and bind him with the cord that has bound the parcels.*)

NICHOLAS. You did well to down a lad of that sort. He is a terrible type of a ruffian.

TIMOTHY. He's one of the old boy's comrades. If you had seen him ten minutes ago, he was all one with a wild beast. (*He binds* DAVE's *feet.*)

KATE. I give him up now. He is a holy terror to the whole world.

TIMOTHY. It would be well to put a gag in his mouth.

JOSEPHINE. He can say nothing. He has his senses lost with the dint of the fall.

TIMOTHY. With the dint of drunkenness. But I now have something to say. Look now the way the room is. He that got hold of the keys—it's likely picked them from your pocket, and he attending you along the road——

KATE. Oh, no! I couldn't hardly believe that!

TIMOTHY. Myself and the little girl being in the kitchen—attending to the work we had to do—and when we came in—there as you see—(*points to chest*)——

KATE. Ah, to look at the way all is tossed and turned. No, but the choice things put within in the basket.

TIMOTHY. He was to bring them away through the darkness——

NICHOLAS. He should be a thief out and out.

TIMOTHY. He'd take the sheet from your side, with respects to you. And when he got at the drink——

KATE. Ah, it should be the drink that did it——

TIMOTHY. He drank the devil into him. He rose the shovel at me to let my blood, and maybe knock out my brains. Only for I have a good coat on my shoulders he'd split me.

NICHOLAS. The Lord be praised he has no family to bring under disgrace!

TIMOTHY. And worse again. He was to put a light in the clothes that's within the chest—and in the rafters, and to burn the house entirely, the way you would not see all he had robbed. He was on the brink of doing it!

KATE (*covering her face with her hands*). Oh, tell me no more. The fire is the last of all!

TIMOTHY (*to* JOSEPHINE). Here's my little girl can bear witness did he call for the pan of sheep's tallow for to give a heart to the flame.

JOSEPHINE (*sullenly*). You can tell your own story without me.

NICHOLAS. I will commit him to justice in the morning. Let the Sheriff come bring him away with his men.

TIMOTHY. It is this very minute he should be brought away. He is that crafty you couldn't trust him not to make his escape. He might rise up in his senses and break his cords and make an attack on us all.

NICHOLAS. It is likely the car-driver went no farther than the post-house at the cross. Out on the car, and the rain down, we got more wet than all the men of the world. You should go around the whole of the province before you would come to the town.

KATE. The flood had us made fools of. The water on the public road had leave to cover the bridge.

Josephine. Oh, let me loosen your cloak, ma'am. You are wet-drowned and perished.

(*She takes* KATE'S *cloak and bonnet and shakes them before the fire.*)

TIMOTHY. To follow the car-driver to the post-house, and to catch him, he could bring word to the barracks to send a sergeant to our aid. Let you go tell him that sir, and I'll stop and mind this lad.

NICHOLAS. Not at all, but you will come holding the lantern. The night is come on, and the road is as slippery as a road of ice. (*To* KATE) We'll be back in a while's time.

KATE. Oh, what way can I stop here in the room after all has happened. The fright is gone into my heart!

(*She takes cloak and bonnet from* JOSEPHINE *and goes through door to kitchen.*)

NICHOLAS (*sarcastically*). The girl Josephine will maybe have the courage to stop for ten minutes, or twelve minutes, of time to guard you against a lad that has lost his senses and is tied with knots and with a rope.

(*They go out,* TIMOTHY *carrying lantern.*)

JOSEPHINE (*stands looking out after them*). I'll go back to my mother's friends in the village. I'm not willing to stop longer in this place, and my uncle beckoning me to tell lies. (*She slips out, knocking over the umbrella that is in her way. Bangs the door after her. The room is almost dark.* DAVE *stirs and moans.* KATE, *coming back, goes over and looks at him. She lights a candle, then goes to him again.*)

KATE. They were surely too hasty and too hard, treating him the way they did. I would hardly believe looking at him he could be so bad as what they say. And if he was itself, is it his fault, being as he was a child without a home? (*She touches his hair.*) There is blood on it, and a sharp wound upon his head.

DAVE (*cries out*). Where am I? Loosen my hands. I cannot move!

KATE. Lie quiet, now, and I will do what I can for you.

(*She takes one of the fine towels from the chest, takes the silver bowl and pours water into it from the kettle.*)

DAVE. Let me up out of this! Are they gone out, the cowards!

My thousand curses on them! Loosen my hands till I will light a wisp in earnest! I'll get my revenge on them! That death may perish them! That I may see them kicked roaring through the provinces! Oh, there is a sting of pain—I cannot move—I cannot see—the blood is coming into my eyes. (*His voice fails as his head sinks back, and he lies still.*)

KATE. Close your eyes now till I'll wash the blood from them. (*She rolls up a sheet, and puts it as a pillow under his head, and washes the blood from his face.*) Here now is a knife. I will cut the cords from your hands (*does so*), and from your feet. (*He moves his limbs, and then lies quite still.*) He is in a doze of weakness. The poor child, all of them telling him he was bad, what way could he believe there was the breath of God in him? (*He moans as she washes the blood from his hair.*) Astray in the lonesome world, he never met with kindness or the love of kindred, to make his heart limber. (*She stoops and listens to his breathing.*) That he may get comfort in his sleep, where he is used to little comfort in his waking! That is all I can do for him now, but to bless him with the sign of Christ's cross. (*She makes the sign over him, and sits down on a chair near the fire and bows her head.*) Oh, King of Mercy come to his help! He is as lonesome as a weaned lamb gone astray among the stones. It is as if he had lost his way in the world, and been bruised on the world's roads. The dust has darkened his eyes, it is hard for him lift his head into the light. He is under clouds of trouble. Bring him to the dawn of the white day. Send a blessing on him from the Court of the Angels! (*She sings*)

> There lust and lucre cannot dwell,
> There envy bears no sway,
> There is no hunger, heat nor cold,
> But pleasure every day.
>
> Thy gardens and thy gallant walks
> Continually are green,
> There grow such sweet and pleasant flowers
> As nowhere else are seen.
>
> Quite through the trees with silver sound
> The flood of life doth flow
> Upon whose banks on every side
> The wood of life doth grow.

There trees for evermore bear fruit,
And evermore do spring;
There evermore the angels sit
And evermore do sing!

(*Music is heard outside as she ceases.*)

There is music outside—sweet quieting music. It might be some poor wandering fiddler going the road through the provinces. (*She stands up and looks at* DAVE, *then sits down again facing him.*) He is sleeping very easy. There is surely someone having a wish for him, in or out of the world.

DAVE (*moves and mutters, then raises himself on his elbow as if listening. He laughs*). I am coming—I could not see the path, but I heard the music and the laughing—merry laughter, not mocking. Is it me you're calling brother? It is long since I was called by that name. Am I your brother, and you with your head held so high? I see the door open—but there is a dyke between us. Reach me out your hand—it is hard to get over the dyke. There is the music again. (*He closes his eyes.*)

KATE. He is maybe listening to the Birds of Heaven. It is sometimes a vision is sent through the passion sleep of the night.

DAVE (*he has moved a little, but is still listening*). I had a bad dream. I dreamed I was on a rough road—with ugly words—with mean company—the mud was splashed on me and the dirt. (*Listens.*) I will, I will do your bidding as it is your will. I will go back till I have leave to come to you—till such time as you will beckon me to come. (*He lays down his head and sleeps again.*)

KATE. He surely got comfort in his sleep. There is a bright appearance on his face.

DAVE (*starting up*). Where am I? What is this place?

KATE (*standing up, and coming nearer*). Where were you, agra?

DAVE. Some good place it was—a very green lawn. It had no bounds to its beauty. (*Puts his hand over his eyes.*)

KATE. It was surely a good dream.

DAVE. There were some that held the hand to me. Who were they? I was to find something. Oh! it is going astray on me! I cannot keep it in my mind!

KATE. It will likely come back to you again.

DAVE. It was as if all the herbs of summer were in blossom—I think no one could be sick or sorry there. I would nearly say it had what should be the sound and the feeling of home.

KATE. It was maybe not in this world you saw that good harbour.

DAVE. And a very laughable thing. It was nearly like as if I was a king's son or a great gentleman. I could not but laugh thinking that. (*He lays down his head.*)

KATE (*moving away*). It is nearly a pity he had not the power to awake at the time that door was open. It is likely he will walk with his head up from this out, for it may be it was himself he saw in that dream.

DAVE (*sitting up on the side of the settle*). Tell me, now, will it ever chance me to get there again?

KATE. It will surely at the last, with the help of God.

DAVE. I will never be content or satisfied till I will come again to that dream.

KATE. You will come to it again surely, and it will be no dream.

DAVE. I want to be in it now.

KATE. Any place that has the love of God in it is a part of that garden. You have maybe brothers under trouble to reach a hand to, and to beckon them to it, as there was a hand reached out to you.

DAVE. What way could I do that, being as I am all badness, without goodness or grace?

KATE. Poor child, it is because they were always putting a bad name on you that you don't know you are good.

DAVE. Good—you are the first ever said that to me.

KATE. It is certain the Man Above never sent you here without some little flame of His own nature being within you.

DAVE. That is a great thought if it is true.

KATE. It is true, surely. Mind you never let that flame be quenched in you.

(DAVE *buries his face in his hands.*)

KATE. You might maybe sleep again. The Lord be with you by noon and by night from this out, in the day and in the darkness! (*Goes taking candle.*)

VOICE OF NICHOLAS (*at the door*). I hear no sound. It is likely his senses are astray from him yet.

VOICE OF TIMOTHY. A great pity it failed us to get word to the sergeant. With all the run I put on myself, the car was gone before me.

(*They come inside.*)

NICHOLAS. It will be time enough to get help in the morning. He is well tied and bound.

TIMOTHY. He to start defaming or blaspheming, it's what we'll put a gag over his mouth. Or to redden the tongs, and threaten him with cruelty. It's little myself for the world would care he never to rise up again. He is a danger to the whole of the universe.

NICHOLAS. Bring in here the lantern before we'll fall over some chair.

(TIMOTHY *brings it in at the same moment as* KATE *comes back with the candle.* DAVE *stands up.*)

TIMOTHY (*going behind* NICHOLAS). His hands are free! He'll do murder on us!

NICHOLAS (*seizing a chair, and holding it up*). Have a care now!

DAVE (*as if surprised*). I have no wish to do hurt or harm.

TIMOTHY. Do not trust him!

NICHOLAS. It is best for you quit this house before any worse thing might come about!

DAVE. I will go. I think I did some foolish thing a while ago. (*Puts his hand over his eyes as if trying to remember*). There was anger on me—I must have done with foolishness.

NICHOLAS. Whether or no, you will go do it in some other place than this.

TIMOTHY. That's right—let him go beg his bread.

(DAVE *goes towards the door.*)

KATE. Ah, Dave, stop awhile! I would be sorry to see you go begging your bread.

DAVE. It would not be for honour, I to go quest or beg. I am going out as I came in, with my spade and the strength of my two hands that are all my estate. I am going in search of—to give help to—(*passes his hand over his eyes*) my people.

TIMOTHY. It is in the gaols you will likely find them, or among those paupers that are rotting with the fever, and are thrown out by the side of the road.

DAVE (*turning back, his eyes shining*). That is it! Those are the ones I will go to! The miserable people the preacher was seeking aid for. I will go look for them in Connacht over, and through the whole wilderness of Connemara!

TIMOTHY. Much good you'll do coming to them, unless drinking and scheming!

DAVE (*taking up his spade and hat*). If it should fail me to earn a handful of meal to keep the life in them, I can show service to the dead. Those that die on the roadside I will not leave to be dragged by a dog, or swallowed down in a boghole. If I cannot make out a couple of boards to put around them, I will weave a straw mat with my hands. If the dead-bells do not ring for them, I will waste a white candle for their wake!

KATE. Oh! You aren't hardly fit for that work, and your cheeks so pale, and the drops of blood on your brow.

DAVE. I give you my word I never felt so merry or so strong. I am like one that has found his treasure and must go share it with his kin. Why wouldn't I be airy doing that? (*Goes out.*)

TIMOTHY. A good riddance. I hate the living sight of him. Strutting out like a lord on the mall!

KATE. Stop your bad talk, Timothy. He is a good boy, and a decent boy, and a boy that doesn't deserve it from God or man.

TIMOTHY. He is a thief and a robber. I will swear to it before any judge. Dave is a lad that belongs to the gallows.

JOSEPHINE (*who has come in and heard his last words*). I hear what you are saying, and it is not truth. I saw Dave going down the road, and I have it in my mind it was your lies turned him out.

(*Comes forward.*)

TIMOTHY. Take care what you are saying!

JOSEPHINE. I know well what I am saying. Give up now to Nicholas O'Cahan what you have your hand on at this minute, and are keeping for your own profit. Hold him, sir! ——

(TIMOTHY *goes towards door, but* NICHOLAS *seizes his arms from behind, and while he struggles she tears his pocket open and bag falls on to floor.* NICHOLAS *picks it up.*)

NICHOLAS. The girl is speaking truth. It is best for you to quit this. It is often it came across me that you, having the bad word so ready on your tongue should have some bad drop in yourself. But I made allowance for you, because of you being of a poor class, and of no ancient family or good blood.

TIMOTHY. Ancient, is it? Let me tell you that if your family is ancient my own is more ancient again! Yourself and your generations and your Battle of Clontarf, that was for driving out the Danes! My own family was of the Danes, and came in with the Danes, and it's likely were long in the country before those families were born that drove them out! The seed and breed of the Loughlans is more ancient, and is seventeen times better than any O'Cahan at all!

NICHOLAS. Of all the impudence! Quit this house before I'll give you up to the Sheriff that will put you in the dock! (*He takes up his book and hurls it at him.* TIMOTHY *escapes by the door. He sinks into an armchair.*)

KATE (*tearfully*). That is best. He had a bad thought of everyone, and that breeds badness in a house.

366

JOSEPHINE. Will you put me out, Ma'am, along with him, or will you let me stop and care you?

KATE (*tearfully*). I'll put no one out. But the world is turned to be very queer. Too many hard knocks, and I do be tired in my legs. I've near a mind to go follow that poor lad that went out, not having a red halfpenny to handle, and wear out what is left of my life poor and banished like himself. And maybe get more respect than ever I got here, with my name not showing out in any old book!

NICHOLAS (*agitated*). What is on you, Kate? Don't be talking about leaving me, and the way the wheel is going around. I take my oath I will never bring down my pedigree upon you again the longest day I'll live! (*Gets up and flings the book on the hearth.*) Let it turn to ashes and my joy go with it, for nothing in the mighty world will ever make me open it again!

KATE. I'm in dread you will be fretting after it yet, and make that a new reproach against my name.

NICHOLAS. Well, will this content you, that I'll give up my own name, and call myself Heniff from this out?

KATE. You cannot do that, and Nicholas O'Cahan being cut in clean letters on the slab you have ordered for your burying.

NICHOLAS. Ah, my poor Kate, what can I do to satisfy you? Listen now, you have leave to call that lad Dave back here from his poverty, if it is your will.

KATE (*goes to the window and looks into the darkness, and then turns back*). I wouldn't ask it. God has surely some great hand in him. He had the look of being very glad in the mind. His head held high, and a light on his brow as bright as the bow of heaven. May friends and angels be around him and steer him to a good harbour in the Paradise of the King!

Curtain.

NOTES AND MUSIC

NOTES AND MUSIC

My First Play:

Colman and Guaire

It was I think nearly thirty years ago that I wrote this, my first attempt at playwriting. I had been staying in Venice, as so often before, with Lady Layard, in her beautiful Ca Capello. But through all the beauty of Grand Canal, its gondolas, its palaces; and all the sunshine and pleasant company, my thoughts kept turning back to the work that had begun in Ireland; the Gaelic League, the Creameries, and especially the Drama. For though our "Literary Theatre" had ended its three years' experiment, the dramatic impulse was living, and William Fay was rehearsing A.E.'s *Deirdre* for the stage. I did not aspire to a stage production, but I thought a little play in rhyme might perhaps be learned and acted by Kiltartan school-children; and it was on the railway journey home, through Italy and the Alps to Calais, that to the rhythm of the engine I began putting into rhyme the legend of Saint Colman's birth, as I had heard it from the old people, my neighbours. Monsignor Fahey, then our parish Priest, was pleased with it, and approved. But I was by that time taken up with the practical work of the Theatre in Dublin, and this was laid aside. I had almost forgotten it until I came upon the manuscript in looking through some papers the other day; and the legends I had gathered have been put into my *Book of Saints and Wonders*. That one which tells of Saint Colman's birth, says that when his mother, Rhinagh, was with child, it was told to King Guaire of Connacht that the child she would bear would be greater than his own son. "And when he heard that, he bade his people to make an end of Rhinagh before the child would be born. And they took her and tied a heavy stone about her neck and threw her into the deep part of the river, where it rises inside Coole. But by the help of God, the stone that was put about her neck did not sink, but went floating upon the water, and she came to the shore and was saved from drowning. And that stone is to be seen yet, and it having the mark of the rope that was put around it. And just at that time there was a blind man had a dream in the North, about a well beside a certain ash tree, and he was told in the dream he would get his sight if he bathed in the water of that well. And a lame man had a dream about the same well, that he would find at Kiltartan, and that there would be healing in it for his lameness. And they set out together, the lame man carrying the man that had lost his sight, till they came to the tree that he dreamed about. But all the field was dry, and there was no sign of water, unless that beside the tree there was a bunch of green rushes. And then the lame man saw there was a light shining out from among the rushes; and when they came to them they heard the cry of a child, and there by the tree was the little baby that afterwards was Saint Colman. And they took him up and they said, 'If we had water we would baptize him.' And with that they pulled up a root of the rushes, and a well sprang up and they baptized him; and that well is there to this day. And the water in springing up splashed upon them, and the lame was cured of his lameness, and the blind man got his sight. And many that would have their blindness cured go and sleep beside that well; and many that are going to cross the sea to America take with them a bit of a blessed board from an old tree that is in that field." And I have been told "He was a great Saint afterwards, and his name is in every place. Seven years he was living in Burren, in a cleft of the mountains, no one in it but himself and a mouse. It was for company he kept the mouse, and it would awaken him when he was asleep and when the time would come for him to be minding the Hours. And it is not known in the world what did the dear man get for food all that time. And that place he lived is a very holy place, being as it is between two blessed wells. No thunder falls on it, or if there is thunder it is very little, and does no injury."

And I have heard of "Many a kindness he has done from time to time, for the people of Aidhne and of Burren". And of all those kindnesses this is the one that pleases me best: "There was a little lad in Kiltartan one time that a farmer used to be sending out to drive the birds off his crops. And there came a day that was very hot and he was tired and he dared not go in, or fall asleep, for he was in dread of the farmer beating him. And he prayed to Saint Colman, and the Saint came and called the birds into the barn. And they all stopped there through the heat of the day, till the little lad got a rest, and never came near the grain or meddled with it at all."

And as to Guaire: "If he was not a Saint he was well worthy to be the brother and the kinsman of Saints, and they would never have been in poverty if he had his way. And he gave alms till his right arm grew to be longer than the left, with the dint of stretching it out to the poor."

And once when there was "a great troop of the poets in Guaire's house in the winter time, a woman of the poet's household had a desire for ripe blackberries. But everybody said there were no blackberries to be got, ripe or unripe, at that time of the year. But as one of Guaire's people was out in the fields he saw a bush that was covered with a cloak, and under the cloak the blackberries were ripe and sound, and they were brought in to the woman, and there was no reproach upon the King's house. This now is the way that happened: King Guaire was going through the field at harvest time, and the thorns of the bush took hold of the cloak he was wearing and held it. And Guaire was not willing to refuse so much as a bush that asked anything of him, and he left the cloak there on the branches. And for that kindness he got his reward in the end."

Legend tells also that one day at Inis-Guaire, a royal banquet having been set out, the King looking at its richness had cried out "God knows I wish all this could be put before some poor starving man!" And with the word the whole feast was carried by invisible hands to the narrow cell on the hills, where the Saint, Colman, lay starved and perishing.

And the King with his people following found him there. And I myself have been shown hoofmarks in the stones, and told they were made by King Guaire's horses on that day.

And as to the King's Vision, an old frieze-coated man sitting by his turf fire told me: "One night I was walking on that mountain beyond that is Slieve-Echtge, and a little chap with me, Martin Lydon, and we came in sight of the lake of Dairecaol. And in the middle of the lake I saw what was like the shadow of a tall fir tree. And while I was looking, it grew to be like the mast of a boat. And then ropes and rigging came at the sides and I saw that it was a ship; and the boy that was with me, he began to laugh. Then I could see another boat, and then more and more till the lake was covered with them, and they moving from one side to another. So we watched for a while, and then we went away and left them there."

January 25, 1930.

The Travelling Man

An old woman living in a cabin by a bog road on Slieve Echtge told me the legend on which this play is founded, and which I have already published in "Poets and Dreamers".

"There was a poor girl walking the road one night with no place to stop, and the Saviour met her on the road, and He said—'Go up to the house you see a light in; there's a woman dead there, and they'll let you in.' So she went, and she found the woman laid out, and the husband and other people; but she worked harder than they all, and she stopped in the house after; and after two quarters the man married her. And one day she was sitting outside the door, picking over a bag of wheat, and the Saviour came again, with the appearance of a poor man, and He asked her for a few grains of the wheat. And she said—'Wouldn't potatoes be good enough for you?' And she called to the girl within to bring out a few potatoes. But He took nine grains of the wheat in His hand and went away; and there wasn't a grain of wheat left in the bag, but all gone. So she ran after Him then to ask Him to forgive her; and she overtook Him on the road, and she asked forgiveness. And He said—'Don't you remember the time you had no house to go to, and I met you on the road, and sent you to a house where you'd live in plenty? And now you wouldn't give Me a few grains of wheat.' And she said—'But why didn't you give me a heart that would like to divide it?' That is how she came round on Him. And He said—'From this out, whenever you have plenty in your hands, divide it freely for My sake.' "

And an old woman who sold sweets in a little shop in Galway, and whose son become a great Dominican preacher, used to say— "Refuse not any, for one may be the Christ."

I owe the Rider's Song, and some of the rest to W. B. Yeats.

The Full Moon

It had sometimes preyed on my mind that *Hyacinth Halvey* had been left by me in Cloon for his lifetime, bearing the weight of a character that had been put on him by force. But it failed me to release him by reason, that "binds men to the wheel"; it took the call of some of those unruly ones who give in to no limitations, and dance to the sound of music that is outside this world, to bring him out from "roast and boiled and all the comforts of the day." Where he is now I do not know, but anyway he is free.

Tannian's dog has now become a protagonist; and Bartley Fallon and Shawn Early strayed in from the fair green of *Spreading the News*, and Mrs. Broderick from the little shop where *The Jackdaw* hops on the counter, as witnesses to the miracle that happened in Hyacinth's own inside; and it is likely they may be talking of it yet; for the talks of Cloon are long talks, and the histories told there do not lessen or fail.

As to Davideen's song, I give the air of it below. The Queen Anne in it was no English queen, but, as I think, that Aine of the old gods at whose hill mad dogs were used to gather, and who turned to grey the yellow hair of Finn of the Fianna of Ireland. It is with some thought of her in their mind that the history-tellers say "Anne was fair like the Georges but very bad and a tyrant. She tyrannised over the Irish. She was very wicked; oh! very wicked indeed!"

Air of "The Heather Broom!"

Shanwalla

Some time ago I was looking through many stories told me on our countryside and given by me later in *Visions and Beliefs*, bearing witness to the consciousness of the presence of the dead, of spirits invisible, for here in Connacht there is no doubt as to the continuance of life after death; the spirit wanders for a while in that intermediate region to which mystics and theologians have given various names. But I felt doubtful as to using them; I hesitated to put them before an audience used to close reasoning and the presentation of proved facts. I feared they might be found inconclusive, trivial, meaningless. But it happened the next day as I was driving to church with one dear to me and now gone from me* we were talking of kindred matters and he said, "I have no doubt at all there will be a return to intuition as in primitive days. Reason took its place, and reason was seized on with passion by the Greeks as a

* Her son, Robert.

new force to be used in every possible field and way. But now it has gone as far as it can go, it has ceased to interest, to satisfy; it is to intuition we must turn for new discoveries."

I said then to myself that my countryside tales are justified. These people of lonely bogs and hillsides have still their intuition, their sensitiveness to the unseen; they do not reason about it, they accept it as simply as they do the sighing of the west wind or the colour of the sky. I believe that what they feel and relate is perhaps of as great importance to that in us which is lasting, as the tested results of men of science examining into psychic things. For none have yet been certainly aware of much more than shadows upon a veil, vague, intangible, yet making the certainty clearer every day that when the veil is rent for us at our passing away, or made thinner for us during our stay in this world, it is not death but life that is to be discovered beyond it.

But as to proof of the return, "How shall they believe if one rose from the dead?" When I was working at this play, where the spirit of the wife returns, imperceptible indeed to the Court where she gives her message, yet able to give it and so to save her man, reason told me that all in that Court should be convinced, that Magistrate and husband and officials would go on their knees in prayer, or call out their belief in this triumph of one of "the cloud of Witnesses." But when it came to writing the scene, I suppose it was either intuition or experience that took the pen and brought it to its present end.

I was talking in a Venice Salon one evening with a well-known English artist and a German Admiral. The artist told us she had once been dining in Kensington Palace with a Royal Princess, and after dinner as they were going upstairs she was left alone for a moment and a clear voice said from below, "Who is there?" She was surprised at anyone thus calling out in such a place, and the Princess came running back, looking scared, and said "Did you hear anything?" "And when I told her, the Princess said, 'Yes, others have heard it too: it is George the IVth.'" This happened in Kensington Palace, and the spirit was that of a King. But the German Admiral, the Reasoner, said "Ach, we hear stories of ghosts, and they are got up by people that want to keep the place for smuggling!"

The Golden Apple

I long had it in my mind to write a play for children, put together from the folk-tales and fairy tales of Ireland. But I did not want

I wish I had the shepherd's lamb, the shepherd's lamb, the shepherd's lamb; I
wish I had the shep-herd's lamb, And Ka-tie com-ing af - ter. Iss
O gur-rim gur-rim hoo, iss gra-ma-chru gon kel-lig hoo, Iss
O gur-rim gur-rim hoo, Sthoo pat-tha gal dho wau-her.

THE GARDENER'S SONG

Colla voce.

Lacrimoso.

CORO. *p*

rall.

THE LITTLE OLD MUD CABIN BY THE HILL

troublesome staging, and it was not till I saw the production of *The Yellow Jacket* that I knew how simply and swiftly changes of scene could be made. If we had put on *The Golden Apple* at the Abbey

377

THE SHAN VAN VOGHT

ERIN, THE TEAR AND THE SMILE

O'DONNALL ABOO

Theatre, I should have needed for the garden scene little but a well head and a little tree, and that could have been a front scene masking the King's bedchamber. The Wood of Wonders is made by the waving of boughs by the Witch and her daughter; and the Giant wants but a step-ladder and a pair of stilts. The cat disguise is always put on out of sight, and need only be head and paws, and a long-tailed grey gown. But I cannot put the play on in Dublin this year, for our earnings have lessened, so that to keep the Company together we have had to send them playing at music halls till better times come with the ending of the war.

We call grey plover filibines, and starlings stairs, and little fish pinkeens, and little sticks kippeens, and hazel rods scollops, in our everyday talk at Kiltartan.

The Jester

I was asked one Christmas by a little schoolboy to write a play that could be acted at school; and in looking for a subject my memory went back to a story I had read in childhood called "The Discontented Children," where, though I forget its incidents, the gamekeeper's children changed places for a while with the children of the Square, and I thought I might write something on these lines. But my mind soon went miching as our people (and Shakespeare) would say and broke through the English hedges into the unbounded wonder-world. Yet it did not quite run out of reach of human types, for having found some almost illegible notes, I see that at the first appearance of Manannan I had put in brackets the initials "G.B.S." And looking now at the story of that Great Jester, in the history of the ancient gods, I see that for all his quips and mischief and "tricks and wonders," he came when he was needed to the help of Finn and the Fianna, and gave good teaching to the boy-hero, Cuchulain; and I read also that "all the food he would use would be a vessel of sour milk or a few crab-apples. And there never was any music sweeter than the music he used to be playing."

I have without leave borrowed a phrase from "The Candle of Vision," written by my liberal fellow-countryman, A.E., where he says, "I felt at times as one raised from the dead, made virginal and pure, who renews exquisite intimacies with the divine companions, with Earth, Water, Air, and Fire." And I think he will forgive me for quoting another passage now from the same book, for I think it must have been in my mind when I wrote of my Wrenboys: "The lands of Immortal Youth which flush with magic the dreams of childhood, for most sink soon below far horizons and do not again

379

arise. For around childhood gather the wizards of the darkness and they baptize it and change its imagination of itself, as in the Arabian tales of enchantment men were changed by sorcerers who cried, 'Be thou beast or bird.' So . . . is the imagination of life about itself changed and one will think he is a worm in the sight of Heaven, he who is but a god in exile . . . What palaces they were born in, what dominions they are rightly heir to, are concealed from them as in the fairy tale the stolen prince lives obscurely among the swineherds. Yet at times men do not remember, in dreams or in the deeps of sleep, they still wear sceptre and diadem and partake of the banquet of the gods."

Air: "Shule Aroon"

The Wrenboys still come to our door at Coole on St. Stephen's Day, as they used in my childhood to come to Roxborough, but it is in our bargain that the wren itself must be symbolic, unmolested, no longer killed in vengeance for that one in the olden times that awakened the sentinels of the enemy Danes by pecking at crumbs on a drum. And, indeed, these last two or three years the rhymes concerning that old history have been lessened, and their place taken by "The Soldiers Song."

Air: "Mo Bhuachailin Buidhe"

I think the staging of the play is easy. The Ogre's hut may be but a shallow front scene, a curtain that can be drawn away. The masks are such as might be used by Wrenboys, little paper ones, such as one finds in a Christmas cracker, held on with a bit of elastic, and would help to get the change into the eyes of the audience, which Manannan's Mullein-dust may not have reached.

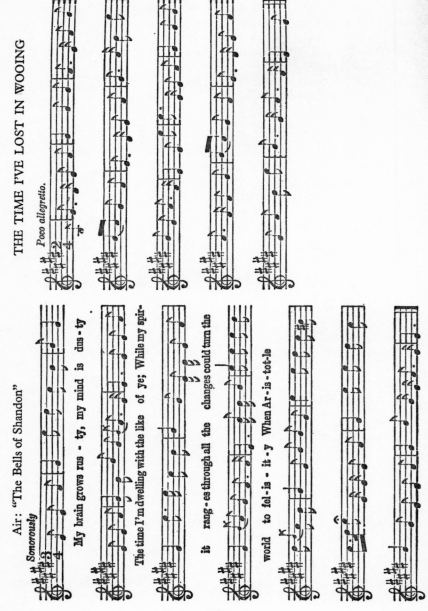

THE TIME I'VE LOST IN WOOING

Air: "The Bells of Shandon"

Poco allegretto.

Sonorously

My brain grows rus-ty, my mind is dus-ty.
The time I'm dwelling with the like of ye; While my spirit rang-es through all the changes could turn the
world to fol-is-it-y When Ar-is-tot-le

Air: "O'Donall Abu"

MY MOLLY O

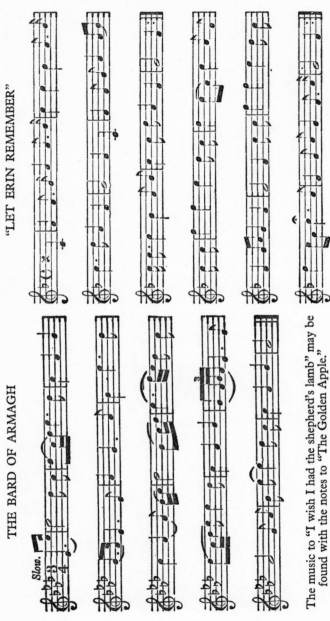

"LET ERIN REMEMBER"

THE BARD OF ARMAGH

The music to "I wish I had the shepherd's lamb" may be found with the notes to "The Golden Apple."

Air: "And doth not a meeting like this"

Air: "Dear Harp of my Country"

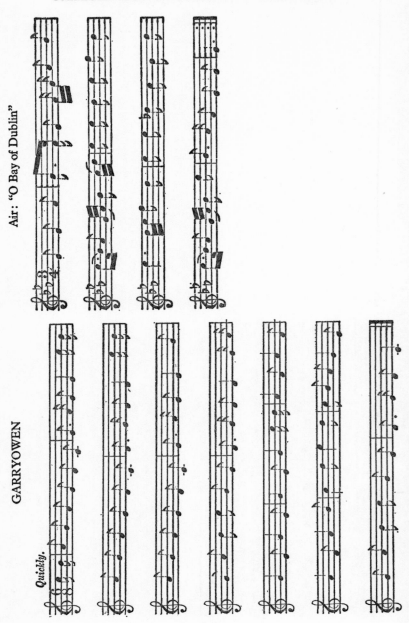

Air: "O Bay of Dublin"

GARRYOWEN

Quickly.

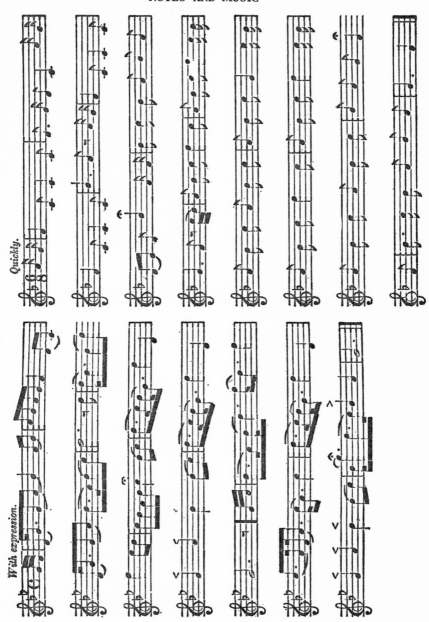

OFT IN THE STILLY NIGHT

THE DESERTER'S MEDITATION

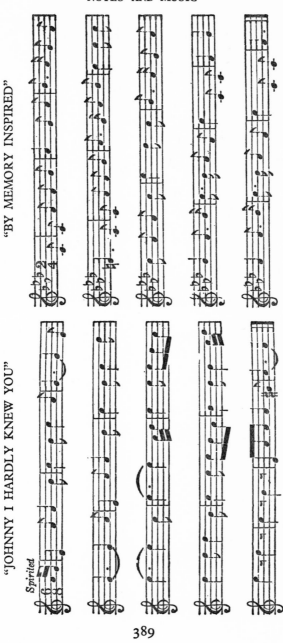

"BY MEMORY INSPIRED"

"JOHNNY I HARDLY KNEW YOU"

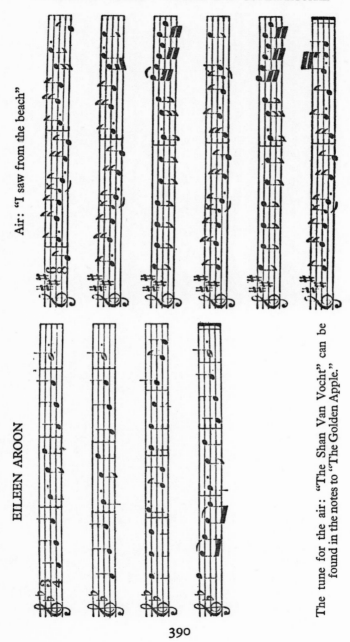

Air: "I saw from the beach"

EILEEN AROON

The tune for the air: "The Shan Van Vocht" can be found in the notes to "The Golden Apple."

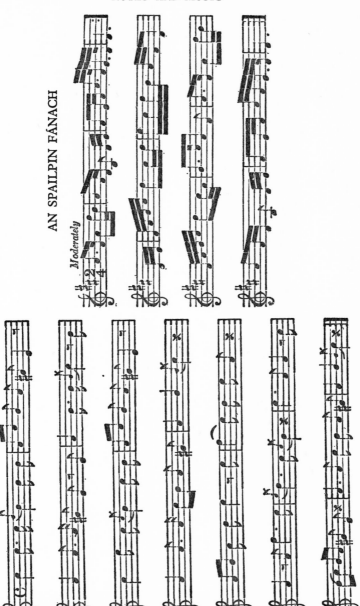

AN SPAILPIN FÁNACH

Moderately

Air: "Silent O Moyle"

Air: "The Last Rose of Summer"

The Dragon

I wrote *The Dragon* in 1917, that now seems so many long years away, and I have been trying to remember how I came to write it. I think perhaps through some unseen inevitable kick of the swing towards gay-coloured comedy from the shadow of tragedy. It was begun seriously enough, for I see among my scraps of manuscripts that the earliest outline of it is entitled "The Awakening of a Soul," the soul of the little Princess who had not gone "far out in the world." And that idea was never quite lost, for even when it had all turned to comedy I see as an alternative name "A Change of Heart." For even the Dragon's heart is changed by force, as happens in the old folk tales and the heart of some innocent creature put in its place by the conqueror's hand; all change more or less except the Queen. She is yet satisfied that she has moved all things well, and so she must remain till some new breaking up or re-birth.

392

As to the frame work, that was once to have been the often-told story of a King's daughter given to whatever man can "knock three laughs out of her." As well as I remember the first was to have been when the eggs were broken, and another when she laughed with the joy of happy love. But the third was the stumbling-block. It was necessary the ears of the Abbey audience should be tickled at the same time as those of the Princess, and old-time jests like those of Sir Dinadin of the Round Table seem but dull to ears of to-day. So I called to my help the Dragon that has given his opportunity to so many a hero from Perseus in the Greek Stories to Shawneen in those of Kiltartan. And he did not sulk or fail me, for after one of the first performances the producer wrote: "I wish you had seen the play last night when a big Northern in the front of the stalls was overcome with helpless laughter, first by Sibby and then by the Dragon. He sat there long after the curtain fell, unable to move and wiping the tears from his eyes; the audience stopped going out and stood and laughed at him." And even a Dragon may think it a feather in his cap to have made Ulster laugh.

Coole, February, 1920.

Aristotle's Bellows

I had begun to put down some notes for this play when in the autumn of 1919 I was suddenly obliged, (through the illness and death of the writer who had undertaken it), to take in hand the writing of the "Life and Achievement" of my nephew Hugh Lane, and this filled my mind and kept me hard at work for a year.

When the proofs were out of my hands I turned with but a vague recollection to these notes, and was surprised to find them fuller than they had appeared in my memory, so that the idea was re-kindled and the writing was soon begun. And I found a certain rest and ease of mind in having turned from a long struggle, (in which, alas, I had been too often worsted) for exactitude in dates and names and in the setting down of facts, to the escape into a world of fantasy where I could create my own. And so before the winter was over the play was put in rehearsal at the Abbey Theatre, and its first performance was on St. Patrick's Day, 1921.

I have been looking at its first scenario, made according to my habit in rough pen and ink sketches, coloured with a pencil blue and red, and the changes from that early idea do not seem to have been very great, except that in the scene where Conan now hears the secret of the hiding-place of the Spell from the talk of the cats, the Bellows had been at that time left beside him by a dwarf from the rath, in his sleep. The cats work better, and I owe their success to the genius of our Stage Carpenter, Mr. Sean Barlow, whose head of the Dragon from my play of that name had been such a masterpiece that I longed to see these other enchanted heads from his hand.

The name of the play in that first scenario was "The Faultfinder" but my cranky Conan broke from that narrowness. If the play has a moral it is given in the words of the Mother, "It's best make changes little by little, the same as you'd put clothes upon a growing child." The restlessness of the time may have found its way into Conan's mind, or as some critic wrote, "He thinks of the Bellows as Mr. Wilson thought of the League of Nations," and so his disappointment comes. As A.E. writes in "The National Being," "I am sympathetic with idealists in a hurry, but I do not think the world can be changed suddenly by some heavenly alchemy, as St. Paul was smitten by a light from the overworld. Though the heart in us cries out continually, 'Oh, hurry, hurry to the Golden Age,' though we think of revolutions, we know that the patient marshalling of human forces is wisdom . . . Not by revolutions can humanity be perfected. I might quote from an old oracle, 'The gods are never so turned away from man as when he ascends to them by disorderly methods.' Our spirits may live in the Golden Age but our bodily life moves on slow feet, and needs the lantern on the path and the staff struck carefully into the darkness before us to see that the path beyond is not a morass, and the light not a will o' the wisp." (But this may not refer to our own Revolution, seeing that has been making a step now and again towards what many judged to be a will o' the wisp through over seven hundred years.)

As to the machinery of the play, the spell was first to have been worked by a harp hung up by some wandering magician, and that was to work its change according to the wind, as it blew from north or south, east or west. But that would have been troublesome in practice, and the Bellows having once entered my mind, brought there I think by some scribbling of the pencil that showed Conan protecting himself with an umbrella, seemed to have every necessary quality, economy, efficiency, convenience.

As to Aristotle, his name is a part of our folklore. The old wife of one of our labourers told me one day, as a bee buzzed through the open door: "Aristotle of the Books was very wise but the bees got the better of him in the end. He wanted to know how did they pack the comb, and he wasted the best part of a fortnight watching them, and he could not see them doing it. Then he made a hive with a glass cover on it and put it over them, and he thought to watch them. But when he went to put his eye to the glass, they had it all covered with wax so that it was as black as the pot, and he was as blind as before. He said he was never rightly killed till then. The bees had him beat that time surely." And Douglas Hyde brought home one day a story from Kilmacduagh bog, in which Aristotle took the place of Solomon, the Wise Man in our tales as well as in those of the East. And he said that as the story grew and the teller became more familiar, the name of Aristotle was shortened to that of Harry.

As to the songs they are all sung to the old Irish airs I give at the end.

August 18, 1921.

The Story brought by Brigit

Last year in looking through old letters I found one from W. B. Yeats, in which he said that Father Hegarty, a priest beloved by the people of Mayo, had said to A.E. that if a passion play should be written (for we were then at the beginning of our dramatic movement) he would be glad to have it put on in his parish. Yeats had then, and later, urged me to work at this. But it was only last summer, when my life seemed to have drifted into a quiet backwater, and I was much alone, that the great subject took hold of me, and so filled my mind that I was forced to get it into words, and into the form I am most used to, of a play.

I knew I could best write it through the voice, as it were, of our own people, and so I have given the story as I think it might have been told by Brigit, "the Mary of the Gael," our great Saint, had she been present during the last days of Him who, tradition tells us, she cherished in his early days. Gaelic Scotland in its folklore makes her the serving maid at the Inn of Bethlehem; but in Ireland it brings the Holy Mother and Child to our own country. Brigit, "shining flame of gold, right foster-mother of Christ," comes often into the hymns and incantations of the Scottish Highlands. "The encompassment of Mary and of Brigit" is asked on herds of cattle and on milking and on churning. She tended sheep, and her protection as "Brigit the fostermother," is asked for the flocks, "to keep them from strangers and from harm," and "from the straight arrows of the women of the sidhe"—the fairy women. "May gentle Mary keep the sheep, may calm Brigit keep them, on the soft land, on the hard land, from the fox and from the wolf." The two names are constantly put together, "calm, generous Brigit," "mild, loving Mary." And in the dedication, the binding, of the young hunter "not to kill a bird sitting, or a beast lying down," he was bade remember "the fairy swan of Brigit of the flocks; the fairy duck of Mary of Peace."

Here in Connacht on her day, the 1st of February, "the blessed Crosses are made of straw, and are put up in the thatch, and the first of the birds begin to make their nests, for the death of the year is done with, and the birthday of the year is begun."

It was a poor woman living on a slope of Slieve Echtge, who told me a while ago "how Brigit helped the Mother of God." "There was a poor man, and a poor woman, living in an ancient place in Ireland, a sort of a wilderness. The man used to be wishing for a son that would be a help to him with the work, but the woman used to say nothing, because she was good. They had a baby at last, but it was a girl, and the man was sorry, and he said, 'We will always be poor, now.' But the woman said, for it was showed to her at that time, 'This child will be the Mother of God.' The girl grew up in that ancient place, and one day she was sitting at the door, and our Saviour sent One to her that said, 'Would you wish to be the Mother of God?' 'I would wish it,' said she. And on the minute, as she said that, the Saviour went into her as a child. The Messenger took her with him, and he put beautiful clothing on her, and she turned to be so beautiful that all the people followed them, crowding to see the two beautiful people passing by. They met with Brigit, and the Mother of God said to her, 'What can we do to make these crowds leave following us?' 'I will do that for you,' said Brigit, 'for I will show them a greater wonder.' She went into a house then, and brought out a harrow, and held it up over her head, and every one of the pins gave out a flame like a candle; and all the people turned back to look at the shining harrow that was such a great wonder. And it is because of that, the harrow is blessed since that time. The Mother of God asked her then what would she do for her as a reward. 'Put my day before you own day,' said Brigit. So she did that, and Saint Brigit's day is kept before her own day ever since. And there are some say Brigit fostered the Holy Child, and kept an account of every drop of blood he lost through his lifetime. And anyway, she was always going about with the Mother of God."

As to the curse put upon Daniel in the play, I wondered sometimes why our country people who are so kind to one another, and to tramps and beggars, that they seem to live by the rule of that old woman in a Galway sweet shop, the mother of the great preacher, Father Burke, "Refuse not any, for one may be the Christ," shun as they do that wandering tribe, tinkers—as they call them, gipsies they may be—who spend their days going along the roads in carts, and sleep at night under their cart, or by the side of a wall. "Some of them that do smith's work are middling decent," I was told; "but the most of them have no trade, but to be going to fairs and doing tricks, and having a table for getting money out of you with games."

"They never go to Mass, they have no religion, or, if they have, it is a wandering one, wandering like themselves." "There was one I knew, I told him I wondered they wouldn't settle down in one place; for if I knew the way to make money, I said, I would make plenty. For they are said to coin money. But he said it made no difference if they had money; they couldn't stop in one place; they must be walking always, and going through the whole country." And then I was given a reason for this ceaseless wandering. "There are some say that when our Lord was on the Cross there could be no tradesman found to drive the nails in his hands and feet till a tinker was brought, and he did it; and that is why they have to walk the world. And I never met anyone that had seen a tinker's funeral."

Other legends have gathered round that story of "the Tree of Passion." One of the most ancient is of the death of Conochar, High King of Ireland in Cuchulain's time. "He had been given at one time a wound in the head in some battle in Connacht. And the wound was sewn up by Fintan, the great healer, with a thread of gold that matched the colour of his hair. And Fintan bade him to be careful and not to give way to anger or to passion, and not to be running, or to go riding on a horse. So through seven years he stayed in his quietness until the coming of the Friday of the Crucifixion. And on that day he took notice of a change that came over the world, and of the darkening of the sun until the moon was seen at the full; and he asked his druid that was with him the meaning of that great change. 'It is Jesus Christ, the Son of God,' said the druid, 'that is at this time meeting with his death by the Jews.' 'It is a pity,' said Conochar, 'that he did not call out for the help of a High King. And that call would bring myself there,' he said, 'in the shape of a hardy fighter, my lips twitching, until the great courage of a champion would be heard breaking a gap of battle between two armies. It is with Christ my help would be; a wild shout going out;

the keening of a full lord, a full loss. I would make my complaint to the trusty army of the high feats, their ready beautiful help would relieve him. Beautiful the overthrowing I would give his enemies; beautiful the fight I would make for Christ that is defouled; I would not rest although my own body was tormented. Why would we not cry after Christ, he that is killed in Armenia, he that is more worthy than any worthy king? I would go to death for his safety; it crushes my heart to hear the outcries and the lamentations!' And with that he took his sword and he rushed at an oakwood that was near at hand, and began to hack and to fell the tree; and it is what he said, that is the treatment he would give them. And from the greatness of the anger that gripped him, the old wound in his head burst open, and the ball started from it, and brought away the brain with it. And that is the way Conochar, King of Ireland, met his death."

The caoine used by the three Women is a little altered from one given in the Religious Songs of Connacht, collected by Douglas Hyde. The notes to which it is spoken have been given to me by Miss Sara Allgood.

Coole, October 16, 1923.

At the first production of this play, in Dublin, the following note was printed on the programme:

Our tradition, and that of Gaelic Scotland, speak of St. Brigit as "the foster-mother of Christ," and I have been told by poor women of Slieve Echtge that she succoured both Blessed Mother and Child when they were brought here by a Heavenly Messenger for safety in Herod's time, and that she "kept an account of every drop of blood He lost through His lifetime." So it is not going very far from that tradition to suppose she may have been present at the end of His life as at the beginning, and have told the story in her own way, as she had seen it in the body or in vision.

CAOINE

Isn't it great the pity, the child she crooned in her arm,

Och, och agus ochone, the spear to be in his side, the dust to be on his head. Och, och, agus ochone, O.

[NOTE.—As to the verses given to the WOMEN, I wish them to be lilted rather than sung. For they have dramatic value, are a part of the play, and any musical setting, however beautiful, that is more complicated than that of the street ballad singer must delay the swift comprehension needed.]

Dave

A thought long dwelling in my mind and that I had heard put by a poor woman in a workhouse into such simple words as, "There is no child comes into the world but brings with him some grain of wisdom of Heaven," was brought nearer to dramatic expression when I saw in the *Irish Statesman* a poem by its Editor, A.E., who has allowed me to print it here and to dedicate the little play to him:

"The Gods have taken alien shapes upon them
Wild peasants driving swine
In a strange country. Through the swarthy faces
The starry faces shine.

Under grey tattered skies they strain and reel there;
But cannot all disguise
The majesty of fallen gods, the beauty,
The fire beneath their eyes.

They huddle at night within low, clay-built cabins,
And, to themselves unknown,
They carry with them diadem and sceptre
And move from throne to throne."

The verses sung by Kate are from an old hymn given in the *Oxford Book of English Verse* as "Song of Mary, Mother of Christ," with the date 1608. I have seen it elsewhere with an earlier date, and attributed to St. Augustine.

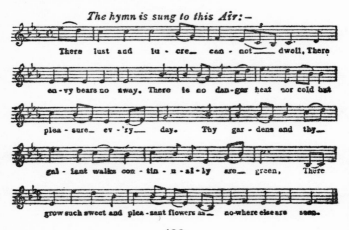

The hymn is sung to this Air:—

There lust and lu-cre can not dwell, There en-vy bears no sway. There is no dan-ger heat nor cold but plea-sure ev-'ry day. Thy gar-dens and thy gal-lant walks con-tin-u-al-ly are green, There grow such sweet and plea-sant flowers as no-where else are seen.

The old Irish Air "The Wheelwright" is the one heard outside the house.

FIRST PERFORMANCES AT THE ABBEY
THEATRE AND THE CASTS

FIRST PERFORMANCES AT THE ABBEY THEATRE

The following plays in this Volume have been performed at the Abbey Theatre and the casts and the date of the first productions are given below:

3rd March 1910
The Travelling Man

Mother	. Sara Allgood
Child	. Elinor Moore
Travelling Man	Fred O'Donovan

10th November 1910
The Full Moon

Shawn Early	. J. O'Rourke
Bartley Fallon	. Arthur Sinclair
Peter Tannian	. Sidney Morgan
Hyacinth Halvey	Fred O'Donovan
Mrs. Broderick	. Sara Allgood
Miss Joyce	Eileen O'Doherty
Cracked Mary	. Maire O'Neill
Davideen	. J. M. Kerrigan

8th April 1915
Shanwalla

Lawrence Scarry, a stable-man . .	. H. E. Hutchinson
Hubert Darcy, his master . . .	. Sydney J. Morgan
Bride Scarry, his wife . . .	Kathleen Drago
Owen Conary, a blind beggar . .	. J. M. Kerrigan
Pat O'Malley	Fred O'Donovan

James Brogan	. Arthur Sinclair
First Girl	. Eithne Magee
Second Girl	. Ann Coppinger
Head Constable	. J. A. O'Rourke
First Policeman	Michael Conniffe
Second Policeman	. Philip Guiry
A Boy	Thomas O'Neill

6th January 1920
The Golden Apple

The King	Peter Nolan
Rury, his son	F. J. McCormick
The Doctor	. Eric Gorman
Simon the Steward	Barry Fitzgerald
The Witch	Christine Hayden
Pampogue, her daughter	. Esme Ward
The Giant	. Hugh Nagle
Briget, his wife	Maureen Delany
The Cook	. Michael Dolan
The Barber	. Bryan Herbert
The Gardener	. Arthur Shields
Muireann, the Enchanted Princess . .	. Eithne Magee

Strangers, Servants, etc.: J. J. Lynch, T. Quinn, Jas. Mahon, H. L. Corrigan, P. Kirwan, J. D. Brennan, etc.

21st April 1919
The Dragon

The King	Barry Fitzgerald
The Queen	. Mary Sheridan
The Princess Nuala	. Eithne Magee
The Dall Glic (The Blind Wise Man) . .	. Peter Nolan
The Nurse	Maureen Delany
The Prince of the Marshes . . .	. J. Hugh Nagle
Manus—King of Sorcha . . .	. Arthur Shields
Fintan—The Astrologer . . .	F. J. MacCormick
Taig	. Eric Gorman
Sibby	. Florence Marks
The Dragon	Seaghan Barlow
The Porter	. Stephen Casey

The Gatekeeper . . . . . Hubert M'Guire

Two Aunts of the Prince of the Marshes { Esme Ward
Dympha Daly

17th March 1921

Aristotle's Bellows

The Mother	Maureen Delany
Celia, her daughter	Gertrude Murphy
Conan, her stepson	Barry Fitzgerald
Timothy, her serving man	F. J. McCormick
Neighbours:	
Rock	. Peter Nolan
Flannery	Michael J. Dolan
First Cat	Seaghan Barlow
Second Cat	. P. Kirwan

April 1924 (Holy Week)

The Story Brought by Brigit

Joel	. Arthur Shields
Daniel	Michael J. Dolan
Marcus	Maurice Esmonde
Silas	Barry Fitzgerald
Pilate	F. J. McCormick
Judas Iscariot	. Eric Gorman
St. John	. P. J. Carolan
St. Brigit	Christine Hayden
First Woman	. Sara Allgood
Second Woman	Maureen Delaney
Third Woman	. Eileen O'Kelly
First Man	. Peter Nolan
Second Man	. Bernard Swan
First Soldier	Gabriel J. Fallon
Second Soldier	F. J. McCormick
Third Soldier	. Tony Quinn
A Young Scribe	Gabriel J. Fallon
An Egyptian Nurse	. May Craig
The Mother	. Eileen Crowe
The Christ	. Lyle Donaghy

407

May 9th, 1927
Dave

Nicholas O'Cahan	Michael J. Dolan
Kate O'Cahan	Maureen Delany
Timothy Loughlin	P. J. Carolan
Josephine Loughlin	K. Curling
Dave	J. Stephenson

Appendices

APPENDIX I

APPENDIX I

18, Woburn Buildings,
Euston Road, W.C.
27th April, 1915.

My dear Lady Gregory,

I wrote to you to-day saying that I had seen Wilson, and that he had asked to have Shan Waller [sic] in the second week. I would have refused in any ordinary year, but I don't want to give even the most cantankerous member of the Company, the chance of saying that we pushed our own wares at the outset. I thought in any case that the extra rehearsal he suggests there would be no harm. I asked Robinson to write me his impressions of the play. He writes as follows: —

"I like the first two acts immensely. They were amusing, pathetic and dramatic, full of surprise, the dialogue capital, and I thought very well acted. I thought the construction of the beginning of the last act bad. I think the audience should be let know as early as possible in it, exactly what had happened since the 2nd Act, exactly who is accused, and what is known, etc.—the first ten minutes are so misty and vague. Then I thought the ghost should not lead the blind man off the stage. She had so little to say, just about the paper, it could have been done on the stage and the blind man could have turned at once and announced the villain. This would have been exciting and dramatic, and in the movement and excitement the ghost could have slipped unobserved out of the door. As it was the paper incident was very flat. Here I think the actors were to blame—I think there was some confusion and 'fluffing' and unless the scene is strongly worked up there, Sinclair's confession at the end, seems a little ridiculous. He makes some general criticisms which I shall keep till I see you as they have no practical value at the moment, and he then says "All this looks as if I hadn't liked the play, but I did—exceedingly. It is the best thing she has done since the Full Moon. I don't think it compares with The Image, but it is more dramatic, but I think the last Act wants clearing up, it's "muzzy". Mrs. Travers Smith liked the play very much, and she has much less feeling for that sort of play than I have and the house was very enthusiastic. I thought the performance capital. Miss Drago was I think, quite strong enough—her frailty, I think was more effective than strength. Kerrigan's blind man was undistinguished, Hutchison very good."

What he says about the opening of the 2nd Act being ineffective, may have been partly because that night, an understudy played one of the two girls, but I feel that his criticism is worth considering. You will remember that when you read it me, I was anxious for a very rapid statement of the essential facts there. You altered it as the result of my criticism. But I remember a feeling of disappointment with what seemed the still too gradual beginning. I did not press this upon you because I said to myself that it was perhaps essential to your art which is more gradual than mine because less logical, being full of folk-lore. His criticism now brings me back to my impression. Apropos about what he says about the ghost, I feel the practical gain of hurrying that scene though the actual entrance of the ghost, goes all right now. The difficulty is that all quality of surprise would of course go if the ghost were to tell him what to do audibly, and that if it first spoke audibly, and then merely whispered, we would get an impossibly artificial scene. The ghost in any case, is not supposed to be heard, so it has no reason to whisper. I'm afraid it would mean your ghost entering without speech though I'm not quite sure. It might remain standing in the door and with two or three sentences, of very few words each, call the blind man towards it. He would then be well up the stage in the doorway and there would be a reason for the ghost speaking in a lower voice, and also a reason for that voice not reaching us. I had an uneasy feeling all through rehearsal that there was no sufficient dramatic reason for the fine poetical sentences you gave the ghost, and that the whole scene ought to be cut down to dumbshow. In fact, the whole action there should go too rapidly for poetry (Binyon says all poetry depends on slowness of movement).

I'm afraid there is something wrong still with the 3rd Act. Wilson tells we that it went well the first night at Manchester, but badly the last night. The first Act always goes splendidly he says, the second Act always well, but the third Act is always the problem. I imagine that the play is much nearer right than Damer was after its first performance, but that it still wants working on. I send you all this criticism on the chance that you may like to work on it before London. On the other hand, you may prefer to let it go to performance as it is and get criticism. I confess to an uneasy feeling that your two young women are too expensive a means of alibi, that we get the alibi at the price of that gradual opening. I have had from the very beginning the feeling that the play ought to rise on the fact made apparent from the first sentence, that your hero has been arrested for the crime, and that we want nothing in the first five minutes except the rubbing in of the fact. I have seen no criticism of the play with the exception of Robinson's.

I find that my imagination goes oftener back to Damer now than any other of your long plays. I am speaking of the stage performances. Why isn't it on the London bill? Was it done last year? If not, it certainly should be done. I feel more and more cross at the thought of that third-rate slough filling up space that we could give to Damer.

I am seeing Ricketts next Friday. He had engagements every night when I was free, but there will be plenty of time, I think. He says that we shouldn't spend nearly as much as you say on Baile's Strand, but give some of the money to a recostuming of The Well of the Saints. I'll find out when I see him whether he is confusing it with Deirdre of the Sorrows. If he has really put his imagination on Well of the Saints, I think it is a peace of luck, and we ought to give him his head.

Last week I began working on The Player Queen, but what I was doing seemed to me faint. I got alarmed that I was not concentrating sufficiently, and so have thrown it aside and so have gone back to my work for you. I shall finish that off now and do nothing but creative work in the summer. I have done a vast quantity of my work for you, but am bothered by my fear that you may want something different, and I don't feel I can change it again. I am rather relieved to come at the end of the book because I think you will let me do as I like in the obscurity of a kind of Appendix. Above all I want to be irrelevant when it amuses me. As irrelevant, let us say as the anatomy of melancholy. That is the way to bore the reviewer and interest the reader. I have gone through your Preface, and to my surprise, discovered that I only object to the opening paragraph about Bret Harte and one later paragraph about Chevy Chase—both seem to me trivial. I do not like the statement that you and I met at Lord Morris's. I knew that some fool would say that we brought in Lord Morris because it sounded grand. It broke the folk atmosphere. The whole Bret Harte paragraph seemed to have strayed out of some late Victorian book of memoirs. With those two omissions, the Introduction is, I think, charming. Furthermore, the restoration of your description of fairy characteristics, will enable me to lighten the commencement of my Essay. Your Introduction is far better in any case for a beginning of the book than mine would have been. Your merit is that you write for those who bring to the book minds with no previous knowledge and mine is that I write for certain special students—my right place is at the end. I'm trying to be a little like Montaigne—a little like the anatomy and neither man could have written a good Preface.

You need not wait for my notes before going on with your work on the book. I am merely putting numbers in brackets here and there on the pages, and writing notes to come at the end of the book to refer to these numbers. My notes can go in any order and there's no finality in the actual numbers. It was no use trying to put final numbers at the present stage because there is yet no final arrangement. Some of your pages for instance, being marked as material not yet sorted. If you approve of my method of working, you can arrange your sections exactly as you like—get the whole book finished and start the printer. I have got to Note 55—there won't be more than 65 in all. Some of the notes are three lines and some of them are ten pages. When you get them, you may decide to do the more usual thing which would be to print the shorter notes at the foot of the pages and leave the longer notes at the end. Or you may prefer to leave all at the end, which for the moment, I prefer. I don't want to be bothered with the general reader at all.

Yours truly
W. B. YEATS

APPENDIX II

SHANWALLA, ACT III

APPENDIX II

SHANWALLA, ACT III

SCENE: *A few days later. Office at Darcy's. A desk, one or two chairs and benches. Two girls coming in with a Policeman.*

2ND GIRL. Is this now the Magistrate's Court?

1ST POLICEMAN. It is so. It is here the Magistrate will find proof who is it is guilty of destroying his horse Shanwalla, the way it would not win in the race.

1ST GIRL. It is Lawrence Scarry done it. The world that is saying that.

1ST POLICEMAN. Keep your mouth quiet. That has yet to be proved.

1ST GIRL. My uncle, that is Pat O'Malley, is laying down it will be proved by sure token.

1ST POLICEMAN. Pat O'Malley! Take care will it be proved against himself.

1ST GIRL. It will not. Aren't we after coming here purposely to prove his alibi?

2ND GIRL. A great wonder it was, Mr. Darcy to bring the horse out to the race and not to leave it in the stable the way it was.

1ST POLICEMAN. They thought there to be nothing on it, and it leaving the yard.

1ST GIRL. Sure, you saw the way it was, that it couldn't so much as raise a gallop, and all the world travelling to Inchy to see him, and all the bets that were on him gone astray.

1ST POLICEMAN. I wasn't in it myself, but sent patrolling the Loughrea road.

2ND GIRL. A great pity you to have missed it. There was no one but had a bet on that horse.

1ST GIRL. I, myself, that put a shilling on him. Word I had from a knacky man that got a tip from the stand. I think I never will chance a bet again.

2ND GIRL. I was late myself coming to the entrance gap, and everyone pressing through it; and there came a great noise of talking among the crowd, that I thought the race to be ended. The throng parted then and the light-weight came passing out, and he wearing Darcy's colours, grey and yellow. Very mournful looking he was, and his eyes going into the ground. Some man that was behind me on the road called out and asked was the honour of Mr. Darcy doing well at the leaps. And the jockey made as if an oath to himself and gave no answer at all.

1ST GIRL. No, but wait till I tell you. I that saw more again. I that went up on some barrels the time I heard great cheers for Shanwalla that was coming the road; prancing up he was and his coat shining. If Darcy had a mind to sell him that time, I tell you he'd have his full price got!

1ST POLICEMAN. It would be lucky for Darcy if he did sell him.

1ST GIRL. The weighty part of the crowd came running to see him, such a welter and such a killing you never saw as was in it; climbing and knocking the wall they were, till there was nothing left standing only gaps.

1ST POLICEMAN. So I saw it myself after; that is the way it was.

1ST GIRL. Shouting Shanwalla they were, that was for Galway, and all Munster against him! But all of a sudden it is to go wild like he did and to stop and to rear up, and Lawrence Scarry that was leading him strove to soother him down. But as he came to the field it is to go into a cold sweat he did, and then he went around in a sort of a megrim, the same as a man that would have drink taken.

1ST POLICEMAN. So he had drink taken . . . of some sort.

1ST GIRL. And is it true, so, that it is to poison him they did?

2ND GIRL. If they did itself, he is as well nearly as he was before. The farrier down from Craughwell that came and attended him. Sure my grandfather was in it that is better again for cures, and that gave me the story down.

1ST POLICEMAN. It is the farrier makes a claim to have brought him round.

2ND GIRL. Shivering he was, and they couldn't keep a drink with him he was that drouthy, and they gave him castor oil, for whatever you put before him, if it was soot and water, he must drink it. But the world wouldn't make him vomit, and it was my grandfather brought him round at the last, giving him a pint of forge water, and whisky and the white of an egg. And everyone that heard it said there was surely poison within in him.

(SECOND POLICEMAN *comes in.*)

1ST POLICEMAN (*To* GIRLS). Go back there now out of the way. And let ye mind yourselves. It is as witnesses ye were brought here, and the less talk you let out of you the better it will be for the cause of justice and for yourselves. (*To* 2ND POLICEMAN.) Did they find another magistrate to sit along with Mr. Darcy?

2ND POLICEMAN. Out searching for one we were the whole of the morning and no one to be found, where they were all gone to the meet of the hounds at Rahasane.

1ST POLICEMAN. It wouldn't hardly be according to law, Mr. Darcy to judge his own case.

2ND POLICEMAN. Sure, he has but to commit whoever is thought to have a hand in it for trial at the Galway assizes. A week is no great hardship in gaol.

1ST POLICEMAN. Did the Head Constable come yet?

2ND POLICEMAN. He did not. He is in pursuit of some trace or track of the guilty person that was put into his hand.

1ST POLICEMAN. Who would he be now?

2ND POLICEMAN. How would I know, and he not willing to tell me? In dread I might catch him myself, I suppose he was. He is one is well pleased to take full credit for all.

1ST POLICEMAN. There was some cause to suspect Pat O'Malley of Canamona they were telling me, and his cousin, James Brogan, from Limerick.

2ND POLICEMAN. I never heard much against Pat O'Malley but that he is poor and has debts down on him. Brogan, though, has the name of being a wild card, a rag on every bush, knocking about here and there.

1ST POLICEMAN. It is likely it's after him the Constable is gone searching.

2ND POLICEMAN (*looking from window*). He should be here by this. Mr. Darcy that is coming in will be vexed not seeing him.

DARCY (*coming in*). Is Lawrence Scarry here?

2ND POLICEMAN. I didn't see him, sir.

DARCY. I'll want him to sift out evidence along with the Head Constable that might help us to find out who was it did this thing.

2ND POLICEMAN. I believe the Constable is of opinion he all to has his hand laid upon the rogue.

DARCY. That's right. It is long to me till I'll have him before me. I won't be long sending him to his rightful place, that is gaol.

1ST POLICEMAN. He'll be best there, surely.

DARCY. He must be a terrible ruffian! I never heard of a worse case in my lifetime! To come breaking into my stables and to try and do away with my horse!

2ND POLICEMAN. It was a very ruffianly deed.

DARCY. To go hurt a *man* you would want to put out of the way it would be bad enough. But I think it seventeen times worse to make an attack on an innocent creature that gave no provocation to anyone. You'd have been sorry to see the way he was!

1ST POLICEMAN. I was well pleased to hear he is at this time on the mending hand.

DARCY. That has nothing to do with it! It's no thanks to the villian if he did escape. There was enough of poison left in the pail he drank from to do away with all the horses on the green of Ballinasloe!

2ND POLICEMAN. So the Constable is after telling me.

DARCY. The black-hearted ruffian! It is crooked law that wouldn't mix that same poison into the diet of the man used it on Shanwalla! He'll get hanging, anyway. There's some justice in that.

1ST POLICEMAN. The law is very severe in those cases.

DARCY. It couldn't be too severe! I wouldn't grudge it to my own brother, and I to have one, and he to have done such a deed!

1ST POLICEMAN. Two men, some are saying, that were in it.

DARCY. It is glad I am to hear that! To give up two of them to the hangman will be some satisfaction, and will show some respect for Shanwalla!

1ST POLICEMAN. Here is the Head Constable coming, and a couple more along with him. They are bringing with them . . .

DARCY. The men they suspect, I suppose. Go tell them to hurry. And try can you find Lawrence Scarry.

1ST POLICEMAN. I'll not have far to go look for him. He is close at hand.

CONSTABLE (*coming in*). I couldn't get here any sooner, sir. I have been searching the whole matter out.

DARCY. That's right. Have you got hold of the man that did it?

CONSTABLE. In my opinion I have.

DARCY. I was in dread you might not be able to put your hand on him.

CONSTABLE. No fear of that. There is one thing sure in this world—when there's a crime there's a criminal.

DARCY. It's not always so easy to find him.

CONSTABLE. In some cases it is not. But it was easy enough this time. I've got him.

DARCY. I thought there were two suspected.

CONSTABLE. O'Malley and Brogan you are thinking of. But they can clear themselves. They have their alibi as good as proved.

DARCY. Who are you going to charge so?

CONSTABLE. It is Lawrence Scarry.

DARCY. Scarry! ... *My* Lawrence Scarry!

CONSTABLE. The same one.

DARCY. Rubbish! You might as well say that I myself did it!

CONSTABLE. The case is strong against him.

DARCY. Some one has made up false witness.

CONSTABLE. There was no need for that. There is proof.

DARCY. There couldn't be proof of what didn't happen. Larry loved that horse!

CONSTABLE. That makes the crime the worse.

DARCY. Where is he? He will be able to disprove it.

CONSTABLE. We have him now at hand. I am making a search in the room at Cahirbohil where he was housed. I found this piece of blue paper stuck under a candle. It was in a tattered condition and smelling of stale porter. It fits in shape and similitude with the twisted paper we found on the stable floor and that had some remains of the poison in it yet. There are some grains of the same sort here. This is the document proves the case through and through.

DARCY. If I thought it possible—but I don't—that he had gone out of his wits and done such a thing I would sooner withdraw the case than have it proved against him!

CONSTABLE. It would be impossible to do that. I have my report made to the inspector. It will be in the hands of the Crown.

DARCY. I tell you he couldn't have done it! It was in the night time it was done, after ten o'clock, between that and early morning.

CONSTABLE. It was within that time sure enough. You took notice yourself, sir, some of the flour was spilled from the box where it was.

DARCY. If I did I thought it might be a rat or a mouse or a thing of the kind. I knew no one could have come in. I had locked the door myself. I had the key all the time.

CONSTABLE. There was no other one, I suppose, has a key?

DARCY. No one—except Lawrence Scarry.

CONSTABLE. So I was thinking. (*Writes note.*) I wasn't rightly sure till now.

DARCY. It makes no difference. He wasn't near the stable. I was expecting him. He never came till morning. He told me he was tired out after the burying—and low-hearted—no wonder . . . and the day over, he had laid down to sleep on his bed.

CONSTABLE. We'll soon know can he give proof of that. I'm not one to rush at a thing without sure evidence.

DARCY. Why don't you go look for proofs against these other men? Had you no information against them? We might be able to prove it. Bring them in.

CONSTABLE. All I heard was, they had bets put on against your own horse in the race. There was ill-feeling against them among those that lost their money. I was advised to make enquiry about them. I did that. I got no information was enough to charge them on.

DARCY. Bring them here, I might make out something. (*They are brought in.* O'MALLEY *is brought forward.*) Now look here, my man, if you were brought in here, it is that there is something against you. What is it? Do you know anything of what happened my horse? Did you ever see him or handle him? Say yes or no.

O'MALLEY. I will. Previous to the day of the races I never laid an eye on him.

CONSTABLE. He says he can give proof he was not out of his own house that night.

O'MALLEY. So I can, too. There are two little girls of the neighbours can bear testimony to that.

DARCY. Who are they? Will they be honest witnesses?

1ST POLICEMAN. Very decent little girls, sir, and well-spoken. Nieces of Pat O'Malley, I believe they are.

DARCY. What have they to say?

1ST GIRL. It was Thursday night....

DARCY. What Thursday night?

1ST GIRL. St. Brigit's Eve for the world. We met Pat O'Malley coming home, where he had been to the burying at Eserkelly; and he having a pain in the jaw and it going athrough his head.

2ND GIRL. That is so. Cold, I suppose he got.

1ST GIRL. We turned into the house with him, and we sat there for a while.

DARCY. For how long?

1ST GIRL. A middling while, and he telling us newses of the burying.

2ND GIRL. Giving us an account of all the people that were in it.

DARCY. That's enough. All I want to know is what time it was.

2ND GIRL. I couldn't know ... only the middling right time.

1ST GIRL. It was just on the stroke of ten o'clock we went in——

2ND GIRL. I was forgetting that. Just up to ten o'clock.

1ST GIRL. The wife put a hot plaster to the jaw and he went in to his bed, and we went away then, and the door was closed after us. Closed and locked; and he never left the house till morning.

2ND GIRL. Till it was time to make a start for Inchy races. We were together going the road.

CONSTABLE. You see, sir, it is hardly worth while going on with this case.

DARCY. Go on then with the other, Brogan. Can he prove where he was that night?

CONSTABLE. That is a thing was laid down against James Brogan. He was seen coming out through a gap in the demesne wall at Cahirbohil about twelve o'clock Thursday night.

DARCY. That is better. He is likely the man we want. Have you any witnesses?

BROGAN. You need bring no witness to that. I did come out that side. I thought it no harm where it was a mile of a short-cut. I had gone in to see a friend.

DARCY. At that time of night?

BROGAN. No, but earlier. I went to visit him. I was coming back from the fair of Loughrea. Darkness overtook me on the road; I went to ask a lodging of him.

DARCY. What friend had you inside my demesne?

BROGAN. I should sooner say kinsman by marriage. His wife's mother and my mother were mixed, blood thick, they were, two cousins. Anyone that has learning can read it on the headstone in Eserkelly. He was Lawrence Scarry.

DARCY. What time was that?

BROGAN. The time I went there it was close on ten o-clock. I stopped a good while, maybe two hours.

DARCY. Then Scarry was in his own room where you were with him all that time! I knew he never left it. I knew he was speaking the truth!

BROGAN. I took my rest there for a while. But I did not say I was with him. I won't tell you one word of a lie. There was no one in the place but myself.

DARCY. Where was he then?

BROGAN. The Lord be praised, I do not know, and that I cannot tell.

DARCY. He might have gone to some neighbour's house.

BROGAN. To be sure he might. That's what I was thinking myself. It will be easy for him call that neighbour to witness.

1ST POLICEMAN. Owen Conary, the dark man that goes questing on the roads was talking abroad in the yard. I heard him give out he himself was the latest person was with Lawrence Scarry on that night.

DARCY. Call him in then. He might settle the matter.

CONSTABLE. He will, I'm thinking. One way or another (CONARY *comes in.*)

DARCY. What time were you with Scarry at Cahirbohil Thursday night?

CONSTABLE. If ever you were there at all.

CONARY. Why wouldn't I be there? I was in it surely. The time I went in it was near to ten o'clock.

CONSTABLE. What way do you know that?

CONARY. I know it by the number of the steps I made, and I coming the road from Kilchriest.

CONSTABLE. And Scarry was in it?

CONARY. He was to be sure.

DARCY. How long did you stop with him?

CONARY. I don't know was it an hour, half an hour? I couldn't be rightly sure.

CONSTABLE. Try and call up your memory now.

CONARY. I wouldn't be sure. My mind was on other things besides time.

DARCY. You maybe stopped with him up to ten o'clock.

CONARY. I did and later, I can be certain of that.

DARCY. This man Brogan says he was there at that time.

CONARY. He did not come in when I was in it. Lawrence Scarry was there in his lone. I talked with him a short while, till being tired and down-hearted he stretched himself in sleep on the bed through the night.

DARCY. That's what he told me. It is certain he slept in his bed last night. This Brogan must be making a mistake or making up a story. He says he came in. You say no one at all came in.

CONARY. No one—unless. . . .

CONSTABLE. Unless who? Tell it out.

CONARY. I thought I saw . . .

CONSTABLE. He is getting away from the truth. You know that you cannot see, and you having the eyesight lost, and being as you are stone dark.

CONARY. I never did before in my natural life. But I give you the bail of my mouth I saw that time, or it seemed to me that I saw.

DARCY. Go on. What did you see?

CONARY. I saw Bride Scarry walking.

426

CONSTABLE. This is superstition and a mockery. We all know her to be dead.

CONARY. I tell you she came in the spirit.

DARCY. I'm afraid his mind is rambling.

CONARY. Why would she not come and the spirit not long gone out of her, where it is known God will blow His breath into those that are dead a hundred or two hundred years?

DARCY. Did you speak to her?

CONARY. I did not; and it is a great pity that it failed me to do it. But it was all strange to me. It is often I coveted to see the flame of the fire on the hearth, and there it was before me, and the walls of the house on every side. And as to her, I saw her as I never saw anyone in this life. But there being no one waking along with me, the fright went into my heart, and it failed me to question her, and I went out the door and made no stop or delay.

CONSTABLE. You are certain it was Bride Scarry? What sort was she?

CONARY. She seemed to me to be coming from the south, and to have on her the lovely appearance of the people of heaven.

DARCY. He is given over to dreams and visions. We are getting nothing from him at all.

CONSTABLE. He was trying to befriend Scarry but there is nothing in what he says that can serve him.

DARCY. Stop a mintue. Scarry did not leave the house? He was in bed asleep when you went out?

CONARY. He laid himself on the bed. But he said he would not be long in it. He bade me waken him. He said he would be going out later in the night.

CONSTABLE. So he did go out later, and did the crime. I was full sure of that.

DARCY. It is hard for me to give up trust in him. He to have turned against me, I will never have faith in any other man in the living world.

CONSTABLE. He will give you his own account now of himself.

SCARRY (*coming in between two policemen*). Will you tell me what is going on, Mr. Hubert, or if it is by your orders it is going on? These peelers dragging me here and there! First they would not give me leave to come to you, and now they are shoving me in, the same as a thief on the road! (*To* POLICEMAN.) Leave go your hold!

CONSTABLE. Keep a quiet mouth now and behave yourself!

SCARRY. What call have you to be putting orders on me? It is Mr. Darcy is my master. I take orders from no other one.

CONSTABLE. It is likely you'll give heed to my orders from this out!

SCARRY. Let you keep that thought for robbers and law breakers! I'm not one of that class! I never gave a summons or got a summons or gave my oath in a court!

CONSTABLE. It is not with a court but with a gaol you will be making acquaintance this night!

SCARRY. Divil a fear of me! Whatever you have against me or make out against me, it is Mr. Darcy is well able to bring a man from the gallows!

DARCY. You need expect no help from me, Scarry, if the grave was there open before you!

SCARRY. What in the world wide! What at all is it you have against me, Mr. Hubert?

DARCY. You will know that at the Assizes when you will be brought before the judge.

SCARRY. Tell me out what it is, and I'll show you I am clear from blame!

DARCY. You'll show me! I would not believe one word coming out of your mouth!

CONSTABLE. There's no use talking. We know what way you passed the night before the race.

SCARRY. Is that it now? Is that what has put you out, sir? You are vexed I did not come to mind the horse. It is very sharp blame you are putting on me for that!

DARCY. You need not try to put a face upon it! You cannot come around me now that I have knowledge of what you are!

SCARRY. I had a right to have come, and you uneasy as you were.

DARCY. That's not it, I tell you!

SCARRY. I told you I thought to come . . . and that I was racked and tormented . . . and maybe I had a drop taken . . . and sleep came upon me.

DARCY. I wish to God you had stopped in your sleep!

SCARRY. I give you my oath, I'll never quit your yard again but to be minding your business night and day.

DARCY. You'll never be helper or head lad again in any stable I may own.

SCARRY. That is hard judgment when all I did was to drowse awhile.

428

DARCY. It is not your drowsing and sleeping goes against you! It is the deed you went out for after your rising up!

SCARRY. What way did you know I went out?

CONSTABLE. There now, he has allowed it.

SCARRY. I never denied it.

CONSTABLE. What time now did you go out?

SCARRY. It seemed to me like the dead hour of darkness, but it might not be so far out in the night.

CONSTABLE. What brought you out at all?

SCARRY. I was troublesome in the mind.

CONSTABLE. You came then to Mr. Darcy's stables.

SCARRY. No, it was not this side I came, but out across the meadows to the north.

DARCY. Speak out. Don't drag this thing on for ever.

SCARRY. It was to the old church of Eserkelly I went, to the side of Bride my wife's grave.

CONSTABLE. You can maybe bring witness to that?

SCARRY. Who would I bring? There was no one in it, unless God, and the dead underneath.

CONSTABLE. What did you go doing there?

SCARRY. Asking her forgiveness I was if ever I was anyway unkind, and saying prayers for the repose of her soul.

CONSTABLE (*to* DARCY). This seems to be a humbugging story, sir, made up to get at your soft side, the way you will get him off.

O'MALLEY. Ah, what getting off! He said one time he was asleep and he says now he was rambling the fields.

BROGAN. Let him tell that story to the birds of the air, for there is no one on the face of the earth will believe it.

SCARRY (*seeing them for the first time*). Is it you yourself, you red rogue, is at the bottom of this mischief? I should have known that where there was bad work you would be in it, yourself and your comrade schemer! (*To* DARCY.) They are two that would swear away a man's life for a farthing candle! There is no nature in them! They are two would think no more of giving false witness than of giving a blow from a pipe. Tell that story to the birds of the air is it! I will and to the magistrate that is my master!

BROGAN. He gave little belief to all you told him up to this.

SCARRY. I have more to tell and maybe he will believe it!

BROGAN. You have nothing to tell but what will bring your own head into the loop!

SCARRY. Maybe it's your own head it will bring into it!

BROGAN. Do your best so, and see will your lies serve you.

SCARRY. What brought you into the house that night? Why did you waken me? What did you ask of me? Was it to come along with you to Darcy's stable?

BROGAN. Stop your slandering mouth!

DARCY. Maybe there is something in it.

BROGAN. I say this man has made up this false witness and this story because we have knowledge of what would hang him twice over, and we being willing to tell it out!

SCARRY. You have nothing to tell against me, if it is not that for one half hour, God forgive me! I consented to your wicked plan.

BROGAN. What I have to say I would sooner not say, because it concerns her that was near in blood to me, if she was mixed in marriage with yourself.

SCARRY. Keep your tongue off her, you villain! Have some shame in you!

BROGAN (*to* DARCY). Have I leave to speak?

DARCY. Go on.

SCARRY. No! It would not be for honour her name to be spoken out of your false mouth, you that are a disgrace to the world! I know what you have in your wicked mind, and what when I was mad and crazed with trouble you made me give credit to for one minute only! I declare to heaven that if you say it in this place it will be the last lie in your throat!

DARCY (*to* BROGAN). Speak out.

BROGAN. It is loth I am to do that, and I would not, without that I am forced by your honour's commands and this man's treachery. I know and I tell you out, it was he himself that made away with his wife!

SCARRY. My God Almighty! (*Stumbles and holds a chair.*)

BROGAN. Look, sir, at the way she died! Gone in the snap of a finger. Well as she was that you would take a lease of her life, as supple walking as a young girl. What was it happened her? Is it that the ladder was settled in a way it would go from under her, and to slip on a slippy flag, the way she would be quiet and dumb and could not hold to her word and tell out to her master that it was Lawrence Scarry himself had engaged for money to put injury on the thing was in his charge!

SCARRY. Let me out till I'll choke him!

BROGAN. Search your mind, sir, did she say she had something to lay before you! Was it he sent her out of the door? Was it he himself brought her in dead? Put away she was, before she could give out that word.

DARCY (*to* SCARRY). You understand what he is saying. What answer have you?

SCARRY. The twists and tricks of a serpent he has! Didn't I speak before and what did it serve me. (BRIDE *comes in and stays near door.*)

DARCY (*getting up*). The case looks bad and black. It has gone beyond me. (*He looks at* CONSTABLE'S *notes; the others whisper together.*)

BRIDE (*coming to* CONARY). Can you hear me what I say, Owen Conary?

CONARY. I do hear you and know your voice, indeed.

2ND POLICEMAN (*touching his shoulder*). No speaking now.

BRIDE. But there is great need for us to talk together. We must have leave to do that. (*Turns and stands a moment near door.*)

A BOY (*coming to door*). The horses are getting uneasy in the stable, let Lawrence Scarry come and quiet them down. (LARRY *starts up.*)

DARCY. No, not you. Never again! (SCARRY *sits down with head in hands.* DARCY *goes out,* POLICE, BROGAN, *and* O'MALLEY *follow him.* GIRLS *go to window and whisper, looking out.* BRIDE *comes to* CONARY.)

BRIDE. Here I am now that you may question me.

CONARY. I will do that, and I give great praise to God that sent you back to me. For I am in no dread of you this time.

BRIDE. You need be in no dread of me, indeed; and it is to save my man I am come, for he is at the rib end of the web, and no woof to be got, and not one to save him without your help and my own.

CONARY. Answer me and tell me now what is to be done for him, and what way can he stand up to the judge, and he it may be going to his hanging tomorrow?

BRIDE. I am come here to stand between himself and his ill-wishers, and the man that put the curse of misfortune upon him.

CONARY. Do that, for he is the worst God ever created, and it is bad is his behaviour and you could not beat upon his cunning. And it is a great wonder the Lord to allow all the villainy is in the world. And that they may meet with all they deserve at this time, and in the cold hell that is before them.

BRIDE. Let you not call out a judgment against them, but let you leave them to the Almighty; and I myself never will put my curse on them; but that He Himself may change everyone for the best!

CONARY. Stretch out now and give aid to the boy that had the sea of the world's troubles over him, since you yourself went from him to the other side, and that was a boy did not deserve it from God or man.

BRIDE. I will do that. For he was fair and honest until the man that is his red enemy put a net around him with lying words, and he broke away from it after. And he was a kind man to me, for a headstrong man, while I was with him, and I liked him well. Do now my bidding and I will leave you my blessing by day and by night, in the light and in the darkness, for from this out I will be free from the world's trouble and at peace.

CONARY. I will do your bidding, indeed. And it is not lonesome I will be from this out, but I to be going the long road it will be as if I did not belong to the world at all; for it seemed to me the time I looked at you, the heavens to have opened then and there! (*They go up to corner. She is seen to be speaking to him. Presently they both go out.*)

1ST GIRL (*leaving window and coming down stage*). They're coming back now from the stables.

2ND GIRL (*looking at* SCARRY *who still sits with head sunk on arms*). Would you ever think now Lawrence Scarry to be such a terrible wicked man, to kill the poor woman stone-dead!

1ST GIRL. Darcy to turn against him—what will it be when he will come before the Judge of Assize and all the counsellors of the Crown?

2ND GIRL. I thought it was but for a bit of funning Pat O'Malley bade us make up the story about him being in the house that night. Sure, what way would I know if he was in it at all? And now they'll be putting it in the newspapers and all around the world.

1ST GIRL. Whether or no, you cannot go back from it now. Well, I declare, I'd near pity the poor man if it was not for the bad deed he has done.

(DARCY, CONSTABLE *and the rest come in.*)

CONSTABLE (*to* SCARRY). Come over here now and hear what Mr. Darcy has to say.

DARCY. There is nothing for me to do but to commit you to gaol.

SCARRY. Is it that *you* give belief to what was said?

DARCY. God knows I would give the half of my estate to have the same thought of you I had yesterday. You never would hear a sharp word from me again. But what stand can you make against the Judge, where I must cast you off, that was your near friend?

SCARRY. My mind is as if gone blind. I can keep no thought in my head. This is surely the crossest day that ever went over me. I can make no stand against such treachery.

CONARY (*coming forward*). Will I get leave to say one word . . . ? A message I am after being given . . .

DARCY. Have you anything new to tell?

CONARY. A message I am after being given for Patrick O'Malley.

DARCY. Has it anything to do with this case?

CONARY. Your honour will know that. I am bidden to tell you, Pat O'Malley, to give up now the thing that is in your hand, that is the sign and the token of your treachery, and of the deed you have joined in and that you have done.

O'MALLEY (*taking his hand from his breast where he had thrust it*). There is nothing in it.

CONARY. Let those that have eyesight say if there is! (CONSTABLE *goes over to* O'MALLEY.)

O'MALLEY (*flinging a letter at* BROGAN). It is you betrayed me! It is you gave it to me! There is no one had knowledge of it only yourself. (CONSTABLE *takes up and gives paper to* DARCY.)

DARCY (*reading*). It is a promise to pay £50 to him so soon as Inchy races will be over, if so be the horse Shanwalla will not have been able to make a start.

O'MALLEY. It was poverty brought me to it, and the children rising around me.

BROGAN. Keep your tongue quiet, you fool!

CONARY. I hear your voice, James Brogan. I am not without a message to yourself.

BROGAN. Some lie you have made up. Who is there in the living world would go send me a message in this place?

CONARY. You will know who sent it, hearing it. It was given to me but now.

BROGAN. There was no one came in or went out. I swear to that.

CONARY. It failed you to see her; but she was here.

BROGAN (*uneasily*). She . . . What are you saying? What are you talking about?

CONARY. She gave me this message: "Were you not a foolish man, James Brogan, to knock the ladder from under me, and I but just after saying to you that it is hard to quench life!"

BROGAN. She did not—she could not——

CONARY. You know well who it was spoke that word. Have a care! She is maybe not far from you.

BROGAN (*falling on his knees and looking at place she had stood*). I give my faith and my solemn oath, Bride, that the time I got wild

433

and faced you I never thought to leave a hand on you, to kill you, but only to put fear on you, the way you would not tell on me, and but to quiet you for a while!

DARCY. Do you understand what you are saying?

BROGAN. "Living or dead I'll be against you," you said, and I threatening to do injury to your man. And if it was for my own profit I did injury to what he had in charge, it is for your own sake I put a revenge on him and strove to destroy him and to bring him down! (*Holds out his arms towards door.*) Are you gone from me now and for ever! Oh, Bride, you were always against me, and you are against me yet, and it is through you I will give myself up to the Judge and will go to my punishment as it is well I have earned it! (*The* TWO POLICEMEN *stand at each side of him as he stands up, and lead him and* O'MALLEY *to door.*)

CONARY (*to* SCARRY). Surely God has some great hand in you, giving leave to the woman to keep her promise for your help. And didn't she behave well, coming challenging through myself your enemies in the court, the way you got over them all, and you so near your last goal!

SCARRY. Through you is it? Stop your raving. She to have left her standing in Heaven it is not with you she would have come speaking, or with any one at all only myself!

DARCY. It is a good thought he had facing them. But it's no wonder he to be apt at riddles, there is great wit and great wisdom in the blind. And it's little he could have done for you, Larry, but for knowing that I myself was on your side.

CONSTABLE (*to the* TWO POLICEMEN). I'm full sure the beggar was in league with them and knew their secrets, and turned on them and betrayed them for his own safety, seeing me searching out the matter to the root.

2ND POLICEMAN. I never heard in my time a spirit to give any aid to the law or to the police.

1ST POLICEMAN. There's nothing in the world more ignorant then to give any belief to ghosts. I am walking the world these twenty years, and never met anything worse than myself!

Curtain.